Death of a Language

Death of a Language

The History of Judeo-Spanish

Tracy K. Harris

DELAWARE

Newark: University of Delaware Press
London and Toronto: Associated University Presses

Associated University Presses
440 Forsgate Drive
Cranbury, NJ 08512

Associated University Presses
25 Sicilian Avenue
London WC1A 2QH, England

Associated University Presses
P.O. Box 338, Port Credit
Mississauga, Ontario
Canada L5G 4L8

The paper used in this publication meets the requirements of the American National Standard for Permanence of Paper for Printed Library Materials Z39.48-1984.

Library of Congress Cataloging-in-Publication Data

Harris, Tracy K.
    Death of a language : the history of Judeo-Spanish / Tracy K. Harris.
        p. cm.
    Includes bibliographical references (p.   ) and index.
    ISBN 0-87413-497-8 (alk. paper)
    1. Ladino language—History. I. Title.
PC4813.H37   1994
467'.9496—dc20   93-39867
                                                             CIP

PRINTED IN THE UNITED STATES OF AMERICA

This book is dedicated
to the memory of my father,
and to my mother and brother.

Contents

Acknowledgments

There are various people who have played an important role in helping to make this book a reality. During my doctoral research, the late Dr. Robert J. DiPietro of Georgetown University and the University of Delaware served as my mentor and guided me through the writing of my original dissertation. I wish to express my gratitude to Dr. Joshua A. Fishman for all of his encouragement and advice throughout the years as well as his suggestion that I attempt such an endeavor. I am indebted to David F. Altabé who for several years has provided me with much information, has corrected many of my errors thus keeping me honest, and who has been a tremendous help in the editing of the manuscript.

Many thanks to Louise (Stori) and Charles MacPhee and to Ethel, Nat, and Sue Stern for their gracious hospitality while I was conducting research in New York, and to Dr. Milton and Margaret Greenblatt who provided me with all the amenities while I worked with informants in Los Angeles.

Debbie Schmidt generously gave of her time to read, correct, and comment on the manuscript in its early stages, and Jim Sullivan patiently worked with me to improve my writing style. Alan Williams was of invaluable help in getting the manuscript into the proper form and in doing much of the computer work. Many thanks to Jay Halio for encouraging me in the book's early stages and to Paul Rieder for his editing expertise at AUP.

Finally, I must thank all of my informants in New York, Israel, and Los Angeles who welcomed me into their homes and into their Sephardic world. They have provided me with many wonderful memories.

Introduction:
Why a Book on Judeo-Spanish?

With a renewed consciousness of ethnicity in the United States and around the world, studies of various ethnic and minority groups and their languages have become increasingly popular. However, not all groups have received the study they deserve. In an editorial on minorities, Lavender is quoted as reporting that "Sephardim are usually neglected by both lay persons and social scientists who study Jews in America" (*Human Behavior,* vol. 5, no. 6:62). Past works on Jewish history and culture have mainly focused on Ashkenazic history, barely touching on the existence or heritage of the Sephardic Jews. And unfortunately when they do, the information, according to Angel, is often superficial and inaccurate (1981:2).

However, the quincentennial anniversary of the expulsion of the Jews from Spain in 1492 has stimulated interest in the history and culture of Sephardic Jews, and the field of Sephardic Studies is just now coming into its own. As Papo writes: "It has only been in the last decade that scholarly attention is finally being directed toward the . . . Sephardim coming primarily from the former Ottoman Empire" (1987:xi).

One of the aims of this study is to call attention to the Sephardim and especially to their language, one of the aspects of Sephardic culture which has not received sufficient consideration in the past. Other goals of this sociolinguistic study of Judeo-Spanish include the following:

(1) to make information concerning Judeo-Spanish, its history, characteristics, and present status available to an English-speaking audience. Previous studies on the language have consisted mostly of historical dialect studies or analyses of specific linguistic features. And these have been written in languages other than English, or they have appeared in journals or books not easily available to the average English-speaking reader. In an effort to provide accessible information, I have therefore translated all foreign language quotations appearing in this work into English.

(2) to present a study of Judeo-Spanish which is geared not only to scholars, but also to nonacademics. Another problem of past studies on Judeo-Spanish is that they have generally been linguistic analyses written in a technical language often difficult for the average nonacademic to understand. I have tried to write this book in a relatively readable style, and although the nonlinguist may decide to skip parts of certain chapters, I trust that even the linguistic examples presented can be understood by the nonspecialist.

(3) to encourage linguistic research on Judeo-Spanish as a dialect of Spanish with possible comparisons between Judeo-Spanish and Spanish dialects of Central and South America, as well as those of Spain. A study of Judeo-Spanish, which developed independently after expulsion, can also reveal various characteristics of Medieval or Classical Spanish.

(4) to provide a case study of what happens to an ethnic or minority language which comes into contact with other dominant languages and cultures. Linguists, anthropologists, sociologists, and psychologists may wish to use Judeo-Spanish as an example in exploring the fate of such languages.

(5) to provide information on the role of language in ethnic identity and its place in the culture and history of a people. Chapter 14 specifically discusses the question of cultural survival after language loss.

(6) to contribute to the study of Jewish languages or Jewish interlinguistics, and especially the study of Sephardic Jews and their language.

(7) to focus specifically on Judeo-Spanish and its characteristics as a dying language, and to examine Judeo-Spanish in the framework of dying languages in general, in hopes that this research will be a contribution to the study of language death.

This work can serve as a reference book on various aspects of Judeo-Spanish. For example, chapters 1, 2, and 9 are useful for a basic definition of the language and provide an account of its current status. Chapters 4, 5, and 10 may be of particular interest to linguists or Hispanicists, while chapters 3, 6, and 11 should attract the attention of historians and sociologists. Chapters 7, 8, and 14 will appeal to those interested in ethnic studies and/or Jewish studies, and chapters 11, 12, and 13 will be of value to the study of dying languages. In short, this book is geared to scholars and nonscholars alike, who wish to learn more about Judeo-Spanish, one of the most treasured aspects of Sephardic culture.

Death of a Language

Part I
Preliminaries: Definition and Historical Setting

1

What is Judeo-Spanish?

In 1492 the Spanish Jews who did not choose to convert to Catholicism were expelled from Spain by King Ferdinand and Queen Isabella. It is estimated that between 100,000 (Papo 1987:7) and 175,000 (Kiddle 1978:75) Jews were forcibly exiled. These exiles became known as Sephardic Jews or Sephardim, from the ancient Hebrew word *sepharad* meaning "Spain." Their knowledge of Spanish, which was basically that of the late fifteenth and early sixteenth centuries, was one of the few possessions the Jews were allowed to take with them from the Iberian Peninsula. They followed three main routes of exile.

Thousands[1] settled in North Africa, especially Northern Morocco, building up sizable Sephardic communities in such cities as Tangiers, Oran, Fez, Tetuan, and Meknes. Their language, which developed into a mixture of Spanish and Arabic, is called *Hakitia*. In a large number of cases it was eventually replaced by a local form of Arabic.

A certain number of expelled Sephardim took refuge in Portugal, but they were subjected to forced baptism or were expelled from there in 1497. Along with other Portuguese Jews, this group went mainly to Holland, France, England, Germany, and other Western European countries. Eventually, Portuguese colonies were established in these countries from which such famous leaders as Spinoza and Disraeli later emerged. These Western Sephardim kept in contact with Spain and Portugal, and were exposed to the literature, language, and other influences of the Iberian Peninsula. Thus, they continued to speak the Portuguese language as it developed in Portugal.[2] However, due to the fact that the Western European countries continued to enjoy a high level of culture, the Western Sephardim were led to drop, by the beginning of the nineteenth century, their mother tongue in favor of the local languages such as Dutch, French, English, and German.[3]

The majority of Jews expelled from Spain in 1492 did not follow the route of exile into Western Europe or North Africa, but instead emigrated to the Ottoman Empire. Thus, their history and language development is quite different from that of the Western Sephardim. It is estimated that about 125,000 exiles (Kiddle 1978:75) settled in various regions of the Ottoman Empire at the invitation of the Ottoman Sultan Bayezid II. These Ottoman settlements were located in the regions of the Balkan Peninsula which comprise the present-day countries of Greece, Turkey, Yugoslavia, Bulgaria, Rumania, and Israel. These Jews who settled in the Empire are referred to as Eastern or Oriental Sephardim. Unlike the Western Sephardim, these eastern or oriental Sephardi communities gradually lost all contact with Spain and Portugal and were thus not exposed to the linguistic influences of the Iberian Peninsula. Their language did not go through the linguistic changes undergone by Castilian Spanish in the sixteenth and seventeenth centuries, and therefore did not share in the development from Old, or Classical Spanish, to Modern Spanish. Thus, the Spanish of the Eastern Sephardim in the Balkans preserved many of the characteristics of the Castilian spoken and written in the late fifteenth and early sixteenth centuries in Spain, which are described in Nebrija's famous *Gramática de la lengua castellana* 'Grammar of the Castilian language' written in 1492.[4]

Besides its archaic features, the language underwent various independent formations and transformations, another result of the Sephardim's isolation from the linguistic developments of the Iberian Peninsula. These new creations in the Empire resulted from analogy based on either the Castilian framework, on Ottoman languages and other foreign influences, or they originated from various Jewish customs or practices. Also, given the fact that it was a language spoken by Jews, the Ottoman Sephardim's Spanish contained a certain amount of Hebrew loanwords and was written in Hebrew characters or Rashi script.[5]

Because the Jews of the Ottoman Empire viewed the surrounding culture to be less advanced than their own, they felt no particular need to learn the local languages. In fact, for a period of time their prestige, especially in the areas of trade, medicine and craftsmanship, was so high that many non-Sephardic Jews, as well as gentiles, learned the language of the Sephardim.

As the Jews of the Balkans moved from region to region, local words and expressions, as well as morphological and syntactic influences, began to infiltrate into their speech. Through the years the Spanish of the Balkan Jews acquired a sizable number of Balkan loanwords and foreign elements, especially Turkish, Greek, and Slavic, which expressed new concepts and objects of the Balkan regions. Italian and French elements were also added to their speech as a result of the introduction of French and Italian schools in the Balkans beginning in the mid 1800s.[6] These local phonetic, morphological and lexical peculiarities soon led to the development of various dialects of the language, depending on the Sephardim's region of residence. The main dialect areas in the Ottoman Empire were located in Salonika (today Thessaloniki), Constantinople (Istanbul), Izmir (Smyrna), Monastir (Bitola), and other areas of Turkey, Greece, Yugoslavia, Rumania, Bulgaria, and Palestine.

The language of the Sephardic Jews has been referred to by a variety of names such as Espanyol, Muestro Espanyol, Djidio, Ladino, and Judezmo, among others. Various scholars (such as this author) refer to the language as Judeo-Spanish (Judeo-Espanyol).[7] In general, Judeo-Spanish is closer to Old Spanish than to the modern Castilian spoken in Spain, but at the same time, it shares similarities characteristic of some of the present-day Spanish dialects spoken in areas of Latin America.

In the Balkans Judeo-Spanish remained the principal language of the Sephardim for four-and-a-half centuries, until the beginning of nationalism in the late 1800s, followed by the Balkan Wars of 1912–1913, World War I, and finally World War II. During the latter conflict Salonika, the largest of the Sephardic communities in the Ottoman Empire, was destroyed by the Nazis in 1943, thus bringing an end to a large part of the Sephardic Jewish life in the Balkans. The only sizable Sephardic community left in the former Ottoman Empire is the Turkish community, especially that of Istanbul. The majority of Sephardic survivors of the various Balkan campaigns and the two world wars presently live in Israel, which is the largest Sephardic community in the world, and the United States. The two largest North American Sephardic communities today are located in New York City and Los Angeles.

Today Judeo-Spanish is spoken mainly by older people and it is in a state of decline. There are very few Sephardim under the age of fifty who can still converse in the language, and it is not being passed on to the younger generations. Figures of the number of proficient Judeo-Spanish speakers in the world today are difficult to obtain, but my estimate is no more than sixty thousand (see chapter 13). Various aspects of the history and current status of Judeo-Spanish will be discussed in the following chapters.

2

The Name of the Language: What Should We Call This Dialect?

The question of what to call the spoken language of the Eastern Sephardic Jews is still not solved today. As Nemer reports, much has been written about "what this language has been called, has not been called, is called, and should be called" (Nemer 1981:6), and various researchers are aware that there are heated debates over the proper name for the language. Fishman points out that, in the realm of sociolinguistics, it is not unusual to have a lack of consensus in certain speech communities as to the name of a language, both on the part of native speakers as well as outsiders who need a term to designate the language in question. He maintains that this lack of consensus has to do with the absence of various higher status functions or uses of the language (Fishman 1985:9). This lack of an agreed upon name can be viewed as one sociolinguistic indicator of the marginal status of Judeo-Spanish. In his research, C. Crantford found a total of eighty-one different names that have been used to refer to the language of the Eastern Sephardim (Crantford 1991). Some of the more popular names include the following: *Ladino, Judezmo (Djudezmo), (E)Spanyol, Muestro (E)spanyol, Djidyo (Jidiyo)* or *Djudyo (Judiyo), Spaniolit, Jargon,* and *Judeo-Spanish (Judeo-Espanyol)*. The following is a discussion of the origins and uses of these names.

Ladino and Judezmo

At present, the most intense and longest running dispute concerns which of the two terms, *Ladino* or *Judezmo* (also spelled *Djudezmo* or *Dzhudezmo*), is the correct name for the spoken language. *Judezmo* is the term preferred by linguists such as Bunis (1975a, b; 1978a, b), Fishman (1985), Gold (1991), and M. Weinreich (1980). Bunis bases his choice on research literature and personal interviews which indicate to him that the term *Judezmo* was used in sixteen major Sephardic communities in the late nineteenth and early twentieth centuries (Bunis 1978b:98). Bunis (1978a, b) and Sephiha (1986) argue that the term *Ladino* should be limited to the written language of the religious texts. Bunis also argues that, since the term *Judezmo* originated among native speakers, it is preferable to a name imposed from outside sources.

Ladino is the most popular or more widely used term today when discussing the language of the Eastern Sephardim (Balch 1980:4), and A. Malinowski writes that "it has a fairly wide currency among nonspecialists as a designation for the modern spoken language" (Malinowski 1979:114). Kalmi Baruch wrote in his article on the Judeo-Spanish of Bosnia (1930:116), that *Ladino* was not only the name given to the language of texts written in Rashi script, but that the term *Ladino* "was also used to designate the current or spoken language." This also seems to be prevalent among my informants in the United States and among several in Israel (Harris 1979, 1987). Almost all of my informants used the term *Ladino* when talking about their mother tongue, even though they generally gave another name when asked specifically how they referred to their native language. I suspect the reason for this discrepancy was that, when presented with the question, they made a conscious effort to respond with the name that they or their parents had used in the Balkans to designate the language. The proponents of the term *Ladino* say that it should be used for the spoken language while *Judezmo,* a term which comes from *judaísmo,* the Spanish word for "Judaism," should be used only in the sense of "Judaism" or "Jewish religion" but not as a name for the language. H. P. Salomon and T. Ryan (1978:155) argue against use of the term *Judezmo* saying that it has become a "misnomer for 'Spanish' under the influence of the word '*Yiddish' (from the German Juedisch-Deutsch),*" which they feel negates the Spanish quality of the language while reducing it to "the status of a ghetto jargon."

It seems that for most Sephardim, the link with their Spanish heritage is an important component of their Sephardic identity. As Stephen Stern (1977, ch. 1) in his research of the Los Angeles Sephardic community discovered, many Sephardim consider themselves not only as Jewish, but as Sephardic Jewish. T. Balch suggests that the Sephardim would therefore prefer a name for their language that embodies this cultural Sephardic identity. While arguing against use of the term *Judezmo* she reports:

A deep-seated pride in being Spanish could be an important factor in the fury at seeing their language characterized as a "Jewish" language which seems to suggest qualities of jargon or substandardness,

and later,

many Sephardic Jews seem to feel that the characterization of their native language as a "Jewish" language overlooks its fundamentally Spanish character which in turn de-emphasizes *their* fundamentally Spanish character. (Balch 1980:8, 9)

According to Professor Haïm Vidal Sephiha, France's expert on Judeo-Spanish and author of much research on the language of which he is a native speaker, *Ladino* is a Judeo-Spanish calque which was the language used to translate holy writings from Hebrew. The distinctive characteristic of this Judeo-Spanish calque is its Semitic syntax and its word for word mirroring of Hebrew while using Spanish words (Sephiha 1986:56, 65). And since it is a translating language, Sephiha emphasizes that "Ladino is not spoken," and should not be confused with the spoken language which he calls *Djudezmo, the Judeo-Spanish vernacular, Djudyo* or *Djidyo, Espanyol, el Espanyol Muestro,* etc. (ibid., 26).

Sephiha describes *Ladino, the Judeo-Spanish calque,* as existing in pre-Expulsion Spain, since it was the method used to teach Hebrew and the basic religious (biblical) texts (ibid., 18). On the other hand, he reports that *Judezmo, the Judeo-Spanish vernacular,* did not really come into existence until about 1620 when the Spanish spoken by the Sephardim in the Balkans began to differentiate itself from the Spanish of 1492 Spain (ibid., 22). This vernacular continued to evolve until after 1860, when it developed, due to the influence of the Alliance Israélite Universelle,[1] into a new form of vernacular which Sephiha calls *le judéo-fragnol* or Judeo-French (ibid., 57, 58). Besides loans from French, *Judezmo* borrowed heavily from Turkish and the other Balkan languages as well as from Italian, depending on the variety of the language spoken. This situation is different from that of *Ladino,* which served only as a translating language and therefore was not susceptible to borrowing. Thus *Ladino* retained its Spanish characteristics, a condition that influenced various Judeo-Spanish speakers to refer to it as "pure" versus the *mesklatino*—"mixture" or "jargon"—that they spoke (Sephiha 1986:77).

Jargon

Jargon (zhargon) was the term used for the language that arose because the speakers were either aware of the great extent of borrowing in their speech or did not, in many cases, believe that Judeo-Spanish was a true language. According to Sephiha, it was a term used by many of the "elite" Sephardim or those who had been educated in schools of the Alliance Israélite Universelle (1986:77). Many members of this Sephardic "elite" became ashamed to speak their language after extensive contact with French and its greater prestige. The great amount of gallicization of Judeo-Spanish was a powerful contributing factor, easily visible to many Judeo-Spanish speakers, in referring to their language as *jargon*.

Spaniolit or Espaniolit

Spaniolit is a term used at times in Israel to designate the present-day language of the Sephardim. It is a combination of the Spanish word *español* plus the Hebrew *-it* suffix which is characteristic of the names of other languages in Hebrew, such as [ivrit] 'Hebrew', [tsarfatit] 'French' and [anglit] 'English.' This writer only saw the word *Spaniolit* in its written form on the masthead of the Judeo-Spanish newspaper *La Luz de Israel,* where the editors described the newspaper in Hebrew as [iton be safa ha Spañolit-Ladino] 'Newspaper in the language Spaniolit-Ladino.' One of my Israeli informants referred to the language as *Spanioliko,* which is a term that adds the Judeo-Spanish diminutive and endearing *-iko* suffix to the term *Spaniolit*.

Djidyo (Ǐidiyo) or Djudyo (Ǐudiyo)

In Ottoman communities such as Bosnia, the everyday language of the Sephardim was not only known as *Espanyol,* but also as *Djudyo* or *Djidyo* (Baruch 1930:117), terms that are varieties of the Spanish word meaning "Jew." It is true, according to various scholars such as Bunis (1975a:32; 1978b:94–95), that in the research literature of the nineteenth and early twentieth centuries the vast majority of Sephardim interviewed were not aware that they spoke

Spanish or a Romance language. They only knew that they spoke "Jewish" or a Jewish language (see chapter 11, Section no. 15).

(E)spanyol, Muestro (E)spanyol

According to Bunis, many members of the first generation of American-born Sephardim report that their parents used to call the language *Espanyol* or *Spanyol* closely resembling the Spanish word *español* (1978b:94–5). This term is frequently qualified by the term *Muestro (E)spanyol* meaning "our Spanish" which differentiates it from Castilian Spanish, while the phrase *Es de muzotros* 'he is (one) of us' was used to distinguish the Sephardim themselves from others. In our research, A. Malinowski (1979) and T. Harris (1979) found that the terms *Espanyol* and *Spanyol* were the most popular choices of our respective informants. Bunis feels use of the term *Spanyol* was influenced by the works of Spanish scholars interested in the culture and language of the Sephardim in the Ottoman Empire who themselves referred to the Sephardim's language as *Espanyol* or *Judeo-Espanyol* (Bunis 1978b:95, 100–101).

Judeo-Spanish or Judeo-Espanyol

Judeo-Spanish is the neutral, self-explanatory, academic term preferred by Romance scholars to refer to the language of the Eastern Sephardim. A few researchers such as Birnbaum (1944:57–58) and Bunis (1978b:94) object to its use since they feel that it is a "pseudoscientific" term introduced by researchers and scholars. However, even though it is an invented academic term, it does embody both the Jewish and Spanish aspects of the origin of the language. And as A. Malinowski points out, "speakers of the language are not in the least uncomfortable with the term" (1979:7). The more recent publications in Judeo-Spanish such as Tel Aviv's weekly newspaper *La Luz de Israel*,[2] and the journal *Aki Yerushalayim* published in Jerusalem, as well as past Judeo-Spanish publications, advertise(d) themselves as either a *jurnal* 'newspaper' or a *revista* 'magazine, journal' *en judeo-espanyol-ladino* or *en djudeo-espanyol*. Malinowski reminds us that even the daily Kol Israel radio broadcast is announced as "nuestra programa en judeo-espanyol" (1979:7–8). The list of scholars both past and present who have used or who presently use the term *Judeo-Spanish* or *Judeo-Espanyol* is quite extensive and includes the following (listed in the Bibliography): Baruch (1930), Malinowski (1979), Nemer (1981), Sephiha (1986) and Wagner (1930), as well as the research of other well-known scholars including M. J. Benardete, H. Besso, C. Crews, A. Danon, M. Luria, J. Nehama, R. Renard, and M. Sala.

Throughout my research I use *Judeo-Spanish,* the neutral researcher's term to refer to the language. However, I do attach great importance to the name used by the speakers themselves to designate their own language. In order to determine the status of current spoken Judeo-Spanish, I interviewed a total of ninety-one native Judeo-Spanish speaking informants (28 from New York, 28 from Israel, 35 from Los Angeles) during the summers of 1978 and 1985. One of the questions I asked concerned the name of the language. The following is a discussion of informant responses.

Informant Responses

When the informants were asked "What name do you use to refer to your native language?" the majority answered with either *(E)spanyol* or *Spanish* or a mixture of two words meaning "Spanish." Table 1 shows the responses of the informants.

It is obvious that *(E)spanyol* was the most popular term used to designate the language. Of the ninety-one informants, sixty-two or 68 percent answered with either *Espanyol, Spanyol* or a variant of the word for "Spanish," while only twelve informants used the name *Ladino.* If we include the use of two name responses when the informants offer *(E)spanyol* plus another language name, or *Ladino* plus another name, we see that seventy informants or 77 percent used *(E)spanyol* or a variant as one or the only name for the language, while twenty-two or 24 percent used *Ladino* by itself or in combination with another name. *Judezmo* was given only five times, always in conjunction with another name (four times with *Ladino* and once with *Espanyol*), and *Djudyo* was given only once by itself and three times with another name.

When asked if the above names were synonyms for the same language, or if certain terms designated the written versus the spoken language, the majority answered that they were synonymous terms for both the written and spoken language. That is, seventy-five or 82 percent of the informants (New York–25, Israel–20, Los Angeles–30) felt that there were no special terms to differentiate the written from the spoken language.

On the other hand, eighteen informants reported that the various names for the language were not synonymous. Many of my infor-

TABLE 1. NAMES USED BY THE INFORMANTS TO
REFER TO THEIR LANGUAGE

Language Name	Total No. of Informants	Informant Distribution		
		NY	Israel	LA
Espanyol	37	14	18	5
Spanyol	14	2	—	12
Spanish	4	2	—	2
Espanyol/Spanyol	3	3	—	—
Espanyol/Spanish	2	—	—	2
Spanioliko	1	—	1	—
Espanyol-Ladino (one name)	1	—	1	—
Ladino	12	2	2	8
Ladino & (E)spanyol	5	2	1	2
Ladino & Judezmo	4	1	—	3
Ladino & Djudyo	1	1	—	—
Djudyo	1	1	—	—
Djudyo & Espanyol	2	—	2	—
Judezmo & Espanyol	1	—	1	—
Judeo-Espanyol	2	—	2	—
No name used	1	—	—	1
TOTAL NO. OF INFORMANTS	91			

mants were very well aware of the use of the term *Ladino* to designate the written language or language of the translations. One
informant stated:

> *Ladino* was used to designate the literal translation from Hebrew, i.e.,
> they were literal translations of the sacred writings from Hebrew syn-
> tax into Spanish. The noun *ladinador* means "translator" while the
> verb *enladinar* means "to translate."

Another informant said:

> *Ladino* was the word they used only when they read the Hebrew. They
> used to say "I'm reading in Ladino" or "I'm translating from Hebrew
> into Ladino,"

while another informant described Ladino as being "pure Spanish"
with no foreign words. *Judezmo,* on the other hand, was considered

as the spoken, mixed language with borrowings depending on the languages with which it had contact.

Other comments about *Judezmo* included:

Judezmo referred to the religion, not the language. That is, *Judezmo* means "Judaism" as in "one practices Judezmo."

Two informants reported that *Judezmo* was used in the same sense as *Yiddishkeit,* and one respondent said that *Judezmo* was a recent name that the Ashkenazim had come up with. Two other informants stated that in both Bulgaria and Monastir, the term *Judezmo* was used to mean the spoken language of the Jews or a Jewish language, but that they started calling it *Espanyol* only after emigrating to the United States. Another informant reported that *Judezmo* was never used to refer the language. However, thirteen informants said that they never heard the terms *Ladino* or *Judezmo* until they emigrated to the United States or Israel. I attribute my informants' relatively high (22 informants or 24 percent) use of the term *Ladino* to its current popularity in the United States, even though in most cases it was not used by the informants until they had emigrated to America. J. Nemer (1981:6) also reports that in her study of the Sephardic community of Indianapolis, the majority of her informants called their language either *Spanish* or *Ladino.*

In Malinowski's studies in Israel (1979) her informants gave responses similar to the ones I received. When asked to name the language they were speaking, she reports that 95 percent of her Israeli informants replied *(E)spanyol.* She also reports that those who recognized the term *Judezmo* said it was either an archaic term or that it referred to the broad concept of "Judaism" rather than specifically to the language of the Sephardim. She suggests that since *Judezmo* is not used as a name for the language, its revival might be considered an "imposition," since it comes from a source outside the living language (ibid.,6).[3]

R. M. Chumaceiro, in her study in Jerusalem in 1971, also reports that *Spanyol* was the most common name that the informants used to designate their spoken language, with the Hebrew derivatives *Spanyolit* or *Sfaradi* (the Hebrew for "Spanish") also offered. She commented that for her informants, *Ladino* was the term given to the language by outsiders and scholars. It was generally a familiar term to the more educated of the informants to signify the written language translations of the Hebrew Biblical texts. But Chumaceiro also reports a similar phenomenon that I found in my studies. She writes that her informants all agreed that *Ladino* is not the name that Spanyol speakers give to their language. However, when they speak to outsiders, they themselves might refer to their mother tongue by the name *Ladino* (Chumaceiro 1982:38). She also states that the terms *Judezmo* and *Judeo-Espanyol* were not known to her respondents even though *Judeo-Espanyol* is the term used in the daily fifteen-minute Judeo-Spanish radio broadcast in Israel.[4]

In Malinowski's study of Sephardim in Istanbul in 1980, she reports that in answer to the same question, 77 percent of her Turkish informants responded with *(E)spanyol* and 23 percent answered *Djudyo*. She also states that each group easily accepted the other term as an alternate name or often quickly added it:

> In free conversation the two terms were used interchangeably, one as frequently as the other (Malinowski 1982a:14).

She also states that several informants offered *djudeo-(e)spanyol* as an alternate name, obviously like my Israeli informants who had come into contact with the term, knowing of its scholarly or academic origins. It is interesting to note that, like most of my informants, none of her Turkish informants spontaneously offered the term *Judezmo*.

Conclusion

The results of my research and that of others, reveal the following four points which need to be summarized:

(1) *(E)spanyol* was the most frequent term given by the informants (mine as well as those of other studies) to designate the name of their language.

(2) Although *Ladino* has traditionally been considered to be the name for the written language of translation from the Hebrew of the Biblical texts, it was a very popular, commonly used term by my United States informants (as well as many from Israel) to also designate the spoken language. However, when asked about the name they used to refer to their native language, most of them answered *(E)spanyol*.

(3) Contrary to the claims of Bunis and others, *Judezmo* was rarely offered as a possible name by my informants, as was also the case with the informants of Malinowski (1979, 1982a) and Chumaceiro (1982).

(4) *Judeo-Spanish* or *Judeo-Espanyol* is generally accepted by

the informants as the neutral, academic term for the language which is used by researchers.

* * *

It is obvious that what to call the language of the Eastern Sephardim is still a very controversial issue. Due to cultural, ethnic, sociological, and linguistic considerations, the question is now, and probably will remain, unsolved. Various informants of different studies could not, or still cannot, agree on a name to designate their language, and even members of the same family often do not hold the same opinions. T. Balch (1980:10) illustrates this confusion with a quote from Barocas who reported that his language was "that nameless dialect I learned to speak since my infancy." For his father it was *muestro espanyol* 'our Spanish', and for the mother of Professor Mair José Benardete it was *la lengua de los djudios* 'the language of the Jews' (Barocas 1976:43, 132, 133).

I do not mean to belittle the sociolinguistic implications of the problem of what to call this language. But I must agree with I. Benabu and J. Sermoneta (1985:xi), who argue that an analysis of the important issues concerning Judeo-Spanish is a more valuable contribution to present and future studies of the language than continued consideration of its nomenclature.

3

History of the Eastern Sephardim: From Pre-Expulsion Spain to World War II in the Levant

In order to comprehend the evolution of a language, an understanding of the historical and sociological factors which have influenced its development is required. The following is a short history of the Sephardic Jews beginning in pre-Expulsion Spain and continuing in the Ottoman Empire until World War II.

The Jews in Pre-Expulsion Spain

The history of the Jews in Spain forms a magnificent chapter in the general history of both the Jews and the Spaniards. Dr. A. Haim writes:

> The Jewish community in Spain (Sefarad) was one of the most unique and important in the Middle Ages, and occupies an outstanding place in the history of the Jews. In Spain there developed during several centuries a Jewish culture that attained the highest pinnacles of creativity and was the most remarkable in the world at the time. (Haim 1988:1)

According to Renard,

> never have the Jews been so progressive or prosperous, never have they participated to such a large extent in the public administration. Never have they exercised such a great influence on the local civilization. Never have the Jews felt so at home . . . and never have they known the relative tranquility of several centuries in which to develop their qualities and resources to engender a veritable civilization,

as they did in pre-Expulsion Spain (Renard 1966a:49). Before 1492 the Jews in Spain enjoyed a very comfortable, if not wealthy, existence. They were indispensable to Spain's economy since they, as merchants, controlled the trade establishing a system of modern commerce with international transactions. As Bendiner points out, it was the Jews, with their connections abroad, their knowledge of foreign languages and customs, and their willingness to travel, who "opened the windows of Andalusia" (1983:97). They were prominent in other vital professions such as medicine, law, moneylending, and artisanship or craftsmanship. They had also distinguished themselves in various scientific fields which included mathematics, astronomy, astrology, and cartography.

Having suffered under Christian rule, the Jews welcomed the Muslim conquest of the early eighth century. Under Muslim rule Jewish culture in Spain enjoyed a "Golden Age," producing classic works in Hebrew poetry, philosophy, ethics, and rabbinic scholarship, especially during the tenth and eleventh centuries and the first half of the twelfth century. Included among the prominent figures of this era are the poet and philosopher Solomon Ibn Gabirol; the great Hebrew poet Judah Halevi; Abraham Ibn Ezra, poet, grammarian, and biblical scholar; Samuel ha Negid, scholar and poet who served as vizier and commander of the army during the eleventh century in Granada; and Moses Maimonides (1135–1204),[1] the great philosopher, who, according to Angel, was the most important figure produced by Sephardic Jewry, and whose works in Jewish law and philosophy remain "classics" to this day (1991:2).

The literary works of Jews or their "crypto-Jewish"[2] descendants formed the basis not only of the Jewish Golden Age of Learning but also of Spain's Golden Age of Literature, which flourished from 1550 to 1650. According to M. Lazar, the two important surviving relics of Jewish poetry in medieval Spain are *Proverbios morales* 'Ethical Proverbs' written by Rabbi Don Santob de Carrión between 1355 and 1360 and the anonymous work *Poema de Yoçef* 'Poems on Joseph,' which dates from the first half of the fifteenth century (Lazar 1972:17). Famous *converso* writers include Juan Alfonso de Baena who compiled *Cancionero de Baena* around 1445, Juan de Mena (1411–1456) who wrote *El laberinto de fortuna* in 1444, Pablo de Santa María (ex Salomon Halevi 1345–1435) and Alonso de Cartagena (1384–1456), the humanist prose writer son of Pablo de Santa María. Famous descendants of *conversos* include Fernando de Rojas (1465–1541), author of *La Celestina* (1499), Luis Vives (1492–1540) who wrote *Introducción a la sabiduría* (1524), Santa Teresa de Jesús or de Avila (born Teresa de Cepeda 1515–1582), author of *El castillo interior* or *Las moradas* (1588) and *Libro de su vida* (1588), fray Luis de León (1527–1591), author of

La perfecta casada (1583), Isaac Cardoso (1604–1683) who wrote *Las excelencias de los hebreos* (1679) and the prolific author/playwright Antonio Enríquez Gómez (1600–1663). Other Jewish writers of Spanish origin include Mateo Alemán (1547–1614?), author of *Guzmán de Alfarache* (Part I–1599; Part II–1604), and León Hebreo (Judah Abravanel 1460?–1521) who wrote *Diálogos de amor* in 1535.

In the Peninsula Jews and Christians lived in an atmosphere of harmony and friendship unknown in the rest of Europe. The Jews enjoyed the favor of kings and noblemen who frequently granted them privileges or protection from violence and oppression. According to Benardete, the Jews formed an *imperium in imperio* (1982:55). Generally they lived in the big cities within the walls of their *aljamas* or *juderías* 'Jewish quarters' where they were able to control their own administration and communal affairs. There were no laws that limited Jewish occupations or place of residence. As Bendiner points out, if the gates of the *aljamas* were closed, it was because the Jews themselves shut them (1983:169).

The Jews also played the role of "civilizer" during the Middle Ages. They contributed much to the integration of the Christian civilization with the Moslem one, which was superior to other European cultures of the time, by serving as the go-between for the Christians and the Moslems. Because of this continual contact with the Moors, the Jews knew Arabic as well as Hebrew and were influenced by Moorish culture and literary works which were of the highest or most advanced level in Spain during this period. The famous School of Translators of Toledo, the majority of whom were Jews (under the reign of Alfonso X, el Sabio "the Wise," 1252–1284), is a fine example of the Jews' crucial role in the development of Spain's culture. In their translations into Castilian (and also into Latin and even Hebrew) of the important works coming from the Greek traditions in the East, the Arabic culture in Spain and the Latin heritage in Europe, they linked Medieval Europe with the Arab world. And at the same time,

> Hebrew literature acquired a cohesion and splendor not surpassed by that existing in any of the Jewish communities in the rest of Europe. (A. Haim 1988:2)

As a result of their high level of intellectual activity, the Jews were the most learned and influential class of fifteenth century Spain. As J. Stampfer points out, the Jews were the "intellectual elite" (1987:17), and the Christian population not only respected them, but envied them as well. Because of their prestige throughout the centuries, intermarriages between Jews and Christians were not unusual. In fact, according to the work of Cardenal Mendoza y Bobadilla (1849), Jewish blood existed in the veins of almost all of the Spanish and Portuguese nobility by the end of the thirteenth century, much to the chagrin of many later in 1547 when the policy of *la limpieza de sangre* 'Spanish blood purity'[3] had become the official policy of the State and prevailed throughout the seventeenth century (Wertheimer 1977:5). Not only was the great inquisitor Torquemada descended from a *converso,* but even King Ferdinand had Jewish blood (Prinz 1973:39).

Unfortunately, life in Spain was to be irrevocably changed. Religious fanaticism soon transformed itself into racism, and an end was put to the high level of civilization not only for the Jews and Arabs, but also for the Spaniards in general. On 4 June 1391, an angry mob attacked the gates of the Jewish quarter in Seville as they killed, looted, and forced the Jews to choose between baptism or death. The pogrom spread throughout the Iberian Peninsula and into the Mediterranean reaching the cities of Madrid, Valencia, Barcelona, and Mallorca. When the riots ended a year later, an estimated one hundred thousand Jews had been killed and more than a hundred thousand Jews had been forcibly converted to Christianity. In the fifteenth century, it was the *conversos* or New Christians who were judged by the Inquisition for backsliding or secretly continuing to practice their former religion. According to Ullman (1991) and Gerber (1991a), 1391 was a more crucial year in Jewish history than 1492 since it served as the basis for the later expulsion edict.

On 31 March 1492, the historical edict of expulsion was signed in Granada by *los reyes católicos* (the Catholic monarchs) King Ferdinand and Queen Isabella, stating that any Jew who did not convert to Catholicism would be expelled or killed. The Jews were granted a four month delay to put their affairs in order and were not permitted to leave the country carrying any money, gold, or silver. Thus they left with few material belongings, but with their most precious possessions: their language, customs, and Spanish-Jewish heritage. Various historians feel that the purpose of the edict was not to expel the Jews, instead it had a primarily religious objective: "to convert the Jews to Christianity" (Kamen 1990). The Catholic monarchs were also struggling against divisive forces in their kingdoms and were desperate for the unification and "purification" of the Iberian Peninsula. Gerber reports that the expulsion edict was "part of a preplanned blueprint for national unity"

(1991b). At any rate, it seems that few believed the Jews would leave the Peninsula in such large numbers and that the consequences to the country itself would be so grave.

The edict of expulsion dealt a fatal blow to Spain's economy, since it was supported almost exclusively by Jews. For example, it was the Jews, such as the *converso* Luis de Santangel, Chancellor, comptroller, and financial advisor to the royal household, who were the principal financiers for Columbus's expeditions. To better understand the crucial position the Jews held in Spain at the time of expulsion, I refer to a quote from Werner Sombart in his book *Les Juifs et la vie économique* (1923: 246–7) who contended that the Jews were the founders of modern capitalism. He wrote that "the expedition of Columbus would not have been possible if the rich Jews had left Spain a generation earlier," since it was the Jews who financed a good part of this expedition. By the same token, he contended that if they had been expelled from the Peninsula a century later, the wealth of the fugitive exiles would not have promoted Dutch, English, and German capitalism, but rather the capitalism of Spain.

At sunset on 2 August 1492, the ships carrying the last Jewish exiles set sail. At dawn on the following day (3 August), the three caravelles of Columbus set out in search of a new world. It is from this auspicious date that the history of the Spanish Jews became external to that of Spain. The Sephardic Diaspora had begun.[4]

The Eastern Sephardim in the Ottoman Empire

According to Wagner (1930:12), the most significant event of the history of the Spanish Jews at the time of expulsion was the invitation extended to them by the Sultan, Bayezid II, who ruled from 1481–1512, to settle in the Ottoman Empire. Bayezid wanted the Jews to colonize the devastated and conquered regions of Macedonia, Thrace, and the territories surrounding Constantinople after the Turkish invasion (Ottoman conquests). This area included the Peninsula of Gallipoli, Adrianople (Edirne), and Rodosto. But more importantly, the Sultan was well aware of the Jewish role in the economy of Spain, and he wanted the Jews to build up the commerce of his empire. Because of the Jews' great accomplishments in the financial and commercial enterprises of Spain, it is easy to understand the following famous quote attributed to Bayezid II on extending his invitation to the Jews to settle in his empire: "What! call ye this Ferdinand 'wise'—he who depopulates his own domin-

ions in order to enrich mine?" (Roth 1970:252). Bayezid ordered
the governors of the Ottoman provinces not to refuse the Jews
entry, and he instructed his border guards not to put any obstacles
in the way of the peninsular refugees. He even provided those who
accepted his invitation with lands and tax exemptions. In return
for settling in his empire and doing for its economy what the Jews
had done for that of Spain, Bayezid II promised to give the Jews
complete religious freedom as well as communal/internal autonomy. He kept his promise and as a result, the Jewish community
or *millet*,[5] which was divided into various local, autonomous communities, had its own administration, courts, jails, hospitals, cemeteries, synagogues, and schools where the Spanish Jews could use
their own language (Spanish) as the medium of instruction. The
Sephardim enjoyed a level of freedom and prestige, and were
granted various privileges not enjoyed by Jews in other parts of
the world. In fact, throughout the centuries, it was not unusual for
Ashkenazic Jews from various Eastern European cities to settle in
the Empire. As Shaw points out, Ottoman Turkey was the major
refuge for Jews not only from Spain, but from all over Europe,
who were fleeing persecution. Life in Turkey was "paradise" compared to what was happening to Jews in the Christian lands of
Europe (1991:11).

One of the main reasons that the Jews enjoyed such freedom in
the Ottoman Empire in the sixteenth, seventeenth, and eighteenth
centuries was because the spirit of nationalism, as it exists today,
was not present in the Empire prior to World War I. As Besso
points out, the Turkish government was based on the idea of a
religious state which did not consider the land and the language to
be forces of unity (Besso 1971:624). With no separation of religion
and state, coupled with no large scale class of landowners, the
policy of the Osmanli State was not to meddle in the religious life
and family customs of its non-Islamic subjects, provided that they
were law-abiding, trustworthy citizens who paid the required taxes
and kept the peace. In fact, as Rodrigue points out, since the non-
Muslim minorities were outside the ruling elite, not only were they
allowed a degree of autonomy in their internal affairs, they were
also "in some respects better off than their Muslim counterparts"
(1990:30). Immanuel suggests that the lack of official anti-Jewish
sentiment was due in large part to the fact that the Jews were
considered the only minority in the Ottoman Empire that did not
have any apparent national aspirations. It is true that they were
active economically, but they generally remained out of politics
and military life (1989:1). And whether it was out of gratitude and/

or respect for Moslem culture and religion, the Jews were, among the *rayas* (the "flock" or taxpaying subjects of the Sultan), the most loyal subjects of the Ottoman Empire (Wagner 1930:13).

According to Besso (1971) and Benardete (1982), this Ottoman governmental concept was one of the reasons Judeo-Spanish was able to survive throughout the centuries in Turkey and in the countries later formed out of the Ottoman Empire. The Turks had no national language requirements, and the Jews were not asked to participate or to cooperate in matters affecting the welfare of the State. For example, non-Muslim Ottoman subjects who were known as *dhimmis* ('protected' subjects), were not obliged to serve in the army until 1909. While this absence of amalgamation with the neighboring peoples made it impossible for the Jews to completely assimilate on the one hand, it enabled them to maintain their language on the other. Various scholars have pointed out that the Sephardim owe much to the Ottoman Empire for allowing them to conserve their language and customs, and that Spain itself should acknowledge the Empire for being the guardian of Spanish traditions. While the ancient Ottoman Empire existed, the use of Judeo-Spanish was never opposed or hindered.

The Sixteenth Century

By the sixteenth century Ottoman Jewry was enjoying a "Golden Age" (Shaw 1991:chap. 2). The main cities in which the Jews had settled were Constantinople (Istanbul), Izmir (Smyrna), Adrianople (Edirne), Monastir (Bitola), Bucharest, Jerusalem, Rhodes, and, above all, Salonika (Thessaloniki), which became the center of Sephardic Jewry in the Balkans. Salonika, with its numerous academies, rich libraries, and archives became the metropolis of all the Orient, and was referred to as "Little Jerusalem," "Mother City of Israel," the "Metropolis of Israel," the "flower of Sephardic Jewry," and the "Sephardic Republic." But it was a center for secular studies as well as religious learning, since the University of Salonika was famous for the teaching of such subjects as mathematics, astronomy, and medicine. Starting from 1545, and until World War II, Salonika was the only Ottoman city in which the Jews comprised the majority of the population. Salonika and Constantinople were the two cities that enjoyed the highest level of culture throughout the Levant. Other Jewish communities subsequently founded by Saloniklis (Jews from Salonika) were in Sofia (Bulgaria), Sarajevo and Skopje (Yugoslavia), and Larisa (Greece).

In the sixteenth century the Sephardic communities in the Ottoman Empire were flourishing. This was apparent in reports made by various travelers of the time such as P. Belon (1588:400), who wrote that the Jews had taken charge of all the commercial traffic and that the wealth and revenue of Turkey was in their hands. He also mentioned the advantage the Jews had of being able to speak and understand all the languages spoken in the Levant. Thus the Jews promoted the economy of the Empire in the same way they had done in Spain and according to the expectations of Bayezid II. They were the merchants par excellence who built up and controlled the trade of the Empire. They had Sephardic contacts in other main cities of the Levant as well as in cities throughout the world. They had a monopoly on luxury items such as jewelry, precious stones, pearls, silk, cotton, sugar, and tobacco.

Besides being merchants, the Jews practiced professions similar to those they had in Spain such as banking, moneylending, and textiles, especially silk and wool weaving. They served as customs officials, interpreters, and diplomatic agents. They taught the Turks to make gunpowder and to manufacture superior weapons such as firearms and cannon, which became a factor in later Ottoman conquests. Medicine was always an important profession for the Sephardim (Franco 1897:39). The fact that the Jews held the post of Imperial Physician for many generations demonstrated the confidence the Muslims had in them. In many instances, according to Shaw, these court physicians also served in an advisory capacity to the Sultans and were able to influence them to favor the Jews when necessary (Shaw 1992:18). Díaz-Mas also points out that acting in their capacity as doctors, interpreters and viziers, it was not rare to see Jews enjoying a certain influence in the Turkish court (1986:60).[6]

In the sixteenth century the Spanish Jews formed a veritable aristocracy in the Ottoman Empire, and their level of education was unquestionably superior. Jewish culture flourished under Ottoman rule. Joseph Caro (1488–1575) wrote his code on Jewish law, the *Shulhan Arukh* (first published in Salonika in 1568), Solomon ha-Levi Alkabes (1505–1584) composed the *Lekha Dodi* (hymn that glorifies the Sabbath), and various kabbalist schools of thought were established throughout the Empire. In fact, it was the Sephardim who introduced printing in the Empire, founding the first Hebrew press in Constantinople in 1493 (see chapter 6, section no. 9). The high prestige that the Sephardim enjoyed resulted in an interesting linguistic phenomenon: non-Sephardic Jews as well as non-Jews (both Greeks and Turks) often learned to speak Judeo-

Spanish for use in their commercial dealings as well as in other relations with the Sephardim (Benardete 1982:119).

In the sixteenth century, under the reign of Suleiman I the Magnificent (1520–1566), a custom was started that was perpetuated throughout the centuries: the sultan invested a Jew with the title of *kâhya* or political defender of the nation. The *kâhya* had free access to the palace to tell of injustices done to Jews anywhere in the Empire (Franco 1897:46). The *kahal* or Jewish community district appointed an official also called the *kâhya,* who was the person of that community in charge of relations with Ottoman officials. According to Shaw, the *kâhyas* also reported births, deaths, marriages, and divorces to the authorities (Shaw 1991:58, 172). And throughout the centuries the Ottomans even protected the Jews against the Blood Libel[7] attacks from Christians and other minorities in the Empire.

But despite the privileges and respect accorded them by the Ottoman government, the Turks did insist on the secular isolation of the Jews. However, as M. Angel points out, the Jews were required by Jewish law to live in their own quarters simply because they needed to be in walking distance of the synagogue (1978:8). They were authorized to live in special Jewish quarters known as *mahalles* or *Yahudi Mahallei* (*juderías* in Spanish), which were local units of the *millet.* Each *mahalle* had its own schools, synagogues, and civil services that were organized under a religious leader who was usually the officially designated representative of the government (Shaw 1976:162). These *mahalles* served to prevent total assimilation, while forcing the Jews to continually maintain their status as foreigners. However, at the same time, this forced isolation helped the Jews not only to conserve their folklore, traditional customs, and liturgical Andalusian music, but more importantly, their language. Estrugo emphasizes that the *juderías* in the Levant were not depressing ghettos like those of the Ashkenazic Jews in Poland, Russia, and other areas of Eastern Europe. Instead, the Levantine *juderías* were pleasant barrios that had their own laws and administrators and consisted of attractive *kortijos* (inherited from Spain), which were large houses built around a central courtyard or patio with orchards and gates, portals, shutters, grating, wells, and other features reminiscent of the ancient *aljamas* in Seville (Estrugo 1958:51).

The Jews' loyalty to their ancestral life can be seen in their regroupment in the Empire. Each city had its different *kales* or synagogues (from the Hebrew word קהל [kahal] "congregation") divided according to the city or region of origin in the Peninsula.

For example, there was a kal de Aragon, kal de Cordoba, kal de Castilla, kal de Barcelona, kal de Toledo, kal de Mallorca, and a kal de Portugal in many cities. Through the years the number of *kales* increased along with the immigration of ever growing numbers of Sephardim to the Balkans. In 1492, for example, there were three synagogues in Salonika: one Romaniote (Greek), one Italian, and one Ashkenazic. By 1536 there were fourteen more and, by the beginning of the seventeenth century, Salonika had thirty *kales*, Constantinople had forty-four and Monastir had five (Renard 1966a:71–72).

The Sephardim spoke their regional dialect in the home, but the Castilian dialect became accepted as the official language, which was used for communal acts, proclamations, business affairs, sermons, relations with other communities, and teaching in the Talmud Torahs (Jewish schools). According to M. Molho, linguistic unity was achieved (i.e., the majority of dialectal elements were assimilated or had ceded to Castilian, especially in the big cities) half a century after exile (1960:2). Thus the Spanish spoken by the Jews in cities like Istanbul and Salonika in the sixteenth century was not so different from that spoken in Spain at the same time. This fact was illustrated by Gonzalo de Illescas, a traveler in the middle of the sixteenth century who wrote in his journal:

> To be sure in the cities of Salonika, Constantinople . . . they do not buy or sell, nor do business in any other language but Spanish. And I met Jews in Venice from Salonika who spoke the Castilian language, though mere lads, as well if not better than I (Gonzalo de Illescas 1606:106–cited in Benardete 1982:61)

The Seventeenth Century—The Beginning of Decadence of Sephardic Life

The privileged life of the Sephardim and their language in the Balkans was not to be long lasting. Since the fate of the Jews was tied closely to that of the Ottoman Muslims, both the Jews and Muslims suffered as the Empire declined starting in the late seventeenth century. Reasons for the decadence of Sephardic life in the Levant include the following:

(1) The Ottoman Empire slowly began to lose its prestige in the economic areas of trade and commerce. In 1669 the taking of the Cretan capital of Candia by the Turks deprived Venice of an essential port of call in the Levant and marked the beginning of the

decadence of Salonika, whose prosperity was linked to its commercial relations with and via Venice. Also, along with other discoveries throughout the world, the Mediterranean ports were losing their importance. This naturally affected the Sephardim, since they controlled the commerce in the Levant.

(2) By the seventeenth century the intellectual life, which had been particularly rich in the sixteenth century, was suffering from the lack of contact with the West, which was then in full renaissance. Also, the abandonment of the Latin alphabet in favor of Hebrew characters hurt the Sephardim intellectually by cutting them off from the literature of the Iberian Peninsula. While the Spanish language was acquiring modern forms and approaching its apogee with its literary *Edad de Oro* (Golden Age), the Spanish speakers of the Levant were clinging to their language which, by the beginning of the seventeenth century, was becoming more archaic than the Castilian Spanish spoken in Spain at that time.

(3) As the years passed, the cultural reserves that the Sephardim had brought with them were being used up. They could not maintain the high level of culture, which was gradually being replaced by another native or indigenous one. Turkey was not able to provide an intellectual stimulation for the Sephardim, who seemed to be caught in a vacuum in which Spanish studies were neglected. While Spanish literature was prospering in Amsterdam in the seventeenth century, thanks to the immigration there of learned *conversos* who wrote in the Latin alphabet, there was very little Spanish literary activity in the Levant. According to Revah, between 1601 and 1729 there were almost no Judeo-Spanish literary works printed in the Balkans except for some liturgical songs and elegies (1964:47). It was only after 1729 that printing in Judeo-Spanish greatly increased.

(4) Saul Mézan points out an interesting factor that contributed to the decadence of the Sephardic culture in the Balkans. He wrote that the happy symbiosis of the Jews, Christians, and Moslems was destroyed in 1492, and that the new refuge for the Sephardim was a refuge for the body but not for the spirit (Mézan 1925:33–34). Not being able to create a new symbiotic relationship, the Oriental Sephardim entered into a period of isolation and decay which endured for three hundred years. A surprising fact is that, after four hundred years of residence in Turkey, the majority of Jews did not learn to read and write in Turkish (Benardete 1982:114). Shaw reports that well into the twentieth century, only a small minority of Turkish Jews knew and used Turkish, since the emphasis was on European languages and customs (1991:165).

(5) The cultural decay and growing poverty, ignorance, and de-spair of this period were the main reasons that the false messianic movement of Shabbetai Zvi was possible. Zvi (1626–1676), who was dedicated to the study of the Kabbalah,[8] was able to persuade a majority of the Balkan Jews that he was the Messiah who would officially come in the year 1666. However, the Turkish authorities saw potential danger in such fanaticism and intervened. Zvi was imprisoned and eventually given the choice by Mehmed IV to con-vert or be executed. He chose the former, and he and his wife converted to the Islamic religion in 1666. The consequences of this movement were disastrous for the Sephardim who were not only ruined economically but were spiritually shattered as well. They also lost the confidence and trust of the Sultans, who allowed the Greeks and Armenians (the other two main minorities of the Em-pire) to take advantage of this period to fill the temporary void left open by the Jews in the areas of commerce. The Greeks and Armenians not only became competition for the Jews in these areas, but even became their employers in certain instances. As M. Angel emphasizes, "If you want to talk about the real decline of the Sephardic communities of the Ottoman Empire, you can pretty much pin the date to 1666" (1987a:83).

The Eighteenth Century—Decline of the Empire and its Jews

The Ottoman decline began to intensify about 1700. The European powers exploited the weaknesses of the Empire with various Ca-pitulations agreements that allowed European citizens to be gov-erned by their own laws, without being subjected to Ottoman authority or taxes. The Ottoman rulers were also ineffective and incompetent, which often resulted in anarchic conditions. Jews and Muslims were driven out of the market place to be replaced by Europeans and Christians, and even advisors to the sultan were being replaced by Muslims and Christians.

Besides a Jewish decline in trade, the Jews suffered intellectually during this period. In the eighteenth century the Sephardic com-munities in the Levant were untouched by the doctrines spreading across Europe, so that for the Diaspora in the Ottoman Empire, the eighteenth century remained part of the Middle Ages. All knowledge outside religion and its literature was considered use-less, and all scientific or philosophical works were rejected (an attitude which had not been true of the seventeenth century). How-ever, Díaz-Mas points out the existence of one cultural bright spot during this period: the publication in 1730 of Jacob Huli's *Me'am Lo'ez,* the famous Sephardic folk encyclopedia (see chapter 6, section no. 6), and the various poetic *coplas* written through the eighteenth century in a general flourishing of Judeo-Spanish literature (1986:66). But unfortunately, these were exceptions in a period of decadence.

As conditions worsened and poverty spread, everyone became completely absorbed in the efforts needed to make a living. As a result, study was neglected and by the middle of the eighteenth century the majority of the needy classes did not know how to read and write except for prayers and simple correspondence. Only the bourgeoisie had some knowledge of the Hebrew language and were capable of understanding an easy text but the majority no longer knew how to read the Bible. The middle classes knew the religious rituals and retained the Ladino, or religious language, as a result of the memorizing technique they used in the schools to recite certain rituals. The girls were excluded from all teaching since it was felt that their purpose in life was simply to become good homemakers. As a result, most of the women were illiterate and thus passed down the culture: *konsežas* (folk tales), *romanzas* (ballads), and *refranes* (proverbs) orally to their children.

At the same time the Jewish community itself was suffering from internal schism and constant bickering due to lack of a strong leadership. Also, many were privy to superstitions of all kinds, since they were still in a state of confusion brought on by the failure of the false prophet Shabbetai Zvi in the seventeenth century.

Because the above factors contributed to reduced prestige of the Sephardim in the Levant, it was rare to find a Jew occupying a functionary position in the administration after the end of the eighteenth century. By that time the Jews had been relegated to a low intellectual level. There was no authority recognized by all that would have been able to impose the necessary means to elevate their intellectual level. The Jewish community had no guide or central institution, only an antiquated organization headed toward failure. Also, the sultans were becoming less inclined to protect the Jews, which resulted in abuses and attacks from the Janissary forces[9] as well as increased accusations of blood libel. Also, there was no policy to aid in the prevention and recovery of certain calamities or natural disasters such as the fires that struck Salonika in 1754 and 1788, and Constantinople in 1756; epidemics that ravaged Salonika (1708–9, 1712–13, 1718–19, 1724, and 1929–30); and earthquakes like the one that occurred in Safed in 1758. Frequent fires, whether accidental or provoked, and diseases did great damage to the Oriental Jewish population.

The Nineteenth Century

Natural disasters continued to plague the Sephardic communities of the Levant in the nineteenth century. New fires, cholera epidemics (lasting from 1832–1913), earthquakes, and more accusations of blood libel (1864, 1872, and 1875 in Izmir, 1866, 1868, 1870, and 1874 in Constantinople, as well as in other cities) all contributed to the further decline of the Sephardic communities.

According to Rodrigue, it was during the reign of Mahmud II (1808–1839) that two events precipitated the fall from grace of the Jewish *sarrafs* (bankers or moneylenders). The abolition of the Janissary corps in 1826, with which the Jewish community had several economic ties, coupled with the murder (ordered by the Sultan) of Behor Isaac Carmona of the famous Istanbul banking family,[10] helped to submerge the Jewish community of Istanbul into "financial chaos" (Rodrigue 1990:27). This financial decline also affected the Jewish communities in Jerusalem and other regions of the Empire. With the Sephardim's loss of economic prominence in banking and commerce, the two other minorities of the Empire once again benefited greatly. The Greeks, and especially the Armenians, began to push the Jews out or to take over areas of Jewish banking dominance. By the first half of the nineteenth century, Judeo-Spanish stopped being the universal language of trade, and there was a weakening of ties uniting the various communities. The Sephardim were also losing contact with the medical and law professions. As medicine degenerated, the Greeks and Armenians were penetrating into Islamic jurisprudence, and the formerly unpursued but now thriving professions of engineering, architecture, and occupations concerned with industry, which had been totally foreign to the Jews. In the first quarter of the nineteenth century Salonika had already lost its principal industry of wool weaving, which fell victim to European competition. Like the rest of Europe, Turkey suffered loss of economic prominence and prestige due to the influence of industry (manufactured products) coupled with foreign capitalistic ventures. As Rodrigue points out, by the mid nineteenth century Western capitalism dominated the Levant (1990:38).

Efforts to modernize the weakening Empire resulted in the age of reforms known as the *Tanzimat,* which aimed to centralize the government. The Empire temporarily revived during the Tanzimat era and many Jews regained their positions of leadership with the help of European Jewish bankers such as the Rothschilds and Baron Maurice de Hirsch (Shaw 1992:19). The Reform Decree *(Hatt-i Humayun)* of 1856 and the citizenship law of 1869 granted equality to all non-Muslims and made them equal citizens under the law. This was an effort to provide a loyal population and, in the words of Rodrigue, "to downplay the importance of ethnic and religious divisions" (1990:32). Such policies negatively affected the Jewish minority and their language, as the autonomy of the *millets* and their individual rights were infringed upon. The Jewish people no longer enjoyed control of all aspects of their life as they had before this new "equality."[11] In the end these reforms did not save the Empire, which by the 1870s was bankrupt, and large sections of the economy were being controlled by non-Muslims and foreigners.

As the Empire declined more and more, Jews were falling progressively into poverty and disfavor. A quote from David Porter, an American traveling in the Ottoman Empire in 1835, sums up the economic situation of a good number of Sephardim in the Balkans during the first half of the nineteenth century:

> I think it will hardly be denied that the Jewish nation in Turkey is in a complete state of indigence, as is sufficiently proved by the mean and vile employments to which individuals devote themselves. (1835:67)

Jewish Education in the Nineteenth Century

The Sephardic schools in the nineteenth century were also in decline. They suffered from a lack of materials, incompetent teachers, old-fashioned pedagogy, vindictive forms of punishment, and unhygienic surroundings. These conditions, combined with a desire for what Rodrigue refers to as a "Western orientation" that promoted Western culture (1990:39), were the main reasons why the schools of the Alliance Israélite Universelle[12] were established in the Balkans after 1860. These schools were meant to enlighten the "backward" Jews in the "backward communities" of the Orient, Turkey, North Africa, and the Middle East (Angel 1987b:104). While these Alliance schools did enable the Jews to reenter the Ottoman society and begin a Jewish cultural revival, they also dealt a fatal blow to Judeo-Spanish since the new language of instruction was French (See chapter 11 section no. 6). The new emphasis was on European languages and cultures (especially French) instead of local or Ottoman Jewish culture and history.

Before the founding of the Alliance Schools, many Jews had attended the Protestant and Catholic schools in the Empire run by missionaries.[13] And although the missionaries were not very successful in converting the Jews, they at least instructed them in the rudiments of conduct, hygiene, and knowledge, while at the same time distributing free food and clothing. The Protestant missionaries also brought something unique to the Sephardim: translations in Judeo-Spanish of the Sacred Scriptures.

End of the Nineteenth Century and Beginning of the Twentieth Century: Nationalism and Division of the Ottoman Empire

The end of the nineteenth century and the beginning of the twentieth century mark the start of nationalism in the Balkans and the vulnerability of the Jews faced with the dismemberment of the Ottoman Empire. The Ottoman Jews were desperate to keep the Empire together and were thus strong supporters of the Ottoman armies against nationalist revolts. However, the various wars and nationalistic movements took a heavy toll. Beginning with the Revolution of Young Turks in 1908, the Balkan Wars of 1912–1913 and World War I, parts of the Empire were annexed and transformed into new countries such as Greece, Serbia, and Montenegro. And each time a fragment of the Empire was detached, thousands of Sephardim lost their political and linguistic cohesion as they were forced outside of the old Ottoman Empire and were subjected to the policies of the new Balkan states. They found themselves with fewer and fewer privileges as the rulers of the new Balkan states were less tolerant than those of the Turkish Empire. Suddenly the Jews had to attend national schools and were forced to learn the local languages. As of 1909, after the Young Turk Revolution, the military exemption tax known as the cizye[14] was abolished, and the Sephardim, who had previously been exempt, were now obligated to do military service. Obligatory military service in the Empire (as elsewhere) served as a catalyst in the elimination of regional dialects or the speech of ethnic minorities such as the Judeo-Spanish of the Sephardim. And since the Jews of the Levant had always been good citizens, many of the Sephardim served as officials and soldiers in the Balkan armies.

At the same time religious intolerance acquired a new strength with the re-Christianization of the newly independent regions. As a result, in the late 1800s and early 1900s many Jewish families left the regions of Macedonia, Greece, and Bulgaria to settle in Turkish cities (especially Istanbul), which they considered more secure and where they would be permitted to conserve their language and customs. During World War I, Jews prospered in Turkey since the other minorities were largely associated with the Ottoman enemies. After World War I, when the Allies occupied Istanbul, the Jewish leaders supported the Turks in the War for Independence (1918–1923) under Kemal Atatürk. With the establishment of the Turkish Republic in 1923, the Jews in Istanbul and other Turkish cities continued to enjoy a certain amount of prestige until 1928, when Atatürk's regime made efforts to remove all foreign influences from the country. In Atatürk's efforts for Westernization, the Arabic script (used for Turkish) was outlawed as the Latin-based alphabet was adopted in November of 1923. Atatürk also devoted much time to "liberating the language from the yoke of foreign languages," which meant eliminating Arabic and Persian loan words from Turkish. Such attempts to remove certain features of the non-Turkish minorities from his country naturally had an effect on minority languages such as Judeo-Spanish since Jews, as well as other minorities, were now encouraged to adopt Turkish as their major language (See chapter 11, section no. 1).

As conditions worsened for the non-Muslim minorities in the Levant, various Sephardim who lived in other territories of the Empire emigrated to Tel Aviv (especially the Saloniklis), Western Europe (London, Paris, Brussels, etc.), and Africa. An appreciable number of Sephardic Jews from the Levant came to the United States after 1900. They also came for economic reasons, since they had heard there was work in America. The advent of the Young Turk Revolution in 1908, political unrest, and wars in the Balkans all combined to cause emigration of considerable proportions between 1908 and 1914. Sephardic communities in the United States were established in New York City (by far the largest community), Rochester, Atlanta, Montgomery, Cincinnati, and eventually on the West Coast in Seattle and Los Angeles. It is interesting to note, that when the Sephardim resettled in Palestine and the United States, they organized themselves once again into *kales,* but this time according to their place of origin in the Balkans, not Spain. Thus, communities of Saloniklis, Stambulis, Izmirlis, Monastirlis, Rhodeslis, Kastorlis, and so on, were founded in different regions of Palestine and the United States.

Those who remained behind in the Empire were not able to resist the pressures which were reducing the domains of their mother tongue. It was especially at this time that Judeo-Spanish became even more weighed down by foreign influences (See chapter 11). Only Salonika remained an important bastion as the mother tongue of the Jews. In all the Jewish schools of Salonika, students were taught to read and write in Judeo-Spanish. Written materials were published in the language, such as novels, histories, folklore, as well as Zionist propaganda and manuals to learn the Hebrew language. At the beginning of the twentieth century Salonika was still exclusively a Spanish-Jewish city where the Jews continued to out-number the Greeks, Turks, and Bulgarians combined. Judeo-Spanish was still the commercial language of trade and was used by the Jews for all correspondence and accounting. The notices of municipal administration were printed in Turkish and Greek but were always accompanied by a translation in Judeo-Spanish (Renard 1966a:79).

But like the other Sephardic centers in the Balkans, Salonika soon lost its status. It began with the great fire in 1917, which destroyed the rich archives of the Talmud Torahs. This was followed by Balkanization after World War I, when Salonika became a part of Greece after the Greek capture of Macedonia. The defeat of the Greeks in Asia Minor and the Greco-Turkish Treaty of 1923 led to population exchanges in which one hundred thousand Greeks from Anatolia and Asia Minor were resettled in Salonika. This new influx of Greek non-Jewish refugees was, according to Elazar, "a deliberate attempt to end the dominant role of the Jewish community" (1989:78). Thus the numerical superiority of the Jews in Salonika was erased. From that time on, the Jewish community of Salonika gradually lost prestige, especially as new laws were passed which favored the Christian holidays. One such law, passed in 1923, required that all businesses be closed on Sundays, a non-Jewish holiday. Later, the official market day was changed from Monday to Saturday, thus excluding the Jews from active participation in normal commercial activities (Donnell 1987:116).[15] Elazar reports that 40,000 Jews left Salonika around this time, many emigrating to Palestine (1989:78). In 1928, there were 62,200 Jews in Salonika, 10,000 of whom left for Palestine in 1932 and 1934 after the pogrom of 1931 (Renard 1966a:79). Shortly thereafter (1932), the Greek government issued a law forbidding the existence of foreign elementary schools located in their territory (except for Hebrew in certain Jewish schools), which brought an end to the Alliance in Salonika. In 1936 the dictatorship of Metaxis of Greece strongly censored all writing, and dealt a fatal blow to Judeo-

Spanish by putting an end to publications in the Rashi script.[16] At this time many Sephardim began leaving Greece for France, Italy, and Latin America.

When World War II broke out, Renard reports that about 56,000 Jews remained in Salonika (1966a:80), the majority of whom continued using Judeo-Spanish as their principal language. In 1941 the Nazis arrived in Salonika, and by 1943, fifty-four thousand Jews had been deported (R. Molho 1992:9), and their libraries, cemetery, and what remained of their archives had been destroyed. Salonika was the last great Sephardic community to be annihilated by the Nazis. From this moment, deprived of its metropolis, Judeo-Spanish, in the words of Renard, was *irrémédiablement condamné* 'irretrievably (or hopelessly) condemned' (1966a:80). The following figures taken from Lestchinsky (1946:12,22) show the devastating effects of the Second World War on the Sephardic Jewish population in the Balkans.

Country	Sept. 1939 Jewish population	Losses	%	1945 Jewish population
Greece	75,000	60,000	80%	16,000
Yugoslavia	75,000	55,000	73.3%	9,000
Bulgaria[17]	50,000	7,000	14%	40,000
Rumania[18]	850,000	425,000	50%	300,000–320,000

The Jewish communities of Turkey, like Spain, were at the margin of conflict in World War II, and since Turkey remained neutral the Turkish Sephardic communities were spared. However, due to the severe hardships brought on by the government's wartime economic measures, the majority of the Balkan Sephardim who survived World War II emigrated to Palestine or the United States. Once again, the Sephardic Jews were uprooted and their history was to continue outside the Levant (except for certain Turkish communities). Even though the history of the Sephardim continues outside of the Levant, their language has declined, and Bumaschny (1968:13) stresses that the decadence of the Judeo-Spanish language coincides with the general decadence of the Eastern or Oriental Sephardic life (See chapter 11).

Concluding Remarks

It must be reemphasized here that refuge in the Ottoman Empire was crucial for the existence and survival of the Sephardic Jews, who have always been grateful for Turkish protection. R. Bortnick writes that after the expulsion from Spain,

> Scores of thousands of our people were lost by way of death or conversion to Catholicism as a result of that expulsion. Thousands more would have perished, indeed Sephardic culture as we know it today would have perished, but for the Ottoman Empire which rescued them and provided them with a safe haven where they could continue their lives, their customs, and their religion in freedom and dignity. (1991:2)

As Shaw (1989) reminds us, in the history of the Eastern Sephardim there was never any official government persecution of Jews in the Ottoman Empire. We also need to emphasize that, while the Ottoman Empire existed, the speaking of Judeo-Spanish was never restricted.

Part II

Description and Survival of Judeo-Spanish: The Language Before and After Expulsion

4

The Language of the Jews in Pre-Expulsion Spain: Did a Sephardic Spanish Exist?

Before their expulsion in 1492, the Jews of Spain spoke the language of the country—that is, Castilian Spanish or one of the other regional dialects. It has been debated for years whether the variety of Spanish spoken by the Jews in pre-Expulsion Spain was different from that spoken by the Christians of the same period. This question has given rise to two conflicting theories concerning this language spoken by the Spanish Jews. One is that it did not become a separate Judeo-Spanish dialect until expulsion led it to acquire the dialectal features distinct from Castilian Spanish. And indeed, it is generally true that when linguists speak of the Judeo-Spanish dialects, they are referring to the various developments of the language in the Balkans after expulsion. This theory assumes that the Spanish spoken by the Jews before 1492 was the same as that spoken by Spain's Christian population at the time. This view is held by such scholars as Kahane (1973:947–48), Peiles (1925:373), Revah (1964:41 and 1970:238–39), Lazar (1972:27), Sephiha (1973b:47 and 1986:54), and Malinowski (1979:4–5).

However, according to other scholars such as Wagner (1930: 29), Blondheim (1925:137), Benardete (1982:58–60), and S. Marcus (1962:129), the language of the Jews in Spain was already different in certain aspects of its lexicon, morphology, and phonology from that of the Christians by the Middle Ages. They base their theory on the evidence from various texts written in Spain before the time of expulsion, and texts published in the Ottoman Empire in the 1500s and 1600s after expulsion, as well as on certain linguistic characteristics found in the speech of Sephardim living in the Balkans and North Africa after expulsion. Various scholars like Spitzer and Lazar present both sides of the argument. In his article on the origin of the Judeo-Romance languages, Spitzer supports the former position: "the Spanish brought to the New World by the *conquistadores* must have been the same language that the

Jews brought with them to the Levant" (1944:179). However, later in the same article, he supports the latter view: "Up until the expulsion of the Jews from Spain there was a kind of differentiated Jewish Spanish" (ibid., 180). He goes on to state that these differences were generally of a religious nature. And Lazar writes:

> Without doubt Jews did intersperse their dialects with Hebrew words and expressions, particularly terms and concepts connected with religion and ethics, and they did tend to preserve archaic words and obsolete forms longer than most other people. (1972:27)

However, he feels that the theory for the existence of a specific Jewish Spanish dialect still lacks adequate serious proof: "It was only after the Expulsion of 1492 that Ladino began to be a specifically Jewish language" (ibid., 27).

It seems that throughout their history the Jews have generally adopted the language of the country in which they are living as their mother tongue while, at the same time, they have introduced a clear linguistic differentiation or Jewish variety (Bunis 1974:2–3 and Mézan 1936:29). These varieties are explained by differences in the mentality and way of life of the Jews. First of all, because of religious reasons, such as the need to be in walking distance of the synagogue, as well as for social convenience, the Jews lived in their own neighborhoods called *aljamas* or *juderías* which were separated from the non-Jewish population. They were usually not exposed to as many varieties of a given language as were the non-Jewish speakers of the same regions, so the linguistic inventory to which the Jews had access probably differed from that of the non-Jewish varieties. For example, language referring to other religions, the military, the government, etc. may not necessarily have had any influence on Jewish speech:

> Items expressing concepts foreign to Judaism might have been rejected, or adopted but given new, specialized meanings. Attitudes toward propriety or modesty in speech may have further distinguished Jewish from non-Jewish speakers. (Bunis 1974:3)

Besides living in their *aljamas,* there was also a disparity in social class and education between the Jews and Christians in pre-Expulsion Spain. Many of the Christians lived in rural areas and were not often well educated, whereas the Jews lived in the cities, were dedicated to commerce and the liberal professions, and many were highly educated. Although they were not part of the aristocracy, the Jews were the most learned or scholarly class in Spain during the fifteenth century (Crews 1935:15). Thus, there was no reason for them to want to model their language after that of the Christians.

The Spanish Jews themselves used two types of Castilian: one for use in the synagogue and the home, and the other to communicate with the gentiles in the markets and in their social and commercial contacts (Benardete 1982:61). Also, because of possible surrounding danger, the Jews had a defense mechanism in the form of a secret language to allow them to communicate secretly with coreligionists. In this instance, they would often use Hebrew and Arabic expressions, some of which have continued to be used as part of a secret language throughout the centuries in exile.

Evidence for postulating both the existence or nonexistence of a Jewish variety of Spanish in pre-Expulsion times comes mainly from the analyses of texts written in Spanish before 1492, and those written in the 1500s and 1600s outside of Spain after expulsion. These texts were generally written in Hebrew characters or Rashi script.[1] I will list some of the texts which have been used for such analyses in the past by various scholars, and will present examples of the language of the Jews which are found in these texts, and which differ in certain aspects from the language of the Christians in pre-Expulsion Spain.

Texts used by scholars for various analyses

A. Medieval poetry
   1. *Los proverbios morales* 'Ethical Proverbs' or *Consejos al rey don Pedro* composed between 1355 and 1360 by Rabbi Don Santob de (of) Carrión[2]
   2. *Poema de Yoçef* 'Poem on Joseph' which dates from the first half of the fifteenth century and is anonymous[3]

B. Religious literature
   1. Bible translations
      a. The Constantinople *Pentateuch* printed in 1547[4]
      b. The Ferrara Bible printed in 1553[5]
   2. Other liturgical literature
      a. The *Sidour* 'Prayerbook' printed in Ferrara in 1552[6]
      b. *Regimiento de la vida* 'Guide for Daily Living' written in 1564 by Rabbi Moses Almosnino[7]
      c. The Spanish paraphrase of the Haftora for the *Ninth of Ab* was composed between 1350 and 1400
      d. The Questions and Rabinnical Responsa of the six-

teenth and seventeenth centuries written by the rabbis of Turkey after expulsion

   e. The *Haggadah of Pesah* printed in Spain prior to expulsion and later in various cities such as Venice in 1522 and Livorno in 1888

C. Statutes and manuscripts
  1. The Statutes or *Taqqanot*[8] written in the Sephardi cursive[9]
  2. The Manuscript of I–I–3 of the Biblioteca Escurial[10]

D. Secular literature
  1. *El cancionero de Baena* was written around 1445 by Alfonso de Baena
  2. The Judeo-Spanish *romanzas* (ballads)[11]
  3. Judeo-Spanish *refranes/reflanes* or proverbs[12]

Differences Between the Language of the Jews and that of the Christians in pre-Expulsion Spain

As S. Birnbaum (1944:64) and D. Bunis (1975a:9) have pointed out, all Jewish languages have two things in common: 1) a merged Hebrew-Aramaic component, and 2) an orthographic system composed of some variety of Hebrew characters. Documents such as contracts, statutes, charters, letters, and poems were written in the Hebrew alphabet and/or Rashi script, whereas the cursive writing or *solitreo* was used for informal writing. Rarely was the Latin alphabet used. It was only in the twentieth century that use of the Latin alphabet increased, especially in the field of journalism. The Rumanian newspaper *Luzero de la Pasensia,* published from 1886–1889 in Turnu-Severin, was the first Judeo-Spanish newspaper to be printed in the Latin alphabet. Below is a discussion of various differences, which can be found in the preceding texts, between the language of the Jews versus that of the Christians in pre-Expulsion Spain.

The Hebrew Component[13]

Since the Jews in Spain lived in Jewish quarters that were isolated from their Christian neighbors, they followed their own religious practices and customs. The necessity was created for a technical vocabulary in the language to describe aspects that were typically Jewish, such as: terms to designate Jewish holidays, dietary laws, utensils of the home and synagogue, religious beliefs, and theories. Such a vocabulary naturally had a Hebrew origin. Thus, Hebrew words and expressions not in current usage in Old Spanish, abound in Jewish texts of the time. Examples of Hebrew words that can be found in some of the previously mentioned texts are:

1. *afilu* 'even (though)' from the Hebrew [afilu].
2. *darush~derasha* 'sermon' from the Hebrew [dɛraša]. The verb *darshar* or *darsar* 'to preach' was also used.
3. *haham* 'rabbi' and/or 'wise' from Hebrew [xaxam].
4. *rav* or *rab* 'rabbi' from Hebrew [rav].
5. *adonay* 'God' from the Hebrew [adonay].
6. *kehila, kehilot* 'community' from Hebrew [kehila].
7. *kohen* 'priest' from Hebrew [kohen].
8. *mazal* 'luck, destiny' from Hebrew [mazal].
9. *malshin~malsin* 'slanderer; informer' from Hebrew [malsin]. According to Koch the Hebrew word *malsin* became part of Castilian as early as 1379 but was eventually dropped from the language (1978:133).
10. *mamzer* 'bastard' from the Hebrew [mamzer]. According to Wagner (1930:32) this word was so well known that the Ferrara Bible version does not translate it. It was the word the Jews used which was equivalent to the Castilian *bastardo* 'bastard.'
11. *tefila* 'prayer' also *livro de tefila* 'prayerbook' from Hebrew [tefila].
12. *talmid* 'student' from Hebrew [talmid] and *talmid(im) haham(im)* 'traditional scholars' from Hebrew [talmid xaxam].
13. Proper Hebrew names like *Reuven* 'Rubin', *Moshe* 'Moses', and *Mitzraim* 'Egypt' were used instead of the Spanish equivalents.

Incorporation of Hebrew Loans—Morphological Influences

1. Hebrew loans were often given Castilian affixes such as the -*ar* infinitive endings in *malsinar* 'to slander' and *darsar* 'to preach' as well as regular verb inflections such as the present tense endings in the verb *darsar: darso, darsas,* etc.
2. Hebrew loans were given the -*ado* participle ending as in *enhermado* 'excommunicated' from the Hebrew [herem]. The modern forms are *enherimado* and *enherimar* (S. Marcus 1962:145).

3. The -ificar ending of certain active verbs was formed under the influence of the Hebrew Hiph'il and Poel causative verbs as in bonificar~aboniguar 'to make better, improve' and fructificar~fruchiguar 'to bear fruit, be productive' (Crews 1935:16).

4. Hebrew loans received adjectival prefixes and suffixes as in lemunyoso from the verb alemuñarse 'to be in mourning, become a widow' derived from the Hebrew [almon] 'widower.' The modern forms are limuño and alimuñarse. Another example of incorporation of both an adjectival prefix and suffix can be seen in the adjective desmazalado 'unlucky' (from Hebrew [mazal] 'luck'). According to Wagner, this word was also used among the Christians for a time and can be found in Cervantes where it means "weak of character" or "ill-fated" (Wagner 1930:30).

5. Spanish noun suffixes were often added to Hebrew words as in meldador 'reader' (in a primary or religious school) and malsindad 'slander'. In some cases, Hebrew suffixes were added to Castilian nouns. For example, the -im masculine plural noun suffix is added to the Spanish word ladrón 'thief' as in ladronim to mean "thieves" instead of ladrones the correct Spanish plural form, and the feminine plural noun suffix -ut is found in the word haraganut instead of the Castilian haraganería meaning "idleness, laziness."

6. An example of a syntactic influence from Hebrew can be seen in constructions like kada uno i uno 'each and every one,' which is a word for word translation of the Hebrew [kol ehad ve ehad]. Other expressions like en kada anyo i anyo 'in each and every year' and en kada kahal i kahal 'in each and every synagogue' (found in the Taqqanot of Valladolid of 1432) reappear according to Revah in the written and spoken language of the Jews (1970:239).

Three other special words or expressions were specific to the Jews, either because of their religious beliefs, or due to Hebrew influence:

1. Use of el Dyo 'God' instead of the Castilian dios which was the word used by the Christians. The Jews dropped the -s ending because they felt it denoted a plural deity, which was contrary to Jewish beliefs.[14] The Jews often used the definite article el before Dyo which has no parallel in Old Spanish. Reasons for this use of the definite article range from a translation of the Hebrew [ha kadoš barux hu] 'the Holy one

blessed be he', whose Spanish equivalent *el Dyo bendicho* may have been shortened to *el Dyo,* to its possible use simply to emphasize the word *Dyo* (S. Marcus 1962:139–40).

2. Use of the expression *dia bueno* 'holiday' from the Judeo-Latin tradition of *bonus dies* or *dies bonus* translated from the Hebrew words [yom tov] 'holiday', literally meaning, "good day."

3. Use of *meldar,* which was originally thought to be derived from the Hebrew [limud] but now considered by various scholars such as Renard (1966a:127) and Sephiha (1986:86) to be derived from the Greek [melatan]. It originally meant the reading of the appropriate prayers of the Mishna especially in memory of one who had died, and also the ceremony of this reading. It could generally be applied to the reading of the Holy Books. In time, the word was extended to mean "to read" in general, and was conjugated like a regular Spanish *-ar* verb. The word also denoted a primary or religious school where children learned to read the Holy Books. The teacher, a reader in such a school, was a *meldador.*

The Arabic Component—Phonological and Lexical Influences[15]

Before 1492 the Jews had a symbiotic relationship with the Christians and Arabs in Spain, serving as an intermediary between these two cultures which otherwise had little or no contact. As a result of this connection with the Moslem culture, the Jews were very familiar with the Arabic language, and thus their phonological repertoire was wider than that of the Christians, who were not influenced by Arabic. For example, the phoneme /h/ or /x/, which was represented by the Hebrew letters Cheth ‫ח‬ or Chaph ‫כ‬ in the written language, existed in the language of the Jews, but was nonexistent in the Castilian of the Christians. This /x/ phoneme corresponded to the Arabic velar spirant [x] and to the Arabic laryngeal spirant [h].[16]

According to M. Molho, the majority of Arabic loans were introduced into Judeo-Spanish after expulsion via the Turkish language (1960:8–9). However, certain Arabic words and expressions were found in the speech of the Jews in pre-Expulsion times, which did not exist in the Old Castilian spoken by the Christians (Wagner 1930:32). Examples of such Arabic loans are:

1. *al had* 'Sunday' from Arabic [alxad] meaning "the first day," as opposed to the Christian word *domingo* which came from

the Latin *dies dominicus* 'the day of God' and signified a Christian god as far as the Jews were concerned.

2. *shara*[17] 'small forest' from Arabic [šajar] 'plants' instead of the Castilian word *bosque*.

3. *hazino* 'sick' from Arabic [ḥazin] 'sad'. The nouns *hazinura*, *hazimiento* and *enhazinimiento* were also used.

4. *alforria* 'liberty' from Arabic [alḥuriya]. This word was often used as part of the idiom *salir a alforria* 'to liberate', especially in regards to a slave.

5. *adefina~adafina* 'Jewish dish' eaten on the Sabbath.

6. *fulano ben fulano* 'someone' from Arabic [fulan ben fulan].

7. *alhasarear* 'to beautify, charm, bewitch' from Arabic [ḥasar].

8. Use of the verb *amanecer* 'to dawn, grow light' in the first person (instead of only the third person singular or impersonal form as in Modern Castilian), modeled after the Arabic (S. Marcus 1962:146).

9. Arabic influence in certain last names such as *Algazi(y)* 'from Gaza' and *Aboulafia* 'he who enjoys health'.

Archaisms[18]

There are scholars like Blondheim (1925:137) who feel that, due to the relative isolation of the Jews in pre-Expulsion Spain, the language of the Jews was archaic in a few aspects with respect to the Spanish spoken by the Christians at the same time. According to S. Marcus, even their literary style was archaic before they were expelled from the Peninsula. An example of a morphological archaism is the use of the *-ante* ending for the present participle found in the I–I–3 Manuscript (S. Marcus 1962:130).

Nontextual Evidence for Differences in the Language of the Jews before Expulsion

Besides the evidence from texts, there is another indication that the language of the Jews in Spain before expulsion was somewhat different from that of the Christians. This evidence stems from the fact that there are instances of the same linguistic phenomena occurring in the spoken language of the Sephardim in both Turkey and Morocco after expulsion, which were nonexistent in the Castilian Spanish of Spain. Since there was almost no contact between the Sephardim of North Africa and the Levant after expulsion, Jochnowitz (1978:65) suggests that we can assume that certain features of their language did exist in pre-Expulsion times. Besides use of the Arabic *alhad,* 'Sunday', *el Dyo* for 'God', and the words *meldar* 'to read', *mamzer* 'bastard', and *malsin* 'slanderer', other examples of morphological forms found in the Judeo-Spanish of both Turkey and North Africa include:

a) the diminutive *-iko, -ika* suffixes in words like *ižiko* 'little son', *mužerika* 'little woman' and *Daviko* 'little David'

b) the subject pronoun forms *mos* 'we' and *vos* 'you' which are older than the modern Spanish *nosotros* and *vosotros.*

Other features present in the language of the Sephardim in both the Balkans and North Africa include: 1) uses of various euphemistic words and expressions to describe the phenomenon of death or taboo words such as the word *blanko* 'white' to mean "carbon" or "black"[19], 2) use of curses saying the opposite of what was intended so as not to invoke the wrath of God, as well as 3) corruptions or transformations of certain words to attain a humorous effect. Examples of such euphemisms and word transformations are presented in detail in the next chapter.

Arguments against the Existence of a Separate Judeo-Spanish Dialect before Expulsion

Problems with Text Analyses

The various scholars who do not believe that a Judeo-Spanish dialect existed before expulsion have also presented their evidence from some of the same texts mentioned above. For example, according to Lazar, Rabbi Shem Tov wrote in the Castilian of the period, and there were very few examples in his writing to be found in what later came to be referred to as Judeo-Spanish dialectical aspects (1972:16).

Haïm Vidal Sephiha (1973b:47 and 1986:18, 151) distinguishes between *Ladino* or the *Judeo-Spanish calque,* which was the language used to translate the Bible and other liturgical texts word for word from Hebrew into Spanish, versus the *Judeo-Spanish vernacular* or the spoken language. Sephiha characterizes the language of the translations as being very literal and often operating at the expense of idiomatic Spanish both lexically and syntactically. When discussing the striking characteristics of both the Constantinople *Pentateuch* of 1547 and the Ferrara Bible of 1553 Sephiha writes that "the translators tried as far as possible to give each Hebrew root a consistent Spanish equivalent, even if this meant twisting the usual meaning of the Spanish" (1971:55). Sephiha feels that Ladino, the translating calque, preceded the spoken Judeo-Spanish vernacular, which developed only after expulsion. In other words, the characteristics of the translating language do not truly reflect the spoken language of the pre-Expulsion era (Sephiha 1973b:47, 1986:20 and Salazar-Caro 1987:62). This then raises the question of the validity of certain text analyses, especially translations, to determine what the colloquial language was like. Sephiha also reminds us that different language varieties were used depending on the audience to which the translation was addressed: "direct Hebrew borrowings are never found in Spanish Bible translations addressed to a Christian audience. Instead, they Hispanicize the Latin terms found in the Vulgate" (1971:57). Naturally, a text intended for a Christian audience will not exhibit the same qualities present in a text intended for a Jewish audience.

In later texts printed in Turkey, Venice, Ferrara, and other places after expulsion, from the middle of the sixteenth century on, we can find examples of Standard Spanish such as *leer* 'to read', instead of the Judeo-Spanish *meldar,* and of *trabajar* 'to work', instead of the Judeo-Spanish *lavorar.* Also, reports by travelers inform us that the language of the Jews was considered the same as that spoken in Spain. For example, Gonzalo de Illescas wrote in his *Historia pontifical* on arriving in Turkey in the mid 1500s, that the Spanish Jews "brought from here (Spain) our language and they still preserve it and willingly use it" (Gonzalo de Illescas 1606:106). And according to Bernardo Aldrete, it was only around 1614 that the post Expulsion language began to show some archaic qualities. He wrote in 1614 that:

> those [Jews] in Italy, Salonika and Africa, those that were from Spain still speak the language that they brought from there and it is recognized as being from that age, different from this time. (1614:263)

Problems with Analyzing Hebrew and Arabic Influences

One argument against using the Hebrew component as evidence for the existence of a pre-Expulsion Judeo-Spanish dialect, is that words dealing with religious terminology can hardly be considered a deviation from the standard language. However, this might be true if the Hebrew loans and influence only denoted religious concepts and objects. But as we have seen, the Hebrew component in the Spanish of the Jews extends to all areas and appears in all kinds of texts from religious ones to *romanzas* and proverbs. In analyzing eighty proverbs from different areas of the Ottoman Empire, this writer found Hebrew words like *gan eden* 'paradise', *hazan* 'hazan', *haham* 'rabbi, wise', and *darshar* 'to preach' appearing constantly. However, other frequently repeated Hebrew words included *sehel* 'intelligence', *haver(im)* 'friend(s)', and *mazal* 'luck' for which there are definite Spanish counterparts, as well as later Turkish, Greek, French, etc., counterparts. And as we have seen, some of these everyday Hebrew words like *mazal* 'luck' and *mals(h)in* 'slanderer' even became a part of the Castilian of the Christians for a certain period of time (Wagner 1930:30–31 and Koch 1978:133). However, their disappearance from Castilian suggests that they were borrowed from the Jews by the Christians at one time and were later dropped, probably coinciding with the effects of expulsion. D. Lida also brings up an inherent difficulty in analyzing Judeo-Spanish proverbs which have counterparts with Castilian proverbs, as well as those which have no equivalent:

> In the first case, does one derive from the other? Which influences which? Is the Sephardic proverb merely a translation of the other? Are those that have no equivalent post-expulsion, or did they exist before solely in the Jewish community? (1978:89)

Many Arabic influences also affected Castilian, so it is often impossible to distinguish the words used only by the Jews, such as *al had* 'Sunday' and *shara* 'forest', as opposed to a word like *hazino* 'sick', which at one time was part of Castilian Spanish before eventually being dropped.

Conclusion

Both theories concerning the existence or nonexistence of a Jewish dialect in pre-Expulsion Spain have some evidence to support their claims. However, it is obvious that more study is definitely needed in this area. One of the problems is the difficulty of obtaining medieval manuscripts written by Spanish Jews which stand out as being particularly Judeo-Spanish from the linguistic point of view. As Lida points out:

> After 1391 and throughout the fifteenth century, the political climate in Spain had deteriorated so much that it was not conducive to the open cultivation of Jewish ethnicity. Also, if we think of some form of Spanish as the language of Hispano-Jewish literature, we have to recog-

nize that the vernacular was not highly esteemed in general as a vehicle for serious writing even as late as the seventeenth century. (1978:83)

Also, most of the copies of the biblical and liturgical translations have almost entirely disappeared. Those not taken by the Jews with them into exile were systematically destroyed by the Inquisition, and those taken out by the exiles were often destroyed by fires, overuse or negligence.

Thus, scholars are still divided on the issue of whether a specific Jewish language did indeed exist in pre-Expulsion times. Arlene Malinowski feels that the evidence for a pre-Expulsion Jewish language should not be based on specific vocabulary which deals mostly with religious loans:

> The existence of such a specialized vocabulary . . . can be viewed and more simply explained as a reflection of the need of the Jewish community to denote accurately certain religious conceptions and practices which the available lexicon could not accommodate without distortion. (1979:4)

Malinowski also considers the textual evidence to be weak. She writes that "there exist no firm textual grounds upon which a conclusive reconstruction of the linguistic behavior of the Jews can be based" (1979:3), and that,

> until 1492 it would be wrong to speak of a Judeo-Spanish vernacular. It is only after the expulsion that the language of the Sephardim begins its independent and unique evolution. (1979:5)

Considering the question from a sociological/historical viewpoint, and given the nature of Jewish communities and their treatment of languages throughout history, it is difficult to deny the presence of some distinctions between the language of the Jews and that of the Christians in pre-Expulsion Spain. These differences manifest themselves in a Hebrew component due to the Jewish mentality and way of life, an Arabic influence resulting from the Jews' unique contact with the Moslem culture, some archaisms due to the isolation of the Jews, plus euphemistic and corrupted forms of lexical items resulting from religious beliefs and superstitions, or to attain a humorous effect. However, I agree with George Jochnowitz who believes that these distinctions cannot be exaggerated since on the whole, the differences were a small part of the features of the language. He writes:

When we say that a Judeo-Spanish type of speech existed before 1492, we do not mean to suggest that it was as recognizably different from Spanish as it is today. . . . What we mean is that the distinctively Jewish features of pre-expulsion Ladino, however minor they may have been, seem to have survived and formed the nucleus of the modern language. (1978:65–66)

5

Post-Expulsion: Judeo-Spanish in the Ottoman Empire

Outline for Chapter 5

I. Phonology and Phonetic Features
   A. Vowels: Differences between Judeo-Spanish and Modern Spanish Dialects
   B. Consonants: Old Spanish Consonantal Distinctions Present in Judeo-Spanish
   C. Other Phonetic Characteristics of Judeo-Spanish

II. Morphology—Word Formation
   A. Verbs
   B. Nouns and Pronouns
   C. Adjectives, Adverbs, and Conjunctions
   D. Agreement

III. Archaisms

IV. New Creations
   A. Analogy
   B. Semantic Alterations
   C. Periphrastic Expressions
   D. Corruptions or Transformations of Words

V. Euphemisms
   A. Words for "God"
   B. Death or Dying
   C. Taboo—Dirty Words
   D. Contrary to Intended Meanings

VI. Proverbs or *Refranes*

VII. Foreign (Non-Spanish) Influences in Judeo-Spanish
   A. The Semitic Component: Hebrew and Arabic

B. Romance Influences: Iberian Dialects and Languages, Italian and French

C. Ottoman Languages: Turkish, Greek, Slavic, and Rumanian

The Judeo-Spanish of the Eastern Sephardim of the Levant is a mixed language characterized by the following features:

(1) In many aspects of its phonology, morphology, and lexicon it is an archaic language based on the Castilian of the late fifteenth and early sixteenth centuries, i.e. pre-classical Castilian or pre-Columbian Spanish as described by the Spanish grammarian Nebrija in his famous *Gramática de la lengua castellana*[1] written in 1492. The Spanish language underwent certain changes in the sixteenth century which marked the transition from Old or Medieval Spanish to Modern Spanish. Since the Jews of the Ottoman Empire were cut off from the Iberian Peninsula, their language did not undergo the same phonetic, morphological, and lexical changes that became characteristic of Modern Spanish. As a result, Judeo-Spanish is characterized by features that went out of use in Spain.

(2) It has undergone independent new formations, reshapings, semantic shifts, and transformations, based on or inherited from the Castilian framework, or originating from various Jewish customs or practices.

(3) A great abundance of foreign elements and loanwords have been incorporated into Judeo-Spanish from other languages such as Hebrew and Arabic, the various Iberian dialects, other Romance languages, especially French and Italian, and various Balkan languages, predominantly Turkish and Greek.

Spitzer describes Judeo-Spanish as:

a genuine Spanish before Columbus and at the same time a kind of kaleidoscope of Balkan and Romance languages; it's an oriental bazaar on top of a genuine Castilian architecture. . . . A mixture of Jewish conservatism and of Jewish molding. (1944:180)

Scholars like Luria (1954:789) and Kiddle (1978:76) have pointed out the advantages of studying Judeo-Spanish. With its distinctive characteristics it gives us a good indication of certain aspects of Medieval Spanish. But other scholars have noted that, even though much study has been made to stress the similarities between Judeo-Spanish and Old Spanish phonology, grammar, and lexicon, little attention has been given to the distinctness of Judeo-Spanish. Nemer and Díaz-Mas remind us that living languages cannot remain unaltered through time and that even though Judeo-Spanish exhibits archaic features characteristic of a language that had been isolated from its source for centuries, it "has also undergone a process of transformation throughout history" (Díaz-Mas 1986:104) and thus "has a history of its own" (Nemer 1981:46). Not only did linguistic changes occur as a natural process through time, but also as a result of contact with other languages, innovations of its speakers, as well as variations due to doubt or uncertainty on the part of the speakers who were not given the opportunity to study their native language in school. Nor did they have sources to refer to concerning questions of usage (see chapter 11).

In the following seven sections of this chapter I will present many of the salient characteristics of Judeo-Spanish as spoken in the Ottoman Empire after expulsion from Spain. In order to give an overview of some of these linguistic features, I will discuss Judeo-Spanish in general, without attempting to deal with language variation according to socioeconomic class, sex, or age of the speakers,[2] or to describe in detail the separate Judeo-Spanish dialects. Even though I have been criticized for the latter in the past (Nemer 1981:180, 187), my purpose here is to give the reader an idea of the major characteristics of the language, or the Judeo-Spanish *koiné* in general, which has developed since expulsion.[3] This means that the various linguistic features discussed in the domains of phonetics, morphology, and the lexicon, did not necessarily occur in all the Judeo-Spanish dialects spoken in the Balkans, nor do they occur in all the regions where Judeo-Spanish is spoken today in the United States and Israel. Syntax will be minimally discussed, since Old Spanish syntax has generally been conserved and thus, the dominant syntactic patterns of Judeo-Spanish are not that different from those of both Old Spanish and Modern Spanish. Various nonsyntactic discrepancies between Judeo-Spanish and Modern Spanish will be presented, and as D. Levy reminds us, many of these features can also be found today in different areas of Spain and Latin America (D. Levy 1952:61).

I. Phonology and Phonetic Features

The Spanish that was carried to the New World by the Spanish *conquistadores* was the same language that the expelled Jews took with them to the Levant, i.e. the Spanish dating from the end of the fifteenth century and the beginning of the sixteenth century. However, the colonization of the Spaniards in America followed a different course from that of the emigration of the Jews to the Balkans. The primary difference was the fact that the Jews of the Balkans were isolated from Spain for centuries, whereas, following the first established colonies in America, waves of Spanish immigrants continually arrived. Thus, according to Rohlfs, the pronunciation of Judeo-Spanish is more archaic than the Spanish of Spanish America since Judeo-Spanish represents the linguistic situation of the fifteenth century, while the Spanish spoken in America has as its base the state of the language of the sixteenth century (Rohlfs 1957:173–74). However, many of the phonetic characteristics of Judeo-Spanish can be found in certain Spanish and Latin American dialects today. As Wagner wrote in 1930,

> I don't believe that in the phonetics of Judeo-Spanish there is one feature that cannot be found in the popular pronunciation of Spanish spoken in Spain or America (1930:17).

A. *Vowels: Differences between Judeo-Spanish and Modern Spanish Dialects*

The stressed vowels of Judeo-Spanish are generally the same as those of Modern Spanish (with variation occurring in unstressed position) with an anticipatory nasalization of vowels before nasalized consonants. However, there are characteristics of vowel usage in Judeo-Spanish which differ from Modern Spanish and include the following.

Differences in diphthongization are quite prevalent. There is an excess of diphthongization in which the diphthongization of stressed vowels has been carried over into unstressed syllables as in *pueder* instead of Modern Spanish *poder* 'to be able', *buendad,* for Modern Spanish *bondad* 'kindness',[4] and *huertelano,* for Modern Spanish *hortelano* 'gardener'.

There is also diphthongization on stressed syllables in Judeo-Spanish words which were diphthongized in Old Spanish but not in Modern Spanish, as in *adientro* for Modern Spanish *adentro* 'within', and *vierbo* 'word' in Judeo-Spanish, which appears in Modern Spanish as *verbo* 'verb'.

There is a lack of diphthongization in accented syllables where Modern Spanish would have it, as in *kero* 'I want' instead of Modern Spanish *quiero, penso* instead of *pienso* 'I think', *ken* versus *quien* 'who', *pasensia* instead of *paciencia* 'patience', *rogo* versus *ruego* 'I ask, request', *konto* for *cuento* 'I relate; count', *ponte* for *puente* 'bridge', and *esforso* instead of *esfuerza* 'effort'. Zamora points out that this lack of diphthongization can also be found in certain Spanish dialects of both Spain and Latin America (Zamora 1974:353).

Another difference is seen in the closure or raising of certain vowels in unstressed or in final position, which was typical of the Iberian dialects, especially in the north (except for the region of Castile). This vowel closure is especially prevalent in the Monastir dialect, but occurs in other Judeo-Spanish dialects such as those of Karaferia, Kastoria, Bosnia, and Bucharest to varying degrees (Zamora 1974:354). The following examples in Judeo-Spanish are followed by their Modern Spanish equivalents in parentheses and their English meaning:

e→i   as in *komis* (comes) 'you eat'; *sieti* (siete) 'seven'; *difindidu* (defendido) 'defended'; *persiguir* (perseguir) 'to follow';

o→u   as in *sinku* (cinco) 'five'; *gatu* (gato) 'cat'; *kusir* (coser) 'to sew'; *brazu* (brazo) 'arm'; *chiku* (chico) 'small child', *difindidu* (defendido) 'defended'; *peru* (pero) 'but' (conj.).

The indirect object pronouns also undergo closure, as in *li* for Modern Spanish *le* 'to/for him/her' and *lis* instead of *les* 'to/for them', as well as the third person reflexive pronoun *si* instead of the modern form *se*. In dialects other than that of Monastir, only the pretonic *o* closes to *u*, as in *arispunder* (responder) 'to respond' and *muzotros* (nosotros) 'we'. In some instances, unstressed *a* has been raised to *e* in word final position and before *s*, as in *kriature* (criatura) 'child', *mansane* (manzana) 'apple', *kazes* (casa) 'houses', and *mientres* (mientras) 'while'.

According to Nemer, in the present-day Indianapolis (Monastir) dialect pre-tonic /e/ and /o/ do not automatically raise to [i] and [u] respectively. They may raise only partially to [I], [ɛ] or [U] (1981:173–74). In fact, she found a tendency for some speakers to use [I] instead of [i] probably due to prolonged contact with English (1981:178). Malinowski found that the degree of vowel closure varied not only from group to group but also from speaker to speaker (1979:21). I also found closure varying in degrees from complete closure [i], as in [komis], to partial closure [I], as in [komIs] 'you eat' (Harris 1979, 1987).

The unstressed *u* or the second element of the *au*, *eu*, and *iu* diphthongs becomes *v* in Judeo-Spanish (which is represented by *b* in Old Spanish of the fifteenth century[5]) following a front vowel and when followed by a consonant:

RULE: au→av   as in *kavsa* (causa) 'cause'

      eu→ev   *devda* (deuda) 'debt'
                 Evropa (Europa) 'Europe'

      iu→iv   *sivdad* (ciudad) 'city'
                 bivda (viuda) 'widow'

This is especially true of the Salonika dialect and could possibly be attributed to Greek influence (Sala 1970a:30). However the same trend can also be found in Castilian Spanish, e.g. Paulo→Pavlo→-Pablo.

A *yod* or a *y* sound is frequently inserted between the two final vowels of a word in order to avoid hiatus, as in *trayer* (traer) 'to bring'; *veyo* (veo) 'I see'; *oyi* (oí) 'I heard'; *kreyu(o)* (creo) 'I believe'; *famiya* (familia) 'family'; *riyo* (río) 'river'; and *miyo* (mío) 'mine' (Renard 1966a:114). Nemer reports the existence of very few vowel clusters on the surface in the Indianapolis (originally Monastir) dialect, thus resulting in an alternate pronunciation in which [y] can appear between two vowels as in [diɛnte]~[diyɛnte] (diente) 'tooth'; and [maɛstru]~[mayɛstru] (maestro) 'master, teacher'; and [diamante]~[diyamante] (diamante) 'diamond' (Nemer 1981:157).

The loss of initial *e-* in *s + consonant* combinations, occurring in certain instances in Judeo-Spanish can be compared to the prothetic *e-* insertion which began to precede *s + consonant* in Modern Spanish (Lathrop 1986:81). This was especially prevalent in Rumanian dialects as in *skrito* (escrito) 'written'; *studiar* (estudiar) 'to study'; *skola* (escuela) 'school'; and *sperans(z)a* (esperanza) 'hope'. Double variants frequently exist as in *skapar~eskapar* 'to finish'. There is a question here as to whether the initial *e-* developed at all, since it did not in Italian as in the Italian words *scritto, studiare* and *speranza*. However, the forms with *es-* were more common in my informants' speech than the forms without initial *e-*.

The phenomenon of vowel assimilation (as opposed to vowel raising) or dissimilation is very common in Judeo-Spanish (Renard 1966a:114) and is found in words like *ĵidiyo* (judío) 'Jew, Jewish'; *render* (rendir) 'to produce; defeat, overcome'; and *vinir* (venir) 'to come' (perhaps also closing of unstressed *e*).

B. Consonants: Old Spanish Consonantal Distinctions Present in Judeo-Spanish

Certain consonants that disappeared from Old Spanish are still found in Judeo-Spanish. According to Lamouche, the presence of the two palatal fricatives /š/ and /ž/ probably contribute the most to giving Judeo-Spanish its distinct phonetic characteristic (1907:982). In Judeo-Spanish these two palatal fricatives plus the palatal affricate /ǰ/ did not undergo the change to the voiceless velar spirant /x/ (spelled *j* or *g*), which only occurred toward the end of the sixteenth century or the beginning of the seventeenth century in Spain. What happened was that the Old Castilian [š], [ž], and [ǰ] sounds became [š] in general Castilian and later changed to the Modern Castilian [x] (Agard 1950:205). The rule can be simply represented by the following:

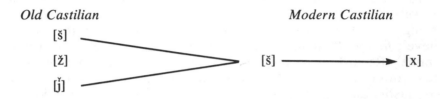

Old Castilian   *Modern Castilian*

Thus in Modern Spanish the written *j* or the *g* before *e* and *i*, as in the words *abajo, mujer,* and *gente* are all pronounced with the velar [x] sound. But since these changes did not take place in Judeo-Spanish, these words retain the original Old Spanish palatal sounds of [š], [ž], and [ǰ] respectively. In the examples given below, the Modern Spanish version is given in parentheses after the Judeo-Spanish word.

The voiceless palatal fricative /š/ was current in seventeenth century Spain as shown by the French transliteration of the Spanish word *Quijote,* which was transliterated into the French as *Quichotte* and pronounced [kišot] (Lathrop 1986:80). Examples of the [š] sound written as *sh* in Judeo-Spanish words are *abasho* (abajo) 'under'; *deshar* (dejar) 'to leave'; *kasha* (caja) 'box'; *pasharo* (pájaro) 'bird'; *disho* (dijo) 'he/she said'; and other past tense preterite forms such as *dishimos* (dijimos) 'we said'; *basho* (bajó) 'he descended'; etc.

The palatalization of *s* to [š] in front of the velar consonant *k,* found in Old Spanish dialects of the sixteenth century, continued in certain Judeo-Spanish dialects. Modern Spanish uses [s] as in *buscar* 'to look for' and *mosca* 'insect' instead of Judeo-Spanish *bushkar* and *moshka.*

With the more frequent use of the [š] sound in Judeo-Spanish, it has been extended to initial position in some instances, as in *shabon* (jabón) 'soap'; *shastre* (sastre) 'tailor'; as well as foreign words such as *shabat* 'Sabbath' from the Hebrew word [šabat], and *shapeau* 'hat' from the French *chapeau* (Umphrey and Adatto 1936:262).

The [š] sound is also found in the second person plural Judeo-Spanish verb forms of all tenses as well as in certain words when the [s] is preceded by the vowel *i* as in tene*sh* (tenéis) 'you (pl.) have'; *avlash* (habláis) 'you (pl.) speak'; *avlatesh* (hablasteis) 'you (pl.) spoke'; *sosh* (sois) 'you (pl.) are'; and *sesh* (seis) 'six'. In these verb forms as well as in the word *sesh*, the palatalization of the final -*s* is due to the influence of the preceding semi vowel *i*, which in turn is absorbed by the palatal (Umphrey & Adatto 1936:262).

The Old Spanish [ž] is the voiced version of [š] and is written in Judeo-Spanish as *z* or *j* mostly in intervocalic position. However, I represent this sound throughout the text as *ž* in order to eliminate confusion with the Modern Spanish letters *z* and *j* (See Appendix A). Examples are *ižo~fižo* (hijo) 'son'; *mužer* (mujer) 'woman'; *kaleža* (calleja) 'street'; *vieža* (vieja) 'old (woman)'; *aženo* (ajeno) 'foreign'; *ožos* (ojos) 'eyes'; and in the perfect forms of *kerer* 'to want'" *kiži, kižitish,* etc. This sound was also found in initial position as in *žugar* (jugar) 'to play'.

Judeo-Spanish is also characterized by retention of the palatal affricate /ǰ/ which became the [x] sound where Modern Spanish writes *j*, or *g* before *e* or *i* in initial position, as in *ǰente* (gente) 'people'; *ǰusto* (justo) 'just'; and *ǰuntos* (juntos) 'together'; or when preceded by a consonant as in *anǰel* (ángel) 'angel'. This sound is frequently found in foreign words such as *ǰurnal* from the French word *journal* 'newspaper' and *tinǰere* from the Turkish word *tencere* 'saucepan'. Canfield considers [ǰ] to be an allophone of /ž/ in initial position and after /n/ (Canfield 1981:85). And both Malinowski and I found a tendency on the part of our informants to reduce [ǰ] to [ž] in certain words such as *joven,* which is often pronounced [žoven] (Harris 1979:49). Malinowski attributes this change to French influence (Malinowski 1979:28).

Retention of Latin initial /f/, which remained throughout the period of Old Spanish, is conserved in Judeo-Spanish (as in Portuguese) in words of certain dialects as in *fižo~fižu* (hijo) 'son'; *fierro* (hierro) 'iron'; and *ferir* (herir) 'to hurt'. This initial *f-* is preserved to a higher degree in the western Judeo-Spanish dialects of Monastir, Skopje and Salonika, rather than in the eastern dialects of Istanbul, Izmir, and other parts of Turkey and Rhodes. This preservation is understandable in that *f-* retention was a characteristic of northern Spain. However, fluctuation of initial *f-* retention was found in centers such as Istanbul and Salonika and can be seen in the speech of some of the informants originally from these areas.

Both Wagner (1923:243) and Lamouche (1907:979), as well as Mali-nowski (1979:32) attributed this to the fact that loss of initial *f-*, which began in Spain in the fourteenth century, was not completely achieved by the time of expulsion. In all the dialects the [f-] sound was more likely to have been preserved by the older generation and, as Bunis points out, was often a characteristic of women's speech in certain areas since women tended to preserve the *f-* longer than men (Bunis 1982a:52).[6] But in the last sixty to eighty years there has been a tendency to drop the initial *f-*, even among the most conservative speakers (Levy 1952). Both Malinowski and Nemer have found in their studies that individuals today frequently use two pronunciations, with /f-/ and /∅/ in free variation in such examples as [favlar]~[avlar] (hablar) 'to speak' and [fižu]~[ižu] (hijo) 'son' (Malinowski 1979:36, Nemer 1981:143–4).

The distinction of bilabial /b/ and labiodental /v/ in initial position in Old Spanish (which was lost by the end of the sixteenth century in Castilian Spanish) is generally retained in Judeo-Spanish, as shown in the contrast of the words *bos* (voz) 'voice' and *vos* (vos) 'to you'-dative (Malinowski 1979:26). In all other positions (except after *m*), especially in intervocalic position, Old Spanish *b* is pro-nounced [v] as in *bivir* (vivir) 'to live'; *bever* (beber) 'to drink'; *palavra* (palabra) 'word'; and *avuela* (abuela) 'grandmother'.

The Sephardic *v* may be explained not only as a survival of a medieval speech sound taken by the Spanish Jews into exile, but it could also be due to the language contact of other Romance languages, especially French, the Balkan languages, or even En-glish today. In Modern Spanish both Old Castilian *b* and *v* became the bilabial spirant [β].[7] According to Nemer (1981:200), there are some instances in Judeo-Spanish where [b] and [β] contrast, al-though Malinowski did not find the bilabial fricative [β] in the speech of her Israeli informants (Malinowski 1979:26). I only found it in the speech of some of my New York and Los Angeles infor-mants who had studied Modern Spanish or who came into daily contact with the language (Harris 1979 and 1987).

The distinction was retained in Judeo-Spanish between intervo-calic /s/ and /z/ from Old Spanish *ss* and *s*. The Latin intervocalic *s* as well as an *s* followed by a voiced consonant remained voiced (i.e. retained the [z] sound) throughout the Middle Ages, after which it became an unvoiced [s]. But intervocalic *ss* which became simplified to *s* as in *passo→paso* remained voiceless or sometimes became the palatalized [š] and later changed to [x] (Lathrop 1986:88). The sound change that began in Spain in the early part of the sixteenth century to devoice intervocalic *s* (which resulted in the entire loss of the voiced element [z]), did not affect the language of the Jews who had been exiled a few years earlier. Thus, in Judeo-Spanish the alveolar sibilant is regularly voiced in intervocalic position within a word, as in Old Spanish. Examples are: *kaza* (casa) 'house'; *kuzina* (cocina) 'kitchen'; *azer* (hacer) 'to do' and *dizir* (decir) 'to say, tell'. Modern Spanish only preserved the voiced [z] when *s* was followed by a voiced consonant as in *desde* pronounced [dezde] 'from', and *mismo* pronounced [mizmo] 'same', which also occurs in Judeo-Spanish.

C. *Other Phonetic Characteristics of Judeo-Spanish*

The existence of *yeísmo* in Judeo-Spanish also appears in various Peninsular dialects (especially in Andalusia) as well as in many Latin American ones. In *yeísmo* the Castilian -*ll*-, that is, the voiced palatal lateral /l/, does not exist. Instead -*ll*- becomes the palatal fricative /y/, as in *eya* (ella) 'she'; *akeya* (aquella) 'that'; *kavayo* (caballo) 'horse'; *se yama* (se llama) 'she/he is named'; *yorar* (llorar) 'to cry'; and also in feminine names such as *Beya* (Bella) and *Estreya* (Estrella).

Metathesis of consonant clusters with *r* is frequent in Judeo-Spanish, especially with the *rd* combination as in the following:

Examples: with *rd:*

tadre (tarde) 'afternoon'	*vedra(d)* (verdad) 'truth'
sodro (sordo) 'deaf'	*kuedra* (cuerda) 'cord'
pedron (perdón) 'pardon'	*akodro* (accuerdo) 'agreement'
godro (gordo) 'fat'	*guadrar* (guardar) 'to keep'
pedrer (perder) 'to lose'	*vedre* (verde) 'green'

Examples: with *br:* *prove* (pobre) 'poor'
  rs: *tres(z)eru* (tercero) 'third'
  dl in imperative forms: *tomalda*[8] (tómadla) 'take it'; *bushkalda* (búscadla) 'look for it'; *daldo* (dadlo) 'give it'; *metelda* (métedla) 'put it'; and *traeldo* (tráedlo) 'bring it'.

However, loanwords from Turkish such as *perde* 'curtain' and *birden* 'suddenly' do not undergo metathesis (Sephiha 1973a:26). In Judeo-Spanish initial *n-* becomes *m-* above all before -*ue*, as in: *muestro* (nuestro) 'our'; *mueve* (nueve) 'nine'; *mues* (nuez) 'nut'; and by assimilation to *mos* (nos) 'us' or reflexive 'we' and *muzotros* (nosotros) 'we'. Sephiha points out that due to French influence, many Judeo-Spanish speakers have reverted back to use of initial *n-* as in *nuestro* and *nozotros* (Sephiha 1986:101).[9]

The absence in Judeo-Spanish of the voiceless interdental fricative [θ], as in the Canary Islands, Andalusia, as well as in most of Latin America, is due to the fact that the change of Old Spanish *c* [ts] to [θ] which took place in Spain in the sixteenth century, did not take place in Sephardic Spanish. Instead, as in various Latin American dialects, the Old Spanish *c* [ts] before *i* and *e* became [s] as pronounced in the Judeo-Spanish words *sielo* (cielo) 'sky', and *selos* (celos) 'jealousy'. The [z] sound before *a* (*amenaza* 'threat'), *o* and *u* (*brazu* 'arm'), which also became [s] in Modern Spanish, remains [z] in Judeo-Spanish due to the distinction discussed above.

The single flap [r] and the trilled [r̄] merged in Judeo-Spanish according to region. In the Izmir and Bucharest dialects both the simple or single [r] and the multiple [r̄] are pronounced as a single [r], even where other Castilian dialects would have multiple [r̄]. Thus, in these two dialects the words *karo* 'dear' and *karro* 'cart' would be pronounced the same way [karo]. However, in Salonika, Constantinople, and Monastir there are variants of *r*, the single orthographic *r* being pronounced as a single [r] and the double orthographic *rr* is usually a multiple [r̄] pronounced with two or three taps. Nemer reports that there is no longer a contrast between [r] and [r̄] in the Indianapolis dialect, since these two sounds are in free variation in word medial position (Nemer 1981:177). Malinowski found that [r] and [r̄] often occur in free variation regardless of the country of origin as in [riko]~[r̄iko] 'rich'. She reports that in Israel, leveling of this distinction has occurred in all varieties of Judeo-Spanish (Malinowski 1979:30).

The tendency in Judeo-Spanish to lose final consonants such as: *-r, -l, -m, -d*, or *-s* as in *pai* (país) 'country'; *liberta* (libertad) 'freedom'; or *miye(ε)* (miel) 'honey'; also occurs in various Latin American dialects as well as in Andalusia. *Liberta* without the final *-d* can also be attributed to Italian origin as in Italian *libertà*.

Medial *-mb-* in Judeo-Spanish is conserved like the Leonese or Gallego Portuguese dialects as in *lombo* (lomo) 'back, loin'; *lamber* (lamer) 'to lick, lap'; and *palomba* (paloma) 'dove'.

Final note: Agard sums up one of the most salient phonological characteristics of Judeo-Spanish. He points out that where Modern Spanish has a two way contrast of the phonemes /s/ and /x/ due to changes occurring in the sixteenth century after the Sephardim had left the Peninsula, Judeo-Spanish preserves a five-way distinction between /s:z:š:ž:ǰ/. These phonological distinctions or features help to give Judeo-Spanish its unique flavor (Agard 1950:205).

II. Morphology—Word Formation

A. Verbs

Agard describes the Judeo-Spanish verb endings as having many traces of Old Castilian forms which have been leveled out in Modern Spanish. At the same time he reports various independent innovations in the Judeo-Spanish verb paradigms that are apparently the result of analogy (Agard 1950:206).

1) In certain regions the first person singular and plural forms of all verbs in the preterite, regardless of the conjugation, end in -i and -imos:[10]

JUDEO-SPANISH FORMS	MODERN SPANISH FORMS	MEANING
avli/avlimos	hablé/hablamos	I/we spoke
komi/komimos	comí/comimos	I/we ate
eskrivi/eskrivimos	escribí/escribimos	I/we wrote

2) The second person singular of the preterite endings is -tes while the second person plural preterite ends in -tesh.[11]

JUDEO-SPANISH FORMS	MODERN SPANISH FORMS	MEANING
avlates/avlatesh	hablaste/hablasteis	you [sg/pl] spoke
komites/komitesh	comiste/comisteis	you [sg/pl] ate
eskrivites/eskrivitesh	escribiste/escribisteis	you [sg/pl] wrote

The transposition of final -s of the second person singular preterite is identical to the Andalusian tomates for tomaste.

3) The second person plural ending of the present indicative and present subjunctive, the Old Spanish -ades and -edes endings, appear phonetically as [-aš, -eš, -iš] (spelled with sh) as in kantash (cantáis) 'you sing'; komesh (coméis) 'you eat'; and eskrivish (escribís) 'you write'.

4) Old Spanish verb forms ending in -o instead of Modern Spanish -oy (or along with the Modern -oy form of certain verbs) are present:

estar	dar	ir	ser
esto (not estoy)	do (not doy)	vo (not voy)	so (not soy)

Lathrop points out that it was not until the sixteenth century that the -y became permanently attached to the do and then spread to the so and vo forms (Lathrop 1986:129).

5) There is a tendency to form the perfect tenses with the verb tener instead of aver (as in Portuguese) plus the past participle as in tengo avlado 'I have spoken'; tengo ido 'I have gone'; or tiene komido 'he has eaten'. This archaic usage is still found today especially in the dialects of Leon, Asturias and Galicia where tener is the preferred auxiliary verb. Malinowski reminds us of the historical connection of these dialects with Portuguese, and she also suggests a possible grammatical explanation. She observes that tener occurs when the auxiliary is in the present indicative, whereas the imperfect of the verb aver (Modern Spanish haber) is used when the auxiliary is in the past or imperfect (Malinowski 1979:68–69).

6) Frequent use of the archaic prothetic prefix a- added to many verbs in Judeo-Spanish also occurs in Portuguese and in the popular speech of various Hispanic countries. Examples are: alevantar (levantar) 'to stand up'; asentar (sentar) 'to sit'; abashi (bajé) 'I descended'; and afumar (fumar) 'to smoke'.

B. Nouns and Pronouns

1) A change of gender occurred in certain nouns. Judeo-Spanish nouns ending in -or are often feminine instead of masculine as in Old and Modern Spanish. Examples are: la kalor 'heat'; la kolor 'color'[12]; la valor 'value'; and la favor 'favor' (Lida 1978:84). Exceptions are: el vapor 'boat'; and el amor 'love'. Other gender changes are el senyal 'sign'; el tribu 'tribe'; la vientre 'belly'; and la fin 'end'. Nouns with initial unaccented a-, which are masculine in Modern Spanish, are feminine in Sephardic dialects for euphonic reasons. Therefore in Judeo-Spanish we have: la asukar 'sugar'; la ave 'bird'; la agua 'water'; and la alfinete 'pin' (for Castilian alfiler).

2) Certain noun suffixes not commonly found in Modern Spanish are used:

(a) The -iko, -ika diminutive noun suffix, which is used in the Aragonese dialect as well as certain Latin American dialects, is very widely used in Judeo-Spanish. The -ito suffix (which is mostly used in Modern Spanish) is rare in Judeo-Spanish. Examples are:

azniko 'little donkey' *mezika* 'small table'
mužerika 'little woman' *manseviko* 'small boy, youth'
kashika 'small box' *kazika* 'small house'

This ending was frequently used with proper names as in *Daviko* 'little David', and *Shauliko* 'little Saul'. According to Kraus, the *-iko* suffix can differentiate meaning in certain instances, as in *ižo* 'son', versus *ižiko* 'child'; or *ventana* 'window,' versus *ventanika* 'ticket window, booking office' (Kraus 1952:413). Wagner also reports that *pasharo* in the Levant meant "bird" as a general class, as well as birds of prey, while *pashariko* designated small or singing birds (Wagner 1930:48).

(b) Noun formations with the *-ižo* suffix as in *kortižo* 'patio' and *empesižo* 'beginning' are frequent.

(c) The *-ada* noun suffix is used as in *mezada* 'monthly salary'; *tadrada* 'evening; party'; and *buena nochada* 'good night'.

3) The third person singular forms *el* and *eya* and the second person dative plural *vos* form for the second person singular polite pronoun of respect, are used. The existence of *usted,* the Modern Spanish singular polite or formal pronoun, is not attested until the seventeenth century, and *os* was also not known in Judeo-Spanish. Nor was the archaic *vuestra merced* known. Examples are: Komo esta *el*? 'How are you?'; Si *eya* me aze el favor. . . . 'If you will do me the favor of. .' A good example of usage of both the third singular and second person plural pronouns for the singular "you" can be found in the following example: "Me adresso a *vos,* komo esta *el*?" 'I'm speaking (addressing myself) to you, how are you?' (Ben-Rubi 1950 in Renard 1966a:122). Speakers used the third person pronouns even when talking with their parents and their spouses in public. Bunis reports that in early modern spoken Judeo-Spanish, women addressed their husbands using the third person *el,* while the men used *vos* to address their wives. The *tu* form was used only in private intimate conversations (Bunis 1982a:52). Children generally never used the *tu* familiar form as they do in Modern Spanish. However, Agard reports that in his research in Rochester, New York he was addressed "with all due respect to the professor" as *tu* (Agard 1950:210). Barocas gives an example of his use of the third person object pronoun *lo* 'him' when talking to his father to show his respect for him: "Asta ke oras ke *lo* espere para komer juntos?" meaning "how long should I wait for you to eat together?" instead of . . . "ke *te* espere" (Barocas 1976:174). Today in current Judeo-Spanish, Malinowski reports that the most common form of second person singular ad-

dress is the pronoun *tu* which is often used in relationships involving frequent daily contact (Malinowski 1979:52).

An example of use of the third person plural pronoun for the second person plural can be seen in the following sentence Barocas used in front of his congregation: "Es kon grande entusiasmo ke todos *eyos* vienen oy aki para . . ." 'It is with great enthusiasm that all of you come here today . .' (instead of "ke todos *ustedes*"). According to Barocas, he used *eyos* as indicative of his respect for his congregation (Barocas 1976:174). A similar phenomenon occurs in Modern Italian as in *che tutti loro vengono qui,* where *loro* in this instance is used as the polite form of "you" instead of its common usage as the third person plural pronoun form.

4) The nonexistence of the forms *conmigo* 'with me'; *contigo* 'with you'; and *consigo* 'with him/her'; since the Modern Spanish -*go* forms were unknown in Judeo-Spanish. Instead, the forms *con mi, con ti,* etc. are used. Examples are: "Eya vino vivir *con mi,*" 'She came to live with me'; and "Penso avlar *con ti,*" 'I intend to talk with you'.

5) Agreement of the relative pronoun *kual* (Modern Spanish *cual*), which also occurs in certain Spanish dialects. The masculine form was *kual,* as in "*Kual* ižo fue?" 'Which son was it?'; the feminine form was *kuala,* as in "*Kuala* mansana keres?" 'Which apple do you want?'' and the neuter form was *kualo,* as in "*Kualo estas aziendo?*" '*What are you doing?*'; or "*Kualo* devo azer?" 'What should I do?' The Modern Spanish relative *cuyo* does not exist in Judeo-Spanish.

C. Adjectives, Adverbs and Conjunctions

1) The archaic use of the definite article with possessive adjectives dates from the fifteenth century and was used frequently in the *romanzas* (Sephiha 1986:108–9). Examples are:

el mi padre 'my father'	*la mi madre* 'my mother'
las mis ižas 'my daughters'	*la su ermana* 'his sister'

Sephiha writes that today a phrase like *la mi ermana* is considered more of a poetic usage when compared with *mi ermana*. This might result from Italian influence, even though Modern Italian drops articles with the names of relatives as in *mio padre* 'my father', but not with other objects as in *il mio libro* 'my book'. It is probable that variations of this rule can be found throughout Spain and Italy today.

2) The combination of the words for "very" and "much" in the phrase *muy muncho* 'a lot' was frequently used.

3) *Ma* meaning "but" is used for Modern Spanish *pero* (from literary Spanish *mas* or borrowed from Italian *ma*), as in "Keria ir *ma* sta aziendo luvia" 'I wanted to go but it's raining' (D. Levy 1952).

4) Invariable *i* is used for the conjunction "and" in all cases, since there is no *e* form as in Modern Spanish,[13] and invariable *o* is used for "or" (there is no *u* form).

D. Agreement

1) In Judeo-Spanish there is frequent lack of agreement of subject and verb as in the following examples:

"Lo *izo* mi padre i su amigo" instead of the plural verb form *izeron* 'My father and his friend did it".

"*Es* las kuatro" instead of the plural form *Son* in 'It is four o'clock'.

"El puevlo non *saven* lo ke keren" instead of the singular *save* "The people (singular) do not know what they want'.

2) Agreement in Judeo-Spanish is often with the possessor, as in Turkish and Hebrew, instead of with the thing possessed, which is characteristic of Romance languages. For example:

"Las konsežas ilustran algunos aspektos de *sus* vida o istoria" (instead of *su* vida) 'The folktales illustrate some aspects of their life and history'.

As Kraus points out, *su* is used to designate "his/her" while *sus* is used to mean "their" even before a singular noun, as in "Los muevos imigrantes estan manteniendo *sus* familias kon *sus* lavoro", 'The new immigrants are supporting their families with their work' (Kraus 1951:268).

There are various Hebrew, Turkish, and French suffixes that are attached to Judeo-Spanish words, and also certain Spanish suffixes attached to Hebrew, French, and Turkish words that are a part of Judeo-Spanish morphology. These forms will be discussed in the section dealing with foreign influences or foreign features that are characteristic of the language.

III. Archaisms

The presence of archaic terms and phrases is one of the most salient characteristics of Judeo-Spanish due to the fact that the

Sephardim were separated from Spain and thus conserved words and expressions that were eventually eliminated from the Castilian lexicon. Renard suggests another source of archaisms, a religious one. The Sephardim had access to the bibles printed in the sixteenth century in Ladino[14] such as those of Constantinople (1547) and Ferrara (1553). The students thoroughly studied these texts and even used to chant by heart various biblical passages:

> This daily contact with these texts considered sacred contributed to fix a good number of ancient formulas in the spoken language and to block the possibilities of the evolution of it. (Renard 1966a:124)

M. Molho also agrees that the bibles in Ladino exercised a profound influence on the language of the Sephardim until the end of the nineteenth century (1960:190). Below are examples of some archaic words and expressions that are common in Judeo-Spanish; I have listed the equivalent Modern Spanish words in parentheses:

1) *adovar* (arreglar) 'to fix, repair', a Medieval Spanish word

2) *aflakar* (adelgazar) 'to make thin, weaken', found in *La Celestina* for *enflaquecer* (Estrugo 1958:92)

3) *agora* (ahora) 'now', Old Castilian word still used in Modern Portuguese

4) *ainda* (aún, todavía) 'yet, still', a Gallego-Portuguese adverb which was frequently used in Spain dating from 1250 (Sephiha 1987a:201)

5) *ande~onde* (dónde) 'where', from Old Spanish as in *De ande vienes?* 'Where are you from?'

6) *ansi* (así) 'thus, so'

7) *alguno* (alguien) 'someone', as in *Ay alguno?* (for *Hay alguien?*) 'Is someone (t)here?'

ninguno~denguno (nadie) 'no one', (found in Galdós) as in *No ay ninguno* for *No hay nadie* 'No one is (t)here' (Estrugo 1958:92–3)

8) *amatar* (apagar) 'to extinguish', used by the Arcipreste de Talavera (Estrugo 1958:92)

9) *atemar~atamar* (acabar) 'to end; to achieve'

10) *atorgar* (consentir) 'to consent, allow' or (confesar) 'to confess', from Old Spanish and Old Catalan. Today it is used in Aragon and Salamanca.

11) *avagar, avagaroso* (despacio) 'slowly', from Medieval Spanish (or Portuguese *devagar*)

12) *bendicho* 'blessed' for modern *bendito*
   Maldicho 'wicked' for modern *maldito,* both found in Old

Spanish. The Modern Spanish forms ending in -*ito* show the influence of Church Latin which was not shared by Sephardic Spanish.

13) *butika~botika* 'small store'; a *bo(u)tikario* is a shopkeeper. *Botica* in Modern Spanish means "drugstore".

14) pan y *conducho* (pan y *condumio*); *conducho* is the Old Spanish word for food served with bread, foodstuffs.

15) *embezar~ambezar* (enseñar), from Old Spanish *avezar, abezar* 'to teach', which was extended to also mean "to study, learn". *Embezar de kavesa* means "to learn by heart".

16) *enladinar, ladinar* 'to translate (Hebrew) texts to Spanish or Ladino', found in *Poema del Cid* (Wagner 1930:20)

17) *eskapar* (terminar) 'to finish, end'

18) *espantar; espanto* (asustar; susto) 'to frighten; fear'

19) *fraguar* (edificar, construir) still conserves the old meaning 'to build, construct' found in the Ferrara Bible. Today it means 'to forge; plot'.

20) *guerko* (diablo) 'devil' from Old Spanish *huerco,* used frequently in medieval literature until classical times.[15]

21) *echos~fechos* (asuntos, negocio) 'affairs, business', found in Cervantes (Estrugo 1958:90)

22) *enchir* (llenar) 'to fill'; in Nebrija's time (1492) they said *henchir los vasos de vino* 'to fill the glasses with wine' (Estrugo 1958:89).

23) *kale* or *kale ke* (for *hay que* or *es necesario que*) 'it is necessary', known in the Castilian of the sixteenth century and conserved today in Catalan and Aragonese. It is used in Judeo-Spanish sentences such as *Kale ke venga* (es necesario que venga, tiene que venir) 'it's necessary that he come'; and *kale vivir a la moda* (hay que vivir a la moda) 'it's necessary to live a la mode—in fashion' (Díaz-Mas 1986:107).

24) *kamareta* (habitación, cuarto) 'room', used by the Archipreste de Talavera in *El corbacho* (Estrugo 1958:91)

25) *las(d)rar* (trabajar duro) 'to work hard, toil, labor, struggle; *"penar i lasdrar"* 'to work and toil very hard'

26) *magazen* (almacén) 'large store', used by Covarrubias in 1610 (Estrugo 1958:92). It might also be attributed to French influence.

27) *mansevo* (joven) 'young' (adj.) or 'youth' (noun), and *mansevez* (juventud) 'youth' in general. Both terms have a limited or predominantly literary use in Spain today (Lapesa 1968:337).

28) *menester* (necesidad) 'necessity'; *es menester* 'it is necessary'

29) *merkar* (comprar) 'to buy', which existed in Old Spanish and is still used in some Spanish American regions today.

30) *orežales* (aretes) 'earrings'

31) *el padre i la madre* (los padres) 'parents', which in Judeo-Spanish meant 'the fathers'. The same thing occurred with *el ermano i la ermana* 'brother and sister', instead of *los ermanos,* which in Judeo-Spanish means more than one brother (Estrugo 1958:88).

32) *pronto* (listo) 'ready', as in *estar pronto* 'to be ready'. The word *listo* was not used by the Sephardim of the Levant since it only became part of the Castilian language around the beginning of the seventeenth century (two centuries after the Sephardim's expulsion from Spain).

33) *topar* (hallar, encontrar) 'to find', as in *topar alguien (alguno)* (dar con alguien) 'to run, bump into someone'. Estrugo informs us that in the time of Cervantes they said "toparon algo" versus the present day "se toparon con algo" (Estrugo 1958:91). Today *topar* has a restricted use in Modern Spanish, predominantly a literary one (Lapesa 1968:337).

34) *trokar* (cambiar) 'to change'

35) *vierbo* 'word' (versus Modern Spanish *verbo* 'verb')

These are just a few examples of lexical archaisms which are found in Judeo-Spanish. However it is important to remember, as Estrugo points out, that in all cases the archaic Spanish of the Sephardim is not as different from Modern Spanish as Old French and Old English are from Modern French and English respectively. Estrugo writes that Judeo-Spanish is more the language of the sixteenth to the eighteenth centuries rather than the eleventh, twelfth, and thirteenth centuries (Estrugo 1958:71).

IV. New Creations

Kraus (1951:265) advises us not to underestimate the creative powers of Judeo-Spanish (versus borrowing) as in all languages, where new words, expressions and concepts are needed. He gives two examples of Judeo-Spanish lexical creations: *komania* 'food', made from the verb *komer* 'to eat' plus the *-ia* noun ending; and *malanyos* 'years of misfortune', made of the adjective *mal* 'bad' + the noun *anyos* 'years'. The following is a discussion of lexical creations due to analogy, semantic alterations, periphrastic expressions, euphemisms and corruptions or transformations of words.

A. Analogy

Because of the Sephardim's isolation from the Iberian Peninsula, coupled with the fact that there was no linguistic standard setting body for the language, it is only natural that various changes in the course of time were due to analogic formations. The following examples were taken from Wagner (1930:25–26), Kraus (1952:412–13), and Renard (1966a:138):

Judeo-Spanish Base	Judeo-Spanish Creation	By analogy with	Modern Spanish
trokar	troka*miento*	-*miento* noun suffix	cambio 'change'
orasyon	orasyon*ar*	-*ar* infinitive ending	rezar, orar 'to pray'
azetuna	azetun*al*	-*al* noun suffix	olivo 'olive tree'
prove	prove*dad*	-*dad* noun suffix	pobreza 'poverty'
justo	juste*dad*	-*dad* noun suffix	justicia 'justice'
aborreser	abores*yon*	-*ción* noun suffix	odio, aborrecimiento 'hate'
muchacho	muchach*ez*	-*ez* noun suffix (as in *mansevez*)	juventud 'youth'
maldad	malaze*dor*	-*dor* noun agent	malhechor 'wrongdoer'
manko	mank*anza,*	-*anza* noun suffix	falta 'lack'
merkar	merk*ida*	-*ida* noun suffix	compra 'buying, purchasing'
tadre	tadr*ada*	-*ada* noun suffix	tarde 'afternoon'

There was also frequent addition of the feminine -*a* and the masculine -*o* endings to adjectives ending in a consonant in an analogical effort to express gender agreement, as in *internasyonala* 'international'. Kraus gives various examples found in the 20 July 1950 edition of *El Tiempo*:[16] *la istoria kruela* 'the cruel history'; *la paz mondiala* 'world peace'; *la politika interiora i exteriora* 'internal and external politics'; and *el brazo el mas joveno de la armada* 'the youngest branch of the navy' (Kraus 1951:265). Sephiha gives other examples: *situasyon sosyala* 'social situation', and *grev ženerala* 'general strike', with *ženerala* agreeing with the feminine French word *grève* meaning "strike" (Sephiha 1986:109).

Estrugo points out an interesting phenomenon when dealing with certain linguistic creations: that despite the distances and lack of communication, many of the same errors and creations appear in different regions of the world, such as in Caracas, Guadalajara, and Seville, as well as in Izmir and Rhodes. It seems that speakers in general take the same or similar liberties with the language when they lack the adequate word or expression for an idea. For example, Estrugo writes that in both Chile and Izmir people say: *Quisiera un "comosellama"* 'I want a whatchamecallit'. Also the verb *comosellamear* has been formed (Estrugo 1958:84–5).

B. Semantic Alterations

Semantic alterations include those words which are semantically altered by frequently giving them a different meaning from the original:

EXAMPLE	ACQUIRED MEANING	ORIGINAL MEANING
topar	to meet	to butt, run into
baldar	to hang	to cripple, incapacitate
mankar	to lack	to maim, cripple

Semantic alterations can also occur because people do not know the original meaning of the word. For example, *teralanya~tiralanya* among Spanish Jews of Constantinople and in the Bulgarian dialects is not only *la telaraña* 'spider web,' but also *araña,* the spider itself. In Constantinople the word *aranya* 'spider' was unknown. In Karaferia (Veroia) *aranya* is the *tela* 'web' and the insect is *aranyero* (Wagner 1930:26–27). In other regions of the Balkans *aranya* is used in a metaphoric sense for a wicked, bad person who sticks his/her nose into other people's business.

C. Periphrastic Expressions

In Judeo-Spanish periphrastic expressions, instead of just one word, were often used to describe various situations. Below are some examples.

1) Instead of simple everyday verbs, paraphrases are used:

fazer luvie 'to make rain' instead of the Spanish word *llover* 'to rain'

dizir mintires 'to tell lies' instead of the Modern Spanish word *mentir* 'to lie'

meterse en medio 'to put oneself in the middle' instead of Spanish *intervenir* or *interponerse* for "to intervene"

2) Abstract words are often replaced by concrete words and expressions:

enganyo de meoyo 'deception of the brain' to mean "deceit"

kara de luna 'face of the moon' to describe a beautiful woman

kara de pokos amigos 'face of (that attracts) few friends' to mean an "unfriendly face"

3) A negative idea is often expressed with periphrastic expressions or poetic phrases since the negative prefix *in-* (meaning 'un' as in the word *inactivo*) of Modern Spanish does not exist in Judeo-Spanish (Camhy 1966:18–19). Some examples are:

esto no se tiene visto 'this has not been seen' to mean "unforeseen, unexpected"

esto no se esperava 'this was not hoped for, awaited', to also mean "unexpected"

no tiene verguenza en kara 'he/she has no shame in the face' to mean "impudent"[17]

no save onde la da ni onde la toma 'he/she does not know where he gives it nor where he takes it' to mean "incoherent"

no le kuadra muncho 'much understanding does not reach him' or *no le bolta el meoyo* 'it does not turn the brains' or *no es seheludo* 'he is not intelligent' from the Hebrew word [sehel] 'intellect' to mean "unintelligent"

4) Periphrastic expressions and general terms were used in Judeo-Spanish for unknown vocabulary as is the case in many languages. For example, since the majority of immigrants to the Balkans had lived predominantly in the cities, they did not speak the Spanish of the rural classes, and thus did not know many vocabulary items dealing with objects of rural life. As a result they used general terms to express certain elements of nature, such as *pasharos* to refer to the general class of large birds and birds of prey versus *pasharikos,* with the *-iko* ending, to designate small or

singing birds in general.[18] Wagner informs us that names of particular birds were taken from either Turkish, Bulgarian or Serbo-Croatian, depending on where the Sephardim resided (Wagner 1930:48). The term *arvol* 'tree' was often used as a generic name for small trees versus *pino* 'pine tree' which was used to designate "tall ramified trees". And for the names of fruit trees the Sephardim frequently used periphrastic expressions such as *arvol d'almendra* 'tree of the almond', and *arvol de mansana* 'tree of the apple', since they did not know the correct Spanish words *almendro* and *manzano* for "almond tree" and "apple tree" respectively.

D. Corruptions or Transformations of Words

The corruption or deformation of words with a humorous or malicious intent was a prevalent practice among the Sephardim (Wagner 1930:49). Examples are:

> *la suziedad* (*sucio* means "dirty") for "society"
> *el rabano* (*rábano* means "radish") for "rabbi"
> *la moshka* (*mosca* means "fly, insect") for "young woman, servant"
> *la nubla* (*nublo* means "cloudy" in South America) for *la novia* 'fiancee'
> *la seka* (*seca* means "dried up, withered") for *suegra* 'mother-in-law' (see the section on proverbs)
> *perros ermanos* (*perro* means "dog") for *primos hermanos* 'first cousins'
> *el tibio* (*tibio* means "lukewarm") for *el tío* 'uncle'
> *la kanesa* (*caño* means "gutter; drain, sewer") for *cabeza* 'head'
> *vinya* (*viña* means "vine") for *la vida* 'life' in the oath *por mi vinya* 'on my life' (Wagner 1930:38)

Proper names were also sometimes changed for a humorous effect, as with the woman's name *Mazalto* 'good luck', which was changed to *Matato* from the verb *matar* meaning "to kill" (Wagner 1930:49).

V. Euphemisms

All languages use euphemistic words and expressions to describe situations such as death, God, taboo words, curses, etc. Judeo-Spanish is no exception. Below are examples of euphemisms regularly used by the Sephardim in the Levant.

A. Words for "God"

Periphrastic expressions were used to express the word for "God", since his name could not be taken in vain:

el Sinyor or *el patron del mundo* 'Master, ruler of the world' (Wagner 1930:51)

El ke no se puede mintar 'He who cannot lie' (Estrugo 1958:89)

El ke no se puede nombrar 'He who cannot be named'

Bendicho El i su nombre 'Blessed be he and his name'

tavan (the Turkish word for "ceiling, roof") as in:

el Tavan ke nos guadre literally "the roof that guards us," meaning "heaven protect us". *Tavan* is used in such expressions as *el Tavan ke me lo pedrone* 'Would that God pardon me' (Nehama 1977:544); or *Bendicho el Tavan* 'Blessed be the ceiling' (meaning "God") (Sephiha 1981:116).

B. Death or Dying

Euphemisms replaced words referring to death and the dead. As in many cultures, the subject of death and dying is a very delicate one and euphemisms are often used for these concepts. The following are examples of some of these euphemisms used by the Sephardim:

el deskansado 'the rested one' is used for *el difunto* 'the deceased'

Hebrew [betaxaim] 'house of the living' is the Judeo-Spanish as well as the Hebrew word for "cemetery".

estuvimos arriba 'we were up(stairs)' was used to mean "we have accompanied the dead one to the cemetery". Since Jewish cemeteries were usually located on top of a hill, the phrase *la punta de la montanya* 'the top of the mountain', was also used for "cemetery" (Wagner 1930:36).

s'arripozo or *ya bolo* 'he put himself to rest', or 'he left—flew away' expresses the idea of "he/she died".

esta mas de aya ke d'aki 'he/she is more there than here' to mean "moribund, dying"

C. Taboo—Dirty Words

Euphemisms were also used for taboo or dirty words. The Sephardim were a very moral, religious and superstitious people, which resulted in their use of euphemisms for taboo words and dirty words as is done in many languages. For example, euphemistic words or expressions were used to designate the sexual organs and sexual acts:

la koza fea 'the ugly thing' or *la koza negra* 'the bad, wicked thing' designated the male genitals.

las verguenzas 'the shameful ones' also designated the genital organs.

errar 'to err' was used for *fornicar* 'to fornicate' in the Ferrara Bible. (See Wagner 1930:38). Various sexual acts as well as certain immoral acts were also designated by Turkish terms.

D. Contrary to Intended Meanings

For superstitious reasons, euphemisms or expressions were used contrary to their intended meanings. Some examples are:

mazal klaro (*klaro* means "light" or "good") to mean "bad luck" instead of *mazal i(o)skuro*

vistozo (de vista) 'having sight' to mean "the blind one"

Bumaschny informs us that in Bosnia a prostitute was referred to as *una muchacha buena* 'a good girl' (Bumaschny 1968:20).

According to Wagner, of all the famous Castilian curses, not one is used in its original form by the Jews in the Levant (Wagner 1930:37). Their curses were expressed by the exact opposite of the meaning intended so as not to invoke the wrath of God. Camhy points out that in order to curse another person one "blesses" him/her as in the following examples (Camhy 1966:19):

El mazal le briye or *la estreya le briye* 'let luck or the star shine on you/him' when calling misfortune on someone's head. *Ke el diablo no os yeva* or *el guerko ke no te yeva* instead of Modern Spanish *Que el diablo os lleve* to mean "may the devil take you".

ke mal mos tenga 'Let wickedness befall us' instead of *ke mal no mos tenga*.

mentar la Ley 'to cite the Law, Torah' was used in the sense of "to curse, insult".

Wagner points out that many of these formulas correspond to the curses having an opposite meaning which are found in the Talmudic books (Wagner 1930:35).

Blanko was the word used instead of *karvon* 'carbon' or 'tar' for euphemistic purposes in order to avoid the word for "black", which had a fatal connotation for the Sephardim. This is a translation of the Arabic term [bIyad] literally meaning "white".[19] Sephiha reminds us that the Judeo-Spanish word *negro* had nothing to do with the color "black", since the Sephardim used the word *preto* from Old Spanish *preto,* which is still used in Portuguese. Rather, the Judeo-Spanish word *negro* carries another connotation, that of "bad" or "wicked". The word *negro* was also combined with the word *malo* 'bad' to mean wickedness in the extreme, and would appear in phrases like *un ombre negro malo* 'a very wicked man', or in the sentence which Sephiha reports that his grandmother often used: *"Este ižiko es negro malo"* to mean "this child is very, very naughty." (Sephiha 1986:103).

VI. Proverbs or Refranes (Reflanes)

Proverbs are an indispensable part of the spoken Judeo-Spanish language. No idea, opinion or story would be expressed without the aid of a proverb. Estrugo believes that there is no other group of people who make such frequent use of the old *refranes* in daily conversation as much as the Sephardim (Estrugo 1958:117). The elders had one for every occasion. The importance given to proverbs is expressed in the following: *Refran(iko) mentiroso no ay* 'There is no refran that lies'. The proverbs were passed on orally from generation to generation. Many are of Spanish origin or have Spanish equivalents, such as *No hay refrán que no sea verdadero* which is the Spanish equivalent of the above proverb and is found in *Don Quijote*.

Other examples of Spanish proverbs or those having Spanish equivalents are:

Dime kon ken vas, te dire ken sosh 'Tell me with whom you walk/go, and I'll tell you who you are'.

Ken mas tiene mas kere 'The more one has, the more one wants' is equivalent to the Castilian *Cuanto más tienes más quieres*.

Ken bien te kere te face (ara) yorar 'He who loves you much makes (will make) you cry'.

Ken nase kon mazal i ventura, ken kon potre i kevadura is equivalent to the Spanish *Unos nacen con estrella, otros estrellados* 'Some are born with good luck, others are destined with bad'.

Other proverbs have a Balkan origin as in:

Ken (el ke) se kema (la boka) en la chorba (Turkish word for "soup") *asopla (en) el yogurt* which is a literal translation of the Turkish proverb *çorbada ağzı yanan yoğurtu üfler* (Benbassat 1987:50), literally, "he who burns himself on (swallowing) the (hot) soup, afterwards (due to fear), blows on his yogurt". This is the equivalent of the Hispanic *gato escalado del agua fría fuye* (Díaz-Mas 1986:146), or the French *chat échaudé craint l'eau froide* meaning that he who has a bad experience becomes more prudent in the future. R. Levy translates it as the English expression "Once burned twice shy" (R. Levy 1987:100). Díaz-Mas also gives us an example of a proverb translated from Rumanian: *Azte ermano kon el guerko fin a (asta ke) pasas el ponte* 'Align yourself or make friends even with the devil until you cross the bridge safely (or until you get what you want)' (Díaz-Mas 1986:146).

Many proverbs are derived from rabbinical and biblical as well as other literary sources such as the folktales—*konsežas* and the *romanzas*. One example is the literal calque from the famous Hebrew expression of Hillel found in the *Pirkei Avot*[20]: *Si yo no para mi, ken para mi, i si no agora kuando?* 'If I am not for me (if I do not defend myself), then who will be for (defend) me? And if not now, when?' Goldberg provides examples of proverbs which served as plot summaries or moralistic tag lines for various ballads, folktales, and the Djoha stories (Goldberg 1993). Others were created by the Sephardim themselves as the need arose. So much of the Sephardic culture and way of life is reflected in the language of the *refranes*. According to Marc Angel, many of the proverbs dealt with the good and bad self-image that the Jews had of themselves. He presents the following two examples (Angel 1978:141–42):

Ĵudiyo bovo no ay 'There is no stupid Jew'.

El Ĵudiyo kuando kevra si asavienta 'When a Jew errs, he learns from his mistakes'.

The following two proverbs are variations on the theme of "to err is human," even for the Jews:

Afilu el hazan se yierra 'Perhaps even the hazan (reader of the religious services) errs', and *I el haham yerra en la teva* 'And even the rabbi makes mistakes'.

Jewish humor, which is an important characteristic of the *refranes,* is expressed in the following proverbs:

El haham por onde kere bolta la oshika 'When the rabbi cannot answer a question, he turns the page and speaks of other things'.

Al Ĵudiyo le viene la repuesta tadre 'The Jew thinks too late' (literally, "to the Jew the answer comes late").

Venga Mashiah, ma no en muestros dias 'Come Messiah, but not in our time' meaning that a long awaited happening should occur at a time when it doesn't affect or inconvenience the speaker.

Bien darsha el senyor haham komo ay ken ke lo sienta 'The rabbi preaches well as if anyone were listening'.

Dos Ĵudiyos, tres kehilot 'Two Jews, three opinions' (literally "communities").

En este mundo sufrimos porke somos J̌udiyos. En el otro mundo sufriremos porke no fuimos J̌udiyos. 'In this world we suffer because we are Jews. In the next world we will suffer because we were not Jews'. Another proverb expressing a similar theme is:

El J̌udiyo es komo el vidro. Se aharvas la piedra al vidro, guay del vidro. Se aharvas el vidro a la piedra, guay del vidro. "Jews are blamed for whatever, they're damned if they do and they're damned if they don't'.

Certain proverbs describe God as exacting but fair as in:

El dyo no aharva kon dos manos 'God doesn't beat you with both hands', and *El dyo es tadrozo ma no ulvidozo* 'God may be slow (late) but he is not forgetful'.

Many proverbs dealt with family members and the importance of familial love as in:

La madre es madre, i lo demas es aire 'The mother is mother and the rest is air', meaning that there is nothing to compare with the love of a mother.

No ay amigo en el mundo mas ke la madre 'There is no friend in the world greater than one's mother'.

Ken no tiene iža, no tiene amiga 'Whoever doesn't have a daughter, doesn't have a friend.'

Ken no tiene ermano, komo si fuera de una mano 'He who has no brother is like a person with one hand'.

Ižos de mis ižos, dos vezes mis ižos 'Children of my children, twice my children' expresses the idea that grandchildren are more dear than children.

However, feelings of familial affection do not seem to extend to in-laws, as in *Suegra ni de barro es buena* 'A mother-in-law, even when made of clay, is no good', and *El amor del yerno es komo sol del invierno* 'the love of the son-in-law is like the winter sun', meaning that a son-in-law's love is half hearted.

Many *refranes* were sympathetic to the poor, since, as Angel reminds us, from the eighteenth century on, the majority of Sephardim were very poor (Angel 1978:141–143).

En dia di luvia pensa en el provi; el tambien tiene frio 'On a rainy day think about the poor man; he also is cold'.

Tanto lavora el provi k'el riko si enrikese 'The poor man (employee) works so hard that the rich man gets rich'.

El prove piedre tiempo en kontando la rikeza del riko 'The poor man wastes time counting the wealth of the rich man'.

En tiempo de ambrera no ay mal pan 'In times of hunger there is no bad bread'.

Other proverbs deal with money, the acquisition of money and its evils (Koen-Serano 1988:39). The term for "money" is expressed by the Turkish word *para* (or *paras* with the Spanish -*s* ending):

La para va i viene 'Money comes and goes'.

Si tenemos paras, tenemos amigos 'If we have money, we have friends'.

La para es avoda zara (idolatrous) 'money is idolatrous work' expresses the idea that we should not make of money an idol or a god.

Guadrar el grosh (piaster) blanko para el dia preto 'Save the white piaster for a black day' expresses the idea of saving for a rainy day.

Amigos i ermanos semos ma a la bolsa no tokaremos literally 'we will be friends and brothers as long as we don't touch the pocket', in other words, "don't let money come between friends".

Dar a los proves es emprestar al Dyo 'To give to the poor is to lend to God' (a proverb from Sarajevo).

Many of the proverbs rhymed, which facilitated memorizing them: *Oy tu por mi, manyana yo por ti* 'Today you for me, tomorrow me for you'.

Pensando a la vežez no gozamos (piedras) a la mansevez 'Thinking (worrying) about old age, we don't enjoy youth' (or 'you lose your youth').

El lavoro a la mansevez da repozo a la vežez 'Work in (the time of) youth gives rest in old age'.

Antes ke te kazes, mira lo ke azes 'Before marrying, look at what you are doing'.

La rikeza kon falsia se akava kon manziya 'Wealth with falseness ends (results) in misfortune'.

Avla la vedrad, piedres la amistad 'Speak the truth and you lose affection (a friendship)', meaning don't be too critical or you're bound to lose a friend.

En tus apuros i afanes, toma konsežo de los refranes 'In your hardships and toil, take advice from the proverbs'.

Other favorite Judeo-Spanish proverbs of mine include:

Ken no entiende avla ažena, no entiende ni la suya 'He who does not understand a foreign language does not understand his own', which was a possible reflection of the multilingual status of the Sephardim in the Levant.[21]

Mas vale (mižor) solo i no mal acompanyado 'Its better to be alone than badly accompanied'.

Prove de moneda no es prove, prove de ideas es prove 'Poor (lack) of money is not poor, lack of ideas is poor'.

Lo preto no se aze blanko 'That which is black does not become white', meaning complete changes in a person's nature are impossible.

El prove i el riko, todos se mezura por un negro piko 'Whether you are rich or poor, you have the same grave'.

Ken es riko? El ke se kontenta kon su parte 'Who is rich? He who is content with his lot in life'.

Deshame entrar, me azere lugar 'Let me in and I'll make room for myself'.

La fortuna no viene solo, kale bushkarla 'Good luck doesn't come, one must seek it'. A variation of this is *La ventura por ken perkura.*

El ke tiene es devdor al ke no tiene 'Whoever has money (or other things) is the debtor to whomever does not have it'.

El gameyo no ve su korkova, ve la de su vižino. 'The camel doesn't see his hump, he sees that of his neighbor', meaning that we never see our own faults.[22]

Kuando te yaman azno mira si tienes kola 'When they call you a jackass, look to see if you have a tail' meaning that they might be correct, but on the other hand, if you don't have a tail, you don't need to pay attention to their criticism.

Un anyo (dia) mas, un sehel mas 'One year (day) older, one year (day) wiser'.

No ay mižor espežo ke el amigo verdadero 'There is no better mirror than a true friend'.

Mas se ambeza en la dolor ke en la alegria 'More is learned from (in) pain than from (in) happiness'.

Kada uno es haham de su ofisio 'Each one is a wise man, in his job'.

El kavod es de ken lo da, no de ken lo toma 'Honor comes from the person who gives it, not from he who takes it'.

Vida sin salud, la muerte es mas dulse 'Life without health, death is sweeter'.

Para el mal i el bien, sehel kale tener 'To do good or evil, it is necessary to be intelligent (have intelligence)'.

Basta mi nombre ke me yamo Abravanel 'It is enough that my name is Abravanel', where the name recalls memories and pride in the Spanish heritage.

The proverbs dealt with all aspects of human life such as love, marriage, death, health, wealth, poverty, daily needs, fatalism, family relations, morality, happiness and sadness. And, depending on the place of residence in the Ottoman Empire, there were often several variations of the same proverb. Goldberg reminds us that the proverbs themselves undergo changes:

And, just as a dialect experiences phonological, morphological, syntactical, and lexical changes, the discourse of its speakers undergoes transformations as well: the collective memory loses some tales and proverbs; new stories create new sayings; some maxims switch contexts, and others seem to gain additional meanings. (Goldberg 1993:114)

Much research has been done and continues to be done on Sephardic proverbs.[23]

VII. Foreign (Non-Spanish) Influences in Judeo-Spanish: The Semitic, Romance, and Ottoman Elements

Along with archaisms and new creations, the most important feature of Judeo-Spanish development has been in the realm of foreign influences, which have contributed to giving the language its mixed quality. The loan words, affixes, and calques, which have become an integral part of the Judeo-Spanish language or code, have been borrowed from the various languages that Judeo-Spanish has come into contact with during its historical development. These borrowings come from the Semitic languages of Hebrew/Aramaic and Arabic, the various Iberian dialects, other Romance languages, especially French and Italian, and the Ottoman languages, most notably Turkish and Greek. Lida (1978:86) points out that, except in the case of most Hebrew loans, about one-half of the words borrowed from other languages often coexist with a Spanish synonym. This fact is confirmed by Yahuda (1915:345), Wagner (1930:38–9), and Hassán (1963:177) for Turkish, and Wagner (1925:197) and Baruch (1930:121) in regards to Greek and Serbo-Croatian borrowings, respectively. However, with the passage of time there are many instances where the original Spanish word is no longer known (or was never known) by the speakers. As Michael Molho wrote:

Many Turkish words have their Spanish equivalents where one or the other is used; but in many cases the Spanish word has been completely substituted by the foreign one. Thus many Spanish words and expressions have fallen into the abyss of oblivion. (1960:5)

The following is a discussion of the Semitic, Romance and Ottoman elements of Judeo-Spanish.

A. The Semitic Component: Hebrew and Arabic

1) HEBREW

The influence of the Hebrew-Aramaic component on Judeo-Spanish has been important, although not as extensive as that of Hebrew on the Yiddish of the Ashkenazic Jews (M. Molho 1960:6).[24] According to Hassán (1963:176), Hebrew loans have mostly been in the form of nouns and adjectives, with a restricted use of verbs. Hebrew words are generally used to render typically Jewish religious concepts, holidays, customs, and institutions as well as proper names. Much of the religious vocabulary is due to the Hebrew liturgical influence on the culture, i.e., religious books and prayers were written in Hebrew, and were often translated into Judeo-Spanish since many (especially the women) could not read or understand spoken Hebrew. Examples of Hebrew loans having to do with religious/Jewish practices are given below:

JUDEO-SPANISH WORD	FROM HEBREW	MEANING
beraha	בּ ר כ ה	blessing
bet haim	בּ י ת ח י ים	cemetery
darush, derasha	דר וּ שׁ , דר שׁ ה	sermon
gan eden	גַ ן ע ד ן	paradise
haham	ח כ ם	rabbi; wise person
kal	ק ה ל	synagogue
kehila	ק ה י ל ה	community
lashon	לשׁ ו ן	language
menora	מ נ ו ר ה	lamp, *menorah*
shabat	שׁ בּ ת	Sabbath, Saturday
Tora	ת ו ר ה	Torah
talmud tora	ת ל מ ו ד ת ו ר ה	religious school
purim	פּ ו ר י ם	Purim
pesah	פּ ס ח	Passover
brit mila	בּ ר י ת מ י ל ה	circumcision

Hebrew expressions such as: *Shabat shalom mevora* 'a Sabbath peace and blessing' was said on the Sabbath, and *Haim tovim* 'a good life', was one of the responses when someone sneezed. Hebrew proper names, such as *Yitshak* 'Isaac,' *Rahel* 'Rachel,' *Moshe* 'Moses,' *Haim* "Chaim,' and *Shaul* 'Saul,' were commonly used in Sephardic families as well as certain proper nouns such as the Hebrew word *Mitzrayim* for 'Egypt.'

However, the Hebrew influence was not present only in the realm of religious or Jewish vocabulary. As M. Molho (1960:6) points out, there is also a sizable number of Hebrew loans which convey nonreligious everyday ideas and concepts such as:

JUDEO-SPANISH WORD	FROM HEBREW	MEANING
azpan	עזפן	insolent
galut	גלות	diaspora, exile
goyim	גוי׳׳ם	gentiles
hamor	חמור	donkey
haver	חבר	friend
kavod	כבוד	honor, respect
malsin, malshin	מלש׳ן	slanderer; informer
mamzer	ממזר	bastard
mazal	מזל	luck
sedaka	צדקה	charity
sehel	שכל	intelligence, prudence
sekana, sakana	סכנה	danger

Díaz-Mas also informs us that the names of the Hebrew months were often used in Judeo-Spanish (1986:108). More recent borrowings from Hebrew include: *knesset* 'parliament,' *olim* 'immigrants,' *sochnut* 'the Jewish Agency,' *tor* 'line' (of people), *kibbutz* 'kibbutz', and other words which became a part of the vocabulary of the new state.

Incorporation of Hebrew elements

(1) Hebrew nouns often acquired Spanish adjectival affixes. In the following examples the Hebrew words are represented phonetically in brackets: *mazaloso* 'lucky' and *dezmazalado* 'unlucky' from Hebrew [mazal] 'luck'; *henosa* 'graceful, charming' from Hebrew [hen] 'grace'; *seheludo* 'intelligent' from Hebrew [sehel] 'intelligence'.

(2) The Spanish *-s* and *-es* plural noun endings were added to certain Hebrew nouns as in:

balabaya(s) 'housewife' from Hebrew [ba'al ha bayit]; *kales* 'synagogues,' from Hebrew [kahal] 'synagogue.'

(3) Hebrew verb forms were given Spanish infinitive and declension endings:

darshar 'to preach' from Hebrew [deruš, deraša] 'sermon' (the conjugated forms have the Spanish verb endings: *darsho, darshas, darsha,* etc.); *malsinar* 'to slander' from Hebrew [malsin] 'slanderer, informer'; *enheremar* 'to excommunicate' from Hebrew [herem] 'excommunication'; *diburear* 'to speak; have knowledge of a foreign language' from Hebrew [dibur] 'speech; word, utterance'; *(a)takanear~(a)takanar* 'to arrange, put in order; repair' from Hebrew [takana] 'remedy, regulation'.

(4) Certain Spanish nouns took on Hebrew endings, such as the masculine plural *-im* ending as in *ladronim* 'thieves' instead of the Spanish *-es* plural ending in *ladrones,* and the feminine *-ut* noun ending as in *haraganut* 'idleness' instead of the Spanish *haraganería* (see chapter 4).

(5) Various mixtures or fusions of Hebrew and Spanish words occurred, such as in the word *afiluke* 'although, even' made up of Hebrew [afilu] 'although' plus the Spanish *que,* and *buen moed* 'good holiday', composed of the Hebrew word [moed] 'holiday', plus the Spanish word *buen* meaning "good". Other periphrastic expressions combining a Spanish and Hebrew component are the following:

azer kavod 'to honor' made of the Judeo-Spanish verb *azer* (Modern Spanish *hacer* 'to do; make') plus the Hebrew word [kavod] 'honor'; *azer~dezir tefila* 'to pray' made of Spanish *azer* 'to make' or *dezir* 'to say' plus Hebrew [tefila] 'prayer'; *dar edut* 'to testify' from Spanish *dar* 'to give' and Hebrew [edut] 'evidence, testimony'; *salir de hova* 'to fulfill one's duty' from Spanish *salir de* 'to leave, go out from' plus Hebrew [hova] 'duty, obligation'; *tornar en teshuva* 'to repent' from Spanish *tornar* 'to change, become' plus Hebrew [xazar bitšuva] 'repent one's sins'; *estar en se(a)kana* 'to be in danger, run a risk' from Spanish *estar* 'to be' plus Hebrew [sakana] 'danger'.

Other fusions included not only Hebrew and Spanish elements, but Turkish ones as well, as in the word *purimlikes* 'Purim gifts' made up of the Hebrew word *purim* plus the Turkish *-lik* noun forming suffix plus the Spanish *-es* plural ending (Bunis 1975a:21). The word for "Hannukah gifts" *hanukalikes* also arose due to morphological analogy to *purimlikes.*

(6) Certain expressions were copied word for word from the literal translations of the Bible (see chapter 4), what Sephiha refers to as the Judeo-Spanish calque (1986:54,63). Some examples are: *kada uno i uno* 'each and every one' which reproduces the Hebrew [kol exad ve exad], and which resulted in other similar expressions such as *en kada fabrika i fabrika* 'in each and every factory'. Other

calques which copy the Hebrew style include *ermoso entre los ermosos* 'beautiful among the beautiful', *pelear una pelea* 'to fight a fight' and *el Dyo bendicho* from the Hebrew [ha kadoš barux hu] 'The holy one, blessed be he', to refer to "God".

Bunis (1975a:14), and Renard (1966a:126) among others, point out that the Hebrew–Aramaic component was often used as a secret language to prevent outsiders from understanding the most significant details of a conversation, especially one concerning business dealings or sensitive group matters. For example, the word *shetika* 'silence' from Hebrew [šetika] was used when a gentile or stranger was approaching (Bumaschny 1968:22). The Hebrew words for numbers as well as the word *kama* 'How much?' were used in commercial negotiations. And the phrase *De bene amenu es?* 'Is he one of us?' (made up of the Hebrew words [ben] 'son' and [amenu] 'ours', plus the Spanish verb *es* 'is' and the preposition *de* 'of' was employed when one wanted to find out if another person was Jewish (M. Molho 1960:7).

2) ARABIC

According to Bumaschny (1968:9) and others, there are two sources of Arabisms in Judeo-Spanish. Early Arabisms were incorporated into the language before expulsion because of the Jews' contact with the Moors, especially in Andalusia. Some examples include *alhad* from Arabic [alxad] literally, "the first day" used to mean "Sunday", *shara* 'forest' from [šajar] 'plants', and *hazino* 'sick' from Arabic [ḥazin] 'sad'.

Later, the majority of Arabisms infiltrated Judeo-Spanish by means of the Turkish language, since one third of the Turkish lexicon was composed of Arabic words and expressions or vocabulary of Arabic origin (Hassán 1963:178) before Kemalist reform.[25]

The words of Arabic origin are naturally less frequent in the Judeo-Spanish dialects of the Balkans than in those found in North Africa, which adopted Arabic words straight from Arabic and not via Turkish. According to I. Molho, the Arabic borrowings mainly apply to botanical and agricultural terms as well as to the fields of commerce and industry, mathematics and science, and to household words designating furniture and utensils (1961:65). Some examples of Judeo-Spanish words derived from Arabic are the following: *alforria* 'liberty', *almenara* 'light, lantern', conserved today with the meaning of "lamp",[26] *kadi* 'Turkish judge or religious authority' versus Spanish *juez* or Hebrew [dayan], *tarifa* 'tarif' and the exclamation *guay!* meaning 'ay!'.

B. Romance Influences: Iberian Dialects and Languages, Italian and French

1) THE IBERIAN DIALECTS AND CATALAN

Renard points out that, at the time of exile "the linguistic unity of Spain was far from realized," since the different regions of the Peninsula spoke very distinct dialects (1966a:128). We know that as the Spanish Jews regrouped in the Balkans, they established their own *kales* or synagogues/communities based on their region of origin. Because of the various phonetic characteristics of the different Judeo-Spanish dialects, Wagner (1930:21) has concluded that the Jews of Constantinople, Adrianople, Izmir and other parts of Turkey, as well as the island of Rhodes, originated from the two Castiles (in central Spain) and speak an oriental or eastern form of Judeo-Spanish; while those from the Balkans (Salonika, Macedonia, Bosnia, Serbia, Monastir, and other parts of Yugoslavia, Rumania, and Bulgaria) originated from the north of Spain including Portugal, Aragon, and Catalonia and speak a type of occidental or western Judeo-Spanish. This theory has been questioned by some scholars such as Revah (1964:44), who does not believe that one can distinguish the language of Salonika and Istanbul on these criteria. He reports that synagogues from the various regions of Spain were established in all the Sephardic centers of the Empire, especially in Istanbul and Salonika. What is important is that the Judeo-Spanish *koiné* which developed in the Ottoman Empire and was based on Castilian, has incorporated numerous regional elements of the Peninsula and thus exhibits qualities characteristic of the various peninsular dialects (Renard 1966a:129).[27]

Examples of such phonetic differences can be seen in the western regions where final *-o, -e* and *-a* have been raised to *-u, -i* and *-e* respectively, while the same regions conserve the initial *f-* relatively well. These traits are related to the northern Spanish dialects of Asturias, Aragon, Leon, Galicia (Gallego), as well as Portugal, and to a certain extent, Catalonia (Wagner 1930:22).

Other examples of Iberian dialectal differences are apparent in the lexicon. In the western regions there are a series of words that have the same form and identical phonetic peculiarities as the northern Spanish dialects. For example, *bezpa* 'wasp' used in Salonika and Bosnia is similar to the Asturian *aviespa,* the Galician *(a)vespa* and the Portuguese *vespa,* while in Constantinople and Bursa they used *bizba* which is equivalent to the Castilian *avispa* (Wagner 1930:22).

Also, certain northern Spanish forms have been generalized in most Judeo-Spanish dialects. For example the word medial *-mb-*, that is, the conservation of Latin *mb* in words like *palomba* 'dove'; *lombo* 'back, loin'; and *lamber* 'to lick'; was originally characteristic of the Leonese and Asturian dialects as well as Gallego and Portuguese. In Castilian these words appear as *paloma, lomo* and *lamer,* respectively.

Examples of loanwords in Judeo-Spanish which come from the various Iberian dialects include the following: *solombra* 'shade, shadow', *mursiegano* 'bat', *shamarada* or *samalada* 'blaze', and *luvya* 'rain' from the Leonese dialect; *bavažadas* 'foolishness, nonsense', which was widely used in the western part of the Peninsula especially in Asturias; *golor* 'smell, odor' also from Asturias; *chuflar* 'to whistle' from either Asturian or Aragonese *chuflar;* and *lonso* 'bear' from Aragonese *onso* which conserved medial *-ns-*. The diminutive *-iko* (Modern *-ico*) suffix also exists in the Aragonese dialect (Díaz-Mas 1986:107).

From Catalan came *kale* or *kale ke* (Modern *cal*) 'it is necessary' which existed in the Castilian of the sixteenth century and is today conserved in Catalan and Aragonese. It is used in Judeo-Spanish expressions such as *kale ke venga* (Modern Spanish *es necesario que venga*) 'it's necessary that he come', and *kale intensifikar los esforsos* (Modern *hay que intensificar los esfuerzos*) 'it is necessary to intensify the efforts'. Other words originating from Catalan are *eskola* 'school' and *assaventar* 'to learn, acquire information' (Bumaschny 1968:9). Catalan also influenced Judeo-Spanish in the use of *an* for *a* + vowel, which was used in Bulgaria, Serbia, Rumania, and Salonika in forms such as *an el* for Modern Spanish *a él* 'to him' and *an'ella* for modern *a ella* 'to her', in order to avoid hiatus (Wagner 1930:24).

2) PORTUGUESE AND GALLEGO

Since many Spanish Jews took refuge first in Portugal before eventually making their way to the Balkan Peninsula, various characteristics of the Portuguese language were integrated into the speech of the Sephardim in the Jewish communities of the Mediterranean, especially during the last two thirds of the sixteenth century.

Because of the similarities between Portuguese and Gallego, it is often difficult to tell the exact origin of a word. Examples of such words that could possibly originate from either language are *agora* 'now', *ainda* 'still' and *chapeo* 'hat'. Also certain words containing minimal linguistic differences approximate closer to the Portuguese form than to the Spanish word. For example, _bucho_ 'guts, belly' with its final -*o* is closer to Portuguese *bucho* than to Spanish _buche;_ and the word *kontente* 'contented, happy' is like the Portuguese *contente* vs. the Spanish *contento*.

Some Portuguese words have been generally used throughout the Judeo-Spanish dialects, such as *akavidarse* 'to take precautions, to be on one's guard' (Spanish *precaverse*).[28] Other Portuguese words are used only in certain regions, such as *faiska* 'flash of lightening, spark', which was used in Bosnia while other Sephardim used *senteya* from Spanish *centella* (Wagner 1950b:193).

There are also Judeo-Spanish words of Portuguese origin that do not exist in most Modern Spanish dialects. Some examples are: _alfinete_ (Spanish *alfiler*) 'pin'; *amanya, amananya* (Portuguese amanhã, Modern Spanish *mañana*) 'tomorrow'; *anojar~anozar* (Portuguese *anojar* vs. Spanish *enojar*) 'to annoy, anger'; and *preto* (Portuguese *preto* vs. Modern Spanish *negro*) 'black'. Other words show differences in diphthongization as in *grego* (Modern Spanish *griego*) "Greek', and *ken* (Portuguese *quem,* Modern Spanish *quien*) 'who, whom'. More words in Judeo-Spanish which are attributed to Portuguese origin are *burako* 'hole';[29] *fronya* (Portuguese *fronha* versus Modern Spanish *funda de almohada*) 'pillowcase'; the Judeo-Spanish verb *embirrarse* (Modern Spanish *enfurecerse*) 'to become furious'; and the derived nouns *birra* or *embirra* 'anger, rage'.[30] An expression coming from Portuguese is *se bebe pipa* for the Spanish *se fuma en pipa* 'to smoke a pipe' (Bumaschny 1968:9).

Two characteristics of the morphology of Judeo-Spanish verbs which have been attributed to Portuguese influence include the compound perfect tenses conjugated with *tener* instead of *aver,* as in *tengo echo* 'I have done' like Portuguese *tenho feito* (instead of Modern Spanish *he hecho*). However, as both Zamora and Renard point out, this use is not only typical of Portuguese but was also present in Old Spanish (Zamora 1974:360 and Renard 1966a:119). The other Portuguese verb feature is the second person plural form of the preterite which ends in -*tes*.[31]

3) ITALIAN

Since Italy was a station on the Sephardim's way to Turkey, Italian influences are prevalent in Judeo-Spanish. Many Spanish Jews went to Naples, Venice, Padua, Rome, Ancona, Leghorn, and Ferrara where the Sephardic communities were particularly prosperous in the sixteenth century. From the time of the Jews' immigration, there were internal commercial relations with several Italian cities, notably Ancona and Venice. In the sixteenth century Venice and Leghorn became centers of Jewish learning, and Kraus informs us that "even the Italian-born Jews used Judeo-Spanish for their discussions in the Talmudic academies" (1951:264). From the first half of the sixteenth century many Sephardic families left Italy following the promulgation of certain expulsion edicts and rejoined their brethren in the Levantine communities, thus contributing in large measure to the infiltration of Judeo-Spanish with Italianisms. On the other hand, as Renard reminds us, those who stayed behind in Italy soon abandoned Judeo-Spanish in favor of Italian (1966a:130).

Italian loans are not spread equally in all the Judeo-Spanish centers. They were greater in the Judeo-Spanish of Serbia because of its trade relations with Venice. Also, Italian influences were particularly numerous in the *villes maritimes* of the Levant due to the fact that Italian served as the language of the ports. For centuries the economic domination of Genoa, Ragusa and especially Venice obliged even Greeks and Turks to adopt Genoese or Venetian expressions. However, Kraus points out that not all Italian loans in Judeo-Spanish were imported directly. The Italians, mainly Genoese and Venetians, had been the uniting bond of union between the Levant and the West dating from the eleventh century. At the end of the twelfth century there were sixty thousand Italians in the Byzantine Empire (Kraus 1952:400). Thus many Italian words penetrated the Greek dialects, from where they passed to the languages of other Balkan nations a long time before the Sephardim established themselves in the Orient (Wagner 1923:231). An example of such a word is *fortuna* 'storm', which came from Italy and went to the west (Catalonia) and to the east (Greece). From Venice came *compagna* 'companion' which passed to Greece, from which the Turks took their *komanya* 'ship's provisions'. Finally, relating the word with the verb *komer* 'to eat', the Sephardim appropriated it (Kraus 1952:400–1). Examples of Italian loans in Judeo-Spanish include the following:

JUDEO-SPANISH NOUNS	FROM ITALIAN	MEANING
dirito	diritto	right
do(u)pyo	doppio	double
dubyo	dubio	doubt
egzempyo	esempio	example

fatcha	faccia	face
genitores	genitori	parents
jornal[32]	giornale	daily newspaper
impiegato(u)	impiegato	clerk, employee
kapatchita	capacità	ability
kapo	capo	chief, head
lavoro	lavoro	work (noun)
lavorante	lavorante	worker
lokanda	locanda	inn
mankanza	mancanza	lack
nona, nono	nonna, nonno	grandmother, -father
palto	paltò	overcoat
perikolo	pericolo	danger
piano	piano	floor, story
porto	porto	port
siekolo	secolo	century
socheta	società	society

VERBS	FROM ITALIAN	MEANING
achetar	accettare	to accept, consent
dober	dovere	ought to
dubyar, dubiar	dubitare	to doubt
lavorar	lavorare	to work
rengrasyar	ringraziare	to thank

ADJECTIVES	FROM ITALIAN	MEANING
blu	blu (possibly from French *bleu*)	blue
kapache	capace	able, capable
libero	libero	free
malato	malato	sick
perikulozo	pericoloso	dangerous
primo	primo	first
steso	stesso	same

PREPOSITIONS, ADVERBS, CONJUNCTIONS	FROM ITALIAN	MEANING
ma	ma	but
fina, fina ke	fino	until
verso	verso	toward
dunke	dunque	then, so
alora	allora	then
kualunke	qualunque	whatever

The Italian loans attest to the contact of the Italians and Jews as well as to the influence of Italian culture on the daily life of the Sephardim. The most recent Italian influences occurred in the last quarter of the nineteenth century when the Italian state founded the schools of the Centro Dante Alighieri in the larger cities of the Ottoman Empire, especially in Salonika and Istanbul. These schools were attended above all by the Sephardim, who drew from the Italian language whenever they felt the need. The scope of the Italian loans led Kraus to conclude that Judeo-Spanish was ready to Italianize itself when the French language came to supplant it (Kraus 1952:400). Kraus wrote that Italian was so influential in the Levant before the establishment of the French Alliance Israélite Universelle schools,[33] that in 1854 when Dr. Albert Cohn, a representative of the House of Rothschild, was sent to help the Jews in Palestine, he stopped off at a meeting in Alexandria where the speeches were given in three languages: Hebrew, Arabic and Italian (Kraus 1952:399–400).

4) FRENCH

French had a certain amount of prestige in the Levant due to the "Capitulations" signed in 1535 between François I and Suleiman the Magnificent, which gave the French the exclusive right to trade with the Turkish coasts. From this time, a few gallicisms were introduced into Judeo-Spanish. But the real French influence became predominant starting from 1862 when the Alliance Israélite Universelle opened schools in the Levant. By 1910 there were 116 Alliance schools throughout the Empire. In these schools French was the language of instruction, and it is obvious that the opening of these Alliance schools sounded the death knell for Judeo-Spanish (See chapter 11 section number 6). Thus it wasn't long before the French language became the language of the elite and Judeo-Spanish was relegated to use as the language of the home and/or as the language of the "klasa basha" or lower class (Sephiha 1986:107). Díaz-Mas describes the new generation of Sephardim who were educated in the Alliance Schools as "los judíos francos" or "franqueados" 'the Frenchified Jews' who dressed and spoke a la franca and who even Frenchified their names (1986:111).

The infiltration of gallicisms in Judeo-Spanish was especially evident in the Judeo-Spanish press dating from the last quarter of the nineteenth century and the beginning of the twentieth century, since the majority of journalists and intellectual Jews of the Levant at this time were francophones. Sephiha reports that this gallicization affected Judeo-Spanish at all levels, not only the lexical level but the phonetic, morphological, and syntactic levels as well. The extent of French influence was so great that Sephiha called this phenomenon *gallomanie galopante* 'galloping gallicization' (1986:107), referring to the French infiltration as if it were a disease.

Below are examples of French loans, many of which were hispanicized and some of which coexisted side by side with Spanish counterparts.

Words Borrowed Outright (the spelling may be changed)

JUDEO-SPANISH WORD	FROM FRENCH	MEANING
avenir	avenir	future
buro	bureau	office
shans	chance	luck
grev	grève	strike
žurnal[34]	journal	newspaper
madam(a)	madame	Mrs., Maam
madmazel, mamuazel	mademoiselle	Miss
musyu, musiu	monsieur	Mr., Sir
malor	malheur	unhappiness
parvenir (a)	parvenir	to succeed; reach
shemendefer	chemin de fer	railroad

French Words Hispanicized

JUDEO-SPANISH WORD	FROM FRENCH	MEANING
aderesso ~ adreso	adresse	address
aferes	affaires	affairs
azardo	hasard	chance, accident
por azardo	par hasard	by chance
buto	but	goal
danžeroso	dangereux	dangerous
desvelopamiento	développement	development
eguardo	égard	respect (to)
a muestro eguardo	à notre égard	in respect to us
elevo,-a	élève	student
enverso	envers	toward
koraže	courage	courage
malorozo	malheureux	unhappy
orozo	heureux	happy
reushita, reuchita	réussite	success
taraza	terrasse	balcony
tradisionel	tradicionnel	traditional

French Verbs Hispanicized

JUDEO-SPANISH VERB	FROM FRENCH	MEANING
ažutar	ajouter	to add
arrivar[35]	arriver	to arrive
demandar	demander	to request
deranžar	déranger	to bother, annoy
esitar	hésiter	to hesitate
posedar	posséder	to possess, own
regretar	regretter	to regret
suetar	souhaiter	to wish (for someone)

Certain Judeo-Spanish verbs have the first conjugation -*ar* infinitive ending instead of their original Spanish -*ir* form (or third conjugation ending) due to analogy of the French verbal equivalents ending in -*er,* which is the first conjugation infinitive ending in French. Three examples are:

JUDEO-SPANISH	MODERN SPANISH by analogy with	FRENCH	MEANING
prefer*ar*	prefer*ir*	préfér*er*	to prefer
repet*ar*	repet*ir*	répét*er*	to repeat
kориž*ar*	corre*gir*	corrig*er*	to correct

An example of phonetic influence from French is the introduction of the *k* sound in words like *akseptar* 'to accept', *aksento* 'accent' instead of the Modern Spanish *s* sound as in *aceptar* and *acento.* An example of syntactic influence from French can be seen in the calque structure *dile de venir,* 'tell him to come' modeled on the French structure *dis-lui de venir* where the infinitive is used instead of the Spanish subjunctive form *dile que venga* (Sephiha 1986:93).

Other French calques can be found in such Judeo-Spanish expressions as *de mas en mas* 'more and more', which is a translation of the French expression *de plus en plus* as opposed to the Spanish *cada vez más.* Another example is *žugar rolo* 'to play a role', taken from French *jouer un rôle* instead of Spanish *hacer/desempeñar un papel.*

So extensive did French influence become in the Judeo-Spanish of the Sephardim in the Balkans, that Sephiha (1986:58) refers to the birth of this new gallicized version of Judeo-Spanish as *judéo-fragnol* (or *judeo-frañol*) 'Judeo-French', a term made up of the three important components of the language: *judéo* 'Jewish', *francés* 'French', and *espanyol* 'Spanish'.

C. Ottoman Languages: Turkish, Greek, Slavic, and Rumanian

1) TURKISH

The majority of Ottoman elements in Judeo-Spanish are of Turkish origin, due to the fact that in the fourteenth and fifteenth centuries the Turks conquered the Balkan centers, imposing on them their political system. The Sephardim arrived in the Balkan Peninsula after these conquests, and Turkish remained the administrative language of the Ottoman Empire until its decay. Other Balkan elements as well as Turkish infiltrated Judeo-Spanish, especially during the course of the seventeenth century, and later Balkan infiltration occurred in the nineteenth century starting from the time that national languages were being imposed on the newly formed Balkan States.

The fact that many Jews and non-Jews of the Levant were bilingual or multilingual also caused linguistic confusion. According to Baruch (1935:177), one must distinguish between the borrowed words and expressions which were occasionally used by the Jews, who also spoke the local regional languages, and the linguistic borrowings and calques that are an integral part of the Judeo-Spanish vocabulary which have replaced the corresponding Spanish words.

There are some two thousand Turkish words or expressions in Judeo-Spanish, especially in the administrative and commercial fields (Renard 1966a:132). Since the Sephardim lived in Jewish quarters or *mahalles,* their relations with the Balkan peoples were often reduced to commercial and administrative ones. Judeo-Spanish is not exceptional in this phenomenon of accepting Turkish words. In fact, it has many words in common with other Balkan languages although, according to Wagner (1930:39) and Renard (1966a:133), Turkish elements in Judeo-Spanish are less numerous than in the other Balkan languages. Below are listed various examples of Turkish loans which are found in Judeo-Spanish and cover not only vocabulary referring to the city and administration, but also everyday terms denoting articles of clothing, the home, professions, foods, plants and animals.

JUDEO-SPANISH WORD	FROM TURKISH	MEANING
Administration, the City, Money		
aga	ağa	title of Turkish official
bakshish	bahşiş	tip, fee
charshi	çarşı	market, shopping district
han	han	inn, commercial building
kira	kira	rent; hire
maale~maala	mahalle	quarter of a town, district
para	para	money (a 40th of a piastre)
pasha[36]	paşa	pasha (Turkish title/post)
Articles of Clothing		
chakshir	çakşir[37]	(Turkish) pants, trousers
chorap(es)	çorap	stocking(s), sock(s)
fez	fes	(Turkish) cylindrical hat
fostan ~ fustan[38]	fistan	dress
kondurya(s)	kundura	shoe(s)
kushak	kuşak	belt, sash
shalvar(es)	şalvar	Turkish baggy trousers
The Home and Utensils		
chanaka	çanak	pot, bowl
kibrit(es)	kibrit	match(es)
mutbak, mupak	mutfak	kitchen
parlak(es)	parlak[39]	match(es)
soba	soba	stove
tabaka	tabaka	story, floor; level
tavan	tavan	ceiling; also "God"; "heaven"
tinǰire ~ tenǰere	tencere	pot, casserole, saucepan
uda ~ oda	oda	room
Foods and Beverages		
buz	buz	ice; frozen
chorba	çorba	soup
dondurma	dondurma	fruit ice, ice cream
karpuz	karpuz	watermelon
kayesi	kayısı	apricot
kebap	kebap	kabob-grilled, roasted meat
kefte	köfte	meat patty; meatball
portokal ~ portukal	portakal	orange (fruit); color
raki	raki	liquor (ouzo-like)
chay	çay	tea

People and Professions

bakal	bakkal	grocer; grocery
buchuk(es)	buçuk	twin(s) ("half" in Turkish)
hamal	hammal	porter, loader, stevedore
kasap	kasap	butcher
mushteri	müşteri	client, customer
musafir	misafir	guest
zarzavachi	zerzevatçı	vegetable peddlar, seller

Plants and Animals

bilbil ~ berbil	bülbül	nightingale
konja	konca	rose, bud
menekshe	menekşe	violet (flower)
zimbul	sümbül	hyacinth

Miscellaneous

haber	haber	news, information
kolay	kolay	easy
kuti	kutu	box
na	na	Behold!, Here is
peshin	peşin	now, immediately
shaka	şaka	joke

Sala points out an interesting phenomenon concerning plant vocabulary: the terms which name cereals, common fruit bearing trees, fruits, and vegetables come from Spanish, e.g. *trigo* 'wheat', *pera* 'pear', *sereza* 'cherry', and *pimienta* 'pepper'. The other Balkan languages conserve the Balkan names for these plants and foods. But when it comes to exotic, ornamental or nourishing plants, in the majority of cases, these terms are borrowings from Turkish in both Judeo-Spanish and the other Balkan languages (Sala 1970e:149–50). It is also the case that, since most of the Jews emigrating to the Ottoman Empire were from the city, their nature vocabulary in general (especially in regard to plants) was sorely lacking.

In the domains of religion and intellectual life, the Turkish influence on Judeo-Spanish was weaker, as it was in the rest of the Balkan languages. This is probably due to the fact that the Turks did not interfere in the religious life of the minorities of the Ottoman Empire, and that contact between the minorities and other Balkan peoples was limited mainly to commercial and administrative relations.

Uses of Turkish Loans

Besides everyday vocabulary, Turkish loans in Judeo-Spanish were also used for the following purposes:

(1) For euphemistic purposes, as illustrated by the use of *kimur* or *komur* for the Turkish word *kömür* 'coal' and 'charcoal' in order not to have to pronounce the offensive word *karbon*.[40]

(2) For acts, deeds and objects which were non-Jewish. For example, Turkish *bayram* was a Moslem holiday or Turkish holy day,[41] while a Jewish holiday was designated by the Hebrew word *moed*. A popular proverb was *Kada dia no es bayram* 'Every day is not a holiday' meaning that a day of work is the general rule. Danon also informs us that the word *yashmak* from Turkish *yaşmak* was the veil of a Turkish or oriental woman, while *dimalo* or *loumar* was the word used to designate the veil of a Jewish woman (1913:11).

(3) For curses, commands or protests in order to give them more force or intensity (Danon 1913:11). Examples are:

Af-edersin 'I ask your pardon, excuse me' from Turkish *affeder-siniz*.

Sus! 'Be quiet!, hush' came from the Turkish command *sus!* 'Shut up, be quiet!' and also the Turkish verb *susmak* 'be silent, cease speaking'.

Ish! was told to children to get them to urinate, from the Turkish *çiş* 'urine', also used as a command for children.

Chush (esp. for a donkey) 'Halt!' from Turkish *çüş* which was the sound made to stop an ass or to deride a man for behaving like one.

kuchi kuchi to call or excite a dog from Turkish *kuçu kuçu* literally "bow-wow", used to call a dog.

(4) Turkish words and idioms were preferred when expressing sarcasm and/or irony (Danon 1913:12):

hortum literally, "elephant's trunk" or "hosepipe", used to mean "glutton".

chamur literally, "mud" was used to designate an unpleasant, argumentative person from Turkish *çamur* 'mud', which was also used to describe an unmannerly person.

Absorption of Turkish Elements

Phonology

Since Spanish does not have the rounded Turkish *ö* or *ü* vowels, the Sephardim substituted Spanish [o] and [u] in Turkish borrowings as well as when speaking Turkish. Examples are:

JUDEO-SPANISH WORD adopted from	TURKISH WORD	MEANING
boreka	börek	filled pastry
mushteri	müşteri	client
tutun	tütün	tobacco

Sometimes there was confusion and [i] replaced Turkish *ö* or *ü:*

bilbil	bülbül	nightingale
kimur	kömür	coal
zimbul	sümbül	hyacinth

Morphology

Spanish suffixes were added to Turkish words:

(1) Transformation of the Turkish infinitive verb endings -*mek* and -*mak* to the -*ear* Spanish infinitive ending, which was most frequently used for the verbs of Turkish origin (Renard 1966a:133):

JUDEO-SPANISH VERB	TURKISH VERB	MEANING
bijirear ~ bejerear	becermak	to succeed, carry out
biterear	bitirmek	to finish, achieve
boyadear	boyamak	to paint, dye
bozear	bozmak	to ruin, spoil
duzudear	düzeltmek	to arrange, order
kolayladear	kolaylamak	to facilitate
patladear	patlamak	to burst, explode
shashear	şaşırtmak	to astonish, confuse

Many Turkish nouns were given the following Spanish suffixes:

(2) The Spanish feminine -*a* ending used to indicate gender:

JUDEO-SPANISH WORD	FROM TURKISH	MEANING
la boreka	börek	filled pastry
la chanaka	çanak	pot, bowl
la maymona	maymun	monkey

(3) The Spanish -*s* or -*es,* plural endings as in:

JUDEO-SPANISH WORD	MEANING
borekas	filled pastries
bakales	grocers
hoteljis	hotelkeepers
konduryas	shoes
chorapes	socks, stockings

(4) The diminutive -*iko* ending as in *bibiliko* 'little nightingale'

(5) The Spanish noun -*ero* ending to designate a profession or doer of an action, as in *kunduryero* 'shoemaker' from Turkish *kondura* 'shoe' (Bunis 1975a:22)

(6) The Spanish -*ión* ending as in *uydurmasion* 'fabrication, lie' from Turkish *uydurma* (Wagner 1930:39).[42]

Díaz-Mas reminds us not to forget Judeo-Spanish lexical creations using Turkish elements, such as the verb *embatakar* 'to muddy, cover in mud' made from the Turkish noun *batak* 'quagmire, marsh, bog'. Another creation was the Judeo-Spanish noun *farfuria* 'porcelain' made from Turkish *fağfur* of the same meaning, from which the name designating sweets, which resemble pieces of porcelain, was derived (1986:110–11).

Certain Turkish suffixes have become productive in Judeo-Spanish:

(1) The derived Judeo-Spanish morpheme suffix -*ji* comes from Turkish -*ci*/-*cü*/-*cı*/-*cu* and was added to words of Latin and other origins to indicate profession, maker, seller or habitual action:

hotelji 'hotelkeeper' (*otelci* in Turkish); *palavraji* 'one who talks a lot' (from Judeo-Spanish *palavra* 'word')

Bunis gives three examples where the Turkish -*ji* ending is added to words of Hebrew origin:

ta(r)buraji 'mischief maker' from Hebrew [tarbut raa] literally, "evil culture, bad manners"; *masaji* 'matza baker' from Hebrew [matza]; *goralji* 'fortune teller'[43] from Hebrew [goral] 'fate, destiny' (Bunis 1975a:19,21)

(2) The Turkish -*achi* suffix and the familiar feminine affectionate ending -*acha* were added to Judeo-Spanish names such as *Bejorachi* (diminutive of the masculine Hebrew name *Bejor*) and *Isterulacha* the feminine diminutive of the name *Ester* (Díaz-Mas 1986:110).

(3) The -*li* ending from Turkish -*li*,-*lü*/-*lı*/-*lu* is used to denote nationality or origin (as in Turkish *Amerikali* 'American' or *Parisli* 'Parisian') to which -*s* is added to form the plural in Judeo-Spanish:

Izmirlis 'those from Izmir'; *Monastirlis* 'those from Monastir'; *Saloniklis* 'those from Salonika'; *Stambulis* 'those from Istanbul'. Díaz-Mas informs us that the Turkish word *chelebi* 'Sir', from Turkish *celebi*,[44] was often put before or after a proper name as a title of respect. (1986:110).

(4) The Turkish noun forming -*lik* suffix was added to Hebrew words to form the fusions *purimlikes* 'Purim gifts' and *hanukalikes* 'Hanukah gifts' (previously discussed in this chapter under Hebrew influences (Bunis 1975a:21). These fusions are made up of three

components: The Hebrew words *purim* and *hanukah* plus the Turkish -*lik* noun suffix plus the Spanish plural -*es* ending.

Sometimes repetition was used to intensify meaning. This occurred with the combination of a Turkish word preceded or followed by its Spanish translation (Wagner 1954:280): *muevo cedid* [ǰedid] 'new' made up of the Judeo-Spanish word *muevo* 'new' followed by the Turkish word having the same meaning; *hiç nada* 'nothing' (used in Salonika) made of the Turkish word *hiç* followed by the Spanish word *nada* both meaning "nothing"; *un ingles buzyelado* 'a phlegmatic Englishman' in which *buz* and *helado* are the Turkish and Spanish words meaning "ice". Wagner heard this phrase in Bulgaria (Wagner 1954:280). This repetition is a phenomenon often encountered in bilingual settings. An example from another language situation is the German-Spanish combination *brotipan* 'bread' (formed from the German word *Brot* and Spanish word *pan* which both mean "bread") found in a German–Spanish speaking community in Venezuela. U. Weinreich also cites Willem's example of cavalho-Pherd, composed of the Portuguese and German words for "horse", used by German immigrants and their descendants in Brazil (1953:52). Other examples can be seen in chapter 10 on code-switching.

Imitation of the Turkish practice of nonsensical rhyming known as *mühmele,* literally 'meaningless words' (as in Turkish *kitap-mitap* 'a quantity of books' or *kuzu-muzu* 'lambs'), also occurs in which a word or part of a word is repeated changing the first consonant of the second word to *m-*. This is used either for emphasis or to attain a humorous effect. Some examples (Wagner 1930:40) are:

Azer shakulas-makulas 'to joke, tell a joke' from the Turkish *şaka* 'joke'; *azer shushushu mushushu* 'to whisper', (heard in Bulgaria) which uses an onomatopoetic form probably coming from the Turkish *sus!* 'Be quiet!' or the verb *susmak* 'be silent', or from Bulgarian [susna] 'to whisper, murmur'. Danon also gives an example of this rhyming found in a *romanza:*

> Levantéis conde,
> Levantéis monde.
>
> (A. Danon 1896:117)

Wagner points out that this rhyming phenomenon is not restricted to Turkish, but appears in other languages such as German, Basque, the French of Istanbul, and even Spanish and Portuguese in isolated instances (Wagner 1930:40, 1954:274). There are other languages in which the initial sound of the second word can be any consonant. We see such an example in American English where the second word begins with the Yiddish *shm-* sound as in *fancy-shmancy*.

Semantic Influences

(1) Some Turkish words were used in a figurative sense reserving their Spanish replacements for the original meaning (Danon 1913:11):

barut 'gun powder' to mean a very hot, spicy food or drink or to describe a volatile, hot-tempered person; *charshi* (Turkish çarsı) 'market, bazaar' also used to mean "affair, thing" as in the expression *es otro charshi* 'that's another story, thing, affair'; *domuz* 'pig' to mean "dirty individual, swine" used as an insult; *meshe-odunu* from Turkish *meşe* 'oak' and *odun* 'log; stupid, coarse fellow' to mean a stubborn, pigheaded person (*meşeodunu* in Turkish means "blockhead").

(2) A Spanish word often acquired the meaning of a Turkish word or its meaning was extended to mean the same as the corresponding Turkish word (Wagner 1954:275–6):

Fuerte in Judeo-Spanish means not only "strong", but also "difficult", which corresponds to the Turkish *güç* 'difficult, hard; strength, force' and to *güçlü* 'strong, powerful'.

Famiya in Judeo-Spanish was also used at one time to mean "wife" since the Turkish words *aile* and *familya* designated both "family" and "wife". Wagner writes: "Evidently this word, which passed from Italian to Greek to Turkish, is related to the conditions of polygamy of the government of the Pashas, the rulers of Old Turkey" (1954:276).[45]

Ora in Judeo-Spanish is used with the double meaning of "hour" and "watch" corresponding to the Turkish word *saat* 'watch'. This concept is also found in various languages of the world.

Gota in Judeo-Spanish means not only "drop" as in Modern Spanish, but also "attack of apoplexy, a stroke-like illness", which is probably modeled after Turkish *damla* which means both "drop" and "apoplexy, paralytic stroke" (also "gout"), as does the Bulgarian [damla] and Rumanian *dambla*. Both words, *gota* and *damla* are often used side by side in Judeo-Spanish (See code-switching examples in chapter 10).

(3) Some idioms and expressions conserved in Spanish form reflect Balkan ways of thinking and are either common to all areas of the Balkans or are translations of Balkan expressions:

es una muchacha abierta means "she is a loose woman" in which *abierta* (literally "open") coincides with the Turkish *açik* which means not only "open", but also "free in manner, licentious, brazen". (Wagner 1930:41)

tener entrada de puerta literally, "to have entrance to the door" means "well-educated", which follows the equivalent expression in various Balkan languages.

The idiom *komer lenya* literally, "to eat wood" was used generally to mean "to receive blows, beatings", and this expression has its equivalent in the Balkan languages but not in the Romance languages. In Turkish the word *odun* 'firewood' also means "beating."

dar a komer literally "to feed" is used in the sense of "to bribe" which is an imitation of Turkish *rüşvet yemek,* literally "to eat the tip", meaning "to accept a bribe".

(4) There were also various expressions combining a Spanish and Turkish word which were calques from Turkish, such as *bever tutun* 'to smoke' literally "to drink tobacco", or *bever (un) sigaro* 'to drink (a) cigarette' from *tütün içmek;*[46] or *echar ashlama* 'to vaccinate' from Turkish *aşlama etmek,* literally, "to make vaccine". Another example of such a calque is *salir abash* 'to succeed' which is a calque of Turkish *başa çikmak* literally "to master, succeed with" (Sephiha 1986:103–4).

(5) Certain proverbs or *refranes* are translations from Turkish and other Balkan languages. One example is *Akeyos polvos trushcron estos lodos* meaning "nothing has changed—only that there's been a transformation" from the Turkish *o toz bu çamur dur* literally, "the dirt of the past is the mud of today" (Wagner 1954:280–81).

It is often difficult to determine the origin of a *refran* since there are many common to both the East and the West. However, Armistead and Silverman have demonstrated in various articles how certain Turkish (as well as Greek) themes have influenced Sephardic folklore, especially the *romanzas* (ballads) and poetry (Armistead and Silverman 1965, 1970).

Concerning the Balkan words of Turkish origin, it is often difficult to tell if the terms in question were taken directly into Judeo-Spanish from Turkish or by the intermediary of one of the other Balkan languages. Of the borrowed Turkish words, some name specific realities of the Balkan Peninsula for which the Sephardim would have no other word, such as *shalvar* (Turkish *şalvar*) 'Turkish baggy trousers', while other borrowed Turkish words exist side by side with the older Spanish terms (depending on the dialect), such as Turkish *çini* 'porcelain, crockery, china' and Spanish *plato* meaning 'dish, plate'. Yahuda wrote that it was not uncommon for Turkish words to be used at the same time as their Spanish counterparts, and he gives the example of two verbs meaning "to finish": Judeo-Spanish *eskapar* and Turkish derived *bitirear* (1915:345). Also, we must remember that the replacement of Turkish words and expressions was not achieved everywhere throughout the Empire in the same proportion. For example, the Judeo-Spanish of Constantinople (Istanbul) where Turkish was the usual language of communication, naturally absorbed more Turkish elements than did the Judeo-Spanish of Bosnia where the Turkish language was used mostly for administrative purposes.

Marius Sala (1970e:154–5) points out that a comparison between words of Turkish origin in Judeo-Spanish and the Balkan languages on one hand, and the words of Arabic origin in Castilian on the other, allows us to observe that the terms of these categories belong to the same fields of activity. That is, by their content the Turkish words in Judeo-Spanish, like the Arabic words in Castilian, almost all designate material objects or concepts which refer to the conquest and the military, civil government, exotic plants and objects of oriental luxury. Thus, as the Spanish took from the Arab civilization, the Sephardim took from the oriental civilization using Turkish words to describe aspects of life in the Ottoman Empire.

2) GREEK

Due to the importance of Greek as a commercial language of trade in all of the Levantine ports, it left its imprint not only on Judeo-Spanish but also on Turkish. However, according to Baruch, the Greek elements in Judeo-Spanish are not as numerous as the Turkish ones, even though contacts between Jews and Greeks were frequent in the course of the centuries (1935:177). Naturally, Greek influence was more prevalent in the Judeo-Spanish of Salonika and other Greek-speaking regions, while there was a reduced number of Greek loans in centers where the Slavic languages dominated, such as in Monastir and other regions of Yugoslavia. Below are examples of Greek loans:

JUDEO-SPANISH WORD	FROM GREEK	MEANING
apotripos[47]	[epitropos]	guardian
aver	[ayeras]	air, wind, atmosphere
argat	[ergatis]	(unskilled) worker

iskularicha(s)~ eskularicha	[skulariki]	earrings
horo	[xopos]	(Greek) dance
mana	[mamɛ]	mother; grandmother
meldar[48]	[meletan]	to read, study
papu	[papu]	grandfather
pinzela	[pizeli]	pea, petits pois
piron[49]	[pirun]	fork
spiritu(s)	[spirto]	match(es)
triandafila	[triandafilo]	rose
vava, bava	[yaya]	grandmother

3) SLAVIC ELEMENTS: SERBO-CROATIAN AND BULGARIAN

The Slavic loan words in the Judeo-Spanish of Yugoslavia and Bulgaria are not as numerous as the Turkish ones, but all of the dialects in these regions have both Balkan and Slavic elements. It is often impossible to know in certain cases from which Slavic language the word originated. Three examples are *gospoža* 'grand lady', *piva* 'beer', and *chay* 'tea' which all appear in the Slavic languages in general.

Before World War II, the four main Sephardic centers in Yugoslavia were Sarajevo, Belgrade, Skopje, and Monastir (Bitola) in which, according to Stankiewicz, four distinct Judeo-Spanish dialects were spoken (1964:231). For the Sephardim of Yugoslavia, Serbo-Croatian was the strongest influence, providing such words as *shkola* 'school', *bina* 'stage', and *brisku* 'peach'. The Judeo-Spanish of Yugoslavia absorbed elements from such diverse languages as Hebrew, Turkish, and Serbo-Croatian. As Stankiewicz wrote: "From an original Spanish dialect, it has thereby evolved into a typical fusion language, typical both as a language of the Jews and as a language of the Balkans" (1964:236). An interesting example illustrating the interaction of the diverse linguistic and cultural elements in Yugoslavia is one of the Judeo-Spanish words for a gentile—*Blax,* which corresponds to the Serbo-Croatian *Vläh.* Stankiewicz informs us that this word was also the term used by Moslems to designate a Christian (1964:235). As in the absorption of Turkish loans, the Judeo-Spanish of Yugoslavia incorporated various Slavic suffixes and phonetic qualities into the language.

Renard informs us that following the Slavic awakening of the nineteenth century, the Bulgarian language left certain expressions in the Judeo-Spanish of Bulgaria, but these influences were localized (1966a:134). For example, *dobruto* is the equivalent of "good morning" and *leka nosht* means "good night" based on the Bulgarian terms having the same meaning. According to Wagner, a large number of Bulgarian loans refer to military life, as in *polk* 'regiment', *polkovnik* 'colonel', and *družina* 'company'. Other Bulgarian loans referred to laic education as in *do(a)skel* or *uchitel* 'professor', *ispit* 'exam', and *diktovka* 'dictation' (Wagner 1930:46).

4) RUMANIAN

Even though Rumanian is a Romance language, I have included it under Balkanisms since its influence was limited only to the Judeo-Spanish spoken in Rumania. An example from Wagner (1909:484) illustrates the mixed character (the Rumanian influences) of the Bucharest dialect of Judeo-Spanish by the end of the nineteenth century. In this example the borrowings from Rumanian are in italics.

> Stuve *unde* el *kroitor*, me tomo la *mazura* d'una *roke*, me la izo tan *potrivita par* ke era *turnat*.

These borrowings would rarely, if at all, be found in any dialect outside of Rumania. Wagner presents this same sentence as it would have been expressed in Constantinople at the same time:

> Estuve donde el shastre, me tomo la mizura para un vestido, me lo ajusto tan bien komo si fuera fondado sobre mi (ibid., 484).

> Translation: 'I was at the tailor's who took my measurements for a dress, he adjusted it so well that it seemed as if it were molded to fit me'.

6

The Survival of Judeo-Spanish for Four-and-a-Half Centuries in the Ottoman Empire

Various scholars have emphasized the uniqueness of the survival of Judeo-Spanish in the history of the Sephardim. After expulsion from Spain, a country in which they had lived in harmony and prosperity for centuries, the Sephardim continued to preserve the Spanish language in other lands. And according to Spitzer, no other Judeo-Romance language has remained so vital as Judeo-Spanish (1944:183). Naturally the following question, which is expressed so well by Jesús Cantera, has been raised:

> How has a non-national language without any relation to the metropolis, been able to survive during nearly five centuries, from 1492 until modern times, at various hundreds of kilometers from Spain and in population centers often isolated and almost always surrounded by non-Romance linguistic communities? (1972–73:107)

What are the reasons for maintaining this language? The hypotheses are varied. Benardete writes of a fundamental sociological principle which he feels has always characterized the Jews:

> Hermeticism to all influences that in the long run would disrupt the quintessence of Judaism; and porousness to all new forms and ideas that possibly could modernize and revitalize the venerable tradition. (1982:8)

Camhy (1971:599) agrees that the sovereignty of Judeo-Spanish in the Ottoman Empire for four-and-a-half centuries was unquestionably a factor of the maintenance of Judaism. Surrounded by communities having other beliefs, customs, and languages, the Sephardim conserved their religious, cultural, social, and political traditions together with the language of their ancestors.

However, Renard (1971:719) reminds us that throughout history, wherever Jews are found, they have generally been marked by their ability for linguistic adaptation. Under Roman, Arab, and Christian occupations they spoke Latin, Arabic, and Spanish dialects respectively. One would assume that after expulsion they would have adopted the language of their new rulers. However, this was not the case. Besso discusses Benardete's theory that one of the curiosities of human psychology is that man's conduct is often in opposition to his feelings and thus often operates against his ideas and actions. Besso points out that this conflict is seen in the Sephardim's preservation of the Spanish language in the Levant, when the logical thing would have been to abandon it altogether (Besso 1971:618).

But reasons for the survival of Judeo-Spanish for four-and-a-half centuries in the Levant go much farther than Jewish conservatism, loyalty to the language of their ancestors and/or psychological conflict. Answers are also found in the historical, political, cultural, and sociological conditions of the Sephardim in the Ottoman Empire after expulsion. Various factors which contributed to the survival of Judeo-Spanish in the Levant are discussed below.

1. The Liberal Nonnationalistic Policies of the Ottoman Empire

In chapter 3 it was pointed out that the Sephardim and Spain owe a great debt to the Turks for the survival of Judeo-Spanish, since no nationalistic tendencies existed in the Ottoman Empire before the end of the 1880s and World War I. As Sephiha (1977:18) points out, in the Middle Ages the tenets of a religion were considered a nation, that is, the Moslem, Christian, and Jewish nations existed. In the Ottoman Empire prior to World War I, the Turkish government was based on the idea of the religious state that did not include other factors such as language or land (Besso 1971:624). Thus, in an atmosphere of religious tolerance, the Judeo-Spanish language was not subjected to political or social pressures. Osmanli policy did not permit interference into the lives of the minorities (the non-Muslim population) of the Empire as long as said minorities paid their taxes and remained loyal subjects, which the Jews unquestionably did. Thus the Sephardim had their own schools and synagogues where Judeo-Spanish was the spoken language as well as the language of instruction. They also enjoyed autonomous control over their own communities. As Rodrigue writes: "a separate *millet* identity survived intact for the Jews" (Rodrigue 1990:170).[1]

Due to the absence of a national language policy during the Empire's existence, the authorities made no efforts to establish Turkish as the national language, nor did they worry about its propagation. This absence of a national language policy on the part of the Turks worked to the advantage of the Jews because it favored the conservation of Judeo-Spanish. Since there was no obligatory military service for non-Muslims,[2] and since the Jews lived in their own districts or *juderías* (Turkish *mahalles*), there was no need to abandon Judeo-Spanish, or to learn Turkish or any of the other local languages. However, this absence of a national language policy did not help to consolidate the Empire, so that one of the first measures Kemal Atatürk passed when he came to power in 1923, was to impose usage of the Turkish language in all communities throughout the country.

2. The Sephardic Quarters or Juderías

According to Cantera (1964b:254), the existence of ghettos or *juderías* in the Diaspora seems to be a universal constant of Judaism. For religious reasons (such as the need to be in walking distance of the synagogue), social convenience, or by edict of the country in which they lived, the Jews inhabited separate quarters in close proximity to each other and separate from the non-Jewish population. These special Levantine Jewish quarters known as *mahalles* (Turkish) or *juderías* were on the whole pleasant, cheerful places, where the Sephardim recreated the streets and atmosphere of their native cities in Spain and Portugal, as opposed to the Ashkenazic ghettos in Eastern Europe. As stated in chapter 3, each *mahalle* had its own synagogues (divided according to the city or region of origin in the Peninsula), schools and civil services with a religious leader who was usually the officially designated representative of the government (Shaw 1976:162). Thus the Jews were not only physically but also socially and culturally isolated from the rest of society. This social and cultural isolation served as the perfect environment for the maintenance of Judeo-Spanish in the Ottoman Empire. The Sephardim conserved their traditions, customs, and language as a kind of instinctive defense, since there was no way to assimilate into their surroundings. Only the men had relations with the outside, and these contacts were limited to commercial or administrative domains.

3. Religion

Religion, or religious spirit, contributed to the Sephardim's cohesion, since it was their religion that separated them or made them different from the rest of society. According to M. Weinreich, religion for Ashkenazic Jewry "was no part-time job . . . it was a way of life and, even more important, an outlook on life" (1953:481). The same can be said for the Sephardic Jews. Their religion helped to shape their conceptual world and their group life, as well as their language.

Their religion also made the Sephardim confer upon Ladino, the written religious language, a character almost as sacred as Hebrew, since various rituals and liturgical literature were written in both Hebrew and Ladino and were recited in both languages. While many Sephardim, especially the women, could not read or write Hebrew, Ladino gave respectability to the spoken everyday Judeo-Spanish (see the following section). As Altabé explains, since so many of the Sephardim did not understand Hebrew, "the decision to use Ladino in the liturgy was motivated by the need to attract people to attend the services" (1981:17). In reality, only a small portion of the service was ever chanted in Judeo-Spanish, while most of the prayers were recited in Hebrew. This liturgical use of Judeo-Spanish differs from the Ashkenazim who used only Hebrew (rather than Yiddish) in their services.[3]

4. Liturgical and Ritual Literature

Liturgical literature, rituals, and songs of the various Jewish holidays were written in Ladino. According to Besso (1971:620), the religious books, prayers, songs, and psalms were some of the most important vehicles of the conservation of Judeo-Spanish. For example, it was the traditional Spanish translations of the Bible[4] that Sephardi students were expected to know by heart. Other religious literature in Spanish included the *Psalms of David,* the *Song of Songs,* the *Proverbs of Solomon,* the pizmonim (religious hymns), the songs of the Sabbath, Passover songs, the *Haggadah,* the *Story of Ruth, Coplas de Purim, Mi Kamoha, Las Coplas de Tu-Bishvat,* Spanish songs for births, circumcisions, marriages, and bar mitzvahs, as well as sermons, rabbinic commentaries, and prayers. Although much of the religious service was conducted in Hebrew in the synagogue, holiday rituals were read, recited, and sung in Judeo-Spanish at home, since the majority did not understand Hebrew.[5] Even in the synagogue the women prayed in Spanish while the men chanted in Hebrew. Scholars such as Henry Besso inform us that at home their family and friends used to sing in Ladino various chapters of the Bible, the Psalms, the *Haggadah* of Passover, the *Song of Songs*, and the poetry of Solomon Ibn Gabirol and Judah Halevi, among others (Besso 1971:620).

5. The *Meldado*

According to Benardete, the *meldado* was one of the religious institutions which also helped to preserve the dialects of Judeo-Spanish communities (1982:133). The *meldado*, equivalent to the *Jahrzeit* ritual for Ashkenazic Jewry, consists of a family reunion to celebrate the anniversary of the death of a loved one. After the appropriate prayer for the deceased had been recited, the rabbi or *haham* would then give an informal discourse or tell a story usually based on Jewish lore. The Judeo-Spanish used in these discourses, and later in the conversations of these social gatherings, was always in the colloquial or everyday language.

6. The *Me'am Lo'ez*

One of the more redeeming creations of the eighteenth century which gave new literary support to the speech of the masses, was the publication in 1730 of Rabbi Jacob Huli's *Me'am Lo'ez*. The *Me'am Lo'ez* was the popular folk encyclopedia of the Oriental Sephardim, which contained Jewish literature (the Bible, Talmud, Zohar, rabbinical literature) and information concerning Jewish history, beliefs, traditions, legends, anecdotes, moral principles, and philanthropic norms in regard to poverty. It was published in Judeo-Spanish in a simple, unpretentious style and in the familiar colloquial language in order to be made accessible to the public, the majority of whom lacked Hebrew tradition at that time. The only Hebrew words used were those that were part of the common language—what everyone understood. The purpose of the *Me'am Lo'ez* was to teach, as well as to entertain, and families used to read a portion of it together each *Shabat* (Sabbath). Others often gathered in cafes to hear parts of it read. Its extensive printing in various volumes and regions of the Balkans from 1739 to 1897 gives an idea of its cohesive force in the Sephardic world. The *Me'am Lo'ez* is considered the most famous work written in Judeo-Spanish, and its popularity helped to preserve the language from decaying or corroding influences.

7. Secular Literature

Other popular Judeo-Spanish literature included the *romanzas* or ballads, formerly transmitted orally, which began to be published in the eighteenth century; the *refranes* or proverbs, which were such an integral part of Sephardic culture (see chapter 5); the *konsežas* or folktales, especially the Djoha stories (see Note no. 9, chapter 9); poetry, and the *romansos* or novels. Publishing in Judeo-Spanish approached its apogee in the twentieth century, when the largest number of books ever was printed in the language. Much of this publication consisted of translations from French, Hebrew, and other languages of many historical, geographic, and literary works edited in Salonika, Constantinople, Izmir, Vienna, and Belgrade. However, a good deal of poetry and several stories and novels were written by Sephardic authors. D. Altabé informs us that at least 115 original works were written in Judeo-Spanish between 1900 and 1933 (1977–78:97). However, it is very difficult to obtain exact numbers since, as Altabé points out, often the *romansos* originally appeared in various Judeo-Spanish periodicals in serialized form and were never published separately. Even though the secular literature of the Sephardim never attained the level of that of the Ashkenazic Jews written in Yiddish, all of these publications in Judeo-Spanish helped to give support to and prolong the life of Judeo-Spanish in the Ottoman Empire, especially since these were the only printed works that most of the Sephardim could obtain and understand.

8. The Judeo-Spanish Press

According to Benardete, the Judeo-Spanish press was also very important to the preservation of the Judeo-Spanish dialects of the Sephardic communities (1982:131–32). The Judeo-Spanish press had its beginning in the nineteenth century in Izmir with the publication of *La Puerta del Oriente* beginning in 1846 and edited by

Rafael Uziel Pincherle. Later, the Judeo-Spanish press in the cities of Constantinople and Salonika soon surpassed that of Izmir. According to Abraham Galante, the main purpose of the Judeo-Spanish press was to report the news within and outside of the country as well as to dedicate itself to Jewish news and to the translation of various articles and literary works (1935:4).

From 1842 to 1959, there were between 296 and 310 different press publications in Judeo-Spanish that appeared in the countries of the former Ottoman Empire (Greece, Turkey, Bulgaria, Yugoslavia, Rumania, Palestine, and Egypt), various parts of Europe (especially Vienna and Paris), and later in Israel and New York (Gaon 1965, Sephiha 1986:142). However, Galante (1935:9) points out that it is often difficult to be precise about the exact dates of publication of various papers. Many of the publications had an "ephemeral existence" only appearing for a very short time or moving from one city to another in the Empire. Several of the newspapers and journals often stopped printing for a period of time due to lack of funds, the death of an editor, or other reasons, before resuming publication. Certain publications were also printed not only in Judeo-Spanish but in other languages as well.

Díaz-Mas divides the years of the Judeo-Spanish press into three different periods (1986:167–8):

a) The first period lasted from 1845 until the revolution of the Young Turks in 1908. Alhadeff reminds us that from the beginning of the nineteenth century, the majority of Jews in the Empire did not read Turkish, Greek, or the other Ottoman regional languages. This, coupled with an ardent desire to get information about Judaism in the world, and later on about Zionism, stimulated the founding of various newspapers in Judeo-Spanish written in Rashi script (1991b:11). But as Díaz-Mas points out, the press had a difficult start during this period, not only because it was a new enterprise, but also due to the conservative character of the Sephardic culture and communities. However, despite these difficulties, some of the better and longer lasting newspapers started publication during this time. They included publications which appeared either daily, weekly, biweekly, bimonthly or monthly. Some examples are listed below according to city of origin.

Salonika

Years of Publication[6]	Title of Periodical	Editor(s)/Publisher(s)
1874–1912	La Epoca	Sa'adi ha-Levi
1897–1916	El Avenir	Moise Aaron Mallah
1900–1918	El Nuevo Avenir	David Isaac Florentin
1913–1918	El Liberal	Albert Matarasso
1914–1920	La Boz del Pueblo	David Isaac Florentin
1918–1925	La Libertad	Elia S. Arditi

Constantinople/Istanbul

1853	La Luz de Israel (Or Israel)	Leon de Hayyim Castro
1860–1870	El Jurnal Israelit became:	Ezekial Gabay
1871–1890	El Nacional	Moise Dalmedico
		David Fresco
1872–1920	El Telegraf(o)	Isaac Gabay
1871–1930	El Tiempo	Isaac H. Carmona
		David Fresco
		Moise Dalmedico
1886	El Amigo de la Familia	David Fresco
	(*Review:* history, literary)	Moise Dalmedico
1909–1922	El Judio (Zionist)	David Elnécavé

Izmir

1871	La Esperanza became:	Rafael Uziel Pincherle
1912	La Buena Esperanza	Aaron de Joseph Hazan
1884	La Verdad	Alexander Benghiat
1889–1922	El Novelista	Yaacov Algrante
1906	El Comercial	Hizikia & Gad Franco
1897–1908	El Messeret	Alexander Benghiat
1908	La Boz del Puevlo	Joseph Romano

Jerusalem

1870	Havazelet	Ezra Benveniste
1902	La Guerta de Yerushalayim	Benzion Taragon
	(literary review)	Salomon Israel Cheresli

b) From 1908 until World War II (1939–1945) was the period when the Judeo-Spanish press flourished, aided especially by less censorship imposed by the Turks. It was during this time that great editors, directors, and journalists surfaced throughout the Empire. Some of the well-known journalists included Moise Dalmedico,

David Elnécavé, Isaac Gabay, Elia R. Karmona, and David Fresco in Constantinople; Sa'adi ha-Levi, Joseph Nehama, and David Isaac Florentin in Salonika; Aaron de Joseph Hazan, Joseph Romano, Alexander Benghiat, and Gad and Hizikia Franco in Izmir; Abraham Galante in Cairo; and Salomon I. Cheresli in Jerusalem.

During this period various humorous, satirical reviews also appeared, which were quite popular in different areas of the Balkans (Díaz-Mas 1986:169). Some of them included:

Salonika

Years of Publication[6]	Title of Periodical or Review	Editor(s)/Publisher(s)
1910–1914	El Kirbatch (Turkish and Arabic word for "whip")	Moise Levi
1916–1922	El Culevro 'wiggling snake'	Isaac Matarasso
1916–1919	El Punchon 'cutting remark'	David Isaac Florentin
1918–1920	La Vara 'the staff'	David Isaac Florentin
1919–1924	Charlo (Charlot) (Fren h word for Charlie Chaplin)	Alexander Peres

Istanbul

1908	El Burlon 'the joker'	Hayyim Mitrani Nissim Behar
1908–1931	El Jugueton 'the clown'	Elia R. Carmona

Izmir

1909	El Kismet Poeta or El Mazaloso 'the lucky one' (humorous supplement in verse of El Messeret)	Alexander Benghiat

During this period the Judeo-Spanish press got its start in New York. Some of the papers are listed below.

Years of Publication	Name of Newspaper	Editor(s)/Publisher(s)
1910–1925	La America	Moise Gadol
1912	La Aguila (lasted one month)	Alfred Mizrahi
1915	El Progresso became:	Albert Torres
	La Bos del Pueblo became:	Maurice Nessim
1920	La Epoca de New York	Alfred Mizrahi

1917	El Emigrante	Albert J. Covo
1921–1922	La Luz	Simon Nessim
		Maurice Ben Rubi
1926–1927	El Luzero (monthly)	Albert J. Levy, Moise
	(cultural & literary review)	Soulam, Albert Torres
1922–1948	La Vara (weekly)	Albert J. Levy
	(enjoyed an uninterrupted	Moise Soulam
	run of twenty-six years)	Albert J. Torres
		(last editor/publisher)

c) From 1945 until the present day was a period which saw the end of most of the Judeo-Spanish press. However, during this period the Judeo-Spanish press of Tel Aviv began publication. The three Tel Aviv papers are listed below.

Years of Publication	Name of Newspaper	Editor(s)/Publisher(s)
1950–1968	El Tiempo	I. Ben-Rubi
1949–1972	La Verdad became:	
1972–1990	La Luz de Israel	Rosa Yaech and Nissim Bueno

The Judeo-Spanish press was important to the maintenance of the Judeo-Spanish language, since not only did it help to keep it alive and vital, but in many instances it was the only means for the Sephardim to obtain news of what was happening in the outside world. It was also often the only reading material in Judeo-Spanish easily available and affordable to the average Sephardi, except for occasional liturgical literature and the *Me'am Lo'ez*. Besides reporting the news, several journals dealt with history, politics, geography, science, and the publishing of literary works in Judeo-Spanish. In fact, the Judeo-Spanish press played an important role in the development of the Judeo-Spanish *romansos* or novels. As D. Altabé writes:

> The Judeo-Spanish novel had its development in the press which inserted serialized translations from novels in other languages. These serials served a twofold purpose; they brought the readers into contact with modern literature, and they helped sell newspapers by keeping interest alive from issue to issue. When a serialized work was successful, it was bound separately and sold as an independent volume. (1977–8:101)

The same went for an original Judeo-Spanish novel. If it was popular enough, it might be published separately.

Sephiha refers to the Judeo-Spanish press as literature in a "period of gestation," which did not have the time or the vigor to develop like Yiddish literature (1986:143–44). Besides the influence of the press on Judeo-Spanish literature, Díaz-Mas emphasizes the value of the Judeo-Spanish press in studying the language since "the language of the press shows the evolution of Judeo-Spanish from the end of the nineteenth century until the present day" (1986:170).

Of the more than three hundred titles published in Judeo-Spanish, only two newspapers still exist today, both of which are only partially written in Judeo-Spanish: *Şalom,* a weekly printed in Istanbul, and *Haber* (temporarily discontinued) which was published weekly in Tel Aviv (See Appendix E). Both papers are written predominantly in Turkish, printing only one or two pages in Judeo-Spanish. *El Mesajero* of Salonika was the last daily newspaper written in Rashi script in the Levant. It ceased publication in 1941 by order of the Nazi occupation leaders. *La Vara,* the weekly published in New York from 1922 until February of 1948, was the very last Judeo-Spanish publication printed in Hebrew characters, not only in America but in the entire world.[7]

9. Sephardic Control of Printing in the Ottoman Empire

It is important to point out that it was the Sephardim who introduced printing into the Ottoman Empire in the sixteenth century. The first Hebrew printing press was founded by the Nahmias brothers in Constantinople in 1493 (the first Hebrew book was published in 1494), followed by later presses in Salonika in 1510, Adrianople in 1554, and in Izmir in 1646 (Sephiha 1977:25). The Sephardim had a monopoly on printing in the Turkish Empire until 1727, and thus had control of all publications. Since there was no printing in Arabic script[8] before the eighteenth century, the Sephardim confined themselves to what was printed in the Hebrew alphabet or Rashi script. They also enjoyed complete freedom in the spread of the printed word, since they were not subjected to censorship until the advent of nationalism in the Balkans and World War I.

10. The Prestige of the Sephardim and its effect on Judeo-Spanish in the Ottoman Empire

For several reasons the Sephardim constituted the dominant cultural and social group in the Balkans until the advent of nationalism in the 1800s (see chapter 3). Renard reports that their sense of organization, their initiative, and their ardor for work, as well as the strong sense of morality that characterized the Sephardim, earned them the highest respect in Levantine society (1966a:185). Culturally, they were far above their Moslem and Christian contemporaries. They had emigrated from Spain, which enjoyed a much higher cultural level than that found in the Ottoman Empire (Sala 1970a:13–14). Even when their cultural level started to decline beginning in the 1700s, the Sephardim were still above the backward state in which the Muslim world of the Empire was stagnating at the time. Not only did the Jews have a monopoly on printing, but the masses themselves could not be considered ignorant. There was a very low proportion of illiterates among the Sephardim at a time when illiteracy was rampant around them (Mézan 1925:85). The Sephardim also outshone the Turks in the arts and professions such as medicine, as evidenced by the fact that they served as the physicians of the court for centuries. And as stated in chapter 3, it was the Spanish Jews who introduced gunpowder to the Empire, and the expertise to make arms and ammunition that were invaluable in later Ottoman conquests.

In economic matters the Sephardim were also far superior to the other members of the Empire, due to the fact that they controlled most of the commercial activity and managed most of the banks. Judeo-Spanish quickly became the universal language of trade, replacing Greek or various Italian dialects (and possibly Lingua Franca or Sabir),[9] which had previously dominated the eastern Mediterranean. Thus a knowledge of Judeo-Spanish was indispensable for all those who wished to participate in commercial transactions.

Because of the Sephardim's superiority in the areas of trade, business, medicine, and printing, as well as their high cultural level, none of the local languages of the Empire, such as Turkish, Greek, Serbo-Croatian, Bulgarian, or Rumanian, enjoyed sufficient prestige to replace Judeo-Spanish. Nor did they have sufficient diffusion or universality to be converted into a language of the whole Turkish Empire, whereas Judeo-Spanish assured communication with all communities situated in the Mediterranean Basin. So it was natural that the Sephardim were able to impose their language not only on non-Sephardic Jews of Greek, Italian, or German origin, but also among the neighboring gentiles as well (Benardete 1982:119 and Sala 1970a:15–16). According to Renard, members of the non-Sephardic community felt the need to imitate the Sephardim in order to better conform to the way of life of a group they recognized as superior (1966a:185).[10] Thus in Salonika it was conceivable that Greeks and Turks, who had business dealings with Sephardim, used Judeo-Spanish for social purposes as well as for business. Judeo-Spanish also affected the local languages, especially Greek and Turkish, which borrowed a few Judeo-Spanish terms, and it even had an effect on Yiddish, the language spoken by the Ashkenazic Jews living in Palestine.[11] Even merchants not living in the Balkans learned some Judeo-Spanish. For example, Benardete reports that a well-educated British merchant named Sir Dudley North (1641–1691), who conducted business in the Balkans, found it necessary (or to his advantage) in the seventeenth century to learn "Balkanized Spanish" or "Giffoot"[12] for handling commercial transactions with the Sephardim (1982:119). And an account written by Lady Mary Wortley Montague, on visiting Adrianople (Edirne) in 1716 and 1717, illustrates the high level of prestige that the Sephardim still enjoyed at that time:

> I observed most of the rich tradesmen were Jews. That people are an incredible power in this country. They have many privileges above all the natural Turks themselves, and have formed a very considerable commonwealth here, being judged by their own laws, and have drawn the whole trade of the empire into their hands. . . . Every pasha has his Jew, who is his *homme d'affaires;* he is let into all his secrets, and does all his business. No bargain is made, no bribe received, no merchandise disposed of, but what passes through their hands. They are the physicians, the stewards, and the interpreters of all the great men. . . . They have found the secret of making themselves so necessary, they are certain of the protection of the court, whatever ministry is in power. (Wharncliffe 1970, 1:321–22)

To sum up: due to the Sephardim's great prestige in the Ottoman Empire until the 1800s, their Castilian-based language (or dialects) triumphed as a language of wider communication over the indigenous Balkan languages. This linguistic triumph, according to Benardete, was "the most significant happening that occurred in the transplanted Hispanic world" (1982:64).

11. The Large Number of Sephardim in the Empire

The importance of the demographic population factor must be emphasized. The Sephardim rapidly constituted numerous communities in relatively sparsely populated regions of the Empire, as well as large neighborhoods in many of the big cities. Salonika was the only city in the Empire whose majority population was Jewish before the advent of nationalism.[13] Also, according to Renard, Sephardic families have been known to be prolific (1966a:186), generally producing more children than Ashkenazic families. Thus the size and location of the Sephardic population determined various features of the spoken language. Renard wrote:

> the law of numbers imposed the quality of the language. A purer form of Judeo-Spanish was found in a city like Salonika where the Sephardim were in the majority. On the other hand, the density of the borrowed words from the local languages into Judeo-Spanish grew with the degree of relative minority status of the Sephardic population. (1966a:186)

12. Judeo-Spanish as the Cohesive Force Uniting the Sephardic Communities Throughout the Balkans

Judeo-Spanish was the universal language of the different Sephardic communities dispersed throughout the Mediterranean (many of which did not know Hebrew) and in other cities of great commercial activity. Thus the language served what Garvin and Mathiot refer to as "the unifying function" (1972:369), helping to unite communities having a common culture. This cohesion of the Sephardim explains in large part their loyalty to their language. As Quilis has stated: "After the blood tie, nothing unites like the language" (Quilis 1970:232).

At the same time, Judeo-Spanish served as a secret language, especially in business/commercial dealings, if the Sephardim did not want to be understood by non-Jewish clientele. When discussing the price of merchandise, more Hebrew and Arabic expressions would suddenly appear in their transactions (Benardete 1982:59. Also see chapter 9).

13. Lack of Strong Influence from Any One Balkan Language

According to Sala (1970a:37), the fundamental reason for safeguarding the Spanish character of Judeo-Spanish was the absence of active bilingualism between Judeo-Spanish and any one particular language with which it came into contact. Thus one of the conditions laid out by Terracini (1951:18–19) for language change to occur was not met; that is, no "true mixture" among the speakers of the languages in contact was attained. The main reason for this was that Judeo-Spanish in the Levant did not come into contact with only one language, but with several—Turkish, Greek, Serbo-Croatian, Bulgarian, and Rumanian, and later with French and Italian—either simultaneously or at different periods. According to Sala, these converging influences seemed to mutually counteract each other, and therefore none was strong enough to modify the structure of Judeo-Spanish (1970a:34–5). However, certain languages were influential in different semantic fields. Turkish and Greek influenced commercial and administrative vocabulary, while French and Italian contributed to modern technology (see chapter 5).

Even Turkish, the most important official language of the Empire, could not replace Judeo-Spanish. The knowledge of Turkish did not necessarily open doors for Jews to advance in the administration. On the contrary, as Danon pointed out, it was even dangerous for the Sephardim to become too visibly involved in administrative affairs or to run for political office, because anti-Semitism often arose among both Turks and the Ottoman minorities (especially the Greeks and Armenians) if Jews were to occupy posts in the place of various Moslems (Pulido 1905:139). Thus the Sephardim's knowledge of Turkish was generally not of the highest level. Benardete reports that

> after four hundred years of residence in Turkey, the majority of Jews could not read or write Turkish. . . . For one thing they knew very little Turkish and for another thing Turkish did not touch their inner being. (1982:114–15)

We must also keep in mind that it was the Sephardim, rather than the majority populations of the Ottoman Empire, who were often considered to be carriers of a superior form of civilization (Sala 1970a:13). Therefore, another of Terracini's conditions was not met for the Sephardim to adopt Turkish. As Terracini explains, an important reason for one speech community to adopt the language of another is if that other community is perceived as having a superior form of culture (Terracini 1951:19).

14. The Conservative Spirit of the Sephardim

In his book (1966a:185), Renard asks whether the conservative spirit of the Sephardim can be explained as a defense or reflex mechanism of an uprooted society, or as an expression of sentimentality or nostalgia for the idea of *Sepharad* 'Spain'. Ramos-Gil (1959:35) and F. Castro (1971:322) believed that the Sephardim of the Balkans were filled with a deep love for Spain and its traditions. Thus, the motives for conserving Judeo-Spanish included pride in their Spanish origin and the language of their ancestors. However, Lamouche (1907:971) felt that Spain evoked no sentiment at all for the Levantine Sephardim.

Renard feels that the Sephardim's general conservatism cannot be overlooked in its role of conserving the language. The Sephardim certainly preserved various Jewish customs and practices in the Levant, and as Renard asks: "Is it not admissible that this (conservative) attitude favored to some extent the maintenance of linguistic traditions?" (1966a:185). However, the Sephardim's maintenance of linguistic traditions might also be explained in large part by the simple fact that people in general are conservative when it comes to language shift. Members of a speech community do not give up their mother tongue easily unless subjected to some form(s) of outside pressure (see chapter 11).

15. The Women's Role in Transmitting the Language

Judeo-Spanish was, in most cases, the only language that Sephardic women in the Levant knew and could pass on to their children. Since they were isolated more than their husbands from relations with the outside world and from Moslem women, where would a Jewish mother have learned Turkish, or another Balkan language, well enough to pass it on to her children? Also, Spanish was, and remains, the language of the *romanzas* and the lullabies that mothers sang to their babies in the cradle. For many of the elderly these *romanzas* represent the umbilical cord which tied them to tradition. There were also stories, proverbs, and riddles in Judeo-Spanish which were recited by mothers to their children on various occasions. According to Besso, the mothers were the principal element in preserving the language (1971:623).[14]

16. The Translations of Protestant Missionaries in the Balkans

In the nineteenth century Protestant missionaries brought translations of the Scriptures in Judeo-Spanish to the Balkans in order to proselytize. Although they did not succeed in getting many converts, their translations, along with the distributions of the Bible

Society of England, aided many Sephardim in the study of their language. The Bible Society also distributed titles in other modern languages, such as French and Italian. This provided the chance for many Sephardim, who did not have the opportunity to attend modern schools, to study another language (Mézan 1925:45).

Part III
Current Status and Characteristics of Judeo-Spanish in the U.S. and Israel: Results of the Research

7

The Sephardic Communities: New York, Israel, and Los Angeles

In order to investigate the present status of Judeo-Spanish, I did research in the Sephardic communities of New York, Israel, and Los Angeles during the summers of 1978 and 1985. I interviewed a total of ninety-one Judeo-Spanish speakers from these three communities. The following is a short description of each community to be followed (in chapter 8) by a description of the informants.

New York

The first Sephardic Jews to reach New Amsterdam came from the Dutch colony of Recife, Brazil. They were descended from Sephardim who had originally fled the Inquisition in Spain and Portugal. In later years, after the Portuguese took over control of the region, the Sephardim were forced to flee Brazil. In 1654 this group of twenty-three Sephardic refugees established Congregation Shearith Israel in New Amsterdam (now Manhattan), which was the first Jewish community, and thus the beginning of Jewish life, in North America.[1] Between 1654 and 1825 Shearith Israel was the only Jewish congregation in New York City. However, within fifty years after the founding of the Spanish and Portuguese Synagogue, Angel informs us that most of its members were made up of Ashkenazic Jews who immigrated to the United States from Germany, Holland, and England. By 1700 there was already a majority of non-Sephardic members belonging to Shearith Israel (Angel 1987b:99). However, the congregation's Sephardic character and traditions were not changed.

In the 1800s and early 1900s, the majority of Jewish immigrants to the United States were Ashkenazic Jews from Eastern Europe who soon greatly outnumbered the modest Sephardic Jewish population. Records show that between 1890 and 1907, a span of seventeen years, only 2,738 Levantine Jews entered the United States (Angel 1974:86). This number is quite small when compared with the four year span between 1904–1908 when 642,000 Eastern European or Ashkenazic Jewish immigrants arrived in the United States (Gartner 1974:42). And by 1924, two million Ashkenazic Jews had arrived in the United States as compared to only thirty thousand to forty thousand Sephardic Jews.

After the 1908 Revolt of the Young Turks in Turkey, additional Sephardim arrived in the United States before American immigration quota restrictions were established in 1924–5. Angel estimates that between 1900 and 1924, approximately thirty-five thousand Sephardic immigrants arrived (1987b:103), and Elazar estimates that twenty-five thousand of these Sephardim from the Balkans and Middle East settled in the New York area (1989:168).[2] Thus, the majority of the Balkan Sephardim emigrated to New York later than the East European Jews. Most of these recent arrivals in the first decades of the twentieth century settled on the Lower East Side of Manhattan where their Ashkenazic Jewish brethren were already a part of what Rischin refers to as the "immigrant Jewish cosmopolis" (Rischin 1962:76).[3]

Many of the Sephardic immigrants had no formal education or vocational skills. Papo reports that although their educational achievements had been equal to the general educational standards prevalent among large segments of the Ottoman population, these standards were not adequate for the needs and pressures of life in America (1987:35). These impoverished and generally poorly educated Jews from Turkey and other areas of the Levant, who had expected to find wealth and streets paved with gold in America, instead found the Lower East Side:

> We live in New York! In an oven of fire, in the midst of dirt and filth. We live in dark and narrow dwellings which inspire disgust. We work from morning to night without giving ourselves even one day a week for rest. We sleep badly, eat badly, dress ourselves badly. . . . We are frugal, saving our money to send to our relatives in the old country. . . . We are losing the best days of our lives, the time of our youth. . . . (Angel 1982:19)

Like their Ashkenazic coreligionists who clustered in *landsmanschaften* societies based on the towns they had emigrated from in Eastern Europe,[4] the Sephardim in New York settled in tightly-knit neighborhoods, establishing their own synagogues, social clubs, coffeehouses,[5] and welfare societies generally based on their region of origin in the Balkans. For example, social organizations were founded by and for Jews from Monastir (Ahavath Shalom— 1907), Kastoria (Hesed veEmet—1910), the Dardanelles (Mekor Hayyim—1910), Salonika and Izmir (Etz Hayyim—1913), and Rhodes (Agudah Achim—1912) (Angel 1974:95 and Papo 1987:302– 305). One of the larger organizations was the Sephardic (Jewish) Brotherhood of America founded in 1915 by Jews from Salonika. Many of the Sephardic groups would rent halls in order to have their own special religious services. Most of these societies concentrated on providing burial services, free loans, social activities, and *tzedakah* (poverty relief). As their members spread out, these societies developed branches in various parts of New York City. Most reached their peak in the 1920s and disappeared with the death of the immigrant generation. The few that still exist today have limited their activities to providing cemetery plots and funeral services or distributing scholarships. However, such organizations, based on and expressing strong regional loyalty, were the main obstacle later on to forming any kind of central Sephardic organization.[6] Elazar points out that the one institution that became the major unifying force in New York's Sephardic community was the Sephardic Home for the Aged in Brooklyn (founded in 1951), since it served a communal need that was too expensive a project for each association to handle alone (1989:171).

After the Sephardim arrived in New York City, they not only had to fight poverty and harsh conditions, but they were often not welcomed by the larger Ashkenazic community who had difficulty accepting them as Jews, since they did not speak Yiddish, nor did they follow all the same religious and cultural traditions. Angel points out that in light of their discomfort caused by these cultural differences, the Sephardim had no choice but to form their own community (1974:91). As Rischin writes: "Levantine Jews maintained an existence independent of Yiddish New York" (1962:106). However, the Sephardic Jews were included in the New York *Kehillah* (the communal organization of the New York City Jews). Papo informs us that by 1913, encouraged by the Federation of Oriental Jews, all but two of the Sephardi societies had become affiliated with the *Kehillah* (1987:48).

However, the newly arrived Sephardim still formed a minority within a minority. Even the few Sephardic organizations that previously existed did not really know what to do with this embarrassing lower class group whom they often referred to pejoratively as "Oriental Jews" (Angel 1987b:102). These newly arrived Sephardim bore no resemblance to the established, well-educated, wealthy, and aristocratic Sephardim, often referred to as "grandees",[7] who were descendants of the original Sephardic immigrants who had come in colonial times. The Sisterhood of Shearith Israel, which especially aided the Balkan immigrants, did set up a settlement house on the Lower East side to help the newly arrived Sephardim, but they were often misguided in their efforts as they looked down upon their more "unfortunate" brethren and could not always understand the psychosocial needs of these newcomers. At the same time the Balkan immigrants were too proud in many instances to accept or to ask for much outside help (Angel 1987b:110).

In an effort to build up the self-awareness and self-esteem of the Sephardim and to correct the misconceptions of them held by the Ashkenazim, Moise Gadol, a Bulgarian Jew, decided to begin publication of a Judeo-Spanish newspaper. *La America* was the nation's first Judeo-Spanish newspaper, published between 1910 and 1923. Editor Gadol wanted his paper to provide help for the immigrants to adjust to life in America. Gadol's paper not only provided local news covering subjects of interest to the Sephardic community, but he also gave advice on every topic imaginable. Gadol even began publishing a Ladino-English-Yiddish dictionary to teach the Sephardim Yiddish so they could advance in America (Angel 1987b:107). Gadol tried very hard to make the Ashkenazim accept the Sephardim as Jews. Later, the Judeo-Spanish press in New York began to flourish. A total of thirteen Judeo-Spanish newspapers were published between 1910 and 1948 (Malinowski 1983:148).[8] Later Judeo-Spanish newspapers included *La Bos del Pueblo, El Luzero Sephardi, La Luz, El Progresso,* and *El Emigrante. La Vara* 'The staff', published by Albert Levy beginning in 1922, enjoyed the greatest support from members of the Sephardic community and was the longest running (twenty-six years) Judeo-Spanish newspaper in the United States. Not only was it the last Judeo-Spanish newspaper to be published in America, it was also the last Judeo-Spanish newspaper in the world printed in Hebrew characters (Sephiha 1977:105). When *La Vara* stopped publication in February of 1948, Albert J. Torres was the publisher/editor. Beginning in the 1930s, various monthly or quarterly Sephardic bulletins have been published in English.

Even though the first years of Sephardic life were difficult, conditions for the Balkan Sephardim began to improve as they did for most other immigrant groups, and there was hope for the future:

The overwhelming majority of the Sephardim were unskilled, struggling, and working long hours as candy peddlers, bootblacks, cloakroom attendants, waiters, and the like. Many sold fruit and vegetables. But it was not long before they began to rise economically . . . in time, bootblacks became owners of shoe-repair shops; fruit vendors opened grocery stores; candy salesmen bought candy concessions in movie theaters, and some went on to buy the theaters as well. (Angel 1974:94)

As the Sephardim became more successful and affluent and were no longer in need of the supporting Sephardic organizations, they moved away from their close-knit communities to areas which had no Sephardic neighborhoods. Eventually they became members of Ashkenazic synagogues and active in the Ashkenazic community. The path of the Sephardim in New York City can be traced in the following stages: after starting out in great poverty on the Lower East Side, they moved to the Bronx and to Brooklyn. Later movements to Queens, Forest Hills, and finally to the fashionable suburbs of Long Island followed (Lida 1962:1038).

Today the Sephardic population of New York is estimated to be about sixty thousand (Elazar 1989:167), which is the largest Sephardic community in the United States. However, as Sitton points out, probably one-half, or about thirty thousand, are from the Arab lands such as Syria, Iraq, and Egypt and are thus not descendants of Judeo-Spanish-speaking Jews (1985:333). In the New York metropolitan area there are about eight Sephardic synagogues whose original members spoke Judeo-Spanish. However, most of these synagogues today have memberships which are at least 50 percent or more Ashkenazic, including Shearith Israel. Of Shearith Israel's membership of approximately five hundred families, Rabbi Marc Angel informs us that about 50 percent are Ashkenazic (telephone interview 7 June 1991). According to Elazar, the second most important Sephardic synagogue in the New York area is Emet Veshalom, the Sephardic Temple of Cedarhurst, Long Island, which was established by the transplanted Balkan community of Brooklyn in the 1950s. It is led by Rabbi Arnold B. Marans and most of its members are Monastirlis or their descendants (Elazar 1989:172).

Given the lowered number of Sephardic members, the use of Judeo-Spanish has diminished. The present use of Ladino in the services of New York Sephardi synagogues is limited to occasional prayers, pizmonim (religious songs), chants, songs, or poems on Shabbat or during the High Holy Days, whereas sixty-five to seventy-five years ago in New York and other American cities, the sermons and oral announcements were regularly given in Judeo-

Spanish. Today, however, English is used "with rare exceptions" (Malinowski 1985:220).

Elazar (1989:172–73) reminds us that, although the Sephardim of New York may not be linked by one particular Sephardic organization, they are involved in common cultural and educational institutions such as Yeshiva University and CUNY's Sephardic Studies Programs, the American Society of Sephardic Studies, the American Sephardi Federation, Sephardic House, and the American Association of Jewish Friends of Turkey.[9]

Israel

Jerusalem is the oldest Sephardic community in Israel, and Yeshaia informs us that there were Sephardic settlements in Jerusalem and Ramleh as early as the beginning of the eleventh century, four centuries before the Jews' expulsion from Spain (1970:100). The first Sephardic Jews came from Toledo, such as the great Hebrew poet Rabbi Judah Halevi who arrived in 1140, and from other Spanish cities such as Cordoba (the family of Maimonides). From Gerona around 1267, came the renowned Talmudic specialist, Torah commentator, and kabbalist, Rabbi Moses ben Nahman (known as Nachmanides and Ramban), who was one of the important leaders and founders of the Sephardic community.

The expulsion of the Jews from Spain and the conquest of Israel by the Turks at the beginning of the sixteenth century provided a new impetus for the arrival of Jews to Jerusalem and the other three main Sephardic centers at that time: Safed, Hebron, and Tiberias. Safed in the Galilee became a center for important religious and literary activity in the sixteenth century, led by Isaac Luria (1534–1572) and his disciples who were responsible for creating the Lurianic Kabbalah, the Jewish religious movement that influenced Judaism throughout the Diaspora. Other famous kabbalists in Safed were Joseph Caro (1488–1575), who wrote the basic code of law known as the *Shulhan Arukh,*[10] and Moses ben Jacob Cordovero (1522–1570).

The Jerusalem Sephardic community, which was led by the Chief Rabbi known as the *Hahambashi,*[11] consisted of rabbinical school students, manual workers and artisans (mostly natives of the country), merchants, and older wealthy people who had come to retire and spend their last days in the holy city. There were only a few Oriental (those Jews originating from Arab and Moslem countries) and Ashkenazic families who were incorporated into the Sephardic community and who spoke Ladino and married Sephardic women (Yeshaia 1964:101).

While the number of Sephardic Jews in Palestine before the 1800s remained relatively static, Ashkenazic immigration increased so much that by 1836 the Ashkenazim of Jerusalem began to separate themselves from the Sephardic community, convincing the Turkish authorities that they were a group apart and should have their own synagogues and special laws concerning Kashrut.[12] After World War I the Oriental Jews in Jerusalem also began to form their own communities. Accompanying these movements was a general cultural decline of the Sephardic Jews resulting from the cultural decadence of the Ottoman Empire. Soon the Sephardic community was no longer the most important Jewish community in Jerusalem.

As a result of the nationalistic movements in the Balkans in the late 1800s and the atrocities of World War II, large scale immigration into Palestine from the Balkan areas occurred. A significant number of Balkan Jews began to emigrate as early as 1939, even though entry into Palestine was difficult due to the constraints of the British Mandate. In 1948, when the State of Israel was formed and immigration was no longer limited, thousands of Balkan Jews emigrated to Israel. According to Sephiha, between 1948 and 1970, 53,288 Sephardim arrived from Turkey, 2,722 came from Greece, 8,063 came from Yugoslavia and 48,642 arrived from Bulgaria (1977:72). In 1977 approximately 300,000 (Sephiha 1977:72) Sephardic Jews resided in Israel making it the largest community of Sephardic Jews in the world.

After the arrival of the Sephardim to the newly formed State of Israel, the Judeo-Spanish press became active. *La Verdad* was published in Tel Aviv from 1949 to 1972, advertising itself as *El uniko jurnal popular independiente en judeo-espanyol* 'the only popular independent newspaper in Judeo-Spanish' (Malinowski 1979:7). *El Tiempo, (Semanal independiente politiko i literario)* 'Independent Political and Literary Weekly,' was also published in Tel Aviv from 1950 to 1968. The successor to *La Verdad* which began publication in 1972 was *La Luz de Israel,* which ceased publication in 1990. *La Luz* was the last newspaper in the world to be published completely in Judeo-Spanish.[13] The only other publication written completely in Judeo-Spanish today is *Aki Yerushalayim,* which is a quarterly journal edited by Moshe Shaul, head of the Judeo-Spanish broadcasts on the Israeli radio *Kol Israel* in Jerusalem. *Kol Israel* broadcasts one daily fifteen-minute program in Judeo-Spanish, and several of the articles in *Aki Yerushalayim* form the cultural element of these broadcasts. The articles in *Aki Yerushalayim* cover all topics of Sephardic interest: information on Sephardic culture and history, news of Sephardi affairs in the rest of the world, poetry, proverbs, *romanzas,* and so on. *Aki Yerushalayim* is written in roman letters.

There are also various Israeli organizations dedicated to the study of Sephardic culture and history, such as the Council of the Sephardi and Oriental Communities, Misgav Yerushalayim, and the Ben-Zvi Institute. (See Appendix E for a list of Sephardic organizations in Israel.)

As in the United States, the Sephardic immigrants to Palestine/ Israel originally settled in neighborhoods and founded synagogues based on their regions of origin in the Balkans. Thus, there is a Stambuli synagogue (Congregation Shaare Razon) in Jerusalem which dates from Ottoman times; the Recanati Synagogue made up mostly of Saloniklis in Tel Aviv where most of the Jews from Salonika settled; an Italian synagogue in Jerusalem; a Monastirli synagogue, Yigdal Yaacov in Mekor Baruch, etc. Today there are approximately six synagogues in Israel whose members are native Judeo-Spanish speakers or who are descended from Judeo-Spanish speakers. The Sephardic centers in Israel today, besides Jerusalem and Tel Aviv, include Haifa and Tiberias, as well as the communities on various yishuvim, moshavim, and kibbutzim. Some of these collective settlements are made up mostly of Jews from Bulgaria and Greece.

However, there is one big difference between the Sephardim of Israel versus those who settled in the United States. The Israeli Sephardim do not appear as divisive as those in New York and Los Angeles, due mainly to the differences of the history of the countries in which they settled. Between the two world wars and until the proclamation of Israel as a Jewish State, the population of Israel was concerned with the building or formation of Eretz Israel, a Jewish homeland and a new national life. This rise of modern Jewish nationalism served to unite the various Sephardic groups who, along with the Ashkenazic Jews, were working toward a common goal: the establishment of a Jewish State. However, these nationalistic efforts also served to diminish the use of the Judeo-Spanish language.[14] Such efforts included service in the Israeli defense forces, a common education where the language of instruction was Hebrew, and the continual absorption of new immigrants from the Diaspora.

As Elazar points out, those who emigrated to Israel after 1948 are now entering their second generation of settlement. During the first generation, like their Ashkenazic coreligionists, the Sephardim were concerned with getting settled, earning a living, and establishing themselves economically as well as in other ways (Elazar 1989:200). And, as in New York, many of the Sephardim in Israel had to overcome incorrect stereotypical ideas held about them by the Ashkenazim.

Throughout this period the Oriental Jews[15] of Israel felt more comfortable aligning themselves with the Sephardic community (Ramos-Gil 1959:33), and today in Israel both communities are considered as one group and are generally referred to as Sephardic Jews, even though the background of the Oriental Jews is not Spanish or Portuguese.[16] However, today in Israel there is a rift, not so much between different Sephardic groups (as in various American Sephardic communities), but between the Sephardic/Oriental communities on the one hand and the Ashkenazic community on the other. In Israel's recent history the Ashkenazim have held more political power in the country, but the majority of the Jewish population today is no longer of Ashkenazic origin. The political and sociological conditions of Israel are changing, but much still needs to be done before this problem is solved. And Elazar points out that despite the past suffering undergone by the Sephardim, they are now well enough established to concern themselves with their status in Israel (Elazar 1989:200).

Los Angeles

The Los Angeles Sephardic community had its beginnings in 1905, when three adventurous Turkish Sephardim arrived in Los Angeles from New York. They were later joined by Sephardic immigrants from the Island of Rhodes and from mainland Turkey. In 1914 the group from Turkey founded the Sephardic *Comunidad* or Community of Los Angeles, which later joined with the Sephardic Brotherhood of Los Angeles, and finally became the Sephardic Temple Tifereth Israel in 1959. In 1917 the group from Rhodes founded the Peace and Progress Society, which in 1935 became the Sephardic Hebrew Center. Here again we see the formation of Sephardic communities and/or synagogues based on the Sephardim's region of origin in the Balkans. In 1937 the United Sephardic Organization of Los Angeles was formed and was later renamed the Council of Sephardic Organizations of Los Angeles. In 1973 the minimally active Council was replaced by the Los Angeles branch of the American Sephardi Federation.

As in New York, the first years in Los Angeles were difficult for many of the early Sephardic settlers. S. Donnell tells us that the main occupations of these Sephardim:

> centered around street-corner activities of peddling flowers, produce and shoeshining. Those who were able, opened stands. In later years, many of these small operations grew into large flower stores or stalls in the wholesale mart or developed into markets or shoeshine concessions in large department stores. (1987:123–24)[17]

By the beginning of World War II Los Angeles, which had been the third Sephardic community in the West after Seattle and Portland, became, due to its growth in general, the largest Sephardic community on the West Coast. Today the Los Angeles community is the second largest Sephardic community in the United States, after New York. It should also be pointed out here that the Los Angeles Sephardim often have close ties with both the New York and Seattle communities. Nearly all of my informants from Los Angeles mentioned relatives or friends in Seattle or New York. These three communities are closely tied resulting from the similar backgrounds of their members.

After World War II new Sephardic immigrants arrived in Los Angeles and joined either one or both of the Sephardic synagogues. Oriental Jewish immigrants from Syria, Iraq, and Morocco also formed their own synagogues at this time.

Today, as in the past, the two main centers for Judeo-Spanish speakers and descendants of Judeo-Spanish speakers are Tifereth Israel, located in Westwood at 10500 Wilshire Boulevard, and the Sephardic Hebrew Center, located in the Ladera Heights section on Fairfax Avenue and West 59th Street. All of my informants belong to at least one of these synagogues, and in fact, many are members and active in the activities of both synagogues.

According to Rabbi Jacob Ott, Tifereth Israel presently has a membership of about 600 families for a total of approximately 2200 people. About 85 to 90 percent of the membership is Sephardic,[18] originating from Turkey (particularly the areas of Istanbul, Izmir, and Gallipoli), Greece, England, and Cuba as well as from other countries. Tifereth Israel is the largest Sephardic congregation west of metropolitan New York (Papo 1987:299). The Sephardic Hebrew Center is smaller, with a membership of approximately 220–250 families including one person families (Elazar 1989:175). The majority, about 95–99 percent, are Rhodeslis from the Island of Rhodes or are descendants of Rhodeslis. The membership also includes a few Cuban families. Of the two synagogues, Tifereth Israel is the more active, with a higher membership attendance for religious services (Donnell 1987:136).

It is interesting to note that the rabbis of Tifereth Israel (Rabbi Jacob Ott) and of the Sephardic Synagogue in Cedarhurst, Long Island (Rabbi Arnold Marans) as well as Rabbi Louis Gerstein, who served as the senior rabbi of New York's Shearith Israel for many years, are/were Ashkenazic. However, as D. Altabé has pointed out, it is not unusual for rabbis of Sephardic congregations to be Ashkenazic.[19] Many of them have not only "contributed to the retention of Judeo-Spanish in the liturgy of their congregations" (Altabé 1981:20), but also have become experts in the Sephardic practices and have encouraged their members to learn about their Sephardic heritage. They have been major forces in preserving the Sephardic heritage of their respective congregations.

However, the use of Judeo-Spanish in both Los Angeles synagogues (as well as the New York synagogues) today is minimal. It is still used in some Friday night and Saturday morning prayers, in some songs and pizmonim chanted on the High Holidays and in some of the *bendichos* sung by the cantor at Tifereth Israel. Occasionally in both Los Angeles and New York some prayers, songs, and poems are recited or sung in Judeo-Spanish from the Sephardic Haggadah used during Passover.

After World War II there were attempts to unite both Sephardic synagogues/communities under the auspices of the Los Angeles Council of Sephardic Organizations. But even though Tifereth Israel and the Sephardic Hebrew Center had much in common, they chose not to merge, a fact lamented by various leaders of the Los Angeles Sephardic community. However, today there is a more positive feeling concerning the merger of both synagogues.

What happened in New York also occurred in Los Angeles. As the Sephardim became more affluent and the city grew in general, many moved away from their original Sephardic neighborhoods. Today neither synagogue is the center of a Sephardic neighborhood, since the Sephardim are dispersed all over Los Angeles, including suburbs from the San Fernando Valley to Long Beach. Papo informs us that, due to the fact that Sephardi educational facilities in the Los Angeles area are minimal,[20] many parents send their children to local Ashkenazi religious schools, and that, "a fairly large number of Sephardi adults in the Los Angeles area are aloof from Sephardi or general Jewish communal life and their children do not receive any Jewish education at all" (1987:296).

Elazar estimates that between 12,000 and 14,000 Sephardim live in the metropolitan area: 80 percent in West Los Angeles, Beverly Hills, Westwood, and the southern sections of the city, while 20 percent live in the San Fernando Valley (1989:174). But we must remember that included in this figure are Jews originating from the Arab/Moslem lands (especially from Syria and Iraq), which have large synagogues in the Los Angeles area, as well as Jews from the far East, India, and Burma none of whom are descended from Judeo-Spanish-speaking Jews. This figure also includes the *Yordim* or the recent immigrants from Israel.

Elazar presents an encouraging view of the Los Angeles Sephardic community even though he admits that there are still organizations which promote their own needs. He writes:

> In comparison to New York City, the Los Angeles Sephardic community exhibits considerable cooperation, a fact most likely related to size. However, even here there is evidence that institutions guard their own interests. (1989:177)

Papo points out that the Los Angeles Sephardim are active in such Los Angeles based organizations as the S.E.C.—The Sephardic Educational Center in Jerusalem, established in 1980; the Maurice Amado Foundation, which makes contributions to various Sephardic institutions; and the Los Angeles branch of the American Sephardi Federation.[21] The Los Angeles Sephardic Home for the Aged known as LASHA (a separate wing for aged Sephardim under the auspices of the Los Angeles Jewish Home for the Aged), also serves as a central uniting Sephardic organization in Los Angeles, as does the Sephardic Home for the Aged in Brooklyn.

Final Note: General Communal Tendencies

All three Sephardic communities share the two following characteristics: A) The first settlements in New York, Israel, and Los Angeles after expulsion were based on region of origin in the Balkans. And in many cases, especially in New York and Los Angeles, the regional loyalties of these communities and synagogues were the main obstacles that hindered or prevented the establishment of a central Sephardic uniting organization. B) As the Sephardim became more affluent in each community, they moved from their original Sephardic neighborhoods to more fashionable areas where there were often little or no Sephardic influences. The most general result has been the assimilation of the Sephardim into the surrounding Ashkenazic communities. Thus the present use of Judeo-Spanish in synagogue services and for other purposes is minimal at best.

8

The Informants

Selection of the Informants

To examine the current status of Judeo-Spanish, I conducted my field work in three different Sephardic communities (see chapter 7). During the summer of 1978 I interviewed twenty-eight native Judeo-Spanish speakers from New York and twenty-eight speakers from the Sephardic community in Israel, predominantly from Tel Aviv and Jerusalem. During the summer of 1985, I interviewed thirty-five native Judeo-Spanish speakers from the Los Angeles Sephardic community. I spent one month in each community collecting data. In the interviews, I elicited vocabulary from a word list (see chapter 10), I asked information concerning language attitudes (see chapter 12), and I recorded samples of free conversation (see chapter 10). The 1978 study was part of my doctoral dissertation at Georgetown University on the current status of Judeo-Spanish in the United States and Israel. Later I added the results of research in Los Angeles for this study.

Since I was dealing with a dying language, I did not know what my speech community population would be like. As Dorian writes:

> The fieldworker who is investigating a dying language has by definition a limited pool of potential informants. This pool may in fact consist of only one person, or it may number a few hundred. (1977:23)

Therefore, from the beginning of the study in 1978, I did not have a specific number of informants in mind, but was hoping to get an equal number from the speech communities of New York and Israel. In my later study in Los Angeles in 1985, I interviewed thirty-five informants and did not worry about matching the twenty-eight informants per community that I had interviewed in the previous studies. Also, since I did not have the luxury of being able to choose from a large pool of Judeo-Spanish speakers, I did not try to obtain equal numbers of informants based on age, sex, profession, or economic levels. As with Woolard's description of her Catalan and Castilian respondents in Barcelona, my informants also had "to be discovered in society" and were "not manipulable by the experimenter" (Woolard 1989:95). However, as it turned out, I did get a fairly representative sample of Judeo-Spanish speakers as far as education, profession, and place of birth are concerned. Only in the age category was the number of older speakers much higher than that of younger ones (84 percent of the informants were over the age of fifty). However, this is natural when studying the population of a dying language which is not being passed on to the younger generations.

Before I went to New York in 1978, I contacted David Bunis of The Judezmo Society (see Appendix E) and requested a membership list. I then wrote to various members (who had Sephardic last names) telling them I was a doctoral student at Georgetown University and asked if I could interview them. Many of the people reported that they could no longer speak the language very well, if at all, and others told me that they had never been able to speak Judeo-Spanish. And some of the good speakers did not even wish to participate in the study. After arriving in New York and beginning the interviews, several informants gave me names of their friends who knew the language, and so I was able to arrange interviews through their recommendations. I also interviewed various residents of the Sephardic Home for the Aged in Brooklyn. Some of the New York informants even provided me with the names of their relatives in Israel which gave me an introduction into the Israeli Sephardic community.

Before going to Israel, I consulted the list of participants of the First Conference of Sephardic Studies (El Primer Simposio de Estudios Sefardíes) which took place in Madrid in 1964 (Hassán 1970), and wrote similar letters requesting interviews. However, after arrival in Israel, I found that many of the participating scholars were already deceased. But once again I was able to get various informants to recommend their friends. The fact that I spoke French and could conduct the interviews in French was a great help, especially with many of the informants who had received their educations in Alliance Israélite Universelle[1] schools in the Balkans and felt that their French was better than their Judeo-Spanish.

In Los Angeles, Rabbi Jacob Ott of Tifereth Israel and Rabbi Kaiser Blueth of the Sephardic Hebrew Center recommended various synagogue members who still spoke Judeo-Spanish. Stephen Stern, who had done a previous study of the ethnic identity of the

Los Angeles Sephardic Community (Stern 1977, 1982), was also quite helpful in giving me a list of possible informants. I also interviewed various residents of LASHA, the Los Angeles Sephardic Home for the Aged. In Los Angeles, as well as in New York and Israel, various informants provided me with the names of their friends or acquaintances who could still converse in the language or who were recommended because of their studies or interest in Sephardic culture, history, and literature.

The Number of Informants

The total number of informants was ninety-one, which may appear to be a small sample when compared to studies done in psychology or sociology. However, for a linguistic study, this number is relatively large. To cite a few examples, in Silva-Carvalán's (1983) study of code-shifting patterns in Chicano Spanish, she interviewed eight Chicano bilingual speakers. In Poplack's (1982) study of code-switching in New York Puerto Rican Spanish as well as language attitudes, she used twenty informants. Malinowski (1979) interviewed sixty informants in her study of Judeo-Spanish in Israel, and as part of Gal's study in Oberwart, Austria, she observed sixty-eight informants (from eight households) and interviewed forty-nine of them concerning their language choice of Hungarian or German (Gal 1979). And in her study of children's language among the Kaluli of Papua New Guinea, B. Schieffelin (1990) focused on the speech of four children and interactions with their respective families.

Linguistic studies examine a speech sample that is made up of representative members of a speech community. Depending on the type of linguistic study, the speech sample can range from one informant,[2] as in anthropological studies where linguists are analyzing a previously unknown or unwritten language, or in studies of dying languages where there are very few living speakers, to several hundred informants, as in studies seeking types of information like that found in census questionnaires, for example, which cover large populations. According to Samarin,

> There is indeed a relation between the kind of linguistic investigation being undertaken and the number of informants who are used. The most obvious kinds of study which require many informants are dialectological and sociolinguistic ones. Where language features are to be correlated with age, class, occupation or any other sociological factor,

a scientific study demands careful sampling. But where one is concerned with determining the structural outline of a language in its broadest form, there is usually no need for more than one good informant. . . . The more one expects diversity in the language at some point or another, the more he needs to have a plurality of informants. (1967:28)

In my study I was not correlating language features or variations with age, class, occupation, or other sociological factors.[3] I was looking for a general picture of the present situation of Judeo-Spanish. What I attempted to accomplish from my interviews was: (a) to look at the current structure and characteristics of Judeo-Spanish; (b) to determine its domains of usage; and, (c) to describe various language attitudes held by present speakers of the language in three different Sephardic communities. And as it turned out, the results of my interviews concerning the language, its use, and the attitudes of the informants were, for the most part, identical in all three communities. Since the trends were the same in each community, demonstrating certain patterns with few deviations, there was no need to obtain a larger sample of informants. I was not measuring the direction or magnitude of sociolinguistic change, nor was I making statistical analyses.

This lack of statistical analysis brings up an important difference between the kind of research techniques used by sociologists and social psychologists versus those used by anthropologists and linguists. And in fact, Fasold does state that this difference in methodology is often a source of disagreement between the social sciences (1984:193). He points out:

> Sociologists and social psychologists are likely to rely on questionnaire data or the observation of people's behavior under controlled experimental conditions. The results are collected as numerical data and statistical analysis is applied to discover if there are significant tendencies. Anthropologists place the highest value on normal, uncontrolled behavior. This leads them to apply a research methodology seldom used in sociology or social psychology—'participant observation.' (1984:192)

He goes on to say that statistical analyses, beyond raw data tabulations and averages, are usually not used in anthropological (or linguistic) studies. This is because anthropologists feel that, due to their involvement with the societies they are studying (participant observation), they are able to better judge what is or is not important without resorting to formal numerical analyses. Such judgements are seen, for example, in Dorian's 1981 study when she found some of the results of her questionnaires to be different from what she knew of the linguistic situation and from what she had observed. I also found similar disparities or discrepancies in my study (see the following chapters) between what Saville-Troike calls "real" versus "ideal behaviors" (1982:120) or what is also referred to as "reported" versus "empirical" data. Such discrepancies are frequently found in linguistic studies. In this study, I only present numbers and percentages of various characteristics and trends.

Below is a description of the native Judeo-Spanish-speaking informants I interviewed from the Sephardic communities of New York, Israel, and Los Angeles. The informants of each community are discussed separately, and then a summary of the total number of informants is presented. The results of the interviews will then be given in the following chapters.

The New York Informants

Of the twenty-eight native Judeo-Spanish-speaking informants living in New York, twenty-four or 86 percent were fifty years old or above: seven ranged in age from fifty to fifty-nine, seven were in the sixty to sixty-nine range, six were between the ages of seventy and seventy-nine, and four were between eighty and eighty-nine years of age. Only four informants were below fifty, ranging in age from thirty-eight to forty-nine. I interviewed seventeen men and eleven women who were from the following areas of the Balkans, or who had been born in New York of parents from these Balkan regions: Salonika, Kastoria, and other Greek cities; Istanbul, Izmir, and other Turkish cities; Monastir, Yugoslavia; Rhodes; and Bulgaria.

As far as educational background is concerned, twelve or 43 percent graduated from high school, and some of the high school graduates attended college for a couple of years. Only six or 21 percent were college graduates, four of whom have advanced degrees. Five informants attended the French schools of the Alliance Israélite Universelle in the Balkans before immigrating to the United States; two did not finish high school, and three had no formal education whatsoever (one of whom is illiterate).

The informants' professions vary a great deal. Eight or 29 percent presently work or worked before retirement (five are now retired) in the garment district. Two work in the import-export business, two are college professors, six are housewives and one is or was engaged in each of the following occupations: executive director of a synagogue, rabbi of a small synagogue who also works as a part-time taxi driver, office administrator, graphic artist, photojournalist, writer, professional singer, millinery designer, telephone operator, and waiter.

The Israeli Informants

In Israel I interviewed twenty-three males and five females who were born in the following regions: six in Salonika; seven in the Bulgarian cities of Sofia (5), Shumen (1), and Dupnitza (1); three in Istanbul; two from Izmir; and one each from Bursa, and Tire in Turkey. One was born in Tel Aviv and seven were born in Jerusalem. Four of the eight informants born in Israel had at least one parent who was originally from Turkey, Greece, or Yugoslavia.

Twenty-one, or 75 percent of the informants were age fifty or above and spanned the following age ranges: ten ranged from ages fifty to fifty-nine, four from sixty to sixty-nine, five from seventy to seventy-nine, and two from ages eighty to eighty-nine. Five informants, or 18 percent of the Israeli informants were in the forty to forty-nine year range and only two informants were between thirty-six and forty years of age.

In general, the Israeli informants had received a higher level of education than did the New York informants. While the majority of New York informants did not attend college, fourteen or 50 percent of the Israeli informants have university degrees. Of the Israeli informants who did not graduate from college, one informant attended some college, twelve informants graduated from high school, and only one did not finish high school. Four of the informants attended Alliance schools in the Balkans before emigrating to Israel, and one informant attended an Alliance school in Jerusalem.

The professions or occupations of the Israeli informants are also quite varied. Five or 18 percent are authors or journalists, seven or 25 percent work in some capacity for the Jewish Agency or the *Sochnut,* two were newspaper editors of *La Luz de Israel,* two are housewives, and one pursues each of the following occupations: folklorist, historian, architect, engineer, insurance agent, accountant, university professor, head of the Judeo-Spanish broadcasting department of the Israeli radio *Kol Israel,* professional singer and music teacher, bank escrow officer, purse manufacturer (now retired), and cafe owner.

The Los Angeles Informants

Of the thirty-five informants, fifteen were men and twenty were women. Thirty-one or 81.5 percent were above fifty years of age. Twenty-five or 72 percent were sixty or above, ranging from ages sixty to ninety-two. Eight were between sixty and sixty-nine, ten were between seventy and seventy-nine, and seven were between eighty and ninety-two. Only ten or 28 percent were fifty-nine or below (six informants were between fifty and fifty-nine while four were below forty-nine years of age), with the youngest informant being thirty-four. Twenty-one of the informants were born in the following regions: eight from the Island of Rhodes, three from Salonika, two from Istanbul, two from Izmir, and one each from Kirklareli, Turkey; Volos, Greece; Shumen, Bulgaria; Israel, London, and Rhodesia. Fourteen were born in the United States, either in New York, Los Angeles, San Francisco, or Seattle, with their parents coming from Salonika, Istanbul, Izmir, and other parts of Greece and Turkey, Monastir, Bulgaria, Rhodes, and Jerusalem.

Twenty-four of the informants attended public schools; nine attended French schools of the Alliance Israélite Universelle in the Balkans; and two went to other private schools. One informant did not finish high school. Only ten of the informants graduated from college and six of those have advanced degrees.

As with the New York and Israeli informants, their professions vary. The professions of the Los Angeles informants include or included (nine are presently retired) the following: four garment industry workers, two secretaries, one saleslady, two flower shop managers, one shoe shop manager, one grocer, one sheet metal worker, one cantor, one gabbai, three school teachers, one teacher's aid, one court interpreter, one printing shop owner, one writer, one accountant, one president of a brokerage house, one escrow officer, one dentist, two physicians and eight housewives.

Summary of All The Informants

Of the ninety-one informants fifty-five were men and thirty-six were women. The majority, seventy-six or 84 percent of the total number of informants, were above the age of fifty, and fifty-one or 57 percent of all the informants were sixty or above. Only fifteen, or 16 percent of the informants, were under fifty years of age. The age range of the total number of informants is as follows:

Age Range		Number of Informants	
34–39	=	4	15 (or 16%) informants below age 50
40–49	=	11	
50–59	=	23	
60–69	=	19	
70–79	=	21	76 (or 84%) informants age 50 or above
80–89	=	12	
92	=	1	

TOTAL	91 Informants

The informants originated from the following regions:

Turkey	(23)	Greece	(17)	Bulgaria	(9)	Yugoslavia	(6)
Istanbul	9	Salonika	12	Sofia	6	Monastir	6
Izmir	6	Kastoria	3	Shumen	2		
Kirklareli	2	Larisa	1	Dupnitza	1		
Çanakkale	2	Volos	1				
Bursa	1						
Tekirdag	1	Rhodes	(14)	Jerusalem	(7)	Tunis	(1)
Tire	1						
Bergama	1	U.S.	(14)[4]				

Education

All but seven of the informants finished high school, and sixty-one informants either did not attend college or did not graduate from a university. Thirty were college graduates (6 from New York, 14 from Israel, and 10 from Los Angeles) and fifteen had advanced degrees. Nineteen of the informants attended Alliance schools in the Balkans for a period of time (5 from New York, 5 from Israel and 9 from Los Angeles).

Professions

The professions of the informants were quite varied and included (either presently or before retirement) twelve garment industry workers, nine writers or journalists, four teachers, three college professors, two physicians, two flower shop managers, two professional singers, two secretaries, two accountants, two importer-exporters, seven workers at the Jewish Agency (*Sochnut*) in Tel Aviv, sixteen housewives, and one of each of the following: grocer, part-time rabbi and cab driver, telephone operator, graphic artist, cafe owner, sales clerk, shoe shop manager, sheet metal worker, printing shop owner, president of a brokerage house, dentist, architect, insurance agent, court interpreter, cantor, gabbai, radio executive, engineer, historian, purse manufacturer, millinery designer, bank manager, bank escrow officer, folklorist, photojournalist, office administrator, executive director of a synagogue, and a waiter.

Chapter 10 will examine the informants' responses to research questions concerning the present usage of Judeo-Spanish, as well as various characteristics of the current spoken language. Informant attitudes toward their mother tongue will be presented in chapter 12.

9

Present Language Domains: When and by Whom is Judeo-Spanish Still Spoken?

The following language uses or domains were discussed with the informants:

1. Reading

When asked if they could read Judeo-Spanish, eighty-one (New York—21, Israel—26, Los Angeles—34) of the informants reported that they could read Judeo-Spanish, but only forty-one (New York—11, Israel—17, Los Angeles—13) said that they could read Rashi script.[1] The greater number of Israeli informants who can read Rashi script is probably due to the fact that those living in Israel are more familiar with the Hebrew alphabet than those living in the United States.

When asked what the informants read in Judeo-Spanish, forty reported that they read letters from Sephardic relatives in other parts of the world, although very few still receive letters today. Twenty-seven of the informants used to read the Judeo-Spanish newspaper *La Luz de Israel*[2] or the journals *Aki Yerushalayim*[3] and *Vidas Largas*[4] which are in existence today. Many of the American informants reported that they used to read *La Vara,* a New York newspaper which ceased publication in 1948, and the Israeli informants mentioned that in the past they had read such newspapers as *La Vera Luz* (Istanbul) and *La Boz del Puevlo* (Salonika), which are now defunct. Some still read editions of *Şalom* which is presently published in Istanbul but is mostly written in Turkish with only one page printed in Judeo-Spanish.[5]

Other reading material in Judeo-Spanish, besides newspapers and journals, includes *romanzas* (ballads) and *refranes* (proverbs), which head the list in popularity with the largest number of readers.

This is not surprising since the Judeo-Spanish *romanzas* and *refranes* constitute the most popular part of Sephardic folklore.

Less popular are the *konsežas* or folk tales and the *Me'am Lo'ez*,[6] which are not as widely known as the *romanzas* or *refranes*, nor are they as accessible. However, in reality, the informants rarely have access (unless they have a special interest) to magazines and other publications in Judeo-Spanish and must be content with the reading of an occasional prayer, proverb, or section of the Haggadah at Passover time.

2. Writing

As far as writing is concerned, sixty-three informants (New York—18, Israel—20, Los Angeles—25) said they could write in Judeo-Spanish in roman letters and that they used to write letters to relatives in other parts of the world. But the actual number of Sephardic informants who write in Judeo-Spanish today is negligible. Many admit that although they could write in Judeo-Spanish in the past, they are out of practice now. In fact, a couple of informants admitted that, on the very rare occasions when they need to write, they do so in Modern Spanish because it is easier. This tendency to replace Judeo-Spanish with Modern Spanish when writing seems to be fairly widespread and is not surprising, since relatively few Sephardim ever received formal training in the Judeo-Spanish language.

3. Speaking

Concerning use of the spoken language, the informants using Judeo-Spanish in all three communities—New York, Israel, and Los Angeles—followed the same trends when speaking to relatives. The greatest number, or seventy-seven of the informants (New York—25, Israel—26, Los Angeles—26), use(d) Judeo-Spanish when speaking to their grandparents. (The remaining fourteen informants did not have the opportunity to know their grandparents). This number progressively decreases in favor of English (in the United States) or Hebrew (in Israel) as we move along a scale of interlocutors from grandparents to parents, to spouses and siblings, to children and finally to grandchildren, with whom only one of the informants speaks Judeo-Spanish today. Table 2 shows the use of Judeo-Spanish versus English (in New York and Los Angeles) and Hebrew (in Israel).

Table 2. Use of Judeo-Spanish with Relatives in New York, Israel, and Los Angeles

People Spoken To	Number Using Judeo-Spanish	Number Using English or Hebrew
grandparents	77	—[7]
mother	79	12
father	75	16
siblings	48	42
spouse	36	54
children	15	70
grandchildren	1*	62**

*The one informant who reports speaking Judeo-Spanish to her grandchildren admits that they don't answer her in Judeo-Spanish but rather in Modern Spanish or French (since the grandchildren live in France).

**Twenty-eight of the informants have no grandchildren but they speak English or Hebrew to their children. Thus we can assume that they would not speak Judeo-Spanish to possible future grandchildren (see Table 3).

The data shown in Table 2 fits into what is known as an implicational scale.[8] In such a scale, use or nonuse of a particular language or linguistic form is placed at opposite ends of the continuum according to the persons with whom it is used. Thus the use of certain forms with other speakers could be implicated from the arrangement of the chart. Table 3 presents the interlocutors with whom Judeo-Spanish is used today. Thus, if informants use(d) Judeo-Spanish when speaking to their parents, it can be assumed that they also spoke it with their grandparents. On the other hand, if they do not speak Judeo-Spanish with their spouses, we can assume that they also do not speak it with their children. In Table 3 the plus and minus signs indicate use or nonuse of the language.

Table 3. Implicational Scale for use of Judeo-Spanish in New York, Israel, and Los Angeles

PEOPLE SPOKEN TO:					
Grandparents	Parents	Siblings	Spouse	Children	Grandchildren
+	−	−	−	−	−
+	+	−	−	−	−
+	+	+	−	−	−
+	+	+	+	−	−
+	+	+	+	+	−

Tables 2 and 3 do not include other languages or language mixtures which were also used with certain relatives, such as Turkish, Greek, Bulgarian, and French, depending on where the Sephardim lived.

One of the important factors dictating the language of communication with various relatives was the age of the relatives. More than likely one used Judeo-Spanish with aunts and uncles who sometimes took the place of grandparents for those informants who never knew their grandparents. And Judeo-Spanish is used with cousins at about the same rate that it is used with siblings.

Since the use of Judeo-Spanish has declined within the family, it is obvious that it is no longer the language of the home as it formerly had been. Various Israeli informants stated that in the past, even when they spoke Judeo-Spanish in the home, they spoke Hebrew or French elsewhere. And an informant from New York reported that, when his family lived in Turkey, Judeo-Spanish was spoken only within the home, never outside of the home.

The important questions today are: With what people might you speak Judeo-Spanish and when is the language still used? Below, the instances or situations in which Judeo-Spanish is most used today are discussed. This information was obtained from the interviews with the informants.

Current Uses of Judeo-Spanish

(A) JUDEO-SPANISH IS THE LANGUAGE USED WITH OLDER PEOPLE.

The majority of informants use(d) Judeo-Spanish when speaking to older people, whether they are/were older relatives such as their mothers, aunts, uncles and mothers-in-law, or older family friends, synagogue members and other elderly people. Various New York informants said that they speak Judeo-Spanish when visiting their relatives and family friends at the Sephardic Home for the Aged in Brooklyn (Judeo-Spanish and English are the principal languages spoken at the Sephardic Home), and Los Angeles informants speak Judeo-Spanish to relatives and friends at LASHA (the Los Angeles Sephardic Home for the Aged). If the informant grew up in a household in which one of their grandparents lived, their knowledge of

Judeo-Spanish is or was fairly good, depending on their age when the grandparent died. Unfortunately, most of them stopped speaking Judeo-Spanish from the time of the grandparent's death. As one informant stated: "If it wasn't for my grandmother, I don't believe I would know Ladino because my mother and father wanted to speak English and kept trying to push back the Ladino." Many of the informants spoke Judeo-Spanish to their grandparent(s) and English or Hebrew to their parents. All of the informants were aware that Judeo-Spanish was a language used with older people and not with the younger generations, and most of them reported that they spoke Judeo-Spanish to older people but English or Hebrew to Sephardim their own age. As one Israeli informant stated: "Hebrew is spoken by the new generation while Judeo-Spanish is spoken by the older generation." Another Israeli informant reported in 1979 that "People under fifty years of age (around the forty to forty-five year range) generally do not speak Judeo-Spanish but they can understand it. People twenty years old and younger don't even understand the language." Today I can write that most of the world's Sephardim under the age of fifty or fifty-five do not understand Judeo-Spanish unless they have studied Modern Spanish in school.

(B) JUDEO-SPANISH IS USED AS A SECRET LANGUAGE.

Judeo-Spanish was often used by parents in the home as a secret language when they did not want their children to understand, and it is still used as a secret or code language today when certain Sephardim don't want anyone else (Ashkenazic Jews, gentiles, or strangers) to understand them. This occurs in business dealings or discussions of a personal nature. One Israeli informant reported that she feels lucky that her parents had so many secrets or else she would not know the little Judeo-Spanish that she does know.

(C) JUDEO-SPANISH IS USED FOR HUMOROUS/EXPRESSIVE PURPOSES.

Occasionally Judeo-Spanish is used for humorous and or expressive purposes when telling jokes or stories, especially the *Djoha* stories.[9] One Israeli informant said that the only Judeo-Spanish he uses with his siblings is for the purpose of telling jokes. Otherwise he speaks with them in Hebrew. A New York informant reported that he uses Judeo-Spanish to tell jokes and funny stories at parties and gatherings. He once headed a Ladino conversation club on Long Island in the early 1960s, which lasted about a year, and as a result he was known in Sephardi circles as the best story teller in Ladino. Another Israeli informant pointed out that Judeo-Spanish expressions are often used to describe the extremes of life, such as disasters and death or great moments of happiness for which, in his opinion, there are no good English or Hebrew equivalents to express such emotions.

(D) JUDEO-SPANISH IS USED AS THE COMMON LANGUAGE AMONG SEPHARDIM.

Judeo-Spanish is still used to communicate with Sephardic relatives living today in the Balkans or Latin America who speak neither English nor Hebrew. Judeo-Spanish also served as the lingua franca among Sephardim of various backgrounds after they emigrated to Israel and the United States from the different areas of the Balkans, since it was the only language they had in common. One Israeli informant, originally from Bulgaria, pointed out that Judeo-Spanish served as the common language for Sephardic Jews from Bulgaria who intermarried with Jews from Greece and Turkey.

(E) JUDEO-SPANISH OR MODERN SPANISH IS USED AT WORK OR WITH NON-SEPHARDIC SPANISH SPEAKERS.

When asked if any of the informants had used or attempted to use Judeo-Spanish with non-Sephardic Spanish speakers, fifty-four reported that they had used Judeo-Spanish in a few instances, and twenty-six reported that they occasionally used Judeo-Spanish or Modern Spanish in their work in some capacity. In New York most of the men who work(ed) in the garment business use(d) Judeo-Spanish when speaking to Puerto Rican workers. They reported that their linguistic ability got them better results from the Puerto Ricans, who were happy to hear some form of Spanish spoken. In fact, in many cases Puerto Rican Spanish influenced Judeo-Spanish, as the Sephardim adopted more and more of the modern Spanish forms (see chapter 10). A salesman used Judeo-Spanish or Modern Spanish with certain customers, and Judeo-Spanish helped a telephone operator in making long distance calls. A photojournalist, who travels often to Spain, also speaks Modern Spanish to neighbors in his apartment building.

In Israel, ten of the informants happen to work in areas where the use of Judeo-Spanish or Modern Castilian Spanish (and/or knowledge of the two) is needed. Two informants work with Sephardic communities throughout the world and also speak Modern Standard Spanish. Three informants use Judeo-Spanish all the time on the job, since two of them regularly broadcast in the language for the Judeo-Spanish department of Israel's national radio station *Kol Israel,* and the third teaches Judeo-Spanish language and literature at Bar Ilan University. Two informants use Judeo-Spanish in their jobs at the Jewish Agency *(Sochnut)* when talking to immigrants from South America; one man uses the language when doing business (he is an engineer) with Argentineans; and another speaks Castilian with clients at his job in a bank. One woman who is a professional singer, includes Judeo-Spanish *romanzas* in her repertoire and thus has a certain familiarity with the language.

Twenty-two informants from Los Angeles also reported that they use(d) Judeo-Spanish with non-Sephardic Spanish speakers, who include(d) business clients or customers, patients, cleaning women (Mexican maids), Mexicans, and Cubans from the temple, and with Mexicans/Chicanos and other Spanish speakers. Most of the informants reported having minimum difficulty understanding these speakers, but ten of the informants reported that these Spanish speakers could understand them provided that the Sephardim, in the words of one informant, "did not use too many Ladino words." Eleven informants from Los Angeles speak and use Modern Spanish. Most of them learned Spanish in school or college, or from contact with business associates, clients or patients, or because they lived for some time in a Spanish-speaking country before moving to California.

One interesting fact must be mentioned here. Various informants from both New York and Los Angeles reported that they often watch the Spanish-speaking television channels and enjoy all of the programs, including the Spanish *novelas* or soap operas. Also the helpers or aids in the Sephardic Homes for the aged in both New York and Los Angeles consist of many non-Sephardic Spanish speakers.

Concluding Remarks

It is obvious that the current domains of Judeo-Spanish are quite limited. Almost none of the informants read, write, or speak Judeo-

Spanish on a regular basis. It has become a language reserved for use with older people or as a humorous or secret language, and it is occasionally used both in and out of the work place with non-Sephardic Spanish speakers.

10

Characteristics of Current Spoken Judeo-Spanish

I. Borrowing and Individual Variation

Even though all aspects of a language are subject to decay, Sala (1970a:45) reminds us that it is in the lexicon where the process of disintegration of a language is seen with greater clarity. Disintegration becomes apparent as the number of words diminishes, often resulting in frequent borrowings from other in-contact languages that eventually replace the original language.

In the case of Judeo-Spanish, a distinction must be made between the foreign influences that are characteristic of the language, what Mackey refers to as integration of foreign elements into the code (Mackey 1970:195), versus the more recent borrowings into Judeo-Spanish that come from the languages of the Sephardim's new countries of residence, that is, the United States and Israel.

The foreign influences which are an integral part of the Judeo-Spanish language were analyzed in chapter 5. These influences include loans from the Semitic languages of Hebrew and Arabic, the Romance component composed of other Iberian dialects and languages as well as French and Italian, and various Ottoman languages such as Turkish, Greek, Bulgarian, and Serbo-Croatian. Even though some borrowings date back to the time of expulsion, and others did not appear until the mid 1800s, many of the informants were aware of the origins of several common Judeo-Spanish words. For example, informants often reported in the word elicitation that words like *kondurya* 'shoe', *musafir* 'guest', *karpuz* 'watermelon', and *buchuk* 'twin' were Turkish; that *shabat* 'Saturday', and *kal* 'synagogue' were from Hebrew; *alhad* 'Sunday' was Arabic; *piron* 'fork' was from Greek; while *shans* 'luck' was of French origin.

On the other hand, foreign words that were not present in the language before the first half of this century, when the majority of

Sephardic Jews began emigrating from the Balkans to the United States and Palestine, are currently replacing Judeo-Spanish words at an extremely rapid rate.

In order to determine the extent of borrowing or foreign interference in current spoken Judeo-Spanish, this researcher analyzed the results of a word elicitation and collection of samples of free conversation from the ninety-one informants. The field work was done in New York, Israel and Los Angeles during the summers of 1978 and 1985 (see chapters 7 and 8).

The Word Elicitation

A total of 124 to 130 Judeo-Spanish words were elicited.[1] The words were given in English, Hebrew, or French (in a few cases) and the informants were asked to respond with the Judeo-Spanish word if possible. Words were presented from different semantic fields, such as names of relatives, professions, clothing, foods, household objects, institutions, common descriptive adjectives and infinitives.

Results

The analysis of the data collected from the word elicitation shows a great amount of lexical and phonological interference:

a) from English in the Judeo-Spanish of the New York and Los Angeles informants;

b) from French and Hebrew in the Judeo-Spanish of the Israeli informants; and

c) massive lexical as well as phonological interference from Modern Spanish in the Judeo-Spanish of both the New York and Los Angeles informants, as well as some borrowings even in the Judeo-Spanish of the Israeli informants who had come into contact with Modern Spanish.

Borrowing from English

Since English is the national language of the United States and is considered to be the most prestigious language in terms of professional advancement, it is easy to understand its powerful impact on all immigrant languages. Table 4 shows examples of frequent

Table 4. Interference from English in the Judeo-Spanish of New York

Judeo-Spanish Word	Most Frequently Offered Response—English Word
rav, rabino	rabbi
maestro, profesor	teacher
charshi, bazar	marketa[2]~market
bet (a)hayim	cemetery
tutun	tobacco
pastel, pan d'Espanya	cake
portokal	orange (fruit)
težado, tavan	roof, ceiling
tabaka, piano	floor (of a building)
kibrites, parlakes	matches

borrowings from English revealed in the word elicitation component of the study in New York.

Other frequent English influences found in the speech of my informants included words like *munpitch* or *mopitch* 'movies' (from English "moving pictures"), *estofa* 'stove,' *trok* 'truck', and *trokožiko* 'little truck', *bloko* 'block' (of a street), *abechar* 'to bet', and *parkear* 'to park'.[3]

Borrowing from French

The French interference in the Judeo-Spanish of the Israeli informants is easier to analyze than the interference from Hebrew.[4] The existing French interference stems from two main sources:

1) French served as a cultural *lingua franca* for the speakers of various languages throughout the Balkans and also with speakers of European languages from many parts of the world;

2) Many Sephardim from the Balkans were educated in French-speaking Alliance schools during the last half of the nineteenth century and the beginning of the twentieth century (see chapter 11, section 6).

Table 5 shows frequent French borrowings in the Judeo-Spanish of the Israeli informants.

Borrowing from Modern Spanish

The Spanish used by the Puerto Ricans in New York and the Chicanos in Los Angeles, as well as the Spanish of other Spanish

Table 5. Interference from French in the Judeo-Spanish of Israel

Judeo-Spanish word	Most Frequently Offered Response—French Word	English Meaning
tia	tante	aunt
tio	oncle	uncle
maale	quartier, banlieu	district
tutun	tabac	tobacco
chay	thé	tea
pastel, pan d'Espanya	gâteau	cake
piano, tabaka	étage	floor, story
regalo	cadeau	gift
komunidad, kehila	comunauté, société	community

speakers in these areas, has had a great influence on the Judeo-Spanish of both New York and Los Angeles. This is due mainly to the similarities of the two languages and the ever-increasing contact of the Sephardim with non-Sephardi Spanish speakers in certain work and school situations (see chapter 9). According to the attitude questionnaire to be discussed in chapter 12, most of the informants considered various forms of Modern Spanish to be more prestigious than Judeo-Spanish. There is even some Standard Spanish interference in Israel in cases where the informants have either studied Modern Spanish, traveled extensively, lived in Spanish-speaking countries, or have used Spanish in their work.

Table 6 shows some of the borrowings from Modern Spanish which were frequently found in the word elicitation of the New York and Los Angeles informants.

Besides lexical borrowing, there is also a great amount of phonological interference from Modern Spanish. Because of the contact between Modern Spanish and Judeo-Spanish speakers in the New York and Los Angeles areas, many of the informants have taken on some of the Modern Spanish pronunciations. The Judeo-Spanish spoken in the Balkans retained several of the sounds characteristic of Medieval Spanish, since the Jews left Spain before many of the sound changes from Medieval to Modern Spanish took place (see chapter 5). For example, in Balkan Judeo-Spanish and in the speech of many of my Israeli informants, the fricative [ž] sound in words like *mužer* 'mother' and *ižo* 'son,' and the affricate [ǰ] sound in words like *ǰente* 'people,' are the norm. However, due to contact with Modern Spanish, the replacement of the [ž] and [ǰ] as well as

Table 6. *Interference from Modern Spanish in the Judeo-Spanish of New York & Los Angeles*

Judeo-Spanish word	Most Frequently Offered Modern Spanish Word	English Meaning
magazen, butika	tienda	store
hazino	enfermo	sick
charshi, bazar	mercado, marketa	market
Dyo	Dios	God
shabat	sábado	Saturday
alhad	domingo	Sunday
piron	tenedor	fork
chapines, kalsados konduryas	zapatos	shoes
mazal, shans	suerte	luck
kibrites, parlakes	fósforos	matches
marido	esposo	husband
ma	pero	but (conj.)
lavorar	trabajar	to work
trokar	cambiar	to change
meldar	leer	to read
merkar	comprar	to buy

the [š] sounds by the voiceless velar fricative [x] is quite wide-spread today in the Judeo-Spanish of my New York and Los Angeles informants. This sound substitution is also fairly common in the speech of several of Nemer's informants in the Indianapolis Sephardic community (Nemer 1981:213–16). Examples include the Modern Spanish pronunciations [ixa, muxɛr, relixiosas, xovɛn] and [xudío] instead of the Judeo-Spanish [iža, mužɛr, reližiosas, ǰovɛn] and [ǰudio].

The word initial and intervocalic labiodental fricative in various dialects of Balkan Judeo-Spanish (excluding that of Monastir) and in many of my Israeli informants' speech was pronounced as a [v], but today, in New York and Los Angeles, it is often pronounced with the Modern Spanish voiced [b] or the voiced spirant [β], as in [βɛnir], [aβia], and [libro] instead of the Judeo-Spanish pronunciations with the [v] sound [vɛnir], [avia], and [livro]. Also, Judeo-Spanish intervocalic [z] has become the Modern Spanish voiceless [s] sound in the speech of many of the informants, as in the following words: [mesa, ɛrmosa, keso, kasa], and [rosa] instead of [meza, ɛrmoza, kezo, kaza], and [roza].

Table 7. Phonological Interference from Modern Spanish in the Judeo-Spanish of the New York and Los Angeles Informants

	Responses of Informants			
Phonetic Representation of Judeo-Spanish Word	*Phonetic Representation of Modern Spanish Word*	*Modern Spanish Word*	*English Meaning*	*Sound Change*
[kaša]	[kaxa]	caja	box	[š]→[x]
[ižo, fižo]	[ixo]	hijo	son	
[mužɛr]	[muxɛr]	mujer	mother	
				[ž]→[x]
[kaleža]	[kayexa]	calleja	street	
[inteližente]	[intelixente]	inteligente	smart	
[ǰente]	[xɛnte]	gente	people	
				[ǰ]→[x]
[ǰovɛn]	[xovɛn]	joven	young	
[livro]	[libro]	libro	book	
				[v]→[b,β]
[ɛstava]	[ɛstaβa]	estaba	(I, s/he, it) was	
[ɛrmoza]	[ɛrmosa]	hermosa	beautiful	
[roza]	[rosa]	rosa	rose	
				[z]→[s]
[kezo]	[keso]	queso	cheese	
[meza]	[mesa]	mesa	table	

Table 7 shows these examples of phonological interference from Modern Spanish in the informants' Judeo-Spanish.

Other phonetic interference from Modern Spanish was commonly heard in the following two words: Modern Spanish *escuela* instead of Judeo-Spanish *eskola* and Modern Spanish *nuestro* and *nos* with an *n-* instead of the Judeo-Spanish *muestro* and *mos*.[5]

Besides my findings of phonological interference from Modern Spanish in the Judeo-Spanish of my New York and Los Angeles informants, Nemer also found similar efforts to "Spanishize" in the Judeo-Spanish of the Indianapolis community: "The most common kind of modification of Judeo-Spanish by the introduction of phonological features is that which tends to 'Spanishize' speech" (1981:213).

My informants were also asked to speak from three to fifteen minutes in order to provide a free conversation sample.[6] The analysis of the speech samples shows two interesting phenomena: 1) discrepancies between the words given by the informants in the word elicitation and those found in the free conversation samples, and 2) a great amount of code-switching in the informants' speech.

Discrepancies between the Vocabulary Used in the Word Elicitation and Speech Samples

In many instances the words given by certain informants in the word elicitation and those used by the same informants in the speech samples did not agree. This was probably due to the fact that when the vocabulary was elicited, the informants had a chance to think about the correct Judeo-Spanish words that were used by them or by family members in the past. In their conversations, on the other hand, the informants did not have the time to consciously make such choices. As a result, the speech samples present a more realistic picture of spoken Judeo-Spanish today and show the extent of interference that has affected the language. Modern Standard Spanish was the source of most of the discrepancies found in the word elicitation versus the conversation samples.

Table 8 lists some of the modern Spanish words found in the free conversation samples of various New York and Los Angeles informants along with the corresponding Judeo-Spanish terms that these same informants gave in the word elicitation. Many of these

Table 8. Discrepancies between the Word Elicitation and Free Conversation Samples: Interference from Modern Spanish

Correct Judeo-Spanish Word Given in the Word Elicitation	Modern Spanish Word Given in the Free Conversation	English Meaning
kamareta, oda	cuarto	room
shabat	sábado	Saturday
tutun	tabaco	tobacco
butika	tienda	store
Dyo	Dios	God
lavorar	trabajar	to work
meldar	leer	to read
eskapar, akavar	terminar	to finish
merkar	comprar	to buy
hazino	enfermo	sick
ma	pero	but (conjunction)

words from Modern Spanish were also words given by various informants in Table 6.

In a few instances the opposite occurred, where informants would give the Modern Spanish word in the word elicitation such as *estudiar* 'to study', or *trabajar* 'to work', but would use the correct Judeo-Spanish *embezar* or *lavorar* in their speech. However, these instances were rare.

Phonological discrepancies from word list elictations were also apparent in the informants' speech samples. Often informants would give the correct Judeo-Spanish pronunciation of a word in the word elicitation such as [ɛskola] 'school', or [mužɛr] 'woman', but in the free conversation samples, these same informants would use these words with their Modern Spanish pronunciations of *escuela* [ɛskwela], and *mujer* [muxɛr], respectively.

Disadvantages of Using Word Elicitation

It is true that word elicitation has its disadvantages. A few informants complained that it was difficult to remember certain words out of context and that they did not have much time to think. However, the object of the word elicitation was to discover the extent of forgotten or unknown words and whether they had been replaced by English, French, Hebrew, or Modern Spanish terms. I wanted to study immediate reactions/responses and did not want to give the informants much time to reflect on their answers.

One informant suggested that one of the reasons for his difficulty was that the word list was not specific enough in some cases. For example, there were many kinds of fines and taxes to be paid in the Balkans, and there were different kinds of cakes or sweets. Thus, confusion resulted because there was not just one word to express the idea of "tax" or "cake." Another suggestion was to study the various phrases in Judeo-Spanish which express certain ideas better than one word. For example, periphrastic expressions like *kara de luna* 'face of the moon' to mean "pretty", versus *kara de karvon* 'face of carbon, coal' to mean "ugly", abound in Judeo-Spanish and are regularly used in place of a single adjective. Such expressions should be the subject of an independent study.

Nemer argues that in my word elicitation in New York and Israel, some of the words were not common ones (1981:53–4). There were a few words like *forest, outskirts,* and *election* that might not be used often in the home. But these words constituted only a small part of the word list.[7] Most of the words on the list were everyday words. For example, very common words such as: *teacher, student, guest, gift, matches,* and *belt* were frequently missed by the informants. Another explanation for the informants' difficulty with the word elicitation can be explained by certain cultural phenomena. One informant pointed out, for example, that Sephardic education in the Balkans in the late 1800s and in the United States in the early 1900s was not as high a priority as it had been in earlier years. This was due to the conditions of poverty the Sephardim were subjected to during and after World War I and later in the United States until they had established themselves. It was interesting to note that the words for "teacher" and "student" resulted in much hesitation on the part of the informants, especially in New York.

Nemer objects to my word elicitation and suggests that I should not consider foreign influences as being synonymous with an impoverished lexicon or examples of interference, but rather as an expansion of the lexicon (1981:54–55). However, given the advanced state of decline of Judeo-Spanish today, I have difficulties with her suggestion. I feel that borrowing, especially on a large scale, has a different significance depending on whether one is referring to "healthy" (Dorian:1981) versus declining languages (see chapter 13).

While Tables 4–8 show only a few instances of English, French, and Modern Spanish interference, they do give an idea of the types of borrowing present in the speech of contemporary Judeo-Spanish speakers living in New York, Israel, and Los Angeles. Because I could not get an equal number of informants of different ages, it was not possible to correlate word elicitation responses with the age of the informants. From previous studies such as those of Dorian (1981), Fasold (1984), and others, it can be presumed that a large number of informants under the age of fifty would exhibit a substantially higher number of English and Modern Spanish borrowings as well as phonological interference in their speech than would older informants. However, it must be pointed out that it is almost impossible to find native Judeo-Spanish speakers today under the age of fifty or fifty-five who can still converse in the language (see chapter 13).

Individual Variation

Another sign of a language in decline, according to Sala (1970b:64), can be found in individual variation. Sjoestedt (1928:101) observes that the number of words subjected to individual variation or fluctuation denotes a pathological state or symptom of a language more than does a high number of borrowings. Phonological variation was quite prevalent in my Judeo-Spanish word elicitation data. But a distinction must be made between variation due to dialect differences and variation that exists across dialects.

Examples of variation due to different Judeo-Spanish dialects can be observed in the words for "son," "book," and "handkerchief." The word for "son" in most Judeo-Spanish dialects is pronounced [ižo], while the word [fižo] with initial f- is especially characteristic of the Salonika dialect. The variants [ižu] and [fižu] with final -u are typical of the Monastir and Kastoria dialects as well as some Bulgarian dialects. The same vowel variation occurs in the word for "book," which is [livro] in most dialects versus [livru] found in Monastir. The closure of the o to u in final position is characteristic of the Monastir and Kastoria dialects but not of the Salonika, Izmir, Istanbul, and other Turkish dialects. The word for "handkerchief" is either [riza], which is found in the Salonika and Kastoria dialects or [rida], prevalent in the Turkish dialects of Istanbul, Izmir, and Bursa as well as in certain Bulgarian dialects (Wagner 1925:198). However, as stated above, the data of various scholars including Benardete (1982) and Malinowski (1979) show these distinctions to be weakening today as a result of the various dialects in contact.

Below are examples of individual variations given for four words. In this data from my word elicitation, variations range from seven to thirteen varieties. The variations are presented phonetically along with the number of informants who used each variety. The correct Judeo-Spanish pronunciation is given first in the list and the final word is the correct Modern Spanish word. Many informants gave more than one variety per term, while others were not able to give the word(s) in Judeo-Spanish at all. While some of the varieties given are due to dialectal differences, most of the variations are due to uncertainty on the part of the informants as to what is the correct form. We must remember that most of the informants never had the opportunity to study Judeo-Spanish, nor do/did they have any dictionaries or sources which could provide the correct forms. Some informants even invented new words.

1. *lawyer*	*# of informants*
avokato (Judeo-Spanish pronunciation)	51
avokatu	2
avokεto	1
avokado (name of fruit)	10

avoká (French pron.)	1
avukat	1
avukato	2
advokato	1
advokat	1
afokato	1
abugada	1
avogado	1
aβogado (Mod. Spanish)	7

2. *school*

ɛskola (Judeo-Spanish pron.)	48
ɛškola	2
ɛskolya	1
skola	23
škola	6
skolya	1
skwɔla (Italian *scuola*)	1
skwela	2
ɛskwela (Mod. Spanish)	9

3. *twin* (from Turkish *buçuk* meaning "half")

bučuk(es) (Judeo-Spanish pron.)	46
bučuki(s)	6
bučok~bučiki	1
bičuk	1
bočko(s)	4
bočkes	1
bočuko	1
buǰuk (-as, -os)	6
bižuk	1
bučikas	2
bučačos	1
medios (from Mod. Spanish *medio* 'half')	3

4. *orange*—the fruit (from Turkish *portakal*)

portukal (Judeo-Spanish pron.)	37
portokal (dialectal difference?)	12
pɛrtukal	2
portugal (Mod. Spanish name of the country)	16
naranja[8]	2
naranxe	1
naranxa (Mod. Spanish)	6

Of a total of 125 words elicited in the data, 50 words or 40 percent of the words lent themselves to individual variation of at least five or more varieties. Seventy-two percent or 90 of the words had three or more varieties. I consider such variation to be a salient feature of present-day spoken Judeo-Spanish, which results from an imperfect knowledge of linguistic forms and is, in this instance, one sign of language decay.

Code-Switching in Contemporary Judeo-Spanish

Code-switching, which often occurs in the speech of bilinguals, is generally defined as the alternation of two languages within a single discourse, sentence or constituent (Poplack 1982:231). However, in the case of Judeo-Spanish, this alternation can also occur between more than two languages. Code-switching is one of the most salient characteristics of current spoken Judeo-Spanish. Data on code-switching was obtained from samples of the New York, Israeli, and Los Angeles informants' speech in their interviews conducted during the summers of 1978 and 1985.

The Free Conversation Samples

In order to determine the extent of code-switching in their speech, the informants were asked to speak from three to fifteen minutes on any of the following topics: their childhood, when they came to the United States or Israel (Palestine), their early days in New York, Israel, or Los Angeles, how they met their spouses, their families or their jobs. If a husband and wife or various family members were being interviewed together, I usually asked them to hold a conversation among themselves. The speech samples generally fell into the five to ten minute range, but many of the informants had difficulty speaking for as long as three minutes. They either did not have the linguistic skills to enable them to speak for a longer period, or they said that it was difficult to talk when no other Judeo-Spanish speakers were present to have a conversation. Often I would ask the informants questions in Judeo-Spanish if they were having trouble thinking of something to say. Thirteen of the total number of informants, or 15 percent, did not feel competent enough in the language to attempt speaking at all, so they gave no conversation samples.

Types of Code-Switching

The analysis of the conversation samples reveals a great amount of code-switching in the speech of the informants. The lexical interference comes mainly from English and Modern Spanish in the

Judeo-Spanish of the New York and Los Angeles informants, and from Hebrew, French, and even some Modern Spanish[9] in the speech of the Israeli informants. In the majority of cases, a foreign word or phrase is inserted into a Judeo-Spanish sentence and pronounced as it is in the foreign language. Three examples are:

English: Estavan *delicious*. 'They were delicious.'

French: Mi padre es *banquier*. 'My father is a banker.'

Hebrew: Viaže kon *aviron*. 'I traveled by plane.'

In the above sentences the English word *delicious,* the French word *banquier* and the Hebrew word *aviron* were pronounced as they are in English, French, and Hebrew, respectively.

Another type of borrowing occurs when a foreign word is inserted into the language, but is given a Judeo-Spanish ending as in:

los kayes yenos de *pushcartes* 'the streets full of pushcarts'

Tiene muchas *partes* de Off-Broadway. 'He has many Off-Broadway parts.'

Nunka *regreto* ser sefardi. 'I never regret being a Sephardi.'

Vo *returnar* aki. 'I am going to return here.'

In the above examples, the Spanish *-es* plural ending was added to the English nouns *pushcart* and *part*.[10] The first person Spanish present tense *-o* verb ending was added to the English *regret* (or the French verb *regretter* depending on its origin), and the Spanish *-ar* infinitive ending was added to the English word *return* (which is pronounced as in English).[11]

In other cases, the English *-s* noun ending is added to Judeo-Spanish or French words as in:

Los *buros* eran aya. 'The offices were there' where a variation of the French noun *bureau* is given the English plural ending and pronunciation, or Spanish words like *komunidad* and *sosiedad* are given the English *-s* ending as in *komunidads* and *sosiedads,* instead of the correct Judeo-Spanish *-es* ending.

The following examples of code-switching that occurred in the speech of my New York, Israeli, and Los Angeles informants were taken from their conversation samples. I have presented examples of lexical interference (which are italicized) from English, Modern Spanish, Hebrew, and French, and have organized them into various types of switching. I divided the examples into the two general categories of single words and short phrases versus larger segments, and also included examples of switches of two or more languages (besides Judeo-Spanish) in the same sentence. After each example, I have put the translation in single quotes. While reading the examples, notice that most of the switched segments deal with everyday common vocabulary which have Judeo-Spanish counterparts.[12]

I. Code-Switching with Individual Words and Short Phrases

A Dates, Numbers and Addresses

1. Mi espozo vino aki *at sixteen* en *nineteen sixteen.* 'My husband came here at age sixteen in 1916'.

2. Vinimos aki en *October.* Al *December* ventiuno desidimos el kazamiento en la sinagoga en un *hall* en *Bedford Avenue, five ninety-seven, Bedford Avenue, Brooklyn, New York.* 'We came here in October. On December 21, we decided to get married in the synagogue in a hall on Bedford Avenue, 597 Bedford Ave., Brooklyn, New York.'

3. Arrivi en Israel en anyo *mil dix-neuf cent quarante huit.* (French numbers) 'I arrived in Israel in the year 1948.'

4. One informant, in discussing his desire to sit with his wife and daughters in the synagogue, said: Yo gusta sentar kon mi famiya—no es *fourteen ninety-two.* 'I like to sit with my family—it's not 1492.'[13]

B Names of Professions

5. El salio *accountant,* muy grande *accountant.* 'He became an accountant, a very big accountant.'

6. La mande a Paris a estudiar i ya es *teacher.* 'I sent her to Paris to study and now she is a teacher.'

7. El yamo a su *lawyer.* 'He called his lawyer.'

8. Mi nuera nasio en Mexico i se kazaron por un *rabbi.* 'My daughter-in-law was born in Mexico and they were married by a rabbi.'

C Names of Places

9. Fuimos para ver este *farm.* 'We went to see this farm.'

10. Estuvimos afuera en la *garden.* 'We were outside in the garden.'

11. El *toilet* estava en el *hall.* 'The toilet was in the hall.'

12. Mi padre estava en el *barber shop* todo el dia. 'My father was in the barber shop all day.'

13. Era mi asosiado aki en este *buro* (French *bureau*). 'He was my colleague here in this office.'

14. Estuve en *bet holim* (Hebrew) serka de Hadera. 'I was in hospital near Hadera.'
15. . . asperando kon "*next*" para entrar al *bathroom*. '. . waiting to hear "next" in order to enter the bathroom.'
16. Vamos al *beach*. 'Let's go to the beach.'

D Names of Countries, Cities, Nationalities, Languages
17. Fuimos a *South America*. 'We went to South America.'
18. Ya vienen de vez en kuando *the South Americans*. 'The South Americans come from time to time.'
19. Todos avlan Ladino o *Arabic*. 'Everyone speaks Ladino or Arabic.'
20. Era un eskrivano *français* (French word and pronunciation) ke era turkofil. 'He was a French writer who was a Turkophile.'
21. Tras esto savia avlar *l'hebreu* (French). 'After this he knew how to speak Hebrew.'
22. Yo parti de *Salonique* (French spelling and pronunciation) or *Selanik* (the Turkish pronunciation) 'I left Salonika'. The term *Salonique* instead of the Judeo-Spanish *Salonika* was used by all the Saloniklis (informants from Salonika) thus showing the strong influence of their French Alliance educations.
23. Arrivi kon la vapor de *la Bulgarie* (French pronunciation). 'I arrived by boat from Bulgaria.'
24. Es komo *la Liberty Statue in New York o la Tour Eiffel à Paris* (French). 'It's like the Statue of Liberty in New York or the Eiffel Tower in Paris.'
25. Avlamos en *ivrit* (Hebrew). 'We speak in Hebrew.'

E Descriptive Adjectives
26. Es *different*. 'It's different.'
27. Era *terrible, disgusting*. 'It was terrible, disgusting.'
28. Estavan *delicious*. 'They were delicious.'
29. Mi mama fue mas *evoluée* (French) porke los Ashkenazis eran mas *evolués* ke los sefardies. 'My mother was more advanced/progressive because the Ashkenazim were more advanced than the Sephardim.'
30. . . . i aya vi las *beautiful* kozas de Amerika. '. . . and there I saw the beautiful things of America.'

31. Bushkamos una koza *suitable*. 'We looked for something suitable.'

F Common Nouns or Expressions
32. Amanya *the grandson* va venir. 'Tomorrow the grandson is coming.'
33. Estuvimos kon la *mishpaha* (Hebrew)[14] 'We were with the family.'
34. Tengo munchos buenos *memories*. 'I have many good memories.'
35. No tenemos *paper*. 'We don't have paper.'
36. *Sand* no es bueno para ti. 'Sand is not good for you.'
37. Tuvimos un *party*. 'We had a party.'
38. *The middle one* (referring to a grandson) estuvo en un *play* la otra semana. 'The middle one was in a play the other week.'
39. Muzotros dishimos *"Good-bye"* a l'escalera. 'We said "good-bye" on the stairs.'
40. La madre de mi papa era komadre i ayudaba kon *baby* kuando una de las mužeres de *harem* tenia un *baby* . . . ke si tenia un *problem* eya le yamo el doktor.' 'My father's mother was a midwife and she used to help with a baby when one of the women of the harem had a baby . . . that if she had a problem, she called the doctor.'
41. Los ke vienen de Atena avlan otro Ladino i otro grego ke la jente ke viene de Volos. Es komo se diže *"more high class."* 'Those that come from Athens speak another Ladino and another Greek than the people from Volos. It is how do you say, "more high class." '
42. Kuando fuimos a la kaza de eya avia un monton de personas para dizer *"Congratulations."* 'When we went to her house there were a lot of people to say "Congratulations." '
43. Kero *something to* komer. 'I want something to eat.'

In the above examples we see very common words such as *grandson, family, baby, problem, memories, paper, good-bye, congratulations* and *something,* all of which have perfectly good counterparts in Judeo-Spanish.

G Conjunctions, Adverbs, and Prepositions

44. Mi papa lavorava en la duana *and* mi mama ayudava al Hadassah i a los proves. 'My father worked in the customs office and my mother helped at Hadassah and (she helped) the poor.'
45. Mi papu era haham en la Turkia *but* aya no avia tanto a komer. 'My grandfather was a rabbi in Turkey but there was not so much to eat there.'
46. Kero merkar livros *aval* (Hebrew) no estan mas baratos. 'I want to buy books but they are not cheaper.'
47. Parti de Rhodesia *because* el situasion (notice gender) no estava muy buena aya. 'I left Rhodesia because the situation was not very good there.'
48. *So,* vine aki. 'So, I came here.'
49. Avlan espanyol, *not* ladino. 'They speak Spanish not Ladino.'
50. Este kortižo fue destruido *during* el tiempo de la gerra. 'This kortižo was destroyed during the time of the war.'

H Idiomatic Expressions, Tags, or Fillers[15]
51. *Aora* (Mod. Spanish), *you know,* no estan aki. 'Now, you know, they are not here.'
52. Akavidate, *believe me,* es verdad. 'I warn you, believe me, it's true.'[16]
53. No savia grego *beklal* (Hebrew). 'He didn't know Greek at all.'
54. Es *hard to take.* 'It's hard to take.'

I Use of both a Judeo-Spanish word and that of another language to express the same word in the same sentence

Silva-Corvalán (1983:82) refers to this kind of shifting as an effort to clarify a message or to make it more precise. This type of switching was very common among my informants. The following are examples:
55. El grande (grandson) tiene un *vapor* i vive en el *boat* en la Marina del Rey. 'The oldest has a *boat* (Judeo-Spanish) and he lives on the *boat* (English) in Marina del Rey.'
56. Entonses mi kunyado avlo kon su *lawyer,* kon el *avokato* suyo. 'Then my brother-in-law spoke with his *lawyer* (English), with his *lawyer* (Judeo-Spanish).'

57. Mi madre vivia kon mi unos kuantos anyos i despues le dio *gota—a stroke* i la metieron en el ospital por tres anyos and then *I had—tuvi* tres kriaturas. 'My mother lived with me for some years and afterwards she had a *stroke* (Judeo-Spanish)—a *stroke* (English)—and they put her in the hospital for three years and then *I had* (English) *I had* (Judeo-Spanish) three children.'

58. Ensenya business en un *adult school—eskola de adultos* para business people. 'She teaches business in an *adult school* (English)—a *school for adults* (Judeo-Spanish) for business people.'

59. Por restriksion de las komidas mi marido *se enfermo—se izo hazino* y en 1944 se murio. 'Due to lack of food my husband *became ill* (Modern Spanish)—*got sick* (Judeo-Spanish) and he died in 1944.'

60. *And* despues no tenia *trabajo*—no tenia *lavoro.* 'And afterwards he didn't have *work* (Mod. Spanish)—he didn't have *a job* (Judeo-Spanish).'

61. Savemos muy bien el *ivrit—el ebreo.* 'We know very well *Hebrew* (Hebrew)—*Hebrew* (Judeo-Spanish).'

62. Dishe *esrim—venti.* 'I said *twenty* (Hebrew)—*twenty* (Judeo-Spanish).'

63. Yo esto kontento lavorar otros uno, dos, o tres anyos *aval* no *yoter*—no *mas.* 'I'm content to work another one, two, or three years but *no more* (Hebrew)—*no more* (Judeo-Spanish).'

II. Code-Switching of Segments larger than a single word or constituent

Hasselmo (1970:182) refers to this as "unlimited switching": the distribution of the segment may vary, that is, it can come in the middle of the sentence, or at the beginning or the end.

64. Despues tuvi un primer chiko *and he was the most spoiled* chiko ke tienes ke ver. 'Afterwards I had a first son and he was the most spoiled child that you have ever seen.'

65. Yo avli kon mi amiga Luisa—eya se grandesio en Seattle, *and I used to go there.* 'I spoke with my friend Luisa—she grew up in Seattle, and I used to go there.'

66. Todos los *ships* ke venian *they (from) all over the*

world i savia munchas idiomas (notice gender) mi
padre. 'All the ships that came—they were from all
over the world—and my father knew many languages.'

67. Mi marido se murio *and so I miss him very much.*
'My husband died and so I miss him very much.'

68. *In fact, in the museum in Seattle in the university*
ay un livro escrito de mano de mi papu de *psalms,*
kantigas. . . . 'In fact, in the museum in Seattle in
the university, there is a book written by hand by
my grandfather of psalms, songs. . . .'

III. Two or more Languages besides Judeo-Spanish used within
the Same Sentence

Unlike many studies of code-switching which involve al-
ternations of one language with another, code-switching in
Judeo-Spanish often includes the interference of two or
more other languages in the same sentence. This type of
switching was very common among my informants. Below
are six examples:

69. Mi padre avlo en ingles *pero* kon *a heavy accent.*
'My father spoke in English but with a heavy accent.' Note the use of Modern Spanish *pero* instead
of Judeo-Spanish *ma,* and *a heavy accent* from English.

70. Fue en un *bicyclette* a la *tienda* de *Mr.* Barash. 'He
went by bike to Mr. Barash's store.' Note French
bicyclette, Modern Spanish *tienda* and the English
title *Mr.*

71. *Aora,* te yevo un *picture* de mi *hijo.* 'Now I bring
you a picture of my son.' Note the Modern Spanish
ahora vs. Judeo-Spanish *agora* and Modern Spanish
pronunciation of *hijo* instead of Judeo-Spanish *ižo,*
as well as English *picture.*

72. Yo te digo ke teniamos muy buen *choir* en el templo
nuestro. 'I tell you that we used to have very good
choir in our temple.' Note the English *choir* and the
Modern Spanish pronunciation *nuestro* instead of
muestro with an *m-.*

73. Lo transferaron (notice conjugation) a una *escuela*
en Harlem kon chikos muncho mas chikos de los ke
tenia *and retarded* tambien, *so* el disho ke no keria

trabajar kon este modo de chikos porke *he had to sort of babysit for them*. 'They transferred him to a school in Harlem with children much younger than those he had, and retarded also, so he said that he didn't want to work with these kind of children because he had to sort of babysit for them.' Note the Modern Spanish word *escuela* instead of the Judeo-Spanish *eskola;* English *and, retarded,* and *so;* Modern Spanish *trabajar* instead of Judeo-Spanish *lavorar;* and the final sentence in English: *and he had to sort of babysit for them*.

74. Yo encontre a mi marido de una amiga ke mi madre konosia. *And he* vino a mi ver en mi kaza *and* despues no tenia *trabajo*. No tenia lavoro *and* despues nos encontremos *and he asked me, well, I'm speaking in English and then we got married after we went for a while* enjuntos. 'I met my husband through a friend that my mother knew. And he came to see me in my house and afterwards he didn't have work. He didn't have a job and after we got to know each other and he asked me, well I'm speaking English and then we got married after we went together for a while.' Note *And* and *he* (English); *trabajo* (Modern Spanish) and then the final two sentences in English.

Code-switching occurred in the speech of all of the informants who were capable of speaking in Judeo-Spanish. As the previous examples show, this code-switching ranged from a borrowed word sprinkled here and there in a Judeo-Spanish sentence, to partial and complete sentences from the interferring language(s). However, one important phenomenon must be emphasized here. The code-switching which occurred among my Judeo-Spanish informants was not the result of knowing more than one language well, but rather the result of having insufficient knowledge of Judeo-Spanish. In contrast to Poplack's previous studies of code-switching, most of my informants did not engage in what she calls "skilled code-switching," which is characterized by a "seeming unawareness of the alternation between languages" and is not accompanied by false starts, hesitations, pauses, metalinguistic commentary, or repetitions of various segments (Poplack 1982:248). As my examples show, this was not the case with the majority of my informants. Their speech was not only full of pauses, hesitations, commentary, and repetitions, but they also expressed a great awareness of what was not Judeo-Spanish. Often during the interviews, they would correct their errors with comments like: "Esto es kasteyano espanyol de Espanya, no es espanyol de muzotros." ('This is Castilian Spanish of Spain, it is not *our Spanish*'). One informant described something that happened one day with: "Un dia estavamos avlando en la marketa en espanyol de muzotros" ('One day we were talking in the market in *our* Spanish'). Another informant expressed her frustrations in the following quote which is a mixture of Judeo-Spanish, Modern Spanish and English when she said: "I'm gonna try to use—avlar espanyol ladino because you all know Castellano tambien i sin kerer me konfundo la lengua." ('I'm gonna try to use—speak Ladino Spanish because you all know Castilian also and without wanting to, I confuse the language').

The code-switching that occurred in the speech of my informants probably would be better classified as "code-shifting," a term used by Silva-Corvalán to describe shifting that occurs when the bilingual speakers have to use the language in which they are self-reportedly less fluent or less competent in order to adapt to the language preference of the listener, in this case, the interviewer (1983:71,81). In the situation of code-shifting, the speaker compensates for insufficient lexical or syntactic knowledge of one of the languages, in this case Judeo-Spanish. This is in opposition to Poplack's view of skilled code-switching which appears to require a large degree of linguistic competence in both languages. According to Silva Corvalán, skilled code-switching is "largely motivated by social and discourse/pragmatic factors," while the primary function of code-shifting has a linguistic communicative function, used when the speaker needs to communicate in a language in which he or she has a limited degree of competence (Silva-Corvalán 1983:85).

Not only did my informants who were capable of conversing in Judeo-Spanish resort to code-switching or shifting, but the extent of the switching was great. There was rarely a sentence uttered by the informants that did not contain some kind of recent borrowing from English, Modern Spanish, French, or Hebrew. And for the most part, the switching appears in situations where everyday vocabulary is used and where a counterpart in Judeo-Spanish exists that the informants do not know or cannot remember. This means that for 100 percent, or all of the New York, Israeli, and Los Angeles informants capable of conversing in Judeo-Spanish, code-switching or code-shifting is a dominant characteristic of their speech. And since the largest Sephardic communities are presently located in Israel and the United States (with New York and Los Angeles being the largest American Sephardic communities), the data suggests that a great amount of code-switching is characteristic of current spoken Judeo-Spanish, no matter where and by whom it is spoken in the world today. Even Malinowski's research in Turkey shows that the Sephardic Jews still residing there often code-switch using a large amount of Turkish and/or French in their speech, that is, if they can still speak Judeo-Spanish at all (1982a:15).

The Significance of Code-Switching

As Poplack has pointed out, code-switching per se is not a phenomenon which is indicative of language death (1983:124). There is also extensive code-switching in the Chicano and Puerto Rican varieties of Spanish in the United States, and one could hardly say that these dialects are in a state of decline. But even though the generational shift from Judeo-Spanish to English or Hebrew follows a similar pattern to that observed for other immigrant languages in Israel and the United States (Fishman 1972 and Malinowski 1983), the case of Judeo-Spanish is different. First of all, there is no home country today where people speak Judeo-Spanish, as is the case for other immigrant languages. This means that there is no new influx of fluent Judeo-Spanish speakers who can help to revitalize the language as it is spoken in the United States or Israel. Since there are no young Judeo-Spanish speakers left, there is no replacing generation of native speakers.[17] Thus there is rare, if any, contact with the spoken language.

I also feel that the code-switching or shifting in Judeo-Spanish does indeed show a trend toward language decay, since for the most part the borrowing occurs in situations where common, everyday vocabulary is used and where good counterparts exist in Judeo-Spanish. This shifting occurs because the informants do not know the equivalent words or expressions in Judeo-Spanish, and therefore the replacement with English, Modern Spanish, French, or Hebrew is necessary to fulfill the function of communication. I might also add that there are no Judeo-Spanish texts and very few dictionaries where a Judeo-Spanish speaker could look up terms if he or she so desired. And there are no university courses offered which emphasize the acquisition of Judeo-Spanish linguistic skills.[18]

But more important is the fact that the majority of my informants reported that they did not possess good linguistic skills in Judeo-Spanish, and they admitted they could not speak the language as well as their parents and grandparents. They all felt more comfortable and preferred communicating in English, Hebrew, French, or even in Modern Spanish in a few cases, rather than in Judeo-Spanish. The informants admitted this while expressing pride in their Sephardic heritage and acknowledging that Judeo-Spanish is an important aspect of their Sephardic identity. But at the same time, however, the vast majority of my informants believe that Judeo-Spanish is a dying language, an opinion which is not shared by other immigrants about their respective languages. They are also doing nothing to perpetuate the language or to insure its survival (see chapter 12).

Concluding Remarks

Today, as the older generation of Judeo-Spanish speakers diminishes, the demise of the language becomes more apparent. The role of code-switching or shifting as a possible stage in the decline of Judeo-Spanish is an important issue to be considered.

Part IV
The Decline of Judeo-Spanish: Sociohistorical Causes and Language Attitudes

11

Reasons for the Decline of Judeo-Spanish in the Levant, the United States, and Israel

Today Judeo-Spanish is a dying language in the United States, Israel, and Turkey, the three countries that now have the largest Sephardic populations in the world. It is a language relegated to the domain of the family and is used almost exclusively among (or with) older people. The younger generations only speak it (if they know how) when they have no other means of being understood by their elders. Generally they speak the languages of the countries in which they live and do not transmit Judeo-Spanish to their children. Judeo-Spanish is being replaced by English in the United States, Hebrew in Israel, and Turkish in Turkey. Today it is very difficult to find fluent native speakers of Judeo-Spanish who are under the age of fifty or fifty-five. The few people under that age who can still speak the language have limited linguistic skills and are not capable of transmitting it to their children or grandchildren. With the passing away of the older generations, the language of the Sephardim will disappear as a living language used for daily communication.

In chapter 6 the reasons for the survival of Judeo-Spanish in the Ottoman Empire for four-and-a-half centuries were discussed. What changes have occurred to cause the recent rapid decline of the language? In this chapter several of the sociocultural factors contributing to the decline of Judeo-Spanish in the Levant, the United States, and Israel are presented.

1. Nationalism in the Balkans

Beginning in the late 1800s, the effects of nationalism were devastating to the Sephardim and to their language. As a result of nationalistic movements, the Balkan Wars, and World War I, the Ottoman Empire was dismembered and distinct republics were established.

These new nationalistic Balkan States were not as tolerant toward the Jews as the former Ottoman Empire had been. The Sephardim were now forced to assimilate to the culture of the surrounding peoples.

Meldares and other private Jewish schools, in which Judeo-Spanish had been the language of instruction, were closed. Even at the rabbinic seminary of Constantinople, all subjects were taught in Turkish starting from 1900. The Jews were now obliged to attend national schools and thus learn the national and local languages in which they were taught (that is, Turkish, Greek, Serbo-Croatian, Bulgarian, and Rumanian). Even the French Alliance Schools were closed after Kemalist reform.

Along with national education, obligatory military service was instituted for all Jewish males who had formerly not been obliged or allowed to serve, or who had been excused from service by the payment of the *cizye* or special exemption tax.[1] In all countries obligatory national education and military service have always been two of the most effective means of spreading the national language, while at the same time aiding in the elimination of the regional speech of the ethnic minorities.

With the New Turkey of Atatürk dating from 1923, more restrictions were placed on the minorities in the area, since his policy consisted of suppressing all foreign elements. Not only did Turkish become the official language of instruction in the schools, but various movements were started to adopt Turkish for everyday family needs in an effort to help the Sephardim and other non-Turkish speaking minorities to assimilate or better incorporate themselves into Turkish unity. This led in the 1930s and 1940s to the founding of the society *Türk Birliği* 'Turkish Unity', whose purpose was to abandon the "corrupted" Judeo-Spanish dialect, as well as French, in favor of Turkish. There were even Jewish institutions which had the following inscription at the entrance of their buildings: *Kardaşlar siz türksünüz ve Türkçe diliniz olmalı dır* 'Brothers, you are Turks and Turkish should be your language' (Farhi 1937:157). Because of such nationalistic policies of the Kemalist government, the Jews of Turkey eventually restricted use of Judeo-Spanish in public life.

In November of 1928 a law was passed in Turkey (part of Kemalist reform) prohibiting the use of non-European alphabets for the writing of Turkish and European languages. Since that time, most Judeo-Spanish publications (books and newspapers) have been printed in the Latin alphabet. In Turkey the spelling system used was modeled after Turkish orthography, examples of which can be seen in Istanbul's newspaper *Şalom*[2], while the Judeo-Spanish newspaper *La Luz de Israel,* published in Tel Aviv until 1990, was based on French orthography (Malinowski 1979:10). In 1936 the Jews of Greece were also forbidden to publish in Rashi script, another restriction which dealt a devastating blow to Judeo-Spanish.

As a result of the advent of nationalism in the Balkans, the traditional Sephardic culture and life style started to crumble and the language was relegated to the intimacy of the family. Thus the decadence of the language coincides with the general decline of the Levantine Sephardim. The Sephardim found themselves caught in a stagnant, hopeless situation for which they could not foresee any improvement. This was added to the fact that in the course of the nineteenth century, the Sephardic communities began to absorb western ideas generally acquired in the French Alliance schools (see section 6). These new ideas encouraged progress, thus motivating them to find new horizons and seek out opportunities in other countries. They finally realized that their long-standing cultural isolation was coming to an end. At this time they began emigrating to Palestine, the United States, and Latin America. Salonika was the only place in the Balkans where Judeo-Spanish continued as a vital language; that is, until 1943, when the Sephardic community was annihilated by the Nazis.

2. Loss of Prestige

The economic upset of Europe in the course of the second half of the nineteenth century dealt a serious blow to the Sephardim in the Ottoman Empire as well as to their language. Because of new international trade agreements as well as new customs restrictions, relations among the Sephardic communities of Salonika, Constantinople, Sofia, and Bucharest, which had been formerly active during the epoch of the Ottoman Empire, became increasingly difficult to maintain. The Jews were put into contact with non-Sephardic merchants and buyers. As a result, the ties which had unified the diverse Sephardic communities were broken, and Judeo-Spanish lost its role as the international cohesive language of the Balkan Sephardim.

The appearance of Turkish, Greek, and Armenian capitalism put an end to the commercial and industrial monopoly of the Sephardim, the majority of whom saw their activities restricted to *petit commerce.* Thus the flow of trade by Jews in the Mediterranean lost its privileged position, as much of the commerce was taken over by the new authorities. Consequently Judeo-Spanish stopped being the trade language in the area and was replaced by others such as Turkish, Greek, French, and Italian. The knowledge of the language of the country became indispensable for the exercising of trade, which had formerly been the fundamental occupation of the Sephardim.

With their loss of economic and political prominence, coupled with a lowering of their cultural level, the Sephardic communities in the Levant lost their prestige. They fell into disfavor and poverty and were relegated to a low intellectual level. Under these conditions the Sephardim either emigrated (as stated above) or made efforts to assimilate. With such a loss of prestige there was no reason for the other groups to learn Judeo-Spanish. Other languages had become more important in the Balkans, and it was now the Sephardim's turn to learn those languages that had gained prestige. Later on, after emigration to other countries, the Sephardim were once again faced with learning another language, such as Hebrew or English. Historically this adoption of other languages is not unusual in the history of the Jews:

> during the course of their historical development, the same political, social, economic and cultural pressures which had originally forced Jews to acquire a knowledge of a particular language (albeit in what at some point probably became a distinctly Jewish form), later often caused them to discard that language in favor of some other language (also probably in a Jewish form) whose speakers had gained greater prestige or power of some kind. (Bunis 1974:4)

In an article illustrating the Sephardim's loss of prestige and its effect on their language, Spitzer wrote of the decaying life style of the Turkish Jews. He reported that the Sephardim of Constantinople in 1939 lived in poor barrios. They were not allowed to hold public jobs, only a small percentage worked in Muslim enterprises, and they were no longer influential in the liberal professions. Those who still spoke Judeo-Spanish belonged to the more humble level of society. The more well-to-do Jewish families had for a while preferred the French language, due to the general prestige of the French and their language propagated by the French Alliance Israélite Universelle schools (Spitzer: 1939:9–10).

3. Assimilation in the Ottoman Empire

Since the economic transformation and nationalism in the Balkans at the end of the nineteenth and beginning of the twentieth centuries led to the disintegration of the Balkan Sephardi communities, the Sephardim found it necessary to assimilate into the new society regardless of any desires to conserve cohesion. The best way not to be eliminated was to be incorporated into the growing bourgeois class. The creation of national schools, more frequent contact with Western civilization, and the ease of communication between cultures all aided in changing Jewish customs and ways of thinking to a more Europeanized ideal. Unfortunately, in the assimilation process the mother tongue often has to take a back seat. As D. Moisés Abravanel wrote, "Assimilation to other communities forces (us) to give a secondary importance to Spanish which can lose much of its value" (Pulido 1905:440). By 1902 Danon reported that the Turkish Jews spoke Turkish as well as the illiterate Moslems did (Pulido 1905:137), an illustration of the fact that the degree of assimilation of a people is often revealed in their linguistic behavior. Where a previous knowledge of Turkish was not necessary for the Sephardim, it now became a necessity for survival and success in the Ottoman culture.

4. Americanization

The most important acculturation factor for ethnic groups in America has been the de-ethnizing or supra-ethnic quality of Americanization, where mass culture encourages conformity and, until very recently, has not tolerated ethnic differences (Nahirny and Fishman 1966:335). The forces of Americanization have nearly destroyed Judeo-Spanish, which no longer serves as a cohesive force for American Sephardim as it did in the Levant. Adoption to the American way of life meant the adoption of English, the vehicle used to "get ahead," as the language of primary socialization. As with all other ethnic groups in the United States, American values have been imposed on the Sephardim:

> the difficulties faced by all American minorities (and by American immigrant minorities in particular) [are] to substantially regulate or moderate the ethnolinguistic influences stemming from the Anglo-American culture that surrounds them and to which they not only *have* but also commonly *seek* easy access. (Fishman 1991:196)

According to Lida, it is the influence of Americanization and democratization which made everyone want to hide the fact that they were first-generation citizens and to appear as "American" as possible (1962:1038). How many first-generation Americans can recall their parents telling them: "We are Americans now, so we speak English." This attitude was also reinforced in the schools, which taught directly or indirectly that the non-Anglo culture the child came from was inferior to the "American" culture. Thus, one did everything to avoid use of a foreign language or observance of customs making him or her different from other "Yankees." Today this American attitude toward other cultures and the use of a foreign language is changing, but unfortunately not in time to save Judeo-Spanish. And as Fishman and Lida point out, this new sophistication mostly applies to the learning of a second foreign language by the English-speaking Americans, rather than to the native language of the ethnic minorities (Fishman 1972:50 and Lida 1962:1038).

The Levantine Sephardim in the United States were encouraged to learn English not only by governmental and school authorities, but were even under pressure from other American Sephardic groups as well. The sisterhood of the Shearith Israel Synagogue of New York ran a neighborhood settlement house on the Lower East Side in the early 1900s, where they emphasized the need for the newly arrived Balkan Sephardim to become Americanized (Angel 1974:104). Other important individuals and groups within the Sephardi community also advocated Americanization and encouraged the Sephardim to study and apply for American citizenship. In the columns of *La America,*[3] America's first Judeo-Spanish weekly newspaper published from 1910 to 1925 in New York, the editor, Moise Gadol, constantly encouraged the Spanish-speaking Sephardim to attend English classes so that they could become good American citizens (Angel 1982:108). He even included English lessons in the pages of *La America.* In Gadol's frequent articles and those of other Judeo-Spanish newspapers and bulletins, as well as in English classes offered by various Sephardic organizations, the value of Judeo-Spanish was rarely, if ever mentioned; nor were there any efforts to promote maintenance of the mother tongue. Thus, Judeo-Spanish was one of the first Sephardi characteristics to disappear as English took over under the powerful forces of Americanization or assimilation.

Another reason for the rapid shift to English is the fact that in the United States (as well as in Israel) the immigrant populations were extremely heterogeneous, possessing no common language which could be shared. Thus English in the United States provided the necessary *lingua franca* to unite the diverse ethnic groups. As Lieberson and Curry suggest, when such diversity (of groups and languages) exists, the resistance to language shift is reduced (Lieberson and Curry 1981:164).

5. Israelization

So much of the cultural and linguistic assimilation into Israeli society on the part of Jewish immigrants is tied up with Zionism, the building of a Jewish State, and the resulting revival of the Hebrew language. Hofman and Fisherman write:

> Uprootedness is one of the basic motives of Zionism. Jews who came to Palestine and later to Israel were in many cases alienated from their countries of origin and often from Jewish culture itself. This was especially the case after the holocaust of World War II. The displaced and disillusioned refugees who settled shortly after the establishment of the State of Israel could not be expected to show much language loyalty. (1972:353)

In an effort to build a Jewish nation, the policy to unite all Jews, and thus the elimination of the main differences between them, was/is supported by Israel's nationalistic tendencies. Zimmels reminds us that in the Diaspora, both Ashkenazim and Sephardim were subjected to the influences of various countries; whereas in Israel, all Jews were governed by the same conditions and closer ties aimed at the development of a more "Israeli" type of Jewry (1958:81). Assimilation has been hastened to a large extent by various factors such as the small size of the country (about the size of the state of New Jersey), urbanization, an excellent system of public transportation which encourages interaction among Israeli citizens, a national system of education and the participation of almost every male in the armed services from the ages of eighteen to fifty-five (Cooper 1985:79). Both the national education and obligatory military service are especially strong homogenizing influences that encourage the use of Hebrew over the various ethnic languages.

The revival of Hebrew was an extraordinary linguistic undertaking that played an important role in Israel's history and became a symbol of Jewish independence.[4] The speaking of Hebrew in Palestine was crucial to the Zionists' vision:

> modern Zionism generally envisioned an internally unified, culturally modernized and homogenized, 'reborn' people, in its old homeland and

not only speaking its old language but speaking *only* its old language, insofar as its internal life was concerned. . . . For most, there could be no question but that only Hebrew could rekindle the Jewish 'national soul' and lead it back to the towering moral and cultural grandeur ('albeit in a modern way') of the classical Jewish past. (Fishman 1991:307–8)

In Hofman's article, he refers to Modern Hebrew, which was revived to serve special needs, as a "deliberately contrived product" that started out as little more than a literary symbol of the religion and has developed into the common denominator of Israeli statehood (1985:51). Later, when discussing the reason for the choice of Hebrew to be the national language of Israel, he writes:

Surely, it would have been more "instrumental" to use one or two of the languages that Jews had traditionally used, such as Yiddish or Ladino, or even a language of wider communication such as German. . . . Yet only Hebrew could be the unifying force needed by the Zionist cause to overcome the many ethnic and linguistic divisions within the immigrating community. (1985:54)

The use of Hebrew in Israel makes the Jews *Israeli Jews* versus Jews from other countries.

For Sephardic as well as other immigrants, to speak Hebrew is a necessity in Israel—it is the *lingua franca* in the Babel of languages where more than thirteen languages are spoken and published. The young Sephardim (if they even know the language) leave Judeo-Spanish to their parents and the intimacy of the home. In fact, many parents did not teach or expose their children to Judeo-Spanish at all, since the speaking of Hebrew was of vital nationalistic importance to the establishment of Israel as a Jewish State. The cry "We're Israeli, speak Hebrew!" was common in many Sephardic homes, even among Sephardim whose family roots had been in Palestine for over two hundred years.

Besides being the national language of Israel, Hebrew is the language needed to "get ahead" as is English in the United States. Hofman and Fisherman remind us that "the all-important need to make a living in a competitive society inexorably strengthens the shift to Hebrew" (1972:364). As far as the Sephardic immigrants to Israel are concerned, there would be no need to maintain Judeo-Spanish except for emotional reasons such as the attachment to the mother tongue. From the moment of arrival in Israel, the emphasis in the government supported *ulpanim* (Hebrew schools for immigrants) was to teach Hebrew to all newcomers, thus discouraging any mother tongue maintenance. And although they appreciate the language and have encouraged studies of it, the organizations which were eventually established to study Sephardic culture and history[5] have never considered the propagation of Judeo-Spanish to be a vital concern.

6. The French Influence—the Alliance Israélite Universelle Schools in the Levant

In 1860 a group of young French Jewish intellectuals gathered in Paris, and, under the initiative of Adolphe Crémieux, formed the Alliance Israélite Universelle to promote universal emancipation and equality among the Jews. One of the goals proposed by the Alliance was the propagation of Western culture and civilization among the Oriental Jews in the Levant and North Africa, which were considered to be underdeveloped countries. The Alliance was the organization which worked the hardest to raise the cultural level of the Jews of the Mediterranean and neighboring countries. Alliance schools were founded in Constantinople/Istanbul beginning in 1865, Adrianople in 1867, Salonika and Izmir in 1873, Shumen in 1870, Sofia in 1879, Monastir in 1895, and Jerusalem in 1882 (Renard 1966a:96, and Israel 1960:53–55, 67). By 1910 there were 116 Alliance schools spread throughout the Balkans, Turkey, Palestine, Morocco, Egypt, and Tunisia (Benardete 1982:150).

The language of instruction in most of the Alliance schools was French, and they refused to teach Spanish (except in Tetuan and Tangiers), even though the Hispano-Levantine Jews spoke Judeo-Spanish at home. As Rodrigue reports, part of the Alliance's "civilizing mission" was to eradicate the use of Judeo-Spanish (1990:85). Obviously the establishment of Alliance schools in the Levant dealt a severe blow to the life of Judeo-Spanish. Benardete, along with others such as Pulido (1905), felt that if the Alliance had understood "the importance of teaching Spanish to the Hispano-Levantines, as she did in the case of the Jews of Tangiers and Tetuan, the Spanish language might then have recovered its vitality in the Orient" (Benardete 1982:149).

There is no doubt that the Alliance did a great job of Westernizing the Sephardim. Whether or not it was intended, the Alliance schools were converted into agents of French imperialism. Little by little the new generations became "frankeados" or Frenchified, as they were introduced to the great French writers: Hugo, Balzac, Rabelais, Racine, Voltaire, and Molière. Albert Matarasso, in one of his manuscripts, describes such Frenchification: "As soon as the Alliance arrived, we took off the skull cap, we set aside the shawl and the phylacteries, and instead of reading the Bible, we began to read the novels of Victor Hugo" (Barocas 1976:151). It was through the French language and French culture that the Levantine Sephardim became familiar with *Don Quichotte* (the French spelling and pronunciation), instead of *Don Quijote*; that is, if they were lucky enough to be exposed to the writers and thinkers of the Spanish Golden Age at all.

According to Renard (1971:721), one cannot overemphasize the importance of the prestige of French in the acceleration of the disintegration process of Judeo-Spanish. Gradually more and more French words penetrated into the speech of the Sephardim, who used French often to demonstrate their elevated cultural level. French influence manifested itself not only in the form of new words, but also in the modification of already existing ones. That is, Spanish words were gallicized and even the syntax became somewhat gallicized (see chap. 5). So well did French penetrate into the *juderías*, that it became very common to give children French names like *Marguerite, Suzanne, Rose, Alber(t), Rober(t),* and *Jak* (from Jacques), which replaced Sephardic names such as *Reyna, Roza, Luna, Gracia, Estrella,* and *Avraham* (Díaz-Mas 1986:111 and Sephiha 1986:96).

French influence was never so apparent as in the Judeo-Spanish press, which was started in the nineteenth century in the Levant (see chapter 6 section no. 8). On examination of various newspaper texts of the time, it is obvious that the majority of the journalists had received their education in Alliance schools. The spelling was *a la franka* or *à la française,* and press words such as *borsa* and *portraito,* versus the everyday Spanish words *bolsa* 'stock exchange' and *retrato* 'portrait,' were common. Various scholars, such as Besso (1970:256), have criticized the press of the end of the nineteenth and beginning of the twentieth centuries because of its "corruption" of the language. They feel that it represents perhaps one of the worst models of Judeo-Spanish, which frustrated its future since it contained so many gallicisms. Due to the extent of gallicization in the Judeo-Spanish press of the time, Dr. A. S. Yahuda wrote that "the modern Judeo-Spanish press and novelesque literature are so Frenchified that perhaps it would be more exact to refer to them as Judeo-French rather than Judeo-Spanish" (Yahuda 1915:343). Max Nordau[6] gave a perfect example of what he calls a "true corruption" due to French influence (Pulido 1905:48). He cited the name of a Judeo-Spanish newspaper published in Salonika from 1897 to 1916. This paper was entitled *El Avenir* 'The Future,' which is a combination of the Spanish definite article *el* plus the French word for "future" *avenir,* instead of the Spanish word *porvenir.* Besides the gallicization of the Judeo-Spanish language, many French newspapers, magazines, and books of all kinds invaded the Sephardic communities at this time.

Sephiha, in talking about the French influence on Judeo-Spanish with the arrival of the Alliance, reports that before 1865, the phonology, lexicon and syntax of Judeo-Spanish remained very close to the Spanish of the fifteenth century (1987b:157). However, after the influence of the Alliance and a heavy Frenchified Judeo-Spanish press, the language underwent so much gallicization that the result was a new state of the language which he calls *judéofragnol* 'Jewish French' (Sephiha 1987b:159). As explained in chapter 5 (Foreign Influences), he uses the term *gallomanie galopante* 'galloping gallicization' expressly because it has medical overtones of a galloping disease, in this case French influence. And he writes of a "contagiousness that revealed itself at all levels: phonetic, morphological, lexical, and syntactic" (1986:107).

Many like Pulido (1905) and Besso (Hassán 1970:389) have criticized the Alliance schools in the Levant for not trying to propagate the Spanish language. But others like Revah and Kahanoff feel that it is not fair to put the blame for Judeo-Spanish's decline completely on the Alliance. Revah points out that toward 1860 the world had changed as a result of scientific, industrial and technical revolutions. A language was needed to describe modern technology. This language could not be Turkish because the Turks had never been interested in spreading their language to the non-Islamic minorities, and besides, they themselves had not yet adapted to modern European life (Hassán 1970:388). Thus according to Kahanoff, the Alliance and the French language filled a void and responded to an urgent need by propagating a vigorous Western culture, which was received enthusiastically by many Sephardim (Hassán 1970:391). A good number of Sephardim realized the backwardness of their culture in the Levant and the mediocrity of their educational system. Therefore, they wanted to participate in the progress accomplished by public instruction in the industrialized countries. The Alliance schools opened new doors to better living conditions, to new professions and business undertakings and to emigration to more progressive regions. And besides, the French language was not only the international language of diplomacy, but was also considered at that time to be the language of modern civilization *par excellence.*

Thus it was not necessary to wait long for the French language to become the language of the elite. At the same time the Sephardim's mother tongue was relegated to the level of a "vulgar and common patois" (Renard 1961:49), to be kept in the intimacy of the home and family:

> The Alliance was hence instrumental in the creation of a Francophone Jewish middle class. . . . Judeo-Spanish remained the language of the home, though it was displaced by French in many cases, while French became the language of culture. (Rodrigue 1990:171–72)

Given this type of bilingual-diglossic situation, it was inevitable that Judeo-Spanish would be greatly influenced by French, and in many cases for the younger generations, replaced by it. As far as the younger generations were concerned, what value could Judeo-Spanish have for them as opposed to French or other European languages like Italian? (see the following section).

7. Other Foreign Influences: A Polyglot Mixture

The Judeo-Spanish press of the nineteenth century is probably the worst example of Judeo-Spanish (as stated above), not only because of the great number of gallicisms but also because of influences from other languages—notably from Italian. The Italian government had established schools of the *Centro Dante Alighieri* in the large cities in the Levant even before the establishment of the French Alliance schools. These Italian schools always had a high percentage of Sephardi students. Thus, from the middle of the nineteenth century, Italian was exercising a notable influence with aspirations to convert itself into the language of Mediterranean trade (see chapter 5).

Italian and French loans often competed with each other and were more effective as soon as Judeo-Spanish was no longer used as a language of instruction or as a liturgical language in the Jewish schools. The Italian and French schools were very well organized with good professors and had access to good materials. They appeared at a time when the Sephardim were ready to be exposed to a new European culture, which the Italian and French languages could easily provide.

Turkish was the Balkan language having the most influence on Judeo-Spanish and from which the Sephardim borrowed many words in order to express certain daily needs in the material and administrative realms (see chap. 5). According to Sala (1970a:16), as this quantity of borrowings increased, the spoken Judeo-Spanish became progressively farther removed from the written language. Kraus informs us that many of the new arrivals to Israel from 1937 to 1952 received whatever education they had in Turkish public schools. And since by this time Judeo-Spanish was rarely spoken in public, it had become more impoverished, and the Sephardim were forced to resort to Turkish words to fill in the gaps (Kraus 1952:406).

As far as Hebrew is concerned, it always enjoyed great prestige as a liturgical language among the Sephardim. But in the seventeenth century, it also triumphed over Spanish as the language of piety in the literary academies of Constantinople and Salonika. Benardete tells us that it was the excessive use of Hebrew in the Spanish of the masses that indicated a highly cultivated person. The use of Hebrew words instead of Spanish words resulted in the diminishing use of Spanish as a daily language, but only among the well educated (Benardete 1982:116).

Hebrew enjoyed a resurrection with the advent of Zionism in the late 1800s and early 1900s. Newspapers such as *Yosset Daath* or *El Progresso* in Adrianople, with articles in Hebrew next to their Judeo-Spanish translations, soon began to appear. Zionist efforts favored the total abandonment of Judeo-Spanish. Tamir informs us that in Bulgaria by 1912, the French Alliance schools were no longer under the jurisdiction of Bulgarian Jewish education, and Hebrew was established as the principal language in Jewish schools (1979:154). Also, in Yugoslavia a strong Zionist colony arose in which Hebrew took precedence over Spanish. Thus, with the upsurge of Zionism, Hebrew began to function as a unifying force for both Sephardic and Ashkenazic Jews in the Balkans.

In discussing foreign influences on the evolution of Judeo-Spanish, we must emphasize the multilingualism of the Sephardim, especially in the Ottoman Empire. Judeo-Spanish was not in contact with just one language in the Balkans, but with several different languages. Wagner reminds us that the Balkans were a linguistic Babylon where many languages interacted. He reported in Constantinople that "any youth from a good Levantine family knows how to express himself in at least six languages" (1930:45). And the six languages *de riguer* were Turkish, Greek, French, Italian, English, and German. The Sephardim were no exception. They spoke Judeo-Spanish in the home, used Hebrew in the synagogue, and their intellectual life was imbued with French or Italian through their schooling. In order to earn a living they also had to speak the language(s) of the region in which they lived; that is, Turkish, Greek, Bulgarian, Serbo-Croatian, or Rumanian. Many of the Sephardim were able to converse equally fluently in all these languages. The result was often "a conglomerated mixture of French, Spanish, Italian, Turkish and Hebrew without internal cohesion and without any efforts toward uniformity of style or eloquence of expression" (Besso 1970:255).[7] The newspaper *Selanik,* published in Salonika from 1869 to 1874, illustrates the multilanguage situation of the Balkans, since it was published in four languages: Judeo-Spanish, Turkish, Greek, and Bulgarian.

According to Sala (1970b:53), given that Judeo-Spanish is declining, it seems to suffer the influence of the languages with which it comes into contact more intensely than does a more vigorous language. The various borrowings into Judeo-Spanish have resulted in a kind of polyglot mixture, which definitely has aided in the disintegration of the language.

8. Absorption by Other Romance Languages

The more similar an ascending language is to a declining language, the faster the latter will decline or be absorbed. And when two languages of the same family come into contact, and one is in the process of disappearing, the disappearing language tends to borrow the common characteristics of the language which is replacing it (Sala 1970c:75). Sala states that when a Judeo-Spanish word is identical or nearly identical in form to the Rumanian or French word, the original meaning of the Judeo-Spanish term is lost by some informants and is generally replaced by the meaning of the Rumanian or French term. He refers to this kind of borrowing as a *calco homofónico* or "homophonic calque" (Sala 1970c:76).[8]

As far as replacement by another Romance language is concerned, Judeo-Spanish disappeared in Italy in the middle of the nineteenth century due in large part to the similarities of Judeo-Spanish and Italian. In Rumania the similarities between Judeo-Spanish and Rumanian have contributed to the almost complete replacement of the former by the latter (Sala 1970a:23). A couple of Sephardi newspapers printed in Rumanian such as *Viata Sefarda* and *Gazeta Evreului Spaniol* definitely hastened Rumanian's entrance into the intimacy of the home.

In Morocco and Latin America Judeo-Spanish was easily absorbed by Modern Spanish. Due to the very close similarities of the two languages, archaic forms and foreign characteristics of

Judeo-Spanish were replaced by the Modern Spanish forms. The influence of Modern Spanish on the Judeo-Spanish of New York and Los Angeles is discussed in chapter 10.

9. Hebrew is Reinforced as the Language of Religion and was Revived as the National Language of Israel

Religion, the main Sephardic institution which resisted assimilation in the Ottoman Empire, was not an effective mechanism in promoting language maintenance for the Sephardim in the United States. This is also true for other ethnic groups in the United States. For first generation Hungarian and Ukrainian immigrants, for example, the Catholic Church did initially offer services in the mother tongue, but eventually the Church took on an increasing de-ethnizing or secular role (Fishman 1966b and Nahirny and Fishman 1966). The Sephardim were faced with a more rapid shift from the beginning, since the use of Judeo-Spanish in the synagogues was rarely encouraged. Except for a few prayers and chants, Hebrew, always the religious language of the Jews, was considered to be the only liturgical language.

With its revival or "vernacularization" (Fishman 1991:291), Hebrew assumed the role of not only the national language of Palestine/Israel, but also the international language of the Jews (see section 5). Hebrew also represented the Jewish language of the future. Sephardic groups themselves started clubs in New York such as the Hebrew Sephardi Club of Harlem (established by the students of the Talmud Torah in 1918) for the purpose of fostering the Hebrew language. Zionist organizations were also formed to encourage the teaching and spread of Hebrew as its revival was taking place in Palestine. Also, the efforts in Palestine/Israel to revive Hebrew as a spoken language naturally insured its place as the predominant language of both religion and daily conversation. But more importantly, Hebrew's position as the international Jewish language raised its prestige level compared with that of Judeo-Spanish.

10. Relaxation of Religious Observances

The decaying of the Sephardic culture in the Balkans, and later in the United States and Israel, was accompanied by a relaxation of religious observances and ultimately a serious movement away from the Sephardi synagogue. As Altabé writes of the Sephardim after coming to the United States:

> The need to work, to earn a living, to establish themselves in their new country, to raise children . . . forced many of them to work on the Sabbath, and to abandon, some to a greater extent than others, the religious practices they had been taught. Their children received, in most cases, even less religious training than they had had. (1981:18)

Thus the youth lost interest in orthodox tenets, traditional services and the Bible, whose translations into Ladino taught many generations their knowledge of Judeo-Spanish (Hassán 1963:178). Religion, which had been the mainstay of Sephardic culture in the Ottoman Empire, was no longer the cohesive force it had formerly been for the Sephardim, a situation which could only have a decaying effect on the language.

In Israel the role of religion has changed. Since the majority of Israelis are Jewish, religion is no longer the crucial identifying characteristic for the Sephardim that it was in their countries of origin. Thus it assumes a secondary role. What has become of primary importance for the Sephardim, as well as for other immigrant groups, is assimilation into Israeli society. This means that the ethnic languages like Judeo-Spanish are replaced by Hebrew.

11. No Sephardic Schools to Promote Religion or Sephardic Culture

Angel points out the Sephardi's lack of ability or interest in fomenting Sephardic culture, practices, and history after emigration to the United States (1974:100–1, 105). Since the Sephardim were too busy trying to establish themselves, they did not have the economic means, time, or talent to set up schools or *yeshivot* for their children. And since they were not equipped to train enough Sephardi rabbis, their children attended Ashkenazic schools under Ashkenazic leadership or went to public schools. Consequently, Sephardic history and culture were rarely taught, which resulted in a lack of awareness of their Sephardi heritage on the part of the children. This means that until fairly recently, the majority of Sephardim (not to mention Ashkenazim) knew/know very little of their post Expulsion history in the Levant. Even in Israel, many of my Sephardi informants, including those whose family roots in Jerusalem go back two or more centuries, told me that the only

Jewish history they had ever studied was Ashkenazic history, rather than Sephardic history (Harris 1979:255).

According to Angel, the older generations have shown their children the external features of Sephardic culture but have not sufficiently passed on the history and philosophy of the Sephardim. Lacking a good religious and Sephardic education, many of the young, educated Sephardim are dissatisfied with what appears to be a superficial culture, and they are disenchanted with Judaism in general (Angel 1971:10–11). They have drifted away by intermarrying with Ashkenazic Jews or non-Jews, by moving into non-Sephardi neighborhoods having no Sephardi synagogues, or by assimilating into the American culture. Thus the younger generation is not vitally interested in the Sephardic community's survival or in the survival of the Judeo-Spanish language. And as sociolinguists Blom and Gumperz point out, it is the identification with peer groups, rather than with the family, which often determines the choice of a language or dialect (Blom and Gumperz 1972:434).

12. No Language Academy or Central Organization to Establish Linguistic Norms

There does not exist, nor has there ever existed for Judeo-Spanish, a central language academy or council (such as in France, Spain, and Israel). Such an organization was desperately needed to establish orthographic norms, uniformity of forms or derivations, coining of neologisms, and the handling of borrowings, all of which became especially chaotic after Judeo-Spanish was transliterated into Roman letters from Rashi script. Nor is there any literary language which can serve as a model. This lack of uniformity aided in the reduction of comprehension among Judeo-Spanish speakers (Sala 1970b:64–65), which may have had the effect on many of encouraging a preference for use of another language. In an article written in 1939 on Judeo-Spanish in Turkey, Spitzer wrote that Judeo-Spanish syntax was "part Turkish and French" and that the language was in such a state that "there is no certainty in the use of words: one Sephardi says *influensa,* another: *influensia* and a third: *influyo,* all referring to the word *influencia*" (Spitzer 1939:10). In my research, I also found a great deal of individual variation or fluctuation of forms.[9] This type of discrepancy or individual variation is a common phenomenon which accompanies languages in decline.

13. Limited Education in the Mother Tongue—Illiteracy in Judeo-Spanish

Besides the fact that no language academy ever existed, another reason for the lack of uniformity in Judeo-Spanish can be attributed to the fact that the mass of Levantine Sephardim were not taught Judeo-Spanish in any methodical way in the schools.[10] It was a language that was learned in the home, while they studied French, Turkish, Greek, Bulgarian, Hebrew, and other languages in schools in the Levant. In fact, there were no accessible published grammar books on the Judeo-Spanish language. Since they rarely received grammatical instruction in the language, the Balkan Sephardim often conjugated verbs erroneously by analogy with either French or Italian conjugations (see chapter 5).

Another result of not having received instruction in the language itself at school, was that many of the Balkan Sephardim were never officially taught to read Judeo-Spanish, a situation similar to that of Pennsylvania German in the United States (Huffines 1980:50). This resulted in a high level of illiteracy in the language. Nehama (1965:339) informs us that by the middle of the eighteenth century, the majority of the needy classes in Salonika did not know how to read or write, the middle classes retained the oral ritual of Ladino, while only the bourgeois class had limited access to printing in Hebrew. He also reminds us that girls were excluded from all education. Therefore, by the time the Balkan Sephardim arrived in Israel and the United States many native speakers were illiterate in Judeo-Spanish, and it was not rare to find people who could not read the Hebrew alphabet at all.

Zengel (1962:132–39) has shown that a literate culture correlates to some degree with a tendency toward linguistic conservatism, that is, literacy tends to act as a regulatory force. This curb or check on the printed word tends to retard change and limit borrowings and other outside influences. Fishman also points out the importance of literacy to the maintenance of a language: "Where literacy has been attained prior to interaction with an 'other tongue,' reading or writing in the mother tongue may resist shift longer than speaking" (1977:79). As the number of illiterates grew, it is only natural that Judeo-Spanish was affected.

Another reason for the low literacy rate in Judeo-Spanish is the fact that the language was written in Hebrew characters or Rashi script until the 1920s, and later in Roman letters, which had no standardized system of orthography (see the following section). According to Huffines, the lack of a standard orthography in Pennsylvania German also contributes to the low literacy level in that language and is one of the reasons for its decline (Huffines 1980:53).

14. Use of the Hebrew Alphabet and Rashi Script instead of the Latin Alphabet

To represent their language in written form, the Sephardim used the Hebrew alphabet, which is characteristically used in all Jewish languages. The form generally used for printed matter is called Rashi script, named after *Ra*bbi *Sh*elomo *I*tshak of Troyes (1040–1105). A type of cursive writing known as *solitreo* was generally used for the everyday writing of manuscripts, business transactions, and personal correspondence. This abandonment of the Latin alphabet had disastrous consequences for the future of Judeo-Spanish after expulsion, since the Sephardim became completely isolated from the West and all contact with the mother country was interrupted. This nonuse of the Latin alphabet caused a total break with the literary development of Spain, which at that time (the sixteenth century) was entering into its Golden Age, thus reducing the possibility of drawing from the lexicon of the Peninsula.

The fact that Jews in the Balkans did not have access to Spanish books printed in Latin characters also contributed somewhat to their intellectual decline. Only the very cultured in the Levant could acquire Castilian materials printed in Spain while others did not even know the Latin alphabet, since no works were published in Latin letters on their presses. Printing in the Latin alphabet did not begin in the Balkans until the latter part of the eighteenth century.

Nehama felt that writing in Hebrew characters instead of the Latin alphabet cut the Sephardim off from the western world as well as from contact with the mother country (1936:206–7). M. Molho goes so far as to state that "the total abandonment of the Spanish (Latin) alphabet was the essential cause of the intellectual decline of Judaism in Turkey" (1960:139). And Camhy refers to Judeo-Spanish as being "locked up in the ghetto of the Hebrew alphabet" (1971:599). Dr. Pulido (1905:332) affirmed that use of the Hebrew alphabet was another factor which contributed to the ignorance of many Sephardim who did not know that they spoke a form of Spanish as opposed to simply a Jewish language (see the following section).

Besides inhibiting cultural and linguistic development, use of the Hebrew alphabet was at times phonetically insufficient or confusing, since certain Hebrew letters could not differentiate between all the consonants while others could represent more than one Spanish vowel. This confusion was yet another factor that led to individual variations which, according to some linguists like Sjoestedt (1928:101) and Sala (1970b:64), denote a pathological state of the language and can, in some instances, result in a lack of comprehension on the part of various speakers (see chapter 10).

15. Complete Break of Relations with Spain

The complete break of relations with Spain resulted in mutual ignorance of the Spaniards in Spain and the Sephardim of the Levant. This mutual ignorance was due in part to the indifference of the Spanish government to *los españoles sin patria,* 'the Spaniards without a country/homeland'.[11] The mother country never tried to establish any cultural contact with the Sephardim after expulsion. According to various scholars such as Camhy (1971:560), a language requires its own soil or land. For Jews, the Spanish language went through the same exile as did the people. Separated from Spain both physically and spiritually, it lost its cultural milieu and thus nourishment from the Peninsular dialects. The Jews in the Balkans never did develop as rich a culture as they had built in Spain.

The break with Spain also produced an interesting result: many of the Sephardim were not aware that they spoke Spanish, a European language. They only thought that they spoke a Jewish language.[12] In a letter dated 8 September 1904 to A. Pulido thanking him for having sent Spanish newspapers (written in Latin letters) to the Sephardic community of Izmir, Rafael Cohen reported that one of the members of the community had asked him, "Is it true that we speak a European language? Don't we speak Jewish?" (Pulido 1905:52). Max Nordau reported hearing a woman in a post office in Belgrade speak to her husband in Judeo-Spanish. When he asked her if she was speaking Spanish she replied: "No, Sir, I'm speaking *Ǧudiyo.*" Her husband then informed Nordau that his wife was not well-educated, because, if she had known, she would say she spoke Spanish (Pulido 1905:47). Luria describes a conversation between two elderly Monastirli women in New York, one of whom was surprised that the language of Spain was similar to that of Monastir. The other woman had to explain to her friend: *Ma somuz ispañolis!* 'But we are Spanish!' (Luria 1930:9).

There are many reported incidents in which the Sephardim, on emigrating to Mexico, Argentina, or Cuba had to correct their erroneous first impression that everyone there was Jewish since they all spoke Spanish (Besso 1970:251). Even the non-Jews of the Balkans associated the Spanish language with Jews. Estrugo (1933:36) informs us that when the Spanish ship *Jaime I* docked in Constantinople in 1924, the Turks and Greeks thought that a Jewish ship had arrived since the crew members spoke the language of the *juderías*. Such instances were common. D. Moises Abravanel wrote that the arrival in Salonika of two singers from Spain caused the citizens to exclaim: "Hear how they speak, they're Jews!" (Pulido 1905:442).

The association of Judeo-Spanish only with a Jewish language rather than also with a European-Romance language was so strong that many older Sephardim felt that anyone who did not speak Spanish was not Jewish. This meant that the Ashkenazim were not considered to be Jews. It must be pointed out here that the opposite occurred in the United States in the early 1900s, when the Ashkenazim felt that anyone (especially the newly arrived immigrants from the Balkans) who did not speak Yiddish could not possibly be Jewish (see section no. 17 and chapter 7). This lack of awareness of the broader origin of their language could only aid in its decline, since Judeo-Spanish in the minds of many Sephardim had a more limited or isolated use. This often resulted in the questioning of its value as a language to be maintained and perpetuated in a broader, ever changing world.

16. No Prestigious Judeo-Spanish Literature

In regard to literature, Judeo-Spanish does not have the prestige that Yiddish has enjoyed. Judeo-Spanish literature, unlike Yiddish literature, has not developed universally, due mostly to the fact that Sephardic culture could only decline in the Balkans where the cultural level was inferior and where political instability reigned. Among the Sephardim there was not the same ghetto mentality resulting in writers like the Ashkenazic authors Mendele Mocher Sforim, Sholom Aleichem, Isaac Bashevis Singer and others. This type of figure is unknown to the Sephardim, since Sephardic life in the Levant more closely resembled Spanish life than Eastern European ghetto life (see chapter 3). According to Malaji (1939:79), these Yiddish writers performed the miracle of transforming a jargon into a language. On the other hand, the Judeo-Spanish literary accomplishments were not as significant.

The most important work in Judeo-Spanish was the *Me'am Lo'ez* of Rabbi Jacob Huli, published in 1730 (see chapter 6 section number 6). Besides the *Me'am Lo'ez, romanzas* (ballads), and *refranes* (proverbs), much of the literature published in Judeo-Spanish consists of translations of works from other languages such as Hebrew, French, German, Turkish, Italian, Greek, and Bulgarian. There are also translations of the Bible and liturgical, ethico-religious, and kabbalistic works, as well as adaptations of novels. A small number of *romansos* or original novels were also written in Judeo-Spanish, but they were not considered to be prestigious works. In interviews with Sephardim who were young adults when they left Turkey and the Balkans immediately before World War I, Altabé reported:

> those who wished to do serious reading would turn to the masterpieces of French literature in the original, or to religious works in Hebrew. The Judeo-Spanish novels were designed for light reading. They were the literature of the masses. (1977–78:104)

This lack of a prestigious written literature resulted in the absence of a linguistic authority or regulator. According to Resnick:

> It is not possible to conserve a language by mere tradition if it is not cultivated in a literary way. The disgrace of Judeo-Spanish lies in not having arrived to be a literary instrument, in not having left its primitive state. Its literary production is insignificant. (1939:5–6)

Another problem caused by the lack of a rich literary tradition in Judeo-Spanish, has been a tendency by many of the most educated Sephardi descendants to lose attachment or fondness for Judeo-Spanish and to look for their spiritual fulfillment, knowledge, and literary stimulation from other sources. It is hard for the Sephardi youth, who are not as devoted to religious tradition as their ancestors were, to be content with the archaic Judeo-Spanish literature. The few current Sephardi writers living in Israel or other parts of the world, such as Elias Canetti, who won the Nobel Prize for Literature in 1981, do not write in Judeo-Spanish. Instead they write in French, German, English, Hebrew, or other languages. Not only has the low literacy rate and lack of a substantial literature discouraged writers and intellectuals from writing in Judeo-Spanish, but, as in the case of Breton (Timm 1980:40), very few scholars in recent years have developed an interest in the language itself for research purposes.

17. Contact with Ashkenazim—Ashkenization

By the early 1900s when the first wave of Sephardic immigrants from the Balkans were arriving in the United States, the Ashkenazic Jews from Eastern Europe were already established in New York City, and the Sephardim found themselves to be a minority within the minority of American Jewry. Since the Ashkenazim form the Jewish majority in America, their brand of Jewishness has come to be considered as a standard stereotype. That is, Ashkenazic foods such as knishes, gefilte fish, blintzes, lox and bagels, as well as Yiddish words and expressions and the Eastern European *shtetl* culture, are considered the only Jewish attributes or characteristics, not only by American gentiles but by the Ashkenazim as well. Sephardic foods such as *borekas* (a pastry filled with cheese, eggplant, spinach or meat), *fritadas* (souffles), *keftes* (meat patties), and other aspects of Sephardic culture such as the *romanzas,* are generally unknown to Ashkenazic Jews. Not only did the Sephardim have different rituals and customs from the Ashkenazim, but they did not speak Yiddish. According to Luria (1930–1:8) and many of my informants, one of the hardest things facing the new Sephardi immigrants after arrival in the United States, was a lack of understanding on the part of the Ashkenazic majority, who could not conceive of the existence of Jews who did not speak Yiddish or at least German or a Slavic language (see chapter 7). Thus the Sephardim were put in the defensive position of trying to prove to the Ashkenazim that they were Jews. Moise Gadol hoped that his newspaper *La America,* which was printed in Hebrew characters, would be influential in making the Ashkenazim believe that the Sephardim were indeed Jews. Occasionally Gadol published articles written in Yiddish expressly intended for the Ashkenazic population. He represented the Ashkenazim as good examples of upward mobility, who attended English and citizenship classes in large numbers and who were becoming "the leading industrialists, teachers, doctors, and lawyers" of the period (Angel 1982:56). Gadol not only urged the Sephardim to follow their example, but he even encouraged them to learn Yiddish, so that they would have an easier time finding a job and working for Yiddish-speaking employers. Gadol even provided the Yiddish equivalent

of Judeo-Spanish words in some of his language lesson sections of
La America.

In Palestine the Ashkenazic immigrants became the majority
population around World War I or shortly thereafter, and they occupied the most powerful government positions as Palestine approached Jewish Statehood. Presently the Ashkenazim still hold
the most important and prestigious government positions in Israel,
but their numbers are decreasing. Today in Israel both Sephardic
and Oriental Jews (those Jews originating from Arab or Moslem
countries) are politically grouped together and are referred to generally as Sephardim (see Elazar 1989). Since these non-Ashkenazic
Jews presently constitute approximately 55 percent of Israel's
population, changes are in the making. However, there are still
many conflicts and problems between Ashkenazim and Sephardim
that need to be addressed.

Also, since very little Sephardi rabbinical training exists, or ever
existed in the United States,[13] the Ashkenazic rabbis of most Sephardic congregations have been limited in their efforts to foster
Sephardic culture.[14] Further, several Sephardic synagogues, such
as New York's Congregation Shearith Israel which was founded
by Sephardim, now have memberships which are about 50 percent
Ashkenazic.[15] Thus the Sephardim in America are slowly becoming
Ashkenazified. To be Jewish in America is to be Ashkenazic. Because of this dilemma, the young Sephardi has three choices according to Rabbi Marc Angel of Shearith Israel:

> He may try to delve into his own history and culture, renewing himself
> as a Sephardi. He may assimilate into the Ashkenazi community. He
> may, tragically, find no tie to Judaism at all, seeing that his notions of
> Judaism are inextricably tied to his Sephardic roots and that these
> roots have now become weakened. (1971:9)

The newly arrived Sephardic immigrants from the Levant were
put in an awkward position due to their lower economic and political status, as well as their general lower educational level, compared to that of the Ashkenazim. The Ashkenazim not only had
difficulty accepting them, but often discriminated against them because they had no idea what to do with these unfortunate Jews
who did not promote the Jewish image the Ashkenazim were trying
to build in America. And as Angel points out, where Ashkenazic
discrimination against Sephardim has been more noticeable, the
Sephardim have tended to think less of themselves and their culture (Angel 1974:134). As a result of these feelings of inferiority,

there were those who were eager to embrace the way of life of the Ashkenazic majority. This included not only adopting Ashkenazic practices and joining Ashkenazic synagogues, but also marrying Ashkenazic spouses.

18. Intermarriage

Much intermarriage also results because larger masses generally absorb smaller ones, and the Sephardic population (Judeo-Spanish speakers and their descendants) in both the United States and Israel is much smaller than the Ashkenazic one. While the Sephardic immigrant generation in the United States had Sephardic spouses, Angel reports that Ashkenazic-Sephardic marriages of third generation Americans are quite common. In fact he writes that "they have become the rule, rather than the exception" (Angel 1974:128). Today about 75 percent of young Sephardim originating from Judeo-Spanish-speaking families marry Ashkenazim (Angel 1982:178).

In Israel there is also a high number of mixed Ashkenazic–Sephardic marriages. In fact, one of my Israeli informants in his seventies, whose wife was Ashkenazic, reported that the spouses of most of his Sephardic friends were also Ashkenazic. And he jokingly said: "All good Sephardic men are married to Ashkenazic women" (Harris 1979:257). Intermarriage naturally affects mother tongue maintenance in a negative way. In the United States, children of a Sephardic–Ashkenazic marriage or Sephardic–non-Jewish marriage speak English as their mother tongue, while in Israel offspring of Sephardic–Ashkenazic unions speak Hebrew.

19. Dispersal of Sephardic (Ethnic) Neighborhoods

As the Levantine Sephardim have become more Americanized and affluent, it has become increasingly difficult to keep the younger generations in the community (see chapter 7). Their ethnic identity has become less important, and thus they feel a diminished need to maintain themselves in a group. As a result, the Sephardim have mingled with the Ashkenazic Jewish majority as well as with non-Jewish Americans in the secular American culture. The existence of the Sephardic communities was crucial to the life of Judeo-Spanish and to the development and propagation of Sephardic culture. Marc Angel quite aptly described the role of the Sephardic community in the past, as compared to the present situation:

The Sephardi neighborhoods—where one lived within walking distance of most relatives; constantly heard Judeo-Spanish chatter; looked to the synagogue as the center of life, and learned and observed Sephardi customs in the course of living—have almost completely disintegrated. People are moving to the more fashionable suburbs. . . . Broadening interests and mobility have sharply decreased the need for neighborhood activities. And, as neighborhoods cease to be the once strong cultural force, the influence of non-Sephardi social patterns naturally becomes stronger. The result is that some Sephardim completely lose their sense of group belonging. (1974:116)

Like other ethnic groups with acculturation and affluence, the Sephardim of New York moved out of their close knit communities on the Lower East Side to go to the Bronx, Queens, and finally to the suburbs of Long Island. In Los Angeles the Sephardim are dispersed throughout Los Angeles county, which includes the San Fernando Valley and Long Beach. The move away from the ethnic neighborhoods dealt a severe blow to language maintenance since the Sephardim no longer heard nor had the chance to speak Judeo-Spanish on a daily basis.[16]

20. No Powerful Movements to Champion the Cause of the Judeo-Spanish Language or its Preservation even on the Part of the Sephardim Themselves

Bunis (1975a:25) points out that, unlike Yiddish, there have been no powerful or strong secular movements to champion the cause of Judeo-Spanish, nor does it appear that any efforts have been made by the more conservative or traditional members of the community to insure future perpetuation of the language (see chapters 12 and 13). The few efforts at perpetuation that were attempted have met with little success. One such movement was spearheaded by Dr. Angel Pulido, a Spanish senator who was a champion for Judeo-Spanish in the early part of this century. He wrote various works on the hopeful renewal of relations between the Spanish government and the Spanish Jews in the Ottoman Empire whom he referred to as *Los españoles sin patria* 'The Spaniards without a country/homeland' (see section 17). Pulido made an impassioned plea before the Spanish Senate on 13 November 1903, for Spanish aid to be given to the Sephardic communities in the Levant to help promote the perpetuation of Spanish (Benardete 1982:179). He suggested ways the Spanish government could renew cultural and economic ties with the Sephardim of the Empire and could set up schools to teach Castilian in the Balkans. He advocated, along with others, the policy of polishing and refining the language. But in general his proposals, as well as those of Juan Eugenio Hartzenbusch,[17] fell on deaf ears. In retrospect, scholars like Camhy (1971:600) realized that a joint effort of Ottoman Judaism, the Alliance, and Spain could have made a world of difference on the present-day language situation of the Sephardim and other Balkan peoples. Renard (1966a:193) also feels that if Spain had not been so indifferent to the fate of the *españoles sin patria,* and had established Spanish schools or at least instruction of Spanish in the Levant, they would have enjoyed considerable success.

Another movement to conserve and "purify" (remove foreign elements from) the written language was started at the turn of the century by a group of Sephardic students and intellectuals in Vienna, who formed the Sephardic cultural society called *Esperanza* 'Hope'. They started a publication entitled *El Mundo Sefardí, Revista para la Vida Social y Cultural* 'The Sephardic World, Magazine for Social and Cultural Life', whose purpose was to return Judeo-Spanish to its use as a cultural language. Unfortunately, this publication was not long lasting.

Ironically, it was the Sephardi rabbis of the Levant who sowed the first seeds for the reduction of publications in Judeo-Spanish. Because of dissension between the clerical and lay elements, a religious council met in Salonika in 1529. In a reaction against secular writings, the council instituted censorship. Publication of any manuscript which was not authorized or revised by a council of rabbis was prohibited. It was not long before Constantinople adopted the same censorship policy as that of Salonika. This policy naturally discouraged writers in both the Spanish and Hebrew languages. From this date Spanish studies began to decline in the Levant. In Salonika only books of the Bible with translations into the Spanish of the fifteenth century were printed. Also the rabbis of the Levant did not allow the importation and circulation of Spanish books printed in Latin characters. In other words it was the rabbis who, in a sense, limited the cultural vigor of the language by their efforts to exclude the Sephardim from Western culture. Henry Besso aptly describes the situation:

The Judeo-Spanish language had been confined in a sort of air-tight cell, as it were, thanks to the pressure exerted by the Rabbis. Due to their power, the religious leaders succeeded in stopping the importation and circulation of Spanish books printed in Latin characters. . . . It was not a question of whether the books existed, but rather a question of not wanting to have them. (1961:1018)

By the twentieth century decay was truly visible. Istanbul's most important biweekly, *El Tiempo,* ceased publication in 1930 and was replaced by *La Voz de Oriente.* The latter was a monthly publication in which Rashi characters were generally replaced by the Latin alphabet with a French system of orthography. Sala points out that in such attempts to restore Sephardic culture with the help of the language, the Sephardim never resorted to Modern Spanish (Sala 1970a:21). Instead they mostly looked to French and Italian (and at times even Turkish) to solve certain linguistic problems such as orthography, adoption of neologisms, etc. Various efforts in *La Voz de Oriente* to purify the language also fell short of their goal, since by that time it was often necessary to translate many of the old Judeo-Spanish words into Turkish for the reader. And Galante informs us that by 1935, it was partially published in Turkish in Latin letters (Galante 1935:10). With the reduction in the number of publications written in Judeo-Spanish, many Sephardim resorted to reading publications printed in other languages.

In the United States and Israel, one of the greatest problems faced by the Sephardim, as well as other ethnic groups, has been the lack of governmental or institutional support for ethnic language maintenance. But more importantly, the Sephardim themselves neither tried, nor were they able to work to maintain or perpetuate Judeo-Spanish. As Malinowski reported in her paper on current Sephardic institutions and activities, there is no "well-conceived and well-organized community-wide program of language maintenance" being pursued anywhere in the United States today (1983:146).

In Israel there are a few Sephardic organizations and publications (see Appendix E). However, they are mostly concerned with promoting aspects of Sephardic culture other than language maintenance. The few efforts aimed at maintaining the language, such as the Judeo-Spanish radio broadcasts[18], are primarily directed to the present speakers of the language who are generally above sixty-five years of age. As this generation of Sephardim passes away, the few educational and cultural Sephardic societies and organizations in both the United States and Israel will concentrate their efforts on aspects of Sephardic culture other than the Judeo-Spanish language.[19]

At the Conference of Sephardic Communities in London, held on May 26 through 28, 1935, the Sephardim realized the poor state of their culture and language. They criticized the lack of religious training for Sephardi rabbis and the fact that Sephardic Jews had left creative research of their past history in the hands of Ashkenazic Jews.

By the time of the First Symposium of Sephardic Studies *El Primer Simposio de Estudios Sefardíes,* held in Madrid in 1964 at the Instituto Arias Montano, and the First International Congress for the Study of Sephardi and Oriental Jewry, held in Jerusalem in June of 1978, the situation had changed. That is, Sephardi, as well as Ashkenazi scholars, were devoting themselves to Sephardic studies. But these efforts were not in time to have any retarding effects on the decline of Judeo-Spanish.

21. No Effective Central Uniting Sephardic Organizations

One of the biggest difficulties in maintaining the Sephardic identity in the United States was that there was no central uniting force. Lida (1962:1039) points out that, although it presented a solid front to the Ashkenazic and non-Jewish worlds, the Sephardic community was divided by dissension from within, due mainly to the conflicts between members from various parts of the former Ottoman Empire. Since the Sephardic immigrants settled in neighborhoods which reflected their countries or cities of origin, a central organization was desperately needed (see chapter 7). However, most efforts to create a central organization for the administration of communal Sephardic life failed. Many Sephardic societies were started, but as J. Papo points out, they were generally short-lived: "Representing disparate regions, and even a variety of languages, and constricted by narrow, localized loyalties, these groups fought each other rather than cooperating for the common good" (1987:263). For example, organizations like the Central Sephardic Jewish Community of America were fairly ineffectual. As the Sephardim made the shift to English and became more and more assimilated into the mainstream of American culture, the original, local Sephardi clubs, coffeehouses and mutual aid societies were no longer needed. They had served their purpose, like the "Little Polands" or "Little Italys," which was to help the arriving immigrants adjust to a new society (Nahirny and Fishman 1966:340). And, as Altabé points out in Mizrahi's (1987:386) study, one characteristic of the Sephardim was that they were not aggressive group organizers. In J. Papo's final analysis concerning the lack of a good central Sephardic leadership or organization, he writes:

> In the end, their dream to achieve a strong, united, viable Sephardi community on American soil was defeated by a combination of forces: those that were external, such as demographic shifts and upward economic mobility; and those that were internal, such as the resistance of the entrenched leaders of the societies and other groups to yielding any of their autonomy, as well as the unwillingness of those who had achieved affluence to join or contribute funds to a united central community. (1987:263)

One important thing to remember is that, during their temporary existence, the local organizations, as well as the Central Sephardic Jewish Community, never did anything to encourage language maintenance among the native Judeo-Spanish-speaking immigrants. But in all fairness to the Sephardim, it must be emphasized that they had numerous problems when they came to a country where English was the prestige language of advancement toward becoming an "American". As stated in chapter 7, the majority of Levantine Sephardim were uneducated, poor, and unskilled, and thus badly prepared to meet the challenges of Americanization. Due to linguistic, religious, and psychological differences, they were isolated, especially since the Ashkenazim did not know what to do with this non-Yiddish-speaking Jewish community. Also, because of their great pride, the Sephardim made it extremely difficult for various groups to help them (Angel 1987b:110). Thus, it took a few generations for the Sephardic community to become relatively comfortable financially while they caught up to the economic status of their Ashkenazic coreligionists. Unfortunately, it is understandable why propagation of the language and central organizations for language maintenance took a back seat to the fight for survival in a new culture. By the time the Sephardim had the leisure to think about maintaining their mother tongue, it was too late.

In Israel, the Judeo-Spanish-speaking Sephardim did the same thing that they did in the United States. That is, they established their own local organizations based on region of origin in Turkey, Greece, etc., which were also not very effective. However, the situation in Israel is different. We must remember that the Sephardic and Oriental Jews in Israel are considered together as one political unit versus the Ashkenazic Jews (see chapter 7). And an important demographic fact is that the Judeo-Spanish Sephardim form only a small percentage of this group which makes up about 55 percent of Israel's total present population. Thus, the organizations which do handle the interests of this large group must concentrate on the needs of the whole group rather than on those of the

Balkan Sephardim. There are some cultural institutions which study the history and culture of the Sephardic and Oriental communities (see Appendix E), but as stated earlier, they have never put much importance on the maintenance of the Judeo-Spanish language.

22. No "Old Country" or Homeland—No Newly Arriving Immigrants

One of the most important reasons for the rapid decline of Judeo-Spanish today is the lack of an "old country" where Judeo-Spanish is the dominant spoken language. The same can be said for the current situation of Yiddish: "it has no 'homeland' across the oceans where the language is still safe and sound, regardless of what happens in the future to its speakers in the USA" (Fishman 1991:215). There is thus a scarcity of new immigrant arrivals. The Sephardim have no original or "old country" from which to glean information about how their language should be spoken. Since 1492 the language of the Sephardim has been a minority language in countries outside of the Iberian Peninsula. Like the Sephardim, American Indians in the United States also have no newly arriving native speakers to help maintain their languages. In his research on Shoshoni and other dying Amerindian languages, Miller wrote: "When an immigrant community switches to English, the language still lives in the old country; but when an American Indian language dies, it is gone forever" (1971:115). The same can be said of Judeo-Spanish in the United States and Israel. When it dies, it will be gone forever.

The lack of contact with newly arriving immigrants makes it impossible to renew ties or to help reinforce the mother tongue. Today there are some Turkish Sephardim emigrating to Israel, but not enough to make a difference for language maintenance. In addition, most of these immigrants speak better Turkish than Judeo-Spanish, if they speak it at all. Nahirny and Fishman point out the importance of immigrants for foreign language maintenance since it is the newly arriving immigrants, as in the past with other ethnic groups, who have been responsible for the maintenance of certain ethnic organizations as well as the ethnic language (Nahirny and Fishman 1966:341). With practically no new immigrants to help revitalize the language in the United States and Israel today, Judeo-Spanish is declining that much faster.

23. Reduction of the Sephardi Population

Through the years the Sephardi population of the world has been greatly reduced. This reduction is due to four main causes:

a. Mass emigration from the Balkans to Palestine, Latin America, and the United States, starting in the nineteenth century, which marked the beginning of the decline of Eastèrn Sephardim.

b. The persecutions, deportations, and massacres of the Sephardim by the Nazis during World War II.

c. Assimilation into other cultures due to the forces of Balkanization, Israelization, Americanization, and intermarriage with Ashkenazic Jews as well as with non-Jews. The offspring of such marriages often do not adopt a Sephardic identity and rarely speak Judeo-Spanish.

d. A drop in the birthrate. Among the Sephardim the birthrate has dropped sharply in the last few generations, especially in the United States, which is a reflection of the changing ideas and attitudes among the Levantine Sephardim under the influence of a secular society. In Israel the drop in birthrate is mainly due to the lack of economic feasibility of supporting large families.

According to Lida, the alarming rapid reduction in the Sephardi population, resulting from either extinction or assimilation, is one of the major phenomena characterizing the Sephardim today. The total decrease of Sephardim in the Levant alone after the Second World War is estimated at some 215,000, out of 281,000 before the war (Lida 1962:1038—also see figures at the end of chapter 3.) These numbers have diminished even further due to emigration. A reduction in the Sephardi population is naturally accompanied by a reduction in the number of speakers of Judeo-Spanish.

24. Reduction of Language Domains or Uses

According to Sala (1970a:17) and others, the disappearance of Judeo-Spanish is due, above all, to the progressive reduction of its sphere of use, that is, its social value as a means of communication. Judeo-Spanish has shifted from being an international trade language and language of prestige in the Levant, to the colloquial language of the home and as a means of communication reserved for older people. As it has become more restricted in usage and thus relegated to the intimacy of the family, Judeo-Spanish has lost its ability to express many abstract notions or elevated ideas or to evoke the contemporary realities of an advanced culture. As a result, its speakers are not able to continue using the language in all circumstances and with the same results as the current language(s) of the region.

The most important phenomenon resulting from this loss of domains of usage has been the growing number of Judeo-Spanish speakers who prefer to communicate in another language. They prefer a language which has more prestige and a wider use and which is better suited to their communicative needs, such as French, Turkish, Hebrew, and English. Due to the deficiencies of Judeo-Spanish and its limited use, many Sephardim have lost confidence in the future of their language.

12

Negative Language Attitudes: Their Role in Language Decline

Introduction

Language attitude studies have been used by linguists to research language and identity as well as various beliefs concerning specific languages. Gardner and Lambert (1972) proved that there is a correlation between favorable attitudes toward a particular culture and its language, and the success with which that language is mastered by others. They distinguished between an integrative attitude (a desire to know and become friendly with the speakers of a language) and an instrumental attitude (a desire to better oneself materially by means of the language). It would appear that the optimal condition for adopting or learning another language is to have a positive integrative as well as a positive instrumental attitude. But as Macnamara (1973:37) points out, this is often not the case, especially in instances of language shift. He reports that instrumental motivation does not necessarily imply an integrative one, and he gives the example of the Irish, Welsh, and Highland Scots who have a positive instrumental attitude toward the adoption of English, while at the same time they have an unfavorable integrative attitude. In these cases as well as others,[1] the necessity to communicate in the language of wider communication has overpowered integrative attitudes.

In cases of language shift, language attitudes of the members of a speech community are also crucial in determining whether or not their own language will be maintained or perpetuated. Negative attitudes toward the mother tongue will help to hasten its decline or death, since the speakers themselves will often choose to adopt another language in its place without making any efforts to maintain it.

Most ethnic groups, who are speakers of minority languages, are faced with negative attitudes concerning their mother tongue as it loses prestige on the way to being replaced by the dominant language(s). The Sephardim are no exception. Negative attitudes toward Judeo-Spanish on the part of its speakers began in the

230

Ottoman Empire as the Sephardic community lost prestige with the beginnings of nationalism in the late 1800s and early 1900s. D. Aaron José Hazan, director of the Izmir newspaper *La Buena Esperanza,* wrote to Dr. Pulido (see chapter 11 section no. 20) on the subject of purifying the language, "You already know how our language is corrupted—It's necessary little by little to bring it nearer to the true language of Cervantes" (Pulido 1905:453). In a 1939 article on the linguistic situation of the Sephardim in Istanbul, Farhi quoted from the manifesto of the Sephardic organization *Türk Birliği* 'Turkish Unity': "We abandon our corrupt jargon (Judeo-Spanish) in favor of the beautiful language of the Gazi (the President of the Turkish Republic, Kemal Atatürk)" (1937:157). Farhi also reported that young Sephardic women and girls were embarrassed in public to speak "the old, distorted family language made up of solecisms and of barbarisms" (ibid., 151). Some of these opinions concerning the language were greatly influenced by schools of the Alliance Israélite Universelle in which the French language and culture were promoted (see chapter 11 section no. 6).

As the Sephardim adopted the national languages in the former Ottoman Empire, many became ashamed to speak Judeo-Spanish outside of the home. Using the language in public signified a lack of assimilation into the surrounding culture, which could be detrimental to desires for advancement or upward mobility. The general feeling was that the language being adopted in its place, whether it was French, Italian, Turkish, another Balkan language, or Hebrew, was a superior language. Many Sephardim felt that Judeo-Spanish had become an inferior or inelegant language incapable of expressing modern or elevated ideas. Several speakers lacked confidence in the future of their language which seemed to have an impoverished vocabulary.

Many of these negative language attitudes, which began in the Levant at the beginning of this century, are still prevalent today among several Sephardim residing in the United States and Israel. This chapter discusses the attitudes toward Judeo-Spanish and its maintenance and perpetuation on the part of the Judeo-Spanish-speaking informants in my studies. The data was collected from the interviews I conducted in New York and Israel in 1978, and in Los Angeles in 1985.

Classification of the Language

When asked how they classified their language, most informants said that Judeo-Spanish was a mixed language that was basically

Old Spanish plus a blend or mixture of other languages, especially Turkish, Greek, Hebrew, French, Italian, and even Yiddish, depending on where the Sephardim had previously lived. It is interesting to note that only one New York informant included English, and only six of the Los Angeles informants mentioned Modern Spanish as having an influence on Judeo-Spanish. This suggests that either the United States informants do not put much emphasis on the present use of Judeo-Spanish, but rather are thinking of the language more in terms of what their families spoke in the Balkans, or they may simply not be aware of the extent to which both Modern Spanish and English have infiltrated their speech.

However, the majority of the informants did know that their language was based on or related to Old Spanish. This was not the case with many of the Balkan Sephardim in the 1800s and early 1900s who were often not aware that they even spoke a Romance language. They considered their language to be purely a Jewish language and were surprised in later years to find out that their native language was related to Spanish, Italian, and French.[2]

The one classification of Judeo-Spanish that suggested a negative connotation was the term *jargon*. One informant reported that the jargon was not "pure" Spanish. Another informant used to call Judeo-Spanish a jargon, thinking that it was not theoretically a language. In Malinowski's studies in both Israel (1979) and Turkey (1982a), the word *jargon* was also used by some informants as a way to define their "inferior" or "corrupt" language. Quotes from various scholars found in Bunis (1978a:10,12) remind us that in much of the literature of the late nineteenth and twentieth centuries, the language was often referred to as a "jargon" or a "corrupted speech form."

Judeo-Spanish as Compared with Other Languages

When the informants were asked if they considered Judeo-Spanish to be an inferior language compared to other languages, the majority answered *no*. But upon further questioning, they generally rated Judeo-Spanish unfavorably when compared with Modern Spanish and considered it an inferior form of speech. They described their language as an impure, incorrect, or non-genuine form of Spanish. Quotes like the following were not uncommon among my New York informants: "I don't speak real Spanish like they do in South America and Puerto Rico," or "Ladino is not pure Spanish like Puerto Rican Spanish is." The emphasis on Puerto Rican Spanish is due to the fact that the Puerto Ricans have been the group of Spanish speakers the Sephardim in New York have most frequently encountered (especially in the working environment) since the 1950s. It makes no difference that other Spanish speakers may not regard New York Puerto Rican Spanish with the same high esteem as the Sephardim do. For the Sephardic informants, including the older speakers, any Spanish other than their own is more prestigious. One couple who had lived in Argentina for three years, and another informant who lived in Cuba as a child before coming to New York, not only spoke the standard Spanish of those countries, but used it in their interviews, were proud of their ability to speak it, and were very well aware of the differences between their standard or "proper" Spanish versus their "incorrect" Judeo-Spanish. In general, however, unless they were language sensitive or had lived in other countries, the New York informants were not very aware of the extent to which Modern Spanish influenced their speech. For example, one informant, a photographer who travels often to Spain and who speaks Spanish to various Latin American friends and residents in his apartment building, had no idea that his speech, which was formerly Judeo-Spanish, is now almost exclusively Modern Spanish. On the other hand, another informant who is a college professor of Spanish, knows that what he speaks now is mostly Modern Spanish.

However, most of the Los Angeles informants were very well aware of the differences between their Judeo-Spanish and Modern Spanish. Several mentioned that when they speak with non-Sephardic speakers, they make conscious efforts to omit the Turkish, Greek, and Hebrew words. Comments like the following were quite prevalent:

When we speak to a Turkino, as we call our Ladino friends, we speak in Ladino. But if I were to speak to a Spaniard I'm guarded and I speak Spanish, the regular Spanish without trying to inject any of the other words.

Another informant stated:

When I was younger I was less aware of the differences than I am now, and so as I've gotten older I've realized that some of the words that we use in Ladino are not the same as the non-Ladino Spanish-speaking people use. And so, when I'm with a non-Sephardi person I try to be careful to use their word. For example: *esposo* instead of *marido* for "husband", or *trabajo* for "work" instead of the Ladino *lavoro*.

Other informants learned about the differences between the two languages when they studied Modern Spanish in school or college. One informant said, "When I was taking Spanish in college I would throw in some Ladino not realizing that I was using Ladino, and the teacher would ask: 'Where did you get that word?'" Another informant stated that even though she did not consider her speech to be inferior, she did consider it to be a handicap when she was working in a school and wanted to communicate with the parents of a Spanish-speaking student and "these Hebrew and Turkish words would crop up into the [her] language and the parents would say 'Huh?'" And another informant stated that when speaking to non-Sephardim, "Occasionally I'll make a mistake, occasionally I'll slip." This consciousness or awareness of the differences between Judeo-Spanish and Modern Spanish, and especially the efforts to correct their language by making it closer to the Modern Spanish variety, is much more prevalent among the Los Angeles Sephardim interviewed in 1985 than among the New York Sephardim I spoke with in 1978. Throughout the interviews, many of the Los Angeles informants often corrected themselves in the word elicitation by saying, for example: "No, *enfermo* is a Spanish word. We [the Sephardim] say *hazino*."

In her study of the Indianapolis Sephardic community, J. Nemer found the same efforts on the part of her informants to make their speech closer to Modern Spanish by adopting certain phonological features: "Since Standard Spanish is considered by many speakers to be a 'real' language, and Judeo-Spanish is not, this modification is an attempt to bring Judeo-Spanish closer to the prestige target" (1981:213).

In Israel Judeo-Spanish was also accorded an inferior status when compared to English and to various European languages, especially French. The Israeli informants who had been educated in schools of the Alliance Israélite Universelle (especially those from Salonika) preferred to conduct their interviews in French rather than Judeo-Spanish. It is difficult to know whether this preference for French was due to its higher prestige in their opinion, or due to their lack of a strong command of Judeo-Spanish and thus their embarrassment in speaking the language imperfectly.

Fluency in Judeo-Spanish

When asked if they were as fluent in Judeo-Spanish as their parents and grandparents were, forty-four (New York—20, Israel—9, Los

Angeles—15) or 48 percent of the total number of informants answered *no*. Of the forty-seven (New York—8, Israel—19, Los Angeles—20) who said that they *were* as fluent as their parents/grandparents, most of them were over the age of sixty-five. The few exceptions who were younger than age sixty-five either work with the language today (as newspaper/journal editors, or in radio broadcasting) or had grandmothers who spoke with them during the day (while their mothers/parents worked), so that in a few instances they felt they spoke better Judeo-Spanish than their parents. However, when questioned further, many of these informants who reported having a high degree of fluency admitted that there are certain domains where their Judeo-Spanish is not as good as their elders. Moshe Shaul, the head of the Judeo-Spanish department of the Israeli radio *Kol Israel,* reported that when he talks about politics he speaks as well as his elders do/did, but he does not speak as well when dealing with topics of folklore and culture. He admitted that his elders had a much better knowledge of the *refranes,* for example, than he does.

I also found, in listening to the speech samples of many of the informants who reported that they were as fluent as their elders, that they used many English, Hebrew, or Modern Spanish words or phrases to express various ideas. It was obvious that their linguistic skills were not, or could not have been, as good as those of their parents or grandparents. This is an example of differences between reported versus empirical data that are common in language attitude studies (see chapter 8). It is difficult to determine whether the informants who reported having as good a level of fluency really believed that they did, or if it was a result of not wanting to admit that their linguistic skills were weak.

The main linguistic reason given for the inferiority of the informants' Judeo-Spanish, as compared with that of their parents/grandparents' speech, was insufficient Judeo-Spanish vocabulary, and thus an inability to express their ideas well. Other deficiencies included lack of knowledge of the grammar, the inability to read and write the language well, and inferior pronunciation and accent. Due to the impoverished vocabulary and a difficulty in expressing certain ideas, code-switching or shifting is one of the most dominant characteristics of Judeo-Spanish speech today.[3] This was often the case in the childhood homes of the informants. Two informants told me that their mothers would speak to them in Ladino while they answered in English. Another informant continually got into trouble with his mother because he kept code-switching in the middle of his sentences. Today, all of the United States informants often revert to English or simply communicate in English because it is much easier for them to speak now. One informant expressed the feelings of many when he said: "I start a conversation in Ladino then mix in English when I'm stumped." Other informants often code switch according to topic, doing what Blom and Gumperz (1972:425) refer to as "metaphorical switching."

Sociological reasons given for the informants' lack of fluency in Judeo-Spanish included: (1) that they had no occasion to use or practice the language, since their parents often wanted to "Americanize" and use English, and their grandparents or older relatives had already died; (2) that they no longer lived in Sephardic neighborhoods or communities; (3) that their spouses were Ashkenazic or non-Jewish and did not know Judeo-Spanish, which was therefore no longer used in the home; and (4) that they no longer needed Judeo-Spanish for conducting business.

One New York informant brought up an interesting point concerning his generation's inferior fluency in the language. He said that he knew Judeo-Spanish only as a means of conversation, while his parents and especially his grandparents not only used the language as the daily language of communication, but they also constantly recited prayers, sang songs and read in the language. A Los Angeles informant expressed the difference in linguistic skills among the different generations in the following statement:

> In my grandparents' case Judeo-Spanish was their language of conversation. I would say that it was the language they used 99 percent of the time. In my mother's case she used it maybe 60 percent or 70–75 percent of the time. I might use it 10 percent of the time.

Another reason mentioned for the lack of fluency was the infiltration or "contamination" of other languages in Judeo-Spanish. One Los Angeles informant stated:

> I used to be [as fluent]. I don't practice often now, but I can still sit with the old people and have a conversation. The problem is now I use Spanish every day in my business. It's probably polluting or diluting my Ladino . . . [causing] my loss of words because I immediately use the Castilian word.

One Israeli informant said that since he has forgotten certain Judeo-Spanish words, he replaces them with Turkish and Hebrew, while another informant uses Bulgarian words. Another Israeli informant stated that Turkish has influenced his Judeo-Spanish vocabulary while Hebrew has influenced his syntax. The French influence is also quite powerful due mainly to the prestige of French in the Balkans and the work of the Alliance schools. One Israeli informant also pointed out that members of the older generation spoke mainly Judeo-Spanish and did not study French, Turkish, or other Balkan languages in school and therefore, were not as influenced by these other languages.

Feelings about Speaking Judeo-Spanish

When asked if they ever felt embarrassed speaking Judeo-Spanish, only thirteen (New York—9, Israel—0, Los Angeles—4) answered *yes*. But other New York and Los Angeles informants admitted that when they were young children they had been embarrassed to speak the language in public places because they wanted to be "American." However, a couple stated that it does not bother them today since the climate for ethnicity in the United States has changed.[4] Four New York and three Los Angeles informants are embarrassed to speak with good Judeo-Spanish speakers because they feel they speak it badly. One informant from Los Angeles made the following comment: "I feel embarrassed sometimes because I can't express myself the way I would like to." Another Los Angeles informant stated, "It never comes out just right. I'm terrible at languages. I think that's why I stopped trying after a while." Other informants feel awkward speaking Judeo-Spanish with native Modern Spanish speakers, since they feel they do not speak correctly because their language is not "pure Castilian." Two New York informants related stories about their Spanish teachers in high school and college, who were either interested in knowing more about the kind of Spanish they spoke or who made fun of their "strange" Spanish. One New York informant said that the only time he has felt embarrassed speaking Ladino was when Yiddish speakers were left out of the conversation, thus showing bad manners on the part of the Sephardim of the group.

Two informants from Rhodes who have always been part of the upper, wealthy class made an interesting comment. Even though they still speak the language at home and are very proud of their Sephardic heritage, and are also very active in New York's Sephardic community, they never speak Judeo-Spanish in a public place like an elevator. This is because they do not want to be mistaken for Puerto Ricans or for what they referred to as "Spanish-speaking refugees," an interesting comment coming from a group of immigrants themselves. This attitude (which can also be found among various non-Jewish Spanish-speaking groups in New York) shows that they consider their culture to be superior to that of other Spanish speakers living in New York City. However, while the Sephardim may consider their culture to be superior, they do not consider their language to be superior. In fact, they feel that the Spanish they speak is not prestigious or else they would not hesitate to use it in public. They know that their brand of Spanish is not the Spanish spoken by the upper class, cultured natives of Spanish-speaking countries, so they prefer to speak English or French in public. This attitude of cultural superiority, as opposed to linguistic superiority, is also evident in current trends of Sephardic studies. For the most part, scholars study such aspects of Sephardic culture as folklore, music (especially the *romanzas*), and history, while research on the Judeo-Spanish language and literature seems to take a back seat. It is difficult to determine whether this lack of research on the language is due to the small number of linguists interested in the topic of Judeo-Spanish, or whether the decline of this nonprestigious language makes it a difficult subject for study.

It is interesting to note that none of the Israeli informants admitted to ever having been embarrassed while speaking Judeo-Spanish. This could be attributed in part to the fact that they became more defensive than the New York or Los Angeles informants when asked this question. And two of the Israelis who answered *no* should have answered *yes,* judging from their comments. One reported that he was embarrassed because he could not speak Judeo-Spanish very well, and the other was embarrassed to speak in front of me because she felt she spoke the language badly. She insisted, however, on playing a tape of her singing in Judeo-Spanish (she is a professional singer) so that I would know she could sing in the language.

Of the informants who stated that they had never felt embarrassed speaking Judeo-Spanish, some expressed a pride in being able to speak this language. One Los Angeles informant and one New York informant stated that they felt it was an honor to speak Judeo-Spanish, and another Los Angeles informant reported that she enjoyed explaining to other Spanish speakers that she spoke an older form of Spanish: "When people ask me what language I'm speaking, I explain to them: 'I speak Old Spanish.' They ask me in amazement: 'Do you know an old Spanish?' and I give it dignity." One Israeli informant felt that various Israeli Sephardim had acquired a new awareness and pride in their language and heritage since 1978, when Yitzhak Navon was elected the fifth

President of Israel. Navon was the first Sephardic president of the country (who served from 1978 to 1983), and he used to sprinkle his Hebrew speech with Judeo-Spanish expressions. This informant implied that many Israeli Sephardim may not have been particularly proud of their language before Navon's election. He felt that this phenomenon of newfound pride in a minority language would also occur in the United States with Spanish, for example, if the Americans were to elect a Spanish-speaking president.

It must be mentioned before continuing, that even though various informants may feel uneasy about speaking Judeo-Spanish, when it is advantageous to use it they do not hesitate to do so. The majority of these occasions occur at work, but there are daily situations where use of Judeo-Spanish with non-Sephardic Spanish speakers can be of help.

Negative Feelings Concerning Judeo-Spanish on the Part of Women

My research in New York, Israel, and Los Angeles uncovered an unexpected source of strong feelings against the language: it was the women, more than the men, who exhibited negative attitudes toward Judeo-Spanish. Other scholars of dying languages such as Dressler and Wodak-Leodolter (1977b:38) and Timm's (1980:36) studies on Breton, and Schlieben-Lange's (1977:104–5) study of Provençal, report the same interesting phenomenon that I also observed in my collection of data: that the women cling to the language to a lesser degree than do the men. Generally we are accustomed to the opposite situation, which is found among many American and Israeli immigrant groups; that is, it is the women who hold on to the ethnic language longer than do the men. But as Labov (1966:495, 489, 312) and Edwards (1985:72) report, women are more aware of prestigious languages and linguistic features than men. Dressler and Wodak-Leodolter suggest that the double inferior status of women is responsible for this attitude. They report:

> In case of a combination of two or more disfavored status roles, one obvious way out is the abandonment of the role that can be changed most easily. Since status roles such as race and sex are immutable, language shift is a solution preferred by persons who combine such minority roles. Therefore women—if they have achieved a certain degree of emancipation—are often significantly more language conscious

and use more hypercorrections than men; they are more inclined to
give in to social pressures toward adaptation. (1977a:7–8)

The mother, who is closer to the child, is almost forced to communicate in the official language which is acquired at school and is
favored by the peer group. In my research most of the women in
general did not speak Judeo-Spanish as well as the men; nor were
they so proud of their language, since they were more aware of its
inferior status. One wife in New York even corrected her husband's
English errors throughout the interview. Of the seven Los Angeles
informants who considered Judeo-Spanish to be an inferior language, six of them were women. They questioned its legitimacy as
a genuine language referring to it as "broken Spanish," "a handicap," "a bastard language," or "not a true language." When initially
contacted by phone, especially in New York and Israel, it was the
women rather than the men who offered the most resistance. Often
they did not want to be interviewed, saying that they no longer
spoke the language or did not speak it well, even though I had
been given information to the contrary.[5] It was their husbands who
were generally more open and willing to be interviewed.

However, in Los Angeles I was struck by the openness with
which I was received, as opposed to the initial reserved reaction
on the part of many of the New York and Israeli Sephardim. Part
of the reason for this may indeed be the more relaxed life style in
Los Angeles, but I also suspect that the general climate concerning
ethnicity in the country has changed in the seven years since I
completed the first interviews in 1978 (see chapter 14). By 1985
my Los Angeles informants did not feel threatened by discussing
their ethnicity or by expressing both negative as well as positive
feelings about their native language. Also, many of them were not
opposed to changing or adopting their style of speech to a variety
of Modern Spanish or switching completely into English.

Attitudes Concerning the Decline of Judeo-Spanish

In answer to the question: "Do you consider Judeo-Spanish to be
a dying language?" seventy-nine of the total number of informants
(New York—24, Israel—24, Los Angeles—31) or 86 percent answered *yes*. This affirmative answer was often accompanied by
qualifying statements such as *Si, malorozamente* 'Yes, unfortunately', *Si, me da pena* 'Yes, it upsets me', "I'm afraid it is," or
"I'm sorry to say so," expressing sadness and regret that the lan-

guage is dying. Two Israeli informants said the language would be dead in three generations, while another said it would disappear within fifty years. Only 13 percent, or twelve of the total number of informants (New York—4, Israel—4, Los Angeles—4), did not consider Judeo-Spanish to be a dying language.

When asked if their children spoke Judeo-Spanish fluently or well, only thirty-three of seventy-nine informants who have children (New York—14, Israel—10, Los Angeles—9), or 41 percent reported that their children could either speak Judeo-Spanish or had a passive knowledge of it. Those who answered *yes* either had older children who were mostly in their fifties or sixties, or children who had studied Spanish in school. However, when questioned further, the informants admitted that in fact most of their children had only a receptive or passive competence in Judeo-Spanish, meaning that they had certain comprehension skills rather than conversational skills. The remaining forty-six informants (who have children), or 58 percent, reported that their children have no knowledge of the language at all.

When asked if their grandchildren spoke Ladino, 100 percent or all of the informants with grandchildren answered in the negative. This means that none of the informants' grandchildren speak Judeo-Spanish, nor do they have a good passive knowledge of the language. We see from this data the apparent misconception on the part of the twelve informants who deny that Judeo-Spanish is dying on one hand, and yet on the other hand report that their grandchildren have no knowledge of the language. This is another example of the discrepancies between reported data and actual empirical data, which are frequently found in language attitude studies (see chapter 8).

In general, there is a strong awareness among the informants that the language will die with the death of the older generation, which is, in most cases, their generation. Statements like the following were not uncommon: "Yes, after we're gone that's [the language] finished," or "Yes, because after our generation our children won't know the language." One informant said, "Unless we transmit it to our youngsters I don't know how that language is really gonna survive unless they teach it in the colleges."

When asked how their children/grandchildren or any young Sephardim that they know feel about speaking Ladino, most believe that the majority of kids today do not really give it much thought. The few young people that do feel strongly about their Sephardic heritage seem to be more interested in aspects of Sephardic culture other than the language, although there are some young people who choose to study Spanish in school because of their Sephardic backgrounds.

Of the informants who did not feel that Judeo-Spanish was a dying language, the four Israeli informants work(ed) for the perpetuation of the language and Sephardic culture. Two of them (Rosa and Nissim Bueno) were editors of Israel's Judeo-Spanish newspaper *La Luz de Israel;* one of them, Moshe Shaul, heads the Judeo-Spanish section of the Israeli radio Kol Israel; and the other, S. Angel-Malachi, was a Sephardi folklorist. They felt that Judeo-Spanish was reviving or renewing itself due in part to the work of organizations such as the Council of the Sephardi and Oriental Communities in Jerusalem (see Appendix E). H. Besso expresses Benardete and S. Levy's opinions that the future of Judeo-Spanish lies in Central and South America, where even Ashkenazic Jews speak a Spanish which is closer to Ladino than to the Modern Spanish of contemporary Spain (Besso 1970:259). S. Levy feels that this Spanish serves as a bridge between the Ashkenazic and Sephardic Jews (S. Levy 1949:51). Because of this linguistic situation in Latin America, Angel-Malachi felt that Yiddish was the language that was dying, not Judeo-Spanish (Angel-Malachi 1978).

Moshe Shaul stated that Judeo-Spanish is in crisis now, and that those at the radio are working to perpetuate it. This idea of the language being in crisis was also expressed by Professor Haïm Vidal Sephiha, France's expert on the Judeo-Spanish language and also head of the *Association Vidas Largas* (see Appendix E). In an interview on 1 July, 1988 in Paris, in which Sephiha spoke in Judeo-Spanish, he said:

> Since 1890 writers and scholars of Judeo-Spanish have said the language is dying and it is now about 1990 and the language has not yet died. It's true that we have experienced very big crises, first with the destruction of the Salonika community, second with the extermination of the Jews (the Judeo-Spanish Jews from Europe who were deported) . . . but since we are only a few in this world who want to save Judeo-Spanish, I don't know if I am/we are going to save it.

Another Israeli informant brought up an interesting point. He stated that if he still lived in Turkey, his children would speak Judeo-Spanish, but since they live in Israel it has been replaced by Hebrew. The same could be said of the informants in the United States whose children's Judeo-Spanish has been replaced by English. Two other Israeli informants qualified their affirmative answers by stating that Judeo-Spanish was definitely dying as a spoken language, but that the Sephardic culture and literary tradition were still strong.

One New York informant answered both *yes* and *no* to the question (in 1978), stating that he was not so pessimistic about the future of Judeo-Spanish as he had been three to five years earlier. He was referring to the recent work being done today to perpetuate Sephardic culture. One New York couple who did not feel Judeo-Spanish was a dying language, reported that their grandchildren were taking up Spanish in school because of the Spanish influence in New York City and because they wanted to learn the language of their parents and grandparents. It is interesting to note that these informants did not appear to make much of a distinction between Judeo-Spanish, their native language that is associated with the Sephardic culture, versus Modern Spanish, which is the language taught in the schools and is associated with Latin/Hispanic culture in general, and with the various countries in the world where Spanish is spoken.

However, even though the four Israeli informants agreed that Judeo-Spanish was not dying, neither their children nor their grandchildren speak the language. Their children may have a passive knowledge of Judeo-Spanish; that is, they can understand it but do not speak it, while their grandchildren do not even understand it. The four New York and four Los Angeles informants who felt Judeo-Spanish was not dying, reported that their children could speak or understand the language, while their grandchildren could not speak any Judeo-Spanish at all, unless they had studied Modern Spanish in school or college. Professor Sephiha also admitted that his son does not know any Judeo-Spanish.

The main reason given as to why the informants' children/grandchildren do not know Judeo-Spanish had to do with the fact that their spouse or daughters/sons-in-law were Ashkenazic or non-Jewish and thus did not speak the language. Conversely, the main reason given for their children's ability to speak or understand the language was the fact that the children spoke Judeo-Spanish to a grandparent who had lived with the family when the child was young. Unfortunately, it was often the case that the children stopped speaking the language from the day that the grandparent died. Another reason given for their children's familiarity with the language was the fact that they had studied Modern Spanish in school or college. In two instances, one informant from New York and one from Israel reported that they now try to speak a little Judeo-Spanish with some of their grown up children who have expressed a special interest in the Judeo-Spanish language and

Sephardic culture. The son of the New York informant does poetry translations from Judeo-Spanish into English. However, his command of the language, like most present day scholars of Sephardic studies who do not speak Modern Spanish, is mostly literary and not conversational, since his parents never spoke to him in Judeo-Spanish while he was growing up.

Attitudes Concerning the Maintenance and Perpetuation of Judeo-Spanish

When questioned about the need to keep speaking Judeo-Spanish and the importance of passing it on to the next generations, fifty-five informants or 60 percent (New York—16, Israel—14, Los Angeles—25) felt that it was necessary to keep speaking the language. However, only forty-one or 45 percent of the informants (New York—8, Israel—3, Los Angeles—30) felt it was important to pass it on to the next generation. And fifty informants (New York—20, Israel—25, Los Angeles—5) or 54 percent did not feel that it was important to pass on the language. It is interesting to note that only eight or 29 percent of the New York informants and three or 11 percent of the Israeli informants felt it was important to pass Judeo-Spanish on to the next generation, as opposed to the thirty or 85 percent of Los Angeles informants who favored perpetuation of the language. This is an obvious contradiction to the previous information concerning the Los Angeles informants' children's and especially their grandchildren's lack of linguistic skills. This illustrates another inconsistency on the part of the informants found in this attitude study.

The reasons given by the informants for maintaining and passing on Judeo-Spanish include:

(1) Knowledge of Judeo-Spanish is important from the standpoint of the culture, history, literary tradition, and heritage of the Sephardim.

(2) Judeo-Spanish is useful as a tie or link to Judaism, especially for non-Hebrew speaking Sephardim. It is a good *lingua franca* that unites the Sephardim throughout the world.

(3) Judeo-Spanish as a mother tongue is part of the Sephardim's personality and is thus part of the Sephardic ethnic group identity and should be preserved.

(4) It is good not to forget one's mother tongue. It is important to keep up the tradition, culture and language of one's ancestors.

(5) It is good to learn more than one language. We should be

bilingual. One Los Angeles informant stated: "Now the only ones who keep up their bilingual identity are the Mexicans."

(6) Ladino is useful because knowing it makes it easier to learn Spanish—i.e., it is helpful in the learning of Spanish, especially since we are so close to Mexico (the Los Angeles informants).

(7) Judeo-Spanish is important like the knowledge of all languages in life. It is considered good to have a second language. (It is not clear here whether the informants considered Judeo-Spanish to be the first or the second language.)

(8) Judeo-Spanish is useful and/or is needed in certain work or business situations.

(9) Judeo-Spanish is a good language for telling jokes and stories. Judeo-Spanish expressions are needed for humorous-expressive purposes.

(10) Judeo-Spanish can be used as a secret language if someone does not want outsiders or children to understand.

(11) Judeo-Spanish is a unique, beautiful and interesting language. It is something to be treasured.

Throughout the interviews it was clear that the informants value Judeo-Spanish and feel a great love and sentimental attachment toward it, and therefore do not want to see it die as a spoken language. One Los Angeles informant stated a feeling expressed by many: "It's a nostalgic thing for us. I have a strong feeling to preserve it—a psychological desire to continue using it." Many of these reasons for wanting to perpetuate the language were often more emotional than practical. The fifty informants (54 percent) who were not in favor of passing it on based their opinions on the following more practical reasons:

(1) There is no need for Judeo-Spanish in daily life. English is the prestigious language in the United States and Hebrew is the official language of Israel.

(2) There are very few people who try to conserve Judeo-Spanish which is a dying language. Since Judeo-Spanish is not being passed on, and there are so few occasions to use the language, and since many of the older Sephardic Judeo-Spanish speakers have died, there will eventually be no great mass of people left to speak it.

(3) The Sephardim are so mixed now. Many of the informants' spouses and their children's spouses are Ashkenazic or even non-Jewish who do not know the language.

(4) The Sephardic communities have disintegrated. Judeo-Spanish has lost its important function in Sephardic society.

(5) In the United States Modern Spanish is more important and

more practical to learn, especially given the growth of the Hispanic population in America and California's proximity to Mexico. Many of the informants would rather have their children/grandchildren learn Modern Spanish, which is taught in the schools and colleges.

(6) Hebrew is the Jewish language that is considered to be the international language of Jews today, which unites Jews from all over the world. One Los Angeles informant stated that Ladino had served a purpose in the past by keeping the Jews cohesive in many parts of the world after expulsion. But today, Hebrew is the language that should take Ladino's place.

(7) Many young people feel that Judeo-Spanish is unimportant. This attitude is reinforced by the fact that it is not a language taught in the schools. In Israel most youngsters want to study English, Arabic, or French in school, while in American schools Spanish and French are the most popular foreign languages studied. When compared to the use of these languages (as well as others), Judeo-Spanish seems unimportant. One Israeli informant reported that many Sephardim feel that Judeo-Spanish is an archaic language and that there are more important things to be done, such as studying the history and culture of the Sephardim (which has traditionally taken a back seat to the teaching of the history and culture of the Ashkenazim), instead of spending money and energy to revive the Judeo-Spanish language.

Many of my informants in New York, Israel, and Los Angeles, as well as those of Malinowski (1982a) in Turkey, feel that Judeo-Spanish has declined to such a degree that it is irretrievable. One of my New York informants reported: "Even the older people here, more frequently than not, speak English." Marc Angel, in his nationwide survey of American-born Sephardim in 1974, reported a similar attitude. About half of his second generation respondents considered the disappearance of Judeo-Spanish to be inevitable while the other half thought the loss of Judeo-Spanish would be a cultural tragedy (Angel 1974:124). Several of my informants expressed directly or indirectly the following idea: that knowledge of Judeo-Spanish is important from the point of view of the culture, history, literature, linguistic tradition, and the heritage of the Sephardim, but not necessarily as a means of communication.

Regardless of the informants' feelings concerning the maintenance and perpetuation of Judeo-Spanish, no efforts are being made to insure its future. The few university courses in Judeo-Spanish which have been or are presently being offered in New York, Israel, or Los Angeles, emphasize(d) the reading and study of Sephardic literature and religious texts or the cultural role of the language in Sephardic folklore, but do/did not provide the linguistic skills needed to speak and pass on the language.[6] Conversation groups which used to meet on Long Island, as well as various Sephardic clubs, no longer exist, since those interested in telling jokes and stories in Judeo-Spanish are passing away.[7] Today, even the Los Angeles Sephardim get together mostly for synagogue functions. Judeo-Spanish no longer performs the important societal functions that it formerly did in the Balkans and in the early days of Sephardic immigration to the United States in the beginning of this century.

Conclusion

The results of this attitude study show that negative language attitudes accompany the impending death of Judeo-Spanish in New York City, Israel, and Los Angeles. Negative language attitudes toward Judeo-Spanish on the part of its speakers are found consistently in various studies of the language. The research of Farhi (1937) in Istanbul, Sala (1970a) in Bucharest, Malinowski in Israel (1979) and Istanbul (1982a), Bortnick in Turkey (1992a,b), Bar Lewaw (1968) in Atlanta and Montgomery, and Nemer (1981) in Indianapolis, all reinforce my findings in New York and Israel (Harris 1979) and in Los Angeles (Harris 1987). Words and phrases like "ugly," "impure," "inelegant," "unimportant," "not chic," "jargon," "corrupt," "inferior," "a bastardized Spanish," "broken Spanish," "not a real language," and "not real Spanish" were commonly used by many informants to describe Judeo-Spanish in the above studies. When compared to English, Hebrew, and varieties of Modern Spanish, as well as other European languages, Judeo-Spanish was generally compared unfavorably and was considered an inferior form of speech.

The great majority (seventy-nine or 86 percent) of the informants consider Judeo-Spanish to be a dying language today. This opinion is reinforced by the fact that 100 percent of the informants' grandchildren do not speak Judeo-Spanish at all, while their children have very limited (if any) conversational skills in the language. Only 45 percent of the informants feel that it is important to pass on Judeo-Spanish, even though in reality nothing is being done to perpetuate the language, and very little is being done to maintain it in the United States and Israel.

Although language attitudes are generally subjective, reported data (versus objective, empirical data) which may or may not have any basis in fact, negative language attitudes must be considered a valid factor in determining whether or not the language is maintained or perpetuated by a speech community.[8] Naturally, negative attitudes are not the only cause of language death or replacement, but they generally are an important phenomenon accompanying the decline of a language. Very few members of a society, who are trying to be upwardly mobile, will invest the time, money, and effort needed to maintain and perpetuate a nonprestigious dying language. And in the United States and Israel, "getting ahead" is of utmost importance. Many Judeo-Spanish speakers feel that the language is not only dying, but that it is beyond the hope of any real rehabilitation:

> Some community members seem to have resigned themselves with little difficulty to the disappearance of the language, believing it to be an unavoidable and quite natural consequence of the process of acculturation. Others regard the loss as regrettable but feel that they are incapable of reversing—even of influencing—the course of affairs. (Malinowski 1983:146)

In the case of Judeo-Spanish in New York City, Israel, and Los Angeles, we cannot deny the influence or impact of negative language attitudes on its decline.

Part V
Language Death and Sephardic Identity: A Sociolinguistic Perspective

13

Judeo-Spanish and Language Death

The Process of Language Death

The general phenomenon of language death or language decline falls into the category of what Fishman introduced as "language shift" versus "language maintenance" (Fishman 1964). Language shift or language replacement occurs when a community makes a total shift to a new language. This means that the replacing language takes over the domains formerly reserved for the original language which is no longer used as a means of communication. According to Fasold, both language maintenance and shift are the results of language choice on the part of members of a speech community: "The members of the community, when the shift has taken place, have collectively chosen a new language where an old one used to be used" (1984:213). Since language shift often reflects pragmatic desires for social mobility and a better standard of living, Edwards reminds us that we should not neglect the powerful influence of the people's own linguistic choices (Edwards 1985:59).

According to Dressler and Wodak-Leodolter (1977a:6), language death affects mostly minority or ethnic languages. These are languages of lower prestige that are spoken by only a small part of the community's population, as opposed to another dominant language or languages of the same community or country. A. Graur (1960:437) points out that no language dies brusquely (except in rare examples of extinction of the members of a speech community). Nor does it occur at the same time for all speakers. It is a gradual process that lasts several years and is accompanied by a long period of unstable bilingualism, which serves as an intermediate stage before the demise of the original language. As Fasold writes, in almost all cases of societal language shift,

> a substantial proportion of the individuals in a society seldom completely give up the use of one language and substitute another one within their lifetime. In the typical case, one generation is bilingual,

but only passes on one of the two languages to the next. (Fasold 1984:216–17)

Edwards, in discussing the decline of Irish, wrote that "bilingualism was usually a way-station on the road to English only" (Edwards 1985:54). During this intermediate bilingual stage, the original language suffers a loss of domains as the dominant language comes to fulfill all of the official, prestigious, and important functions of the community, while the ethnic language becomes relegated more and more to use in the home, for religious purposes, and for cultural traditions and events. Often in these reduced functions the dying language is used side by side with the replacing language. Edwards writes that Gaelic is often used with English (Edwards 1985:60), and in her Breton studies, Timm writes that French coexists with Breton in several domains (Timm 1980:38). As the language functions diminish and the original language declines, the dominant language eventually replaces the original mother tongue minority language in all domains, even that of primary socialization.

For immigrant ethnic languages in the United States, as well as in Israel, the shift to the dominant language usually takes place over the course of three generations. The first generation (or grandparents) speaks the original language or mother tongue fluently and uses it most, if not all, of the time. The second generation (or parents) is bilingual in the mother tongue and the replacing language and often begins to feel more at home in the new language. This generation of speakers is referred to as "semi-speakers" by Dorian (1981:156). It is this bilingual generation that passes on the replacing language to the third generation as its new mother tongue. The members of the third generation (or grandchildren) understand or speak the native language of their parents very little, if at all, since they use the replacing language almost one hundred percent of the time. One of my New York informants described this situation quite well when she said that she felt caught in the middle of three worlds: her parents spoke Judeo-Spanish fluently; she does not speak it so well but she understands it and can get along in it; while her children do not speak it at all (Harris 1979:293).

Terracini writes that the necessary prerequisite for the change from one language to another is that the two civilizations and languages in question should not only be distinct in the consciousness or realization of the speakers, but more or less opposed to each other. When this consciousness exists the change of languages is rapid and radical (Terracini 1951:21). Dorian refers to this phenomenon as culture conflict (1981:9), and Edwards writes of language contact and conflict where one language supplants another (1985:49). Denison emphasizes that when social prestige and the number of speakers of the dominant language are higher than that of the minority language, then the survival of the original language is in question (1977:16). Ethnic/immigrant minorities throughout the world are constantly competing with the surrounding dominant (and often more modern) cultures which they wish to join and to which they often have easy access (Fishman 1991:196). And Dorian points out that the adaptive strategy of the speakers of the minority language is to achieve membership in the dominant culture as quickly and as easily as possible:

> the adoption of a dominant-culture language (even to the exclusion of their own) by the members of a subordinate or peripheral culture is an adaptive, or coping, strategy. It provides linguistic access to the dominant culture, with all the attendant possibilities of incorporation into that culture, if only at the fringes. (1981:40–41)

This adoption of the dominant language can be attained without great financial expense, as opposed to changing one's life style, wardrobe or diet, for example. According to Denison, "it is as though a culture (speech community) . . . sometimes 'decides', for reasons of functional economy, to suppress a part of itself in the process of onward transmission" (1977:21). Thus Denison has coined the term "language suicide," which occurs when speakers of the original, low prestige language consciously choose not to transmit it to their children, who in turn are not motivated to learn it. Also, one cannot minimize the role of the children themselves who resist use of the mother or ethnic tongue. Among many immigrant groups in the United States for example, it is often the case that the parents speak the ethnic language to the children who respond only in English.

Fasold (1984:218) reminds us that even though Fishman introduced the concept of language maintenance and language shift in 1964, not many in-depth studies on language shift have been done. This is somewhat puzzling when we consider Edwards's observation that "history shows that language shift is the rule, not the exception . . . virtually *all* groups have language shift somewhere in their past" (1985:96). By the same token, not much research has been done on language extinction, even though, as Swadesh pointed out, "the disappearance of languages, when viewed in the broad sweep of history, is no uncommon phenomenon" (1948:226).

Some examples of ancient languages which have died and been replaced by others include Egyptian, Sumerian, Phoenician, Aramaic, Hittite, Etruscan, Oscan, Umbrian, Thracian, and Pictish. Languages such as Sanskrit, Latin, Old Church Slavonic, and Classical Arabic died as spoken languages but have been maintained for religious purposes.

Nancy Dorian also reminds us that "linguistic extinction, or 'language death,' . . . is to be found under way currently in virtually every part of the world" (1981:1). Languages that have died in the last century or are presently in the process of dying include: (a) American Indian languages such as Yahi, Chitimacha, Tiwa, Natchez, Catawba, Mashpi, Lake Miwok, Shoshoni, Penobscot, Cupeño, and Luiseño; (b) Celtic languages such as Cornish and Manx as well as the presently declining Gaelic in Ireland, East Sutherland Gaelic in Scotland, and Breton in Brittany; and (c) Romance languages such as Provençal in Southern France and Istro-Rumanian in Rumania.

In chapter 11, various reasons for the decline of Judeo-Spanish were discussed. But how does one know when a particular language is in fact dying? What is the tangible evidence? Below I will present a few of the most obvious signs of the impending death of Judeo-Spanish. Later I will consider Judeo-Spanish in the framework of dying languages in general.

Signs of the Impending Death of Judeo-Spanish

(A) DIMINISHING DOMAINS OF USAGE

The reduction of language domains is one of the most visible signs of language decline. Today Judeo-Spanish, like other dying languages, has only three main functions, which are minimal at best. It is reserved: (1) for use with the elderly, (2) as a secret language when the speakers do not want children or outsiders to know what they are saying, and (3) for entertainment purposes, such as telling jokes, stories, reciting proverbs, and singing ballads or *romanzas*. Fishman points out that one of the principle Yiddish domains for second generation Ashkenazim is humor (Fishman 1965:50), and Huffines also reports that her informants use Pennsylvania German as a form of entertainment "for fun, to tease, to make jokes" (Huffines 1980:54). Fishman refers to this vestigial existence of the original language in an advanced stage of language shift as a metaphorical function which cannot last. He writes that the language

> is used (by those who still know it) primarily in exceptional circumstances: to designate humor, irony, satire, affect, or to put it even more broadly—to indicate symbolic contrastivity to normal functioning. However, the predominance of *such* usage is itself an indication of shift. . . . Metaphorical usage is not intergenerationally continuous but, rather, fleeting, changeable, marginal and nonreciprocal. . . . Language maintenance is clearly impossible on a metaphorical basis alone. (Fishman et al. 1985:63)

(B) A VERY SMALL NUMBER OF JUDEO-SPANISH SPEAKERS

The rapid reduction of speakers is a result of either: the passing away of the older generations; the drop in population due to disease, war, extermination, immigration, assimilation; or the actual renunciation of the use of Judeo-Spanish in favor of another language. Figures of the number of proficient Judeo-Spanish speakers in the world today are very difficult to obtain. In 1966, Renard estimated the number of Judeo-Spanish speakers in the world to be 360,000 (1966a:105). As of 1979, I estimated that there were about 160,000 speakers (Harris 1979:352). Given the passage of fourteen years since this last estimate, and the fact that many older Sephardim have passed away, I would suggest that a more realistic estimate of proficient Judeo-Spanish speakers in the world today is closer to 60,000.

(C) NO YOUNG JUDEO-SPANISH SPEAKERS

Besides reduction of language domains and the small number of speakers, probably the most important sign of impending language death is the absence of young Judeo-Spanish speakers. Today it is almost impossible to find native speakers of Judeo-Spanish who are under the age of forty or fifty in Israel (Malinowski 1979, Harris 1979) and the United States (Harris 1979, 1987). Malinowski also could not find any young Judeo-Spanish speakers in Turkey (Malinowski 1982a). The few people of that age who have some knowledge of the language have limited linguistic skills and are not capable of transmitting Judeo-Spanish to their children or grandchildren.

As I reported in chapter 12, only 42 percent (33 of 79) of the informants' children could speak or had a passive knowledge of the language, while 100 percent of the informants' grandchildren could not speak Judeo-Spanish at all. As Fasold writes, "If there is a genuine shift taking place, it would certainly show up in the larger proportions of older speakers using the declining language than younger speakers" (1984:215). Judeo-Spanish is used almost exclusively by older people since they constitute the only remaining group of skilled speakers. It is often the case that in the process of language shift, different generations of the same family use different languages. For example, often the grandparents will use the immigrant, ethnic language, while the grandchildren answer in the replacing, more prestigious language.

(D) NO MONOLINGUAL SPEAKERS

The absence of monolingual speakers of the original language is another important sign of impending language death. In Dorian's (1977:24,31) and Hill's (1978:47) studies, there were no monolingual Gaelic, or Cupeño or Luiseño speakers respectively. In Malinowski's studies in Israel and Turkey (1979, 1982a), Nemer's study in Indianapolis (1981), and my studies in New York, Israel, and Los Angeles (Harris 1979, 1987), there were also no longer any monolingual Judeo-Spanish speakers.

(E) LACK OF INSTITUTIONAL/COMMUNITY SUPPORT

The lack of institutional/community support for Judeo-Spanish is also a sign of language decline. Fishman emphasizes its important role in language maintenance, and he concentrates on what he considers to be the four principle language maintenance institutions: the ethnic mother tongue press and publications, ethnic language broadcasting on both radio and television, non-English ethnic mother-tongue schools, and local religious units utilizing languages other than English (Fishman et al. 1985:195–282).

Judeo-Spanish in the United States no longer has the advantage of any of the above institutions. The Judeo-Spanish press ended in 1948, when the last New York newspaper, *La Vara*, ceased publication. There are a few American publications which deal with Sephardic culture, but none are written in Judeo-Spanish. There is no regular radio or television broadcasting in the language, and there are no schools in which Judeo-Spanish is the language of instruction or is taught as a subject. While there are local Sephardic synagogues, Judeo-Spanish is rarely used (except in songs, stories, an occasional prayer, and by older members of the congregation), and services and cultural events are not held in Judeo-Spanish.

In Israel the institutional supports are minimal, and these are in danger of disappearing. For example, in 1978, the Judeo-Spanish newspaper *La Luz de Israel,* published in Tel Aviv, was a biweekly paper with about 80,000 readers in Israel and throughout the world.[1] In 1985, it became a weekly paper, and in 1990, it ceased publication altogether. Of the more than three hundred Judeo-Spanish newspapers which formerly existed throughout the world, only one remains in existence today, and it is written mostly in Turkish. *Şalom,* the Jewish weekly published in Istanbul, is eight pages in length with only one page printed in Judeo-Spanish (see Appendix E).

Today the Jerusalem based quarterly *Aki Yerushalayim* (See Appendix E), which American Sephardim also read, is the only journal in the world today that is written completely in Judeo-Spanish. There are a few other journals dedicated to Sephardic topics such as *Los Muestros,* published in Belgium, and *Vidas Largas,* published in Paris, but the majority of their articles are written in languages other than Judeo-Spanish.

In 1978 radio station Kol Israel in Jerusalem had a morning news program in Judeo-Spanish and a fifteen minute evening broadcast that was a commentary in Judeo-Spanish on subjects of interest concerning Sephardic folklore, culture, and so forth. Now there is just one nightly program in Judeo-Spanish covering both the news and topics of Sephardic interest (see Appendix E). However, in his 1991 interview with Rachel Bortnick, the director of the Judeo-Spanish section of Kol Israel, Moshe Shaul, talked about the "precarious" position of that fifteen minute program whose budget had been cut by the government. He reported that they were being pressured to shorten or totally give up these Judeo-Spanish broadcasts which he felt (along with several others) was unfair, since broadcasts in other languages were receiving generous support from the Israeli government (Bortnick 1992a:4). However, appeals were made that have resulted in the retention of the broadcast, at least temporarily.

Structural Signs of Language Decay

A dying language undergoes structural changes in all parts of its grammar. Linguists such as Hill (1978), Dressler and Wodak-Leodolter (1977a), Dorian (1973, 1981), Sala (1970b), and others write

of obligatory phonological rules becoming optional, both morphological and syntactic analogical leveling, simplification of grammatical structures, loss of rules, language reduction in general,
polysemy, and other linguistic changes. All of the above structural
changes often impair the communicative efficiency of the original
language and can be signs of impending language death. Some examples of structural change in Judeo-Spanish are the following:

(A) PHONOLOGICAL LEVELING

Judeo-Spanish has undergone a great extent of phonological leveling in both the United States and Israel, due to continuous contact between the Sephardim of different dialectal communities and
the need for a common language or dialect in which they could
easily communicate with one another. Malinowski reports that today in Israel most phonological signs of regional differences have
generally disappeared, with leveling of such features as vowel raising, retention of initial *f-*, and distinctions between single [r] and
trilled [r̄] (Malinowski 1979:22,30,35). She also found individual
differences which she feels should be considered only as stylistic
variations. D. Levy (1952), Hirsch (1951), and Benardete (1982:169)
write of the development of a *koiné* in New York. According to
Bunis, this leveling of earlier variations in Judeo-Spanish has resulted in a "supraregional, unofficial 'standard' variety" which is
heard today in New York and Tel Aviv and is evident in existent
Judeo-Spanish publications. This phonological variety more
closely resembles the dialect of Istanbul and its surroundings (and
the Turkish dialects of Izmir, Edirne, Gelibolu, and Bursa) and is
known as *(e)stambulesko* (Bunis 1982b:393).

(B) INDIVIDUAL VARIATION

Another sign of a language in decline, according to Sala
(1970b:64), can be found in individual variation. Sjoestedt
(1928:101) observes that the number of words subjected to individual variation or fluctuation denotes a pathological state or symptom
of a language more than does a high number of borrowings. Phonological variation, not due to dialect differences, was quite prevalent
in my Judeo-Spanish word elicitation data.[2]

According to Mackey, "in any evolving code the degree of individual variation is a function of the rate of change" (1970:197).
Variation across Judeo-Spanish dialects gives an idea of the inse-
cure speech of the informants who have an imperfect knowledge

of the language. This is due to their lack of exposure to Judeo-Spanish, its present state of decline, and also to the fact that there is no standard norm. (Remember that Judeo-Spanish was a language that was not studied in school[3]).

(C) BORROWING AND CODE-SWITCHING

The Judeo-Spanish lexicon is the structural aspect which has changed the most, since it is made up not only of archaic Castilian words, but has borrowed heavily from Hebrew and Arabic, Romance languages (especially French and Italian), various Balkan languages with which Judeo-Spanish came into contact, and more recently from Modern Spanish, English, and Modern Hebrew (see chapter 10). When analyzing this extensive lexical borrowing, Dorian's point should be considered here: that we must examine the question of how long after its introduction does a loanword remain an instance of interference (Dorian 1981:100). That is, we must distinguish borrowing from integration into the code (Mackey 1970:195). This is often a difficult thing to do in Judeo-Spanish. Also, one must distinguish the variations of lexical items given by the informants which were due to the speaker's region of origin and particular Judeo-Spanish dialect spoken. Although Malinowski and I found such variation in the choice of lexical items, it did not seem to hamper comprehension, since as she points out "only rarely did an informant fail to recognize as a possible synonym the forms popular in varieties of Judeo-Spanish other than that of his own native land" (1979:104). And Malinowski predicts that if the current trends and current mixing of dialect speakers continues, leveling in the lexicon will also occur.

My informants in the United States substituted a large number of words and phrases from English and Modern Spanish into their samples of free conversation, while my Israeli informants used many Hebrew and French words. All of my informants who were able to give samples of free conversation resorted to frequent code-switching. Since it was such a common phenomenon in the speech of the informants, I posited code-switching[4] as one of the dominant characteristics of Judeo-Spanish today as spoken in New York, Israel, and Los Angeles. This large extent of code-switching might be considered as one sign of decay of the Judeo-Spanish language. However, we must remember that code-switching per se is not necessarily a sign of language death in general, or of language shift, since it often functions as one of the important aspects of conversational strategies; that is, when speakers make conscious or unconscious choices of the linguistic forms they use (DiPietro 1976:203).

(D) HESITATIONS, HALTING SPEECH, FEAR OF MAKING MISTAKES

In his Bucharest study Sala recorded numerous hesitations and corrections in pronunciation and word choice on the part of his informants, which he attributes to lack of a consolidated norm (1970a:21, 40–45). For Sala this hesitation represents the most salient peculiarity of the Judeo-Spanish of Bucharest. D. Levy wrote that confusion and vagueness resulting from the inefficient phonetic writing system (which was not based on Castilian and was used after the abandonment of the Hebrew alphabet[5]), actually characterized the degeneration and corruption of the New York Izmir dialect (1952).

I also found a great deal of hesitation and halting delivery in the speech of my informants. This is most probably due to linguistic insecurity brought on by insufficient exposure to Judeo-Spanish. Another characteristic of my informants was an unwillingness to make mistakes. Terracini quotes Vendryes who wrote in regards to Latin, that "a language begins to die when people make mistakes." However, Terracini adds, "it would be better to say: when most people not only make mistakes, but are afraid to make mistakes" (1951:35). This fear of making mistakes was especially prevalent in the speech of my female informants.[6] The lack of correct Judeo-Spanish vocabulary was the main reason given by the informants for their inferior Judeo-Spanish skills, as compared with those of their elders. This lexical deficiency was the only structural weakness that most informants were aware of, since it did impair their ability to express certain ideas.

Judeo-Spanish within the Framework of Dying Languages in General

In the process of language death or replacement, changes in the original culture (see the following chapter), as well as in certain structural aspects of the original language, make the retrieval of a dying language almost impossible. The study of a dying language will not revive it; however, various scholars have suggested an organized study of Judeo-Spanish for linguistic, historical, and cultural purposes, especially to contribute to the emerging field of research known as "Jewish interlinguistics" (Herzog 1978:54 and Gold 1981). We can also put Judeo-Spanish within the framework of dying languages and language shift or replacement in general. Studies of the various Judeo-Spanish dialects can offer the field of linguistics certain knowledge on the manner in which a language dies or the mechanism of language death. As Jane Hill has pointed out, "surprisingly little has been written about the events, both social and linguistic, which surround the death of a language" (1978:45). A study of Judeo-Spanish can shed light on just such events. Various sociological and linguistic variables or conditions that surround the decline or disappearance of Judeo-Spanish are present for language death and language replacement in general. The different studies done on other dying languages, such as the Amerindian languages (Swadesh 1948, Miller 1971, etc.); Celtic languages including Gaelic (Macnamara 1971, Agnew 1981, Edwards 1984a, 1984b, 1985), East Sutherland Gaelic (Dorian 1973, 1977, 1981), Welsh (Lewis 1978), and Breton (Timm 1980, Dressler and Wodak-Leodolter 1977b); Provençal (Schlieben-Lange (1977); Pennsylvania German (Huffines 1980), and others, all show that these languages are influenced by the same or very similar sociolinguistic factors. Dorian refers to the sociolinguistic "profile" of a dying language (Dorian 1981:112–113), and Huffines writes of "a paradigm" for a dying language (Huffines 1980:54). I have formulated a list of sociolinguistic features whose presence in various combinations eventually contribute to language death or replacement. These variables have been taken from this and the preceding two chapters, but are now being presented in a more comprehensive form to cover dying languages in general. The following is by no means an all inclusive list, and the features are not presented in any particular order.

Sociolinguistic Features Contributing to Language Death

1. Nationalistic movements that do not favor cultural or linguistic pluralism.
2. Forces of assimilation such as Americanization or Israelization.
3. Reduction or narrowing of language domains or functions of the original language.
4. Loss of prestige of the original language.
5. Negative attitudes on the part of the speakers concerning the original language, which they consider to be inferior in certain ways.

6. Refusal of women to speak or pass on the language to their children.
7. Resistance of youth to speak the language or even to be identified with it.
8. Isolation from the mother country and culture.
9. Lack of close-knit neighborhoods or speech communities where the original language is dominant.
10. Influences of other languages and cultures (on the original language and culture) resulting in a great amount of cultural change in the community.
11. Lack of a central unifying force in the community.
12. No attempts to preserve the language by speakers of the language themselves.
13. No effective organizations or movements to champion the cause (maintenance and perpetuation) of the language.
14. No language academy or central organization to establish linguistic norms.
15. Use of an inefficient writing system to represent the language.
16. Illiteracy or a low literacy rate of speakers of the language.
17. No good secular literature (or a very limited amount) written in the language.
18. Relaxation of religious observances or of religious importance in the community, especially if the language has now, or previously had religious functions.
19. No governmental support for teaching the language, which results in no instruction of the language itself in schools or universities.
20. Very limited or no institutional support such as ethnic mother-tongue press, radio and television broadcasts, ethnic mother-tongue schools, other schools where the ethnic language is taught, and local religious units which encourage use of the language.
21. No more monolingual speakers of the language.
22. No young speakers (under the age of forty or fifty) of the language.
23. Intermarriage with speakers of other languages and members of other ethnic groups.
24. Reduction of the population who speaks the language.
25. Fear on the part of the speakers to make mistakes, resulting in much hesitation and a halting delivery.
26. Individual variations or fluctuations in the use of forms due

to confusion on the part of the speakers as well as to a lack of standardized linguistic norms.

27. A large amount of code-switching in the speech of all or most of the speakers.
28. No possibility of, or very limited contact with fluent speakers.
29. No mother country or heartland. That is, the language has no territory of its own where it is used across a broad range of domains.
30. No continual (or sizable) influx of newly arriving immigrants.
31. Great diversity of the immigrant population of a country resulting in the need for a common language.

Concluding Remarks

Various scholars such as Fishman (1964), Dorian (1981), Gregor (1980), and Edwards (1985) agree that no one factor is responsible for language death or language replacement, nor do speakers of the language necessarily exhibit the same linguistic characteristics. Language death is caused by a "chain of events" (Denison 1977:21) where different combinations of factors can bring about or hasten the process of language extinction. In future studies we must weigh the significance of each factor of change and conduct research to determine where and when certain features are present. Even though we know the variables that are generally present in cases of language shift, it is still difficult to predict shift. As Fasold points out, there has been very little success in using any combination of factors to predict language shift, and there also seems to be a great deal of consensus that we do not know how to predict language shift (1984:217).

To aid in deciding the status of various languages, I wish to emphasize the "critical" period or stage in the history of a language which signifies that the language is in the process of dying or being replaced. This critical period is reached when the great majority, if not all, of the speakers of a language in a particular society or speech community are above the age of forty. This means that the childbearing generation of a community is not passing on the language to their offspring. For whatever reasons: whether the parents don't know the language well enough, whether due to nationalism, low prestige, intermarriage, or the fear that the mother tongue will be an obstacle to their child's advancement, the parents have consciously chosen not to pass on the language. Once this stage is reached the trend is irreversible, and it is almost impossible to revive the language for use as the everyday means of communication (barring extraordinary circumstances as in the unique case of Hebrew in Israel).[7]

Today Judeo-Spanish has reached this critical stage, and so has Yiddish, the language of the Eastern European Ashkenazic Jews. There are various Yiddish supporters who may argue that the language is not declining on the grounds that there appear to be many surviving Yiddish speakers,[8] and that there are still isolated pockets in the world where children are learning the language. However, Fishman makes a clear distinction between ultra-Orthodox Yiddish speakers and secularists. The small groups of ultra-Orthodox, who live in sections of New York and Jerusalem, continue to use Yiddish as their daily means of communication and thus to pass it on to their children.[9] However, for the majority secular Ashkenazic community, Fishman writes:

> It is fair to say that there is virtually no societally structured intergenerational ethnolinguistic community among Yiddish secularists in New York today (and even less outside of New York) and such meager continuity as does still obtain exists on an atypical and individual family basis alone. (1991:202)

Thus he reports that the attrition of Yiddish in the United States is quite advanced, and he suggests that what happens to Yiddish in America will have effects on the future of the language throughout the world (Fishman 1991:194). While it is true that currently Ashkenazic Jews far outnumber Sephardic Jews in the world, the number of young Yiddish speakers is extremely small. The reality is that the current average age of the secular Yiddish speakers worldwide, like Judeo-Spanish speakers, is in the high seventies (Fishman 1991:199). Thus both Yiddish and Judeo-Spanish have not been transmitted to the younger generations in most Jewish communities of the world for the past forty-five to fifty years. As Dorian writes:

> The home is the last bastion of a subordinate language in competition with a dominant official language of wider currency. An impending shift has in effect arrived, even though a fairly sizable number of speakers may be left, if those speakers have failed to transmit the language to their children, so that no replacement generation is available when the parent generation dies away. The pattern of the shift is almost monotonously the same in diverse settings: the language of wider cur-

rency is recognized as the language of upward mobility, and as soon as the linguistic competence of the parents permits, it is introduced into the home. (1981:105)

Although various factors are present in language decline, scholars such as Saville-Troike (1982:193), Edwards (1985:50), and others agree with Denison who concludes that "the direct cause of 'language death' is seen to be social and psychological: parents cease transmitting the language in question to their offspring" (1977:22). Denison also reminds us that it is not languages themselves which live and die, but the people who speak them; it is speech communities which live and die (1977:13). Edwards describes the process more extensively when he writes:

Languages themselves obviously obey no organic imperatives, but their speakers do. Languages do not live or die at all. . . . Yet they clearly *do* have an 'allotted life' which is granted, not by the laws of nature, but by human society and culture. The fortunes of language are bound up with those of its users, and if languages decline or 'die' it is simply because the circumstances of their speakers have altered. The most common scenario here is that involving language contact and conflict: one language supplants another. (1985:49)

Future studies on disappearing/dying languages should include research on the generational spread of the speakers of the language in question; that is, which generations, both old and young, still speak the language and are passing it on. In-depth analyses of the semi-speakers should be undertaken. As Dorian suggests, we need to study how the speech of semi-speakers compares with other reductive language systems such as child language or pidgins (Dorian 1981:155). Studies are needed in an attempt to discover universals of linguistic change which occur in the process of language death. A structural feature analysis of phonological, morphological, syntactic, and lexical aspects as well as trends which can be observed in dying languages could be attempted. Much work still needs to be done on both the linguistic and sociological aspects of dying languages. It is hoped that certain procedures and analyses made in this research may prove useful in future studies of language death.

14

Prospects for Judeo-Spanish and Sephardic Ethnicity

Is a Judeo-Spanish Revival Possible?

The reasons for the decline of Judeo-Spanish as well as present signs of impending language death have been presented in chapters 11, 12 and 13. In the United States and Israel Judeo-Spanish is a language relegated to use with and by older people, and it presently has very limited domains. Today there are no monolingual speakers or young Judeo-Spanish speakers left with the exception of scholars of the language. Judeo-Spanish has reached what I referred to in chapter 13 as a critical stage in its history since it is not being passed on to the younger generations. Fishman writes that threatened languages whose "intergenerational continuity is proceeding negatively, with fewer and fewer users (speakers, readers, writers and even understanders) or uses every generation" (1991:1), are often beyond the help of efforts to reverse language shift.[1] He suggests that such efforts must be accomplished first at the intimate family and local community levels, primarily by the minorities themselves (Fishman 1991:3–4). As we have seen, this is not the case with Judeo-Spanish, which receives no maintenance support from its speakers or from any institutions.[2] Due to its present status, the chances of reviving Judeo-Spanish as a language of daily communication are almost nonexistent.

Edwards questions the validity of language revivals suggesting that such efforts are artificial endeavors since language decline does not occur in a vacuum, but takes place along with changes in society, and that the original milieu in which the language once flourished no longer exists. Also, by the time that people are aware that a language is threatened by extinction, it is generally too late to save it. He also points out that language boards, agencies, committees, and so forth are often signs that a language is in danger (Edwards 1985:72, 83). Given the lack of success of revival movements in the past with such languages as Gaelic, Welsh, and Breton, Nahir reports that all language revival efforts have failed with the exception of the Hebrew revival in Israel (1977:111).[3]

We must remember that, throughout the history of Judeo-Spanish in the United States and Israel, there have never been any positive efforts to maintain the mother tongue. Even with the establishment of various Sephardic organizations to study Sephardic culture, history, etc., the propagation of Judeo-Spanish has never been an important concern. And on an individual basis, the desire to continue speaking Judeo-Spanish is, as Fishman found in his studies of Yiddish, more attitudinal than behavioral (1965:50). In other words, the speakers themselves know that Judeo-Spanish is a dying language and they do not choose to make any efforts on behalf of language maintenance. We must not forget that it is the members of a speech community themselves who have consciously chosen to give up the mother tongue. As a result, the speakers of declining languages do not get as upset over language decline as do concerned outsiders or some group leaders (Edwards 1985:98). And as Gellner points out, language is a relatively easy thing to change: "Changing one's language is not the heart-breaking or soul-destroying business which it is claimed to be in romantic nationalist literature" (1964:165).

Since Judeo-Spanish is in a state of decline with no possibility for language maintenance or revival, what are the prospects for Sephardic ethnicity in general? How does the present climate for ethnicity in the United States and Israel affect the mother-tongue language and group identity? What were the results of the ethnic revival in America? I will examine these questions in the following sections.

The Ethnic Revival and Ethnic Identity

As Fishman et al. (1985), Edwards (1985), and others report, there is an extensive amount of evidence pointing to an ethnic revival that occurred in the United States (as well as in other parts of the world) from the mid-sixties and mid-seventies and which declined by the end of the seventies. The evidence for this revival in the United States consists of

"across the board" increases in non-English mother-tongue claiming; increases in the number of ethnic community mother-tongue periodical publications . . . schools . . . local religious units utilizing languages other than English in some part of their total effort; increases in the number of radio stations and television channels broadcasting in languages other than English . . . increases in ethnic studies (courses, departments) at American colleges and universities; ethnic awareness . . . ethnic pageants and festivities . . . and increased ethnic concerns in the mainstream press and other mass media as well as increased ethnic "sensitivity" on the part of mainstream political parties. (Fishman et al. 1985:489)

This movement in the United States was influenced by various Black and Hispanic movements that resulted in a change of climate for ethnicity in general, in that it was no longer threatening, unpopular, or unpatriotic to speak a language other than English or to espouse and manifest ethnic beliefs and practices. These trends resulted in the United States Congressional passage of the Ethnic Heritage Studies Act in 1972, which promoted the study of the cultural heritage of various ethnic groups and encouraged ethnic identity as a positive force in American society (Mizrahi 1987:42, 58). This "new ethnicity" was primarily a movement lead by second, third, and fourth generation Americans trying to rediscover their "roots" (Fishman 1973:226).

The cultural behavior, beliefs, values, and traditions of a people help to define their membership in a particular ethnic group. How people dress, what they eat, and the type of work they do, are examples of overt ethnic markers. Language behavior, especially mother-tongue use, is also generally considered to be ethnicity related. In fact, Fishman writes that language and ethnicity have been "naturally linked in almost every age of premodern pan-Mediterranean and European thought." (Fishman et al. 1985:12). With this in mind, should it not follow that a linguistic revival would accompany an ethnic revival? We need to relate language shift to ethnicity to understand what ethnic revivals really accomplish.

Various scholars think that the word "revival" may not be the most appropriate term. First of all, ethnic revivals are not really movements of return to the past. As Edwards points out, "there is no 'going back' for most people. . . . There is no evidence at all that people *en masse* wish to escape modernity, least of all the 'ethnics'" (1985:101). He also reminds us that not only is "going back" not a viable option, but also that a romantic view of the past disguises harsh conditions that we would not want to duplicate. A. Smith considers the recent ethnic resurgence as a "development and transformation of pre-existing, if submerged, ethnic ties and as the recent phase of a long historical cycle or ethnic emergence and decline, which has been going on since the dawn of recorded history" (1981:86). And Fishman agrees since he refers to ethnic revivals as "ethnicity repertoire changes" that are really not revivals at all, but rather awakenings and reforms (Fishman et al. 1985:515). These reforms have contributed to a broadening of the limits of what is acceptable in the designation of being "American." He writes:

> it is now not only possible to "be American" in a variety of different ethnic ways, but sidestream ethnicity *per se* has also become much more modern and American. The spirit of the times is different and the vast majority of Americans reveal sidestream ethnicity-associated ways of doing, feeling and knowing within their total repertoire of social behaviors. (ibid., 502)

Fishman later writes that sidestream ethnicity or exhibiting some form of ethnicity is even expected today as a feature of an American identity.

Gans suggests that an ethnic revival has not taken place, but rather a new, more visible way of expressing one's identity has emerged, and that the current needs for ethnic identity have changed. They are neither frequent nor intense, nor do they resemble the ancestral European heritage (Gans 1979:193, 195). His hypothesis is that while ethnic ties continue to diminish, the third generation still perceives itself as ethnic:

> in this generation, people are less and less interested in their ethnic cultures and organizations—both sacred and secular—and are instead more concerned with maintaining their ethnic identity, with the feeling of being Jewish or Italian or Polish, and with finding ways of feeling and expressing that identity in suitable ways. (ibid., 202)

Gans points out that this ethnic identity can be expressed in various ways, but that given the degree to which the third generation has already acculturated and assimilated, they will look for easy or convenient ways to express their ethnicity. According to Gans, this involves the use of symbols such as various holidays, ethnic foods and promoting certain causes. He refers to the third generation's pursuit of identity as "symbolic ethnicity," and the symbols chosen to represent ethnicity may vary (ibid., 204–6). For example, Mizrahi suggests that although a Sephardi may show strong affinity and be aligned to Sephardim in general, he or she may not necessarily behave in ways which are considered typical of the Sephardic group, such as eating specific "typical" foods, for example (Mizrahi 1987:344). The Sephardi is free to choose the particular symbols he/she wants to embrace. This "symbolic ethnicity" results in an increased tolerance for and acceptance of a more visible manifestation of ethnic diversity: "Ethnicity is freer to express itself" (Edwards 1985:101).

What kind of ethnicity is exhibited today in the United States? D. Matza informs us that after coming to the United States, the Levantine Sephardic immigrants tried to duplicate their way of life and their institutions of the Levant (1990:338). However, this was accomplished with an American twist or flavor. In fact, what happens with most ethnic groups in the "new country" is that the ethnic identity changes and adapts to the dominant way of life:

> The distinctive cultures of these ethnic groups are to a large extent creations growing out of their experience on American soil, not mere transplants from other countries. Chow mein, the St. Patrick's Day parade, and the "Afro" hairdo are all American products. . . . (Sowell 1978:233)

The result for Sephardim is a different manifestation of certain traditional ethnic markers plus modern American and Israeli influences. The Sephardic identity in both the United States and Israel is a combination of life in the Levant and the new country. In S. Stern's article on the Sephardic Jews of Los Angeles, he emphasizes the Sephardim's efforts to find a common ground between the old and new cultures. He writes that the American born or younger generations are always looking for

> avenues of creativity in order to make Sephardic life relevant to American culture . . . and . . . to clarify those aspects of the Sephardic identity that can be made compatible with American values. (1982:140–41)

Keeping the comments of Gans, Sowell, and Stern in mind, the question arises as to what markers of ethnicity does a particular ethnic group choose to maintain? The obvious answer is that they will be the markers that do not hinder social mobility, economic advancement, and acceptance into the mainstream society. It appears that in the assimilation process, the more public or visible markers that might stigmatize group members will disappear before those markers that are less visible and are restricted to the more private domains. According to Edwards the survival of the private markers of ethnicity is due to the fact that they are subjected to fewer external pressures (1985:97). Thus, visible markers such as ways of dressing, hairdos, and language are more likely to disappear than culinary or religious practices. At the same time, various group markers can also disappear as ordinary daily markers, but be retained as symbolic ones appearing only for special festivals or functions.

Language and Identity

Where does the ethnic mother-tongue language fit into this process of repertoire change? First of all, it is obvious that language is a very visible ethnic marker. And even though language is symbolic of ethnicity, it is, as a daily means of communication, an element of identity very susceptible to change. Bunis (1974:2) and Matza (1990:344–45) remind us that throughout history the Jews have always tried to become good citizens and learn the languages of their respective host countries. Sherman feels that Jews have habitually carried within themselves more than one culture at a time; their Judaism, which they carry within their spiritual and psychic being, and the other culture, which they have worn like an "outer garment": "Each time they trod new ground, they changed their outer garment, but always they succeeded in retaining at least in part their inner culture" (1965:123). Language is part of this changeable "outer garment." Edwards reminds us that the linguistic behavior of a group depends on pragmatic concerns of adjustment to new requirements and conditions of acceptance (1985:92). As Fishman writes, "the language with stronger rewards and sanctions associated with it wins out" (Fishman et al. 1985:45).

In the United States the adopted dominant language of more prestige is English, and in Israel it is Hebrew. So what is the future for Sephardic identity/ethnicity as Judeo-Spanish disappears? Does the impending death of Judeo-Spanish as a language of communication mean that Sephardic culture and identity will also die? Various scholars answer this question negatively, since studies have proven that ethnic culture and identity are not dependent on language. As Fishman writes:

> no matter how all-embracing language is experienced to be as the vehicle or as the symbol of the total ethnocultural package, it is really only a part, and a detachable part at that, rather than the whole of that package. (Fishman et al. 1985:506)

And Edwards agrees with Fishman:

> since identity essentially rests upon the continuation of boundaries which, in turn, depend upon a maintained sense of groupness, the

erosion of an original language—at least in its ordinary, communicative aspects—does not inevitably mean the erosion of identity itself. (1985:48)

Eastman expresses the same argument:

When we stop using the language of our ethnic group, only the language use aspect of our ethnic identity changes; the primordial sense of who we are and what group we think we belong to for the remainder remains intact. (1984:261)

We need only to examine the behaviors of ethnic groups who have replaced their original language with a dominant language of wider communication and prestige, to see that the link between original language and identity is not essential.

The Irish of both Ireland and the United States, while most of them do not speak Gaelic, have maintained their heritage throughout other cultural changes. As Edwards wrote about those in Ireland: "The Irish as a group seem not to have lost their national identity, but to have enshrined it in English" (1985:62). And certainly in the United States, Irish ethnicity is alive and well as represented by the commercialism of St. Patrick's Day and its American product (according to Sowell 1978:233), the St. Patrick's Day parade. Even though Gaelic is not being passed on to the younger generations, Edwards (1985:61) reports that most Irish value it as a symbol of national or ethnic identity or cultural distinctiveness, and Macnamara (1971:83) also reports positive attitudes exhibited by the Irish toward Gaelic. Edwards writes that informants from Brittany have adopted the same attitude as the Irish toward their original languages: that Breton and Gaelic are to be valued as cultural possessions, but they do not need to be personally acquired (1985:68). I also found in my research that many informants feel the same way: that Judeo-Spanish is important from a cultural and historical point of view, but that it is not necessary to speak it (Harris 1979, 1987).

An example closer to home is that of today's younger generation of Ashkenazic Jews whose parents or grandparents were/are native Yiddish speakers, but who themselves do not speak the language. However, they do not feel less Jewish because of their lack of linguistic skills. Among most of the Yiddish activists in Fishman's study, Yiddish was not considered the most important factor in Jewish ethnicity or identity (Fishman et al. 1985:287). They felt that Jewish ethnicity could survive without Yiddish and admitted that there were more pressing problems for many of the communi-

ties than maintenance of the mother tongue. Such problems included economic and social mobility and acceptance. These same
problems were also considered as more important than mother-
tongue maintenance by members of the Sephardic communities in
my studies (Harris 1979, 1987). In Mizrahi's study of eight different
Sephardic groups in the Greater New York and New Jersey area,
language also does not seem to be an important variable in the
Sephardim's concept of Sephardic ethnicity since the majority of
her respondents speak English at home. Instead, she examines
various markers other than language that contribute to Sephardic
cohesiveness and identity (Mizrahi 1987:172).

The above examples illustrate the central theme of Edward's
book (1985): that cultural identity survives language loss. Even
though identity can radically change, it is not "inexorably bound
up with language" (Edwards 1985:67). The fact is that most groups
will switch languages if it is in their best interests. However, Fishman (1991), Edwards (1985) and others admit that communicative
language shift, which can also result in language death, does entail
cultural changes of the identity of the group. Otherwise there would
be no reason for the original language to be lost. As stated earlier,
the Sephardic Jews living in Israel and the United States today do
not live the same way they did in Turkey and the Balkans. This
is largely due to the forces of Israelization and Americanization,
respectively. The disintegration of the Sephardic life, which began
with the dismemberment of the Ottoman Empire, is today an irreversible movement to which there is no "going back." The culture
has changed to such an extent that the mother tongue no longer
performs the same important functions that it originally did. As
Professor David Altabé, President of the American Society of Sephardic Studies, said, "Language, like other social institutions, has
a function in a particular society, and as it loses this function, it
becomes less and less important" (Harris 1979:302). Social conditions change, people move, and demands alter, which result in a
community's pragmatic desire for communicative language shift.
In other words, language use of a person or group changes to
accommodate the communicative needs of the mainstream society
(Eastman 1984:263).

However, an ethnic group's pragmatic choice of English in the
United States or Hebrew in Israel as the language of daily communication, does not necessarily mean that it has lost its attachment
to the mother tongue. On the contrary, the mother tongue usually
retains a strong symbolic value, which, according to Fishman, can
"hang on" at purely symbolic or very low levels of daily use (Fish-

man et al. 1985:235). This can be seen in the "vestigial" uses of Judeo-Spanish for the singing of *romanzas* and for humoristic purposes. Eastman has introduced the idea of an "associated" language, which is a language connected with group identity but not necessarily used on a regular basis, or it may not even be used at all (Eastman 1984:259). In fact, Eastman questions whether language is even a proper vehicle for preserving ethnic identities.

Fishman also points out that, as mother-tongue language varieties become more restricted in domains of usage, the attitudes toward them often become more positive. In fact, younger members of the second and third generations often put a positive value on their mother tongue, which he refers to as "attitudinal haloization" (Fishman 1977:105). However, as Saville-Troike emphasizes, these positive attitudes toward Yiddish, Gaelic, Breton, and other ethnic mother-tongue languages that are declining, are not accompanied by increased use. Nor do positive attitudes enhance the chances for mother-tongue language survival (Saville-Troike 1982:197). And Fishman agrees that positive attitudes and intellectual admiration for a language "do not and cannot, by themselves, lead to language learning, language use, language fluency or language transmission to another generation" (1991:203). Certainly, most of my informants regretted the loss of Judeo-Spanish, which they felt was something very precious, but they are doing nothing to perpetuate the language.

In language shift, the loss of the mother tongue is not achieved without a price. But as Edwards points out:

> change and transition are social realities for most people. The alternative is a stasis which very few have been prepared to accept. Change may not always be welcomed, of course. Adjustments made for perceived advancement are not without cost, but usually the cost is less than that which would ensue if change were not made. (1985:97)

The decline of Judeo-Spanish should be regarded not as a tragedy, but as a natural result of such change. According to one of my informants, Shelomo Avayou, the Balkan specialist for the Archives of the History of the Jewish People located at Hebrew University, the phenomenon of language death or language replacement should be considered as a natural result of progress. "Language death coincides with cultural change which is inevitable since life itself is not a static phenomenon" (Harris 1979:301). And one of Professor Haïm Vidal Sephiha's eighty-two-year-old informants originally from Turkey, Madame Baratz Bejarano, described the situation: "If we have lost our language it is because we have suffered the fate of all people—grandeur and decadence". She goes on to say that due to the results of war, extermination, mixed marriages, and assimilation, the Sephardim have been forced to learn the languages of the countries that gave them a home. She ends by saying, "It was necessary for us to choose between survival or the ancestral language. We have chosen life" (Sephiha 1977:115).

Renewal of Interest in Sephardic Culture

While it is indisputable that language shift has reached an advanced stage in Sephardic communities throughout the United States and Israel, and there is also no chance to maintain or revive Judeo-Spanish as a language of daily communication, there are definite signs of a revived interest in Sephardic culture. As Stern points out, one of the most important results of this new ethnic consciousness is that all generations of Sephardim feel a need to recognize and utilize their Sephardic identity in some way:

> This phenomenon stems, in part, from the increasing need of American ethnic groups to trace and publicize their ethnic roots. Another major determinant in this emphasis is the ever increasing recognition by Ashkenazim that Sephardim *are* Jewish and are a special unique form of Jewishness, at that. (1982:137)

According to Mizrahi's (1987) study, American Sephardim feel they are misperceived not only by American gentiles, but by American Ashkenazim as well. Her respondents feel that gentiles do not understand that there are differences between Ashkenazic and Sephardic Jews or that they sometimes even confuse them with the Israeli Sephardic group. Mizrahi writes:

> It is understandable that American Sephardim are misperceived or poorly known. To begin with, Sephardim are a tiny minority. They comprise only 3% of all American Jews, who themselves are only 3% of the total population. Furthermore, American Ashkenaze Jews are dynamic and visible. They excel as writers and educators, are active in the media, and are prominent in show business, both behind the scenes and as performers. Given these characteristics and especially in light of the relative numbers, it is perhaps inevitable that American Gentile understanding of "Jewish" is based on an Ashkenaze mold. (1987:320)

The respondents in Mizrahi's study also feel that American gentiles, Ashkenazim, and many Sephardim do not understand the role of the Sephardim in America's history. As many have pointed out, teaching in America (as well as in Israel for that matter) has been geared toward the Ashkenaze tradition with the total absence of a Sephardic dimension. According to Mizrahi, this lack of information is a loss

> for Americans in general, who may not be aware that Jewish history is interwoven with American history from the presence of Sephardic sailors on Columbus's ships and continuing through to Colonial days when Sephardim were substantially involved in America's development. It is a loss for American Ashkenazim, who may not be aware of the cultural diversity and early roots of American Jewry. . . . Finally. . . . [it] is also a loss for American Sephardim themselves, who may be deprived of access to information about their own group and validation by others of their distinctiveness. (1987:22–23)

Because of this lack of Sephardic education, Angel feels that the Sephardim were not really aware of their cultural roots, and therefore did not understand Sephardism (1974:120).

However, with the ethnic revival, American Sephardim are becoming more aggressive in their desire to be recognized as both Jewish and Sephardic. One of the most visible signs of this renewed interest in Sephardic culture is manifested in the course offerings at the university level and also in adult education programs of Sephardic organizations and synagogues. The greatest number of courses being offered today are courses in Sephardic history, folklore, culture, religious practices, music, and cooking. Also very popular are events supported by congregations and organizations like Sephardic House,[4] which foster Sephardic culture and traditions. Programs include lectures on Sephardic themes, Sephardic festivals, and entertainment such as films, concerts and plays. Such cultural events in the United States and Israel are not carried on in Judeo-Spanish, but rather in English or Hebrew, due to the limited number of speakers left in the language. Fishman reports the same phenomenon occurring when it comes to Yiddish events. The younger Jews who show a positive attitude toward Yiddish and Ashkenazic culture, are much more likely to attend English translations of original Yiddish plays and songs, and to read Yiddish novels and short stories in English translations rather "than to savour the originals or to prepare themselves to ever be able to do so" (Fishman 1991:198). Timm (1980) in her Breton studies and Edwards in his Gaelic research in Nova Scotia (1982), reported a similar lack of emphasis on language in cultural activities. The resulting advantage, as Edwards suggests, is that it enables non-speakers to participate in traditional events (1985:67–68).

There have even been a few courses on the Judeo-Spanish language itself. American colleges and universities which have offered courses on Judeo-Spanish in the last fifteen years include New York's Columbia University (Bunis 1982b), New York University, Yeshiva University, the Jewish Theological Seminary as well as Sephardic House, the University of Washington (experimental college) in Seattle, the University of Miami at Coral Gables, and the University of Judaism (adult education division) in Los Angeles. In Israel the Hebrew University of Jerusalem, the University of Haifa, Bar Ilan University, and Ben Gurion University have also offered courses in the language (see note number 5, chapter 12). However, the emphasis in these courses has been on the reading of Judeo-Spanish literary works or on the history and characteristics of the language, instead of the acquisition of linguistic skills.[5]

Today there is more scholarly interest and research being carried out on all aspects of Sephardic culture than before the ethnic revival. There are many more Sephardic cultural events and activities, and a general Sephardic awareness is much more prevalent. As Lavender points out, the Sephardic Jews already identify with a fertile Sephardic culture, and they are now at the stage of perpetuating that culture instead of working to develop a cultural consciousness (Lavender 1977:307). However, we must point out that even with all this new Sephardic awareness and cultural promotion, very little research is currently being done on the Judeo-Spanish language, nor is language maintenance or perpetuation an important concern.

Concluding Remarks

Even though the majority of my informants in both the United States and Israel do not feel that it is necessary to pass Judeo-Spanish on to their children, they do feel that maintenance of Sephardic culture is important and that research on the Sephardic heritage should be promoted (Harris 1979, 1987). Today the movements in both the United States and Israel to study what Matza (1990:354) refers to as the "most tangible aspects of culture," such as Sephardic history, literature, religious practices, philosophy, folklore, music, and cooking, are presently being embraced by the Sephardic community and will continue to be accepted in the future. These movements can help to encourage pride in a Sephardic identity which is crucial for ethnicity maintenance. In her study, Mizrahi shows that an intense pride in being Sephardic, pride in Sephardic traditions and history, as well as exhibiting a strong affinity for other Sephardim, were three important components which define Sephardic identity (Mizrahi 1987:305–6).

As Fishman observed, ethnicity maintenance, like language maintenance, requires strong institutional support (Fishman et al. 1985:48). And even though the emphasis is not on the Judeo-Spanish language, Sephardic culture is now being strongly supported by various Sephardic organizations, synagogues, and study programs in both the United States and Israel (see Appendix E). Concerning the future of ethnicity in general, Fishman predicts that

> Most probably there is no "non-ethnic tomorrow" in the offing . . . only a tomorrow in which the ethnic and the supraethnic (the sidestreams and the mainstreams) will be more intimately linked, as they are in the United States today. . . . Minority ethnicity is constantly restructuring and recreating itself and its future, all around us, well into and beyond the third generation. (Fishman et al. 1985:517)

I also cannot foresee the disappearance of a Sephardic identity or ethnicity. In fact, in my most recent research in Los Angeles (Harris 1987), I found my informants to be enthusiastically active in the maintenance and promotion of Sephardic cultural activities. As more information is made available, many more Sephardim (as well as non-Sephardim) are likely to enjoy a revival of interest in the Sephardic heritage.

However, as far as Judeo-Spanish is concerned, the shift to English in the United States and to Hebrew in Israel is almost complete. With the passing away of the older generations, the language of the Eastern Sephardim will disappear as a living language used for daily communication. Present and future studies of Judeo-Spanish will help us to value it as one of the most precious aspects of Sephardic culture.

Appendix A: Phonetic Symbols and Spelling

Consonants

Phonetic Symbol	Equivalent To	Modern Spanish/ English Example	Judeo-Spanish Spelling	Judeo-Spanish Example
[p]	Modern Spanish	premio	p	premio
[t]	Modern Spanish	también	t	tambien
[k]	Modern Spanish	cuanto, que	k	kuanto, ke
[b]	Modern Spanish	barco	b	barko
[d]	Modern Spanish	después	d	despues
[g]	Modern Spanish	grande	g	grande
[f]	Modern Spanish	factor	f	faktor
[v]	English	very	v	livro
[s]	Modern Spanish	cielo, sin	s	sielo, sin
[z]	English	zebra	z	meza, razon
[š]*	English	share	sh	bushkar, disho
[ž]*	English	treasure	ž	ižo, mužer
[č]*	Modern Spanish	chico	ch	chiko
[ǰ]*	English	just	ǰ	ǰusto
[h,x]	Modern Spanish	jabon, gente	h	haham
[m]	Modern Spanish	mesa	m	meza
[n]	Modern Spanish	número	n	numero
[ñ]	Modern Spanish	año	ny	anyo
[l]	Modern Spanish	luz	l	luz
[r]	Modern Spanish	caro	r	karo
[r̄]	Modern Spanish	carro	rr	karro
[y]	Modern Spanish	ya, llama	y	ya, yama

Vowels

[i]	Modern Spanish	mi	i	mi
[e]	Modern Spanish	de	e	de
[ɛ]	Modern Spanish	quiero	e	kero
[a]	Modern Spanish	español	a	espanyol
[ɔ]	Modern Spanish	oro	o	oro
[o]	Modern Spanish	boca	o	boka
[u]	Modern Spanish	comunidad	u	komunidad

---

*Because there has never been any authority to dictate academic standards or norms for Judeo-Spanish, the spelling of the language has been a constant source of problems for the scholar. The difficulties are especially apparent in the four palatal sounds represented phonetically by [š], [ž], [č], and [ǰ]. To help solve this problem, I consulted the Judeo-Spanish weekly *La Luz de Israel,* which was published in Tel Aviv from 1972 to 1990, and the cultural biannual journal *Aki Yerushalayim,* which is still published in Jerusalem (see Appendix E). These are the two most popular and recent publications in Judeo-Spanish.

The [š] sound is represented as *sh* in *Aki Yerushalayim* and as *ch* in *La Luz.* I have chosen to use the *sh* orthography.

The [č] sound is represented by *tch* in *La Luz* and by *ch* in *Aki Yerushalayim.* I use the *ch* spelling which is the same as that in Modern Spanish.

The voiced [ž] and [ǰ] present greater problems in Modern Judeo-Spanish orthography. [ž] is represented as *j* (mu*j*er) or *z* (vi*z*ino) in both *Aki Yerushalayim* and *La Luz de Israel.* I represent this sound both phonetically and orthographically as *ž*. The [ǰ] sound is spelled as *j* in *La Luz* and *dj* in *Aki Yerushalayim.* I use the *ǰ* symbol for both the phonetic and orthographic representations. I chose to use the *ž* and *ǰ* symbols for spelling (as well as for phonetic representation) in Judeo-Spanish so that these sounds would not be confused with the letter *z* or with the Spanish [h,x] sound which is spelled in Modern Spanish with the letters *j* or *g* before *e,i*.

The Modern Spanish bilabial spirant [β] and the English front, high-mid, lax vowel [I] are found in certain varieties of Modern Judeo-Spanish spoken in the United States. See chapter 10 (Table 7) and chapter 5 (Vowels).

Appendix B: Map of Sephardic Communities in the Ottoman Empire

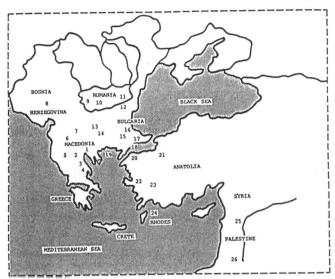

The numbers on the map represent the following Sephardic communities in the Ottoman Empire. The present-day name of the city (if there has been a change) is enclosed in parentheses followed by the name of the present-day country.

1. Salonika (Thessaloniki), Greece
2. Karaferia (Veroia), Greece
3. Larisa, Greece
4. Volos, Greece
5. Kastoria, Greece
6. Monastir (Bitola), Yugoslavia
7. Skopje, Yugoslavia/Macedonia
8. Sarajevo, Yugoslavia
9. Turnu Severin, Rumania
10. Craiova, Rumania
11. Bucharest, Rumania
12. Ruschuk (Ruse), Bulgaria
13. Sofia, Bulgaria
14. Plovdiv, Bulgaria
15. Adrianople (Edirne), Turkey
16. Kirklareli, Turkey
17. Constantinople (Istanbul), Turkey
18. Rodosto (Tekirdag), Turkey
19. Gallipoli (Gelibolu), Turkey
20. Çanakkale, Turkey
21. Bursa, Turkey
22. Izmir, Turkey
23. Tire, Turkey
24. Rhodes
25. Tiberias, Palestine (Israel)
26. Jerusalem, Israel

Appendix C: Informant Questionnaire

1. Age _____ 2. Sex _____ 3. Place of Birth _____

4. What country and city did you come from? _____

5. What countries and cities have you lived in? _____

6. When did you come to the United States/Israel? _____
   How old were you? _____

7. If you are a native of the United States/Israel, where did your parents
   come from?   mother _____   father _____

8. Occupation _____

- -

9. *Education:*

Type of School (public, private, Alliance?)	Location	Language of Instruction	Did you study J-S (Judeo-Spanish)?	
Primary	_____	_____	YES	NO
Middle	_____	_____	YES	NO
High School	_____	_____	YES	NO
University	_____	_____	YES	NO

   List degrees if any: _____

- -

10. Can you read J-S (Judeo-Spanish)?   YES   NO
    If YES, do you read Rashi script?   YES   NO
    Do you read Latin characters?   YES   NO

11. Do you read J-S newspapers?   YES   NO

I asked the questions orally in either English, French, Hebrew, or Spanish, depending on the informant's background and linguistic skills. The interviews were taped.

If YES, which one(s)? _____
If NO, did you ever read J-S newspapers?   YES   NO
If YES, which one(s)? _____

12. Do you read any of the following materials in J-S?
    _____ books
    _____ translations of religious works
    _____ the *Bible*
    _____ *Me'am Lo'ez*
    _____ prayers
    _____ the Haggadah
    _____ letters
    _____ ballads *(romanzas)*
    _____ proverbs *(refranes)*
    _____ folktales, stories *(konsežas)*
    _____ poetry
    _____ magazines, reviews, newsletters, bulletins
           If YES, which one(s)? _____
    _____ other _____

13. Can you write in J-S?   YES   NO
    If YES, do you write in Rashi characters?   YES   NO
              Do you write in Latin letters?   YES   NO

14. Are there any professional associates-colleagues
    with whom you speak J-S?   YES   NO
       with whom you write?   YES   NO
    Are there any relatives to whom you write?   YES   NO

15. Do you, or did you, listen to J-S radio broadcasts?   YES   NO
    If YES, how often? _____
    What did you listen to? _____ (news, music, drama, other)

16. What other languages can you speak? _____
                                  read? _____
                                  write? _____

17. Which language(s) do you feel most comfortable speaking? _____
    reading? _____ writing? _____

18. What language do/did you use when speaking to:
    maternal grandmother _____   maternal grandfather _____
    paternal grandmother _____   paternal grandfather _____
    mother _____   father _____
    sister(s)/brother(s) _____
    aunts and uncles _____
    spouse _____
    your children _____   your grandchildren _____
    other relatives _____
    good friends _____   your rabbi _____

19. To what other person might you speak Judeo-Spanish? _____

20. Do you know any Judeo-Spanish:
    _____ *romanzas* (ballads)   _____ *kantigas* (songs)
    _____ *refranes* (proverbs)   _____ *konsežas* (folktales)
    _____ poetry   _____ prayers

21. Are there any events or occasions for which you use J-S expressions such as: "Vengan en la buena ora" or "Bivas, kreskas, enfloreskas"?   YES   NO

    If YES, give the expression(s) and occasion(s):
    _____

22. Do you know any swear words in J-S?   YES   NO
    What language do you curse in? _____

23. What name do you use to refer to your native speech?
    _____ Judeo-Espanyol   _____ Judeo-Spanish
    _____ Espanyol   _____ Ladino
    _____ Judezmo   _____ (D)J̌udiyo or (D)J̌idiyo
    _____ Spanish   _____ Spaniolit
    _____ Other? _____

24. Are the above names synonymous, that is, are they all names for the same language?   YES   NO
    If NO, is one used only for the spoken language?   YES   NO
        If YES, which one? _____
    Is one used only for the written language?   YES   NO
        If YES, which one? _____

25. Do you consider your variety of speech to be:

_____ an independent language

_____ a mixed language—If YES, what languages is it composed of? _____

_____ a dialect—If YES, what language is it based on or what languages is it related to? _____

_____ a jargon

_____ slang

_____ other _____

26. In your opinion, is your speech variety a corrupted or inferior language as compared to Spanish, French, Italian, etc.?   YES   NO

27. Are you as fluent in J-S as your grandparents were?   YES   NO
    As your parents are/were?   YES   NO
    If you answered NO to any of the above, in what ways is your speech inferior?

_____ vocabulary

_____ grammar/syntax

_____ pronunciation

_____ ability to read and/or write

_____ ability to express certain ideas? Please elaborate:

_____

28. In your opinion, is J-S a useful language for communication with Jews all over the world?   YES   NO

29. In your opinion, is J-S an important language to know for all or any of the following reasons?

_____ cultural

_____ religious

_____ ethnic

_____ other? _____

30. Do you consider J-S to be a dying language?   YES   NO
    Why or why not? _____

31. Do you feel it is important to keep speaking the language?
                                          YES   NO
    Why or why not? _____

32. Do you feel it is important to pass the language on to the next generation?   YES   NO

    Why or why not? _____

33. What language(s) would you like your children/grandchildren to study in school?
    _____ Judeo-Spanish   _____ Arabic   _____ Italian
    _____ Russian   _____ German   _____ other
    _____ Portuguese   _____ Spanish
    _____ Hebrew   _____ French

34. Do your children speak J-S fluently or well?   YES   NO
    Age of children: _____ , _____ , _____

35. Do your children have a receptive competence in J-S? That is, do they understand it when spoken to but do not answer in J-S?
                                                    YES   NO

    If YES, in what language do they answer? _____

36. Do your grandchildren speak J-S?   YES   NO
    If YES, how well? _____
    Age of grandchildren: _____ , _____ , _____

37. If your children/grandchildren do not speak J-S (fluently or well), does it bother you?   YES   NO

    Why or why not? _____

38. How do your children/grandchildren or any young Sephardim you know feel about speaking J-S? _____

39. Have you ever felt embarrassed speaking J-S?   YES   NO
    Can you recall/describe the situation/circumstances? _____

40. Are you or were you ever conscious of differences between J-S dialects?   YES   NO
    If YES, which dialect has/had more prestige in your opinion? _____

41. Have you ever attempted to use J-S with non-Sephardic Spanish speakers here in New York? Los Angeles? Israel?   YES   NO
    If YES, could you understand them easily?   YES   NO

Could they understand you easily?   YES   NO
With what Spanish speakers did you speak J-S? (from Spain,
Puerto Rico, Mexico, Cuba, etc.) _____

42. Do you know the region of Spain your ancestors originated from?
                                                      YES   NO

If YES, which region? _____
How do you know? (last name, synagogue in Turkey/Greece, relatives told you, etc.) _____

43. What is your first name? _____ What do your friends and family
call you? _____

44. Is your spouse Sephardic?   YES   NO
If NO, is your spouse _____ Ashkenazic _____ non-Jewish

45. Do you think research on J-S is important?   YES   NO
Why or why not? _____

Appendix D: Word List

mother   _____

father   _____

grandmother   _____

grandfather   _____

daughter   _____

brother   _____

aunt   _____

uncle   _____

- -

dress   _____

pants (slacks)   _____

overcoat   _____

shoes   _____

stockings, socks   _____

shawl   _____

handkerchief   _____

earring   _____

pin   _____

belt   _____

- -

synagogue   _____

rabbi   _____

prayer book   _____

blessing   _____

holiday   _____

God   _____

I asked the words orally in either English, French, or Hebrew, depending on the preferred language of the informant.

The word lists used in New York and Israel in 1978 and in Los Angeles in 1985 were the same, except for the following six words which I omitted from the 1985 list: *sister, sermon, forest, outskirts* (suburbs), *parliament,* and *opportunity.*

- -

grocer, shopkeeper _____

butcher _____

doctor _____

lawyer _____

teacher _____

student _____

worker _____

tailor _____

director, manager _____

stevedore, loader _____

- -

market _____

grocery (store) _____

store _____

restaurant _____

street _____

cemetery _____

school _____

- -

intelligent _____

tired _____

sick _____

unlucky _____

beautiful _____

ugly _____

happy _____

sad _____

- -

government _____

community _____

liberty, freedom _____

election _____

immigration _____

tax _____

- -

sun   _____
rain   _____
wind   _____
storm   _____
rose   _____
cat   _____
dog   _____
donkey   _____
- -
tea   _____
tobacco   _____
bread   _____
cheese   _____
meat   _____
cake   _____
orange (fruit)   _____
watermelon   _____
ice   _____
rice   _____
eggs   _____
coffee   _____
- -
now   _____
tomorrow   _____
yesterday   _____
night   _____
Sunday   _____
Wednesday   _____
Saturday   _____
hour   _____
- -
to read   _____
to work   _____
to study   _____
to sell   _____
to buy   _____

to dance   ———
to warn   ———
to eat   ———
to finish   ———
to change   ———

- -

room   ———
bedroom   ———
kitchen   ———
stove   ———
pot, casserole   ———
fork   ———
table   ———
garden   ———
window   ———
roof   ———
floor (room)   ———
floor (building)   ———

- -

news   ———
book   ———
language   ———
work (noun)   ———
box   ———
matches   ———
newspaper   ———
gift   ———
goal, purpose   ———
honor, respect   ———
luck   ———
danger   ———
friend   ———
man   ———
woman   ———
owner (house)   ———
guest   ———

party   ———————
price   ———————
twin   ———————

- -

Appendix E: Sephardic Organizations, Publications, and Projects

The following is a list of the main Sephardic organizations and their publications, as well as various projects being undertaken in the field of Sephardic Studies in the United States (New York and Los Angeles), Israel, Turkey and Europe.

New York

1) The Jacob E. Safra Institute of Sephardic Studies
   Yeshiva University
   Furst Hall, Suite 419
   500 West 185th St.
   New York, N.Y. 10033-3201
   (212) 960-5235
   The Haham, Dr. Solomon Gaon, Director
   Rabbi M. Mitchell Serels, Director, Sephardic Community
     Activities Program, Yeshiva University

was established at Yeshiva University in 1964

   to help preserve the rich Sephardi heritage and develop rabbis, teachers and other key leaders for the Sephardic Jewish community.

The program provides courses on the history, culture, and traditions of Sephardic Jewry, which are integrated into the regular program of study at Yeshiva University and other educational institutions in New York. This program includes a rabbinical training program in the Sephardic tradition (RIETS—The Rabbi Isaac Elchanan Theological Seminary) and also provides informational, educational, and cultural community services for Sephardic congregations throughout the United States and Canada. The program is headed by the Haham Rabbi Dr. Solomon Gaon and Rabbis Herbert C. Dobrinsky and Mitchell Serels. Rabbi Dobrinsky is the managing editor of *The American Sephardi,* which is the journal of the Sephardic Studies Program and contains articles concerning the history, literature, and culture of the Sephardic Jews.
The Sephardic Community Program of Yeshiva University is also a

major resource for all the other national and local Sephardic organizations and conducts an average of twenty-three major annual Sephardic cultural events throughout the United States. In cooperation with the National Tourist Office of Spain, the Sephardic Community Program of Yeshiva University sponsors *Semana Sepharad,* which is an annual Sephardic Cultural Festival consisting of one week of meetings and includes scholarly presentations, entertainment and Sephardic food at various locations in New York and New Jersey.

2) The American Society of Sephardic Studies (ASOSS)
   Yeshiva University
   500 West 185th St.
   New York, N.Y. 10033
   (212) 960-5235
   Professor David F. Altabé, President

was founded in 1967 to encourage the study of all aspects of Sephardic culture. The Society holds an annual conference at which scholarly papers are presented, and it publishes *The Sephardic Scholar,* a journal dedicated to the advancement of the Sephardic heritage, its literature, customs, and culture as experienced in the Diaspora.

3) The American Sephardi Federation (AFS)
   305 Seventh Avenue, 11th Floor
   New York, N.Y. 10001-6008
   (212) 366-7223
   Leon Levy, President

was founded in 1973 and is the North American affiliate of the World Sephardi Federation. Its purpose is to promote and strengthen Sephardic and Jewish identity, as well as instill awareness and pride in the Sephardic heritage by encouraging and stimulating cultural and educational projects of Sephardic interest. It strives to keep Americans informed of all Sephardic events and all aspects of Sephardic life and culture in the United States and abroad, as it educates other Jews and non-Jews on the Sephardim. The ASF considers itself to be the unifying voice of American Sephardim within the Jewish community as well as with the media. There are other active branches of the ASF outside of New York on the West coast, in the Midwest, the Pacific Northwest, Florida, and other states.

The ASF holds an annual national convention and has begun a Sephardic Resource Center with a speaker's bureau, whose goal is to provide guidelines and information to people interested in teaching and learning about Sephardic history and culture as well as participating in various Sephardic cultural festivals. The quarterly publication of the ASF is *Sephardic Highlights* and the monthly ASF *Action Update* reports to members on organizational activities. The Young Leadership Division of the

American Sephardi Federation publishes a quarterly publication entitled *Sephardic Connection.*

4) Sephardic House—Institute for Researching and Promoting
    Sephardic History and Culture
    2112 Broadway, Suite 200A
    New York, N.Y. 10023
    (212) 496-2173
    Dr. Janice E. Ovadiah, Executive Director
    Rabbi Marc D. Angel, Chairman of the Board

formerly based at Shearith Israel, is now an independent organization dedicated to researching and promoting Sephardic history and culture. Sephardic House was founded in 1978 and sponsors a wide variety of classes, lectures, and public programs on different aspects of the Sephardic experience (culture, folklore, history, literature, etc.), as well as concerts, film festivals, exhibits, symposia, and various projects of Sephardic interest. Sephardic House has also published and distributed several books and pamphlets on Sephardic themes as well as tapes of Sephardic music.

Sephardic House has well over one thousand members from throughout the country and also has an outreach program to communities outside of the New York area. Sephardic House has a lecture and program bureau to serve various organizations and communities throughout the country with programming ideas and resources as well as a listing of qualified lecturers, entertainers, story-tellers, exhibits, videos, cassettes, books, and other resource materials. The *Sephardic House Newsletter* appears monthly.

5) Adelantre! The Judezmo Society
    4594 Bedford Avenue
    Brooklyn, N.Y. 11235

was founded by David M. Bunis and Stephen Levy in June 1975

in the hope of stimulating popular and scholarly interest in all facets of Sephardic linguistics, literature, history, music and folkways.

Ke Xaber? 'What's New?' is the newsletter published irregularly by *Adelantre!,* which contains news about activities, publications, recordings, and institutions of Sephardic interest in the United States and abroad. The last issue of *Ke Xaber?* appeared in the late 1970s. *Adelantre!* has also published various works in cooperation with the American Sephardi Federation in a series entitled *Working Papers in Sephardi and Oriental Jewish Studies.*

6) The Institute for Sephardic Studies
Graduate Center, CUNY
33 W. 42nd St., Room 1439
New York, N.Y. 10018
(212) 790-4404
Dr. Jane Gerber, Director

was established in 1985 and is

dedicated to furthering research and publications on the history and culture of Sephardic Jewry and encouraging the teaching of Sephardic civilization.

Activities of the Institute include public lectures, conferences, teacher training, and scholar exchanges.

7) The Foundation for the Advancement of Sephardic Studies and
Culture (FASSC)
17 Grenfell Drive
Great Neck, N.Y. 11020
(516) 482-4037
Louis N. Levy, President

was founded in 1963 by Louis N. Levy with the collaboration of the late David N. Barocas and the late Professor Mair J. Benardete. The Foundation encourages scholarly pursuits and has published a number of tracts under the general title of *The Sephardic Storm Lamp,* which deal with various aspects of Sephardic literature, history, and the Judeo-Spanish language.

8) American Association of Jewish Friends of Turkey, Inc. (AAJFT)
17 Grenfell Drive
Great Neck, N.Y. 11020
(516) 482-4037
Louis N. Levy, President

is a cultural and educational association founded in 1989 for the promotion of Turkish-Jewish support of the Sephardic culture as it evolved in the Ottoman Empire, and for the expression of Jewish gratitude to the Turks for receiving over 100,000 exiles from Spain five hundred years ago. The AAJFT promotes conferences, publications educational materials, research, etc., on all aspects of Sephardic life and culture in the Ottoman Empire and Turkish-Sephardic relations during the past five hundred years.

The *AAJFT Newsletter,* edited by Rachel A. Bortnick, promotes articles on the historical friendship of the Jewish and Turkish peoples and on Sephardic culture. It also provides news and information on the Jewish community of Turkey and the activities in conjunction with the five hundredth anniversary of the arrival in the Ottoman Empire of the Sephardic Jews who were expelled from Spain in 1492.

9) Sephardic Home for the Aged
   2266 Cropsey Avenue
   Brooklyn, N.Y. 11214-5797
   (718) 266-6100
   Michael New, Director

was established in August of 1951

to fill the needs of the Sephardic Jews who came from the Eastern Mediterranean areas, especially Greece, Turkey and neighboring countries.

It has a capacity of 271 beds with programs and services catering to the needs of the residents. The entire Sephardic community of New York participates in the activities of the Home, which include all kinds of fund raising events. Sephardic entertainment is provided, and traditional Sephardic religious practices and festivals are maintained for the residents of the Home. The Sephardic Home is one of the richest sources of information concerning the Judeo-Spanish language and Sephardic culture in general, since the majority of the residents are native speakers of the language who lived a good part of their lives in the Balkan regions and who are very familiar with Sephardic music and folklore. The monthly newsletter of the Home is called *The Sephardic Home News* and contains information about activities in the Home as well as items of general interest to the Sephardic community.

10) Congregation Shearith Israel—The Spanish and Portuguese
    Synagogue
    8 West 70th St.
    New York, N.Y. 10023
    (212) 873-0300
    Rabbi Marc D. Angel

Shearith Israel, the most famous Sephardic synagogue in New York, was the first Jewish synagogue founded in the United States in 1654. Shearith Israel has always been active and at the forefront in promoting Sephardic culture, and was also an important institution in helping newly arriving Sephardic immigrants to New York, especially in the early years of this century. Shearith Israel, together with Sephardic House, also sponsors the Annual Sephardic Festival and Fair, which features Sephardic food, entertainment, artisans, and craftspeople who display and sell their

works, and also the sale of books of Sephardic interest. The Shearith
Israel *Bulletin* is published monthly by the congregation.

Los Angeles

1) The Sephardic Educational Center (S.E.C.) in Jerusalem and
   Worldwide
   6505 Wilshire Blvd., Suite 403
   Los Angeles, CA 90048
   (213) 653-7365
   José A. Nessim, M.D., President and Founder
   Dr. Michael M. Laskier, Executive Director

The S.E.C. is

dedicated to the preservation, enrichment, and perpetuation of Sephardic education, culture, and religious values, and sponsors and coordi-
nates programs for Sephardic and other Jewish communities around
the world.

Dr. Nessim says that the S.E.C. is

the only international educational center that Sephardim have actually
founded, financed and operate.

The objectives of the S.E.C. are to present Sephardic culture to all Jews
and to serve as an educational bridge between the Sephardic and Ashkenazic worlds and to educate, especially Jewish youth. The S.E.C. sponsors an annual academic international conference on Sephardic topics as
well as educational/travel programs in Israel each summer for youth and
young adults from all over the world. The participants of such programs
experience first hand all aspects of Sephardic life.
    The S.E.C., founded in 1979, has chapters around the world including
those in New York, Miami, Seattle, Toronto, Montreal, Madrid, Buenos
Aires, Mexico City, Rio de Janeiro, Caracas, and Bombay. The quarterly
newsletter of the S.E.C. is *Hamerkaz* ('The Center' in Hebrew).

2) Los Angeles Sephardic Home for the Aged (LASHA)—part of
   Jewish Home for the Aging of Greater Los Angeles

Main Office	*Eisenberg Campus*
Grancell Village Campus	
7150 Tampa Ave.	18855 Victory Blvd.
Reseda, CA 91335	Reseda, CA 91335
(818) 774-3200	(818) 774-3000
Lou Hasson, President	

LASHA is a partnership between the Sephardic community and the Jewish Home for the Aging of Greater Los Angeles and serves as a support group for the Sephardic residents of the Home. There are two homes or campuses: Grancell Village and the Eisenberg Campus. Like the Sephardic Home for the Aged in Brooklyn, these two homes provide all kinds of services for aged Sephardim and include various types of Sephardic entertainment. The Sephardic community of Los Angeles, like that of New York, is quite active in maintaining the two LASHA homes and in participating in various fund raising activities. Members of the two main Sephardic synagogues in Los Angeles (see below) often sponsor activities such as annual picnics and parties for the LASHA residents of the Home. *Lashon* is the bimonthly publication of the Home.

3) Sephardic Synagogues
   a. Sephardic Temple Tifereth Israel
      10500 Wilshire Blvd.
      Los Angeles, CA 90024
      (213) 475-7311
      Rabbi Jacob Ott

Tifereth Israel is the largest Sephardic synagogue in Los Angeles with a membership of about six hundred families. Most of the members emigrated from or are descended from areas of Turkey, Greece, and the Balkans. Tifereth Israel sponsors all kinds of activities promoting Sephardic culture such as lectures, concerts, and festivals, including a lecture series in their continuing adult education program. Tifereth Israel's monthly bulletin is *El Shofar.*

   b. Sephardic Hebrew Center
      4911 West 59th St.
      Los Angeles, CA 90056
      (213) 295-5541
      Rabbi Robert J. Rome

This is the smaller of the two Los Angeles Sephardic (Judeo-Spanish-speaking) synagogues with a membership of about 250 families. Most of the members are Rhodeslis (from the Island of Rhodes) or are descended from Rhodeslis. This synagogue, like Tifereth Israel, also promotes Sephardic activities, and its monthly bulletin is *Sephardic News.*

4) The Maurice Amado Foundation
   3600 Wilshire Blvd. - Suite 1228
   Los Angeles, CA 90010-2605

   P.O. Box 429497
   Cincinnati, Ohio 45242-9497
   Dr. Tamar Frank, Program Consultant

was established in 1961 in Los Angeles "with the aim of supporting activities that emphasize the Sephardic Jewish heritage." The foundation has made philanthropic contributions to various organizations such as Temple Tifereth Israel in Los Angeles and the Sephardic Home for the Aged in New York. It has awarded grants to institutions such as the Technion in Haifa, the Jewish Museum in New York, and has endowed a chair in Sephardic Studies at UCLA. In 1989 the Foundation created the Sephardic Education Project, which funds educational and cultural programs that deal with the Sephardic heritage.

Israel

1) The Council of the Sephardi and Oriental Communities of
     Jerusalem
   Rehov Havazelet 12
   Jerusalem, ISRAEL
   (02) 226-461

has as its purpose to promote interest in the language and culture of Israel's Sephardic and Oriental Jews. The Council publishes studies on all aspects of Sephardic culture and also provides grants and scholarships to researchers in the field of Sephardic studies.

2) Misgav Yerushalayim—Institute for Research on the Sephardi
     and Oriental Jewish Heritage
   46, Jabotinsky Street
   P.O. Box 4035
   Jerusalem 91040
   ISRAEL
   Tel: 972-2-619034/5
   Dr. Galit Hasan Rokem, Director
   Nitza Genuth, Deputy Director

was founded in 1973 by the Hebrew University of Jerusalem, the Council of the Sephardi and Oriental Communities of Jerusalem and the World Sephardi Federation. Its goal is the study of the Sephardi and Oriental Jewish heritage. Misgav Yerushalayim provides grants and scholarships for such research, it endows a chair at the Hebrew University, and it publishes and disseminates studies. Beginning in 1978, it has convened an international congress every four years. In general, it is a resource center for scholars in the field, with an extensive library containing all kinds of literary and cultural publications relating to Sephardi and Oriental Jewry. The Institute is presently involved in the writing of a seven volume documentary history of the Sephardi communities from the fifteenth century onward.

3) The Ben-Zvi Institute
P.O. Box 7504
Jerusalem 91070
ISRAEL
Professor Michel Abitbol, Director

was founded in 1952 under the auspices of the President of Israel at the time, Yitzhak Ben-Zvi, for the purpose of studying the Jewish communities of the Orient and the Middle East. The Institute contains a rich library of literary and other publications in Judeo-Spanish, as well as studies written on the language and on all aspects of Sephardic culture and the Sephardic experience. The Institute also edits an annual research journal entitled *Sefunot*.

4) The world headquarters of
The Sephardic Educational Center (S.E.C.)
Batey Machasseh, #1
P.O. Box 14326
Old City, Jerusalem
ISRAEL 91142
Tel. 972-2-282-344

began in 1980 in the Old City and sponsors educational activities for Sephardic youth and young adults around the world (see explanation of the S.E.C. in Los Angeles). The S.E.C. in Jerusalem has also established a Sephardic rabbinical seminary in Israel, which has graduated more than two dozen young rabbis who presently serve in the Diaspora.

5) The Judeo-Spanish Department of Radio Israel—*La Emision en Djudeo-espanyol de Kol Israel*
9 Heleni Hamalka
Jerusalem, ISRAEL
Moshe Shaul, Director

has existed since 1948. Kol Israel airs a fifteen minute broadcast in Judeo-Spanish every evening from 7:45 to 8:00 P.M. Israeli time. This broadcast includes news items and a commentary or discussion in Judeo-Spanish concerning Sephardic folklore, culture, history, literature, or other topics relating to Sephardic culture or Israeli life in general. The playing of Sephardic music (*romanzas, kantigas,* etc.) is also a very popular part of this daily broadcast. These Judeo-Spanish broadcasts are not only heard in Israel, but are also broadcast daily in various European countries located in the Mediterranean region.

In 1978, *La Emision en Djudeo-espanyol de Kol Israel* began the *Proyekto Folklor Djudeo-espanyol* 'Judeo-Spanish Folklore Project', for which they have taped and transcribed more than 4000 authentic Judeo-Spanish songs and their different versions, making it one of the richest collections of Judeo-Spanish music in the world.

In 1985, *El Premio España de la RNE* 'The Spanish Radio Award' was awarded to *La Emisión en Djudeo-espanyol de Radio Israel*

in recognition for its sustained efforts to preserve the Judeo-Spanish language and culture.

This award also recognized the contributions of *Aki Yerushalayim*, the publication of the Judeo-Spanish Department of Radio Kol Israel (see below).

6) *Aki Yerushalayim*
   P.O. Box 8175
   Jerusalem 91080
   ISRAEL
   Moshe Shaul, Editor

la sola revista kulturala en djudeo-espanyol publikada aktualmente en el mundo 'the only cultural publication in Judeo-Spanish presently published in the entire world'

is the biannual cultural journal, which began publication in 1979 in conjunction with the Judeo-Spanish radio program *La Boz de Israel*. It is edited by Moshe Shaul, the head of the Judeo-Spanish broadcasts of Israel Radio *Kol Israel*. The purpose of *Aki Yerushalayim* is "to stimulate and help to renew . . . literary and folkloric activity in Judeo-Spanish". This journal averages eighty pages and is the only publication in the world today written entirely in Judeo-Spanish. It includes articles about the history, culture, folklore, and language of the Sephardim. It also has selections from Judeo-Spanish literature and poetry, book reviews, Sephardic recipes, and notices of activities of interest in Sephardic communities throughout the world. *Aki Yerushalayim* is printed in Latin letters, which makes it readable by anyone with a knowledge of Spanish.

7) *Haber* ("news" in Turkish, "friend" in Hebrew)
   Emet Editorial Ltd.
   Lilienblum 21/11
   P.O.B. 1260
   Tel Aviv 65132
   ISRAEL
   Yakup Barokas, Editor-in-Chief

With the demise of *La Luz de Israel*, the only Judeo-Spanish newspaper published in Israel from 1972 to 1990, a young group of Turkish Israelis started publication of the new weekly *Haber*. *Haber* consisted of six pages in Turkish and two pages in Judeo-Spanish (Ladino). It was full of news and commentary on events about, and of special interest to the more than 100,000 Israelis of Turkish background, as well as to all Turkish Jews and Sephardim. Articles included news and information about Turkey, Turkish–Israeli relations, as well as news on Sephardim throughout the world, and articles concerning Sephardic culture. The first issue appeared on 6 September 1991. Unfortunately, due to high printing costs and limited circulation, HABER ceased publication in May of 1992. The closing has been described as "temporary," and there is talk that it may reappear as a monthly. However, the future of this publication is not promising.

8) SEFARAD: Society for the Preservation and Dissemination of
   Judeo-Spanish Culture
   P.O. Box 8175
   Jerusalem 91080
   ISRAEL

was founded in Jerusalem in 1981 for the promotion of Judeo-Spanish culture. The Sefarad Society along with Misgav Yerushalayim, started El Atelier Djudeo-Espanyol de Yerushalayim, which meets once a month and is dedicated to the Judeo-Spanish heritage. The Sefarad Society has worked together with Radio Kol Israel on the *Proyekto Folklor Djudeo-espanyol* (see number 5 above) to tape thousands of transcriptions of Judeo-Spanish songs.

9) Centre de Recherches sur le Judaïsme de Salonique—El Instituto
   para la Investigasion del Djudaizmo de Salonika (Research
   Center for the Study of Salonikan Jewry)
   3 Zangwill St.
   Tel Aviv, ISRAEL

is a small research center whose purpose is to encourage studies on the Sephardic community of Salonika. In 1975 the Centre established at the University of Tel Aviv the Chair for the History and Culture of the Jewry of Salonika and Greece. A Sephardic synagogue dedicated to the Jews of Salonika, Hechal Yehuda Recanati Synagogue, has been constructed at 13 Rehov Ben Sruk in Tel Aviv. This houses a library and cultural center dedicated to the Salonikan Jewish community.

10) MORIT—Foundation for the Heritage of Turkish Jewry
    P.O. Box 1300
    Bat Yam 59112
    ISRAEL
    Gad Nassi, President

is comprised mostly of Turkish immigrants from the early 1970s and was founded in mid-1985 to promote the history and culture of Turkish Jewry. MORIT sponsored the First International Congress of Turkish Jewry in October of 1989 in Tel Aviv. The organization hopes to sponsor more conferences, issue publications and films and generally to make the Israeli public more aware of the Turkish-Jewish heritage. One of MORIT's principal projects is the construction of a Turkish Cultural Center in Herzliya that would include a museum, an auditorium, a library and archives, a synagogue, and meeting facilities. MORIT's bulletin is *Sesimiz* ("Our Voice" in Turkish), edited by Gad Nassi, which is written in Turkish, Hebrew, Judeo-Spanish, and French. It emphasizes the history and culture of the Jews of Turkey.

11) La Asosiasion de los Djudios de Turkia en Israel–Itahdut Yotsei
    Turkia (Association of Turkish Jews in Israel)
    P.O. Box 3362
    Bat Yam
    ISRAEL
    Isak Kohen, former President (deceased 29 July 1992)

is a center for the conservation of the cultural heritage of the Jews from Turkey. Its monthly bulletin, edited by Isak Kohen, is *Dostluk* ("friendship" in Turkish). It is written primarily in Turkish with a few pages in Judeo-Spanish and provides information on events in Israel, especially in the Turkish Jewish community, as well as information on the history and culture of this community.

12) The Center for Spanish Jewish Studies
    Levinsky Institute (College) of Education
    15, Shoshana Persitz Street
    Tel Aviv, ISRAEL
    Dr. Aviva Doron, Director

is an institute started in 1989 for the training of school teachers in Sephardic education. The Institute is associated with Tel Aviv University.

Turkey

1) *Şalom* (Hebrew "shalom")
   Atiye Sok.
   Polar Apt. No. 12/6
   Teşvikiye
   Istanbul, TURKEY
   Silvio Ovadya, Editor-in-Chief
   Salomon Bicarano, Ladino Editor

is the weekly Jewish political and cultural newspaper in Istanbul which has been in existence for forty-five years. It appears every Wednesday and is eight pages in length, with seven pages written in Turkish, and only one page written in Judeo-Spanish (since September of 1984). It was originally written completely in Judeo-Spanish, but today very few young Turkish Jews are fluent in the language. *Şalom* contains news, interviews and articles concerning the language, folklore, literature, and other aspects of Judeo-Spanish culture, as well as information on the Turkish Jewish community. As of 1990 its circulation was approximately 3,500.

2) Quincentennial Foundation of Istanbul 1492–1992

New York branch	*Istanbul*
Information Center	Foundation Headquarters
305 Seventh Ave., 11th floor	500. Yil Vakfi
New York, N.Y. 10001	Cemal Sahir Sokak 26-28
(212) 229-1451	Mecidiyekoy
Jak V. Kamhi, Chairman	Istanbul, TURKEY
	Tel: (90.1) 175-3944
	Naïm Güleryüz, Vice Pres.

was established in 1989 by a group of Turkish citizens, both Jews and Moslems, to celebrate the five hundredth anniversary of the welcoming of the Jewish people to the Ottoman Empire after their expulsion from Spain and to commemorate five hundred years of peaceful living on Turkish lands by these Jews. Founded and headquartered in Istanbul, with branches in the United States, the United Kingdom, France, and Italy, the Quincentennial Foundation is planning a three year cultural and academic program designed to bring the diverse and rich legacy of Turkish Jewry to a greater audience. Events are planned for Turkey, the United States, Europe, Britain and Mexico. The program not only celebrates the five hundredth anniversary of the arrival of the Sephardic Jews on Turkish soil, but also the remarkable spirit of tolerance and acceptance which has characterized the entire Jewish experience in Turkey. The Quincentennial Foundation will sponsor and arrange a diverse program of activities, including exhibitions, symposia, films, books, as well as music, dance, folklore, and other theater performances to commemorate this anniversary. As part of the 1992 celebration, the Quincentennial Foundation is establishing a Jewish museum in Istanbul. The foundation publishes a quarterly newsletter called *The Quincentennial Quarterly*.

France

1) Association Vidas Largas—Association pour le Maintien et la Promotion de la Langue et la Culture Judéo-Espagnoles

(Association for the Maintenance and Promotion of the Judeo-
Spanish Language and Culture)
37 Rue Esquirol
75013 Paris
FRANCE
Haïm Vidal Sephiha, President

is an association dedicated to promoting Sephardic cultural and linguistic studies and activities. Since 1974, it has sponsored monthly Ateliers Judéo-Espagnoles at the Rashi Center (Centre Rachi) in Paris. The publication of the Association, also named *Vidas Largas,* publishes research on the Judeo-Spanish heritage and various Sephardic topics, which cover the life and culture of Sephardic communities throughout the world in both the past and present. Most of these articles are written in French; however, *Vidas Largas* also publishes stories, poems, proverbs, and songs in Judeo-Spanish. Vidas Largas sponsors a weekly radio program entitled *El Judeo-espanyol sovre las ondas* 'Judeo-Spanish on the (air)waves,' which broadcasts on FM radio for a half hour.

President Sephiha reports that *Vidas Largas* has about seven hundred members throughout France, but he has also received requests from about five thousand people worldwide for books, information, etc. on Sephardic topics.

2) Alliance Israélite Universelle
   45 Rue La Bruyère
   75009 Paris
   FRANCE
   Tel: 4280-35-00

was established in 1860 by French Jews who felt that their coreligionists in the Ottoman Empire, the Balkans, and the Middle East needed a more western education. Many of the Sephardim in their sixties and seventies today throughout the world received their education in such schools (see chapter 11 section no. 6). Today the Alliance is very active and is responsible for the maintenance of 124 schools in various parts of the Mediterranean. The Alliance has branch offices in other countries as well as in both New York and Los Angeles.

Belgium

1) *Los Muestros, la Boz de Los Sefaradim—La Voix des
   Sépharades—The Sephardic Voice*
   Moïse Rahmani, ed.
   25 Rue Dodonée
   B—1180 Brussels
   BELGIUM

is a new quarterly magazine begun in 1990 in Brussels. It is dedicated to all aspects of Sephardic history, culture, language, and religion, and publishes articles written in English, French, Judeo-Spanish, and Modern Spanish.

Spain

1) Instituto (Benito) Arias Montano
   Duque de Medinaceli 6
   28014 Madrid
   SPAIN
   tel: 429-20-17
   José Luis Lacavé, Director

was founded in 1939–40 and was originally dedicated to Hebraic studies. In 1962, along with the World Sephardi Federation, the Institute created the Instituto de Estudios Sefardíes (Institute of Sephardic Studies), which is today integrated into the Instituto de Filología (Institute of Philology) of the Consejo Superior de Investigaciones Científicas or CSIC (the Supreme Council for Scientific Studies). The Instituto Arias Montano is dedicated to the study of Sephardic language and literature and has published many scholarly works in these areas, including Joseph Nehama's famous *Dictionnaire du Judéo-Espagnol* in 1977. The Institute houses the Biblioteca de Estudios Sefardíes (Library of Sephardic Studies), which contains an important collection of books, manuscripts, newspapers, etc., dedicated to Sephardic topics. The Institute organized and published (in 1970) the proceedings of the First Symposium of Sephardic Studies *(el Primer Simposio de Estudios Sefardíes),* organized by CSIC in Madrid in June of 1964, and also founded the Museo Sefardí de Toledo (The Sephardic Museum of Toledo) in 1969. *Sefarad,* the quarterly journal of the Institute, is devoted to Sephardic history and culture.

2) *Sefarard,* Radio Exterior de España
   Apt. Correos 156.202
   28080 Madrid
   SPAIN
   Matilde Gini de Barnatan, Program Director

broadcasts a program in Judeo-Spanish called *Sefarad* each Thursday from 7:45 to 8:15 P.M., which is directed toward the countries located in the Mediterranean and the Middle East. On Fridays there is a twenty minute program directed to North and South America. The broadcasts present interviews, talks, etc., on the history, literature, folklore, music, and other aspects of Sephardic culture.

Notes

Chapter 1. What is Judeo-Spanish?

1. Kiddle estimates that approximately fifty thousand exiles went to either North Africa or to Portugal (Kiddle 1978:75).

2. By the seventeenth century, Portuguese was the spoken language of the Western Sephardim, while Spanish remained the language of the literature and prayer books as well as the official language for relations with other communities.

3. According to Alhadeff, the Sephardim in Western Europe were in contact with an advanced Christian society and thus quickly lost their Ladino tradition. The opposite phenomenon occurred with the Eastern Sephardim in the Ottoman Empire who were separated from populations that had a lower cultural level and a liberal regime, which allowed them to have their own communal autonomy (Alhadeff 1991a:9).

4. Nebrija's *Gramática sobre la lengua castellana* was not only the first Spanish grammar written, which helped to solidify Castilian as the strongest language in Spain, but it was also the first scientific grammar of a vernacular language in Europe. This work, together with his later *Reglas de ortografía castellana* 'Rules of Castilian orthography' written in 1517, helped to standardize Castilian usage and spelling.

5. A characteristic of all Jewish languages is that they are written with some form of Hebrew characters and have a Hebrew-Aramaic component (see Bunis 1975a:9). Rashi Script was the typeface designed to resemble the print used by the Sephardim in medieval Spain. It is named after the commentary of Rashi (*R*abbi *Sh*elomo *I*tshak of Troyes 1040–1105) and appeared in the first Hebrew book printed in 1475. Rashi script was used to print books and newspapers in Turkey until the 1920s and in Salonika until World War II (Perez 1992:33).

6. Italian schools of the Centro Dante Alighieri and French schools of the Alliance Israélite Universelle were established throughout cities of the Ottoman Empire dating from the mid 1800s. See chap. 11, sections no. 6, no. 7.

7. See chapter 2 for a discussion of the names of the language.

Chapter 2. The Name of the Language

1. In 1860 a group of French Jewish intellectuals formed the Alliance Israélite Universelle to educate and raise the cultural level of the Jews in the Levant and North Africa which they considered to be underdeveloped regions. Between 1860 and 1910, 116 Alliance schools were established throughout the Balkans, Turkey, Palestine, Morocco, Egypt, and Tunisia (Benardete 1982:150). See chapter 11, section no. 6.

2. *La Luz de Israel* which was started in Tel Aviv in 1972, ceased publication in 1990.

3. Bunis offers this same argument against use of the terms *(E)spanyol* and *Judeo-Spanish* because they have been introduced by outside influences (Bunis 1978b).

4. The Israeli radio station Kol Israel (Voice of Israel) broadcasts one daily fifteen minute program in Judeo-Spanish. The programs consist of news reports and topics on Sephardic culture like music, literature, folklore, cooking, et cetera. See Appendix E.

Chapter 3. History of the Eastern Sephardim

1. The family of Maimonides left Spain for Jerusalem in 1146 after the fanatic Muslim Almohades conquered parts of Spain.

2. In response to various pogroms and other anti-Jewish demonstrations in Spain in the late 1300s (especially after the anti-Jewish massacres of 1391), many Jews converted to Christianity and became known as *conversos* 'those who converted' or *cristianos nuevos* 'New Christians,' who were distinct from the original Old Christians. However, many of these conversos continued to practice Judaism secretly and were also referred to as *Crypto-Jews* and later as *Marranos* (literally "pigs").

3. The blood purity laws required that all public officials had to be people of Old Christian ancestry. In other words, they could not hold office if they had any *converso* or Jewish blood (Gampel 1987:49).

4. The terms *Sepharad I* and *Sepharad II* have been used by various scholars like M. Weinreich (1980) to refer to the two main periods in Sephardic Jewish history. *Sepharad I* designates medieval Spain or the pre-Expulsion period, while *Sepharad II* refers to the Sephardic Diaspora or the period dating from expulsion (1492).

There are also two terms which are often used to refer to the Sephardic Diaspora: *Diaspora I* designates the first countries where the Jews settled after expulsion (which include the Ottoman Empire, Northern Africa, Portugal, and other Western European countries), and *Diaspora II* refers to the countries of settlement dating from the end of the nineteenth century and beginning of the twentieth century (especially Palestine/Israel and the United States).

5. The Ottoman Empire was organized into a system of *millets,* which were separate religious communities that enjoyed autonomous self-government under a religious leader. Each millet had various local branches. Thus the Empire was divided into the Muslim *millet* as well as the Jewish, Armenian, and Greek Orthodox (which also included Slavs) *millets.* For further discussion of *millets* see Shaw (1976:59, 151–52) and Rodrigue (1990:29).

6. The Mendes Nasi family was one such family who had a great influence on the politics and economy of the Ottoman Empire in the 1500s. When Doña Gracia Mendes (1510–1568) emigrated to Constantinople from Portugal (via Amsterdam and Venice) after the death of her husband, she became one of the leaders of Turkish Jewry and a spokeswoman for the Marrano diaspora. She was instrumental in organizing a commercial boycott against the Italian port of Ancona, after this city burned several Marranos at the stake in 1555. She even got the sultan, Suleiman the Magnificent, to intercede on behalf of various imprisoned Marranos. Doña Gracia's nephew and son-in-law, Joseph Nasi (1524–1579), later became a political advisor to Suleiman's son and successor Selim II (1566–1574). Selim II deeded to Nasi land in and around the area of the Lake of Tiberius in Palestine

where he hoped to build settlements for fellow Marranos in the Holy Land and to raise silkworms to develop a silk weaving industry to rival that of Venice. However, even though both the Ancona boycott and Joseph Nasi's plans for Zionist developments in Tiberius were not successful, Prinz does point out the value of Mendes' and Nasi's preliminary efforts to help their coreligionists in distress (Prinz 1973:149). Later, Selim II bestowed upon Nasi the title of Duke of Naxos and presented him with the Aegean Island.

7. Blood Libel—the accusation that Jews used the blood of Christians (especially that of babies or children) for their religious rites in the preparation of unleavened bread for Passover. The blood libel myth has existed in various parts of the world throughout the history of the Jews.

8. Kabbalah (also spelled *cabala*)—One of the mystical traditions of Judaism whose school had flourished in the Iberian Peninsula before expulsion. After expulsion the city of Safed in Palestine became one of the most important centers of Jewish mysticism from which originated such famous students as Joseph Caro, who wrote the *Shulhan Arukh* (the basic code of law), and Isaac Luria and his successors.

9. The Janissary forces were the elite corps of Turkish troops who were organized in the fourteenth century and abolished in 1826.

10. The Carmona family rose to financial prominence during the second half of the eighteenth century. Moshe Carmona established a banking enterprise in Istanbul and was friendly with Selim III, the Sultan from 1789–1807. Behor Isaac, his grandson, increased the family fortune and was the banker and money lender of various high Janissary officials as well as for Esma, the sister of Mahmud II. Behor Isaac was very influential in the Turkish court as evidenced by the fact that he had the power to obtain the required permission from the Turkish authorities for the Jewish community to build new synagogues. He was a philanthropist, founding *yeshivot* (rabbinical schools) in Izmir, Jerusalem, and Bursa as well as contributing money to aid the poor Jews and heading an organization which sent money to Palestinian Jewish communities. When the Janissary corps were abolished in 1826, the Sultan ordered the murder of Behor Isaac and the confiscation of his fortune (Rodrigue 1990:27).

11. For a discussion of what happened to Turkish Jews after they were granted equality and citizenship, see Rodrigue (1990:31–35) and Shaw (1991: chapter 4).

12. See chapter 2, note 1 on the Alliance Israélite Universelle. See also chapter 11, section 6.

13. The London Society for Promoting Christianity amongst Jews opened its first school in 1829 in Izmir and two schools in Istanbul in 1855 and 1864. The Church of Scotland established schools in 1846 and 1873 in Izmir and one in Istanbul in 1873 (Rodrigue 1990:37).

14. The *cizye* was originally a poll tax that was abolished in 1856. It was reinstated in 1857 as a military exemption tax *(bedel-i askeriye)* to be paid by non-Muslims. In 1909 after the Young Turk Revolution it was finally abolished and all males were subject to military conscription (Rodrigue 1990:32).

15. In the past, since the Sephardim were the business/commercial leaders, many non-Jewish shops had also remained closed on Saturdays.

16. See chapter 1, note 5 on Rashi script.

17. Most of the Bulgarian Jews survived World War II because Bulgaria was an ally of Germany. However, after the Communist takeover, most Bulgarian Jews emigrated and resettled in Israel.

18. The majority of Rumanian Jews were Ashkenazic Jews.

Chapter 4. The Language of the Jews in Pre-Expulsion Spain

1. See note 5, chapter 1 on Rashi script.

2. Don Santob de Carrión was also known as Rabbi Shem Tov.

3. *Poema de Yoçef* is a poetic adaptation of the story of Joseph and his brothers. Both *Poema de Yoçef* and *Proverbios morales* were written in Spanish. *Los proverbios morales* was later translated into Hebrew.

4. The Constantinople *Pentateuch* was written in both Spanish and Greek and was transcribed into Hebrew characters.

5. The Ferrara Bible was printed in Latin characters.

6. The *Sidour* contains vestiges of Old Spanish translations of prayers in Latin characters which are conserved among the documents of the Inquisition of the fifteenth century concerning the Marranos.

7. *Regimiento de la vida* was written in Rashi characters. It contains specific rules of conduct and discusses human virtues. The Amsterdam version was written in Latin letters and printed in 1729.

8. The *Taqqanot* were ordinances regulating the life of the Jewish community. They dealt with schools, synagogues, courts and judges, taxes, the sale of wine, holidays, clothing, and community meetings. The language of the *Taqqanot* is Spanish interspersed with quotations from the Bible and the Talmud in Hebrew and Aramaic.

9. The Sephardi cursive known as *solitreo,* written with Hebrew letters, was used for everyday business transactions and personal correspondence. It evolved from a cursive script used by the medieval Spanish Jews and was taught in Jewish schools in the Levant for writing not only Judeo-Spanish but also Hebrew-Aramaic material by hand (Bunis 1975b:1–2).

10. The Manuscript I–I–3 was written in the Castilian of the sixteenth century which, according to Unamuno, reflects the archaic style of the Jews (S. Marcus 1962:130).

11. The Judeo-Spanish *romanzas* are the traditional Spanish ballads which were generally a continuation and adaptation of the traditional *romancero* of both the Middle Ages and the Renaissance. Later on, new *romanzas* were created in the Ottoman Empire.

12. The Judeo-Spanish proverbs contain the names of Jewish holidays and various Hebrew words, some of which have counterparts in Castilian (Lida 1978:89).

13. See chapter 5 for a more detailed discussion of the Hebrew component in Judeo-Spanish.

14. Renard points out a curious and interesting fact: the most common word form in Hebrew to designate "God" is the word [ɛlohim] which is a morphologically plural noun (1966a:126).

15. See chapter 5 for more discussion on Arabic influences.

16. The Arabic laryngeal spirant [ḥ] occurs in Judeo-Spanish in words of Hebrew and Turkish as well as Arabic origin.

17. According to I. Molho, *shara* and *alhad* were not used at all by the Spanish Christians (I. Molho 1961:64).

18. See chapter 5 for a more detailed discussion of archaisms.

19. The word *blanko*, literally "white," was used in Judeo-Spanish to mean "carbon" or "tar" and later "black," which has a fatal connotation for the Sephardim. This euphemistic use of the word *blanko* to mean "black," corresponds to the Spanish Arabic (and North African Arabic) word [blyad] literally "white,"

which also means "carbon," "tar," and "black." According to Wagner, there is no other analogous situation in other Jewish traditions. He concludes that this euphemism can only be a translation of the Arabic usage of the same word (Wagner 1930:33). Also, since this euphemism was found throughout diverse Sephardic communities after expulsion, it must have been common in the speech of the Spanish Jews before expulsion.

Chapter 5. Post-Expulsion: Judeo-Spanish in the Ottoman Empire

1. See chapter 1, note 4.

2. For a detailed account of nonregional variation in early Modern Eastern Judeo-Spanish, see Bunis (1982a:41–70).

3. The following is Entwistle's definition of the Judeo-Spanish *koiné:*

> the common basis of the existing dialects is a *koiné* established since the dispersion, into which have crept new regional differences corresponding to the location of the speakers in Constantinople, Salonika, Skoplje, Monastir . . . (Entwistle 1951:180).

Wagner informs us that the Jews from all the different communities were able to understand each other using this Sephardic *koiné* and that it was "the language of the books and of the newspapers and also of the conversation of the educated Jews among themselves" (Wagner 1930:21).

4. D. Levy suggests that this is probably diphthongization by analogy to *puedo* and *bueno* respectively (D. Levy 1952).

5. Spaulding points out the use of Old Spanish *b* with the value of consonantal u = v as in the standard Old Spanish forms *debda = deuda,* 'debt'; *cibdad = ciudad,* 'city'; and *cabteloso = cauteloso,* 'cautious'. He reports that the consonant had not yet become vocalized in the first half of the sixteenth century. (Spaulding 1965:80).

6. Bunis reports that initial *f-* is still found among some of the older women from the areas of Yugoslavia, Greece, Rumania, and Bulgaria, but is rarely found among men (Bunis 1982a:52).

7. The b—v distinction also occurs in some South American Spanish dialects.

8. Estrugo reminds us that forms such as *daldo* and *tomaldo* were seen in the Peninsula as late as 1610 in the writings of Covarrubias, and before that in those of the Arcipreste de Hita (Estrugo 1958:83).

9. According to Umphrey and Adatto, phenomena such as *yeísmo,* metathesis, and *m* before *ue* are more or less colloquial and often are characteristic of the Spanish spoken by the uneducated or illiterate in various countries, as opposed to simply being archaic (Umphrey and Adatto 1936:263).

10. D. Levy writes that this is most likely the result of analogy of the first conjugation to the second and third conjugations (D. Levy 1952).

11. According to Spaulding, the second person plural *-tes* ending of the preterit was the customary ending even in seventeenth century texts (Spaulding 1965:166).

12. Estrugo points out that both forms *la calor* and *la color* were also feminine in the time of Cervantes (Estrugo 1958:89).

13. See Estrugo for an example illustrating that *e* was also not used in the writings of the Arcipreste de Hita (Estrugo 1958:91).

14. According to Sephiha (1986), *Ladino* is the Judeo-Spanish calque which

was the language used to translate holy writings from Hebrew to Spanish. See chapter 2.

15. In *La Celestina* it is spelled *güerco* and *g* is the velar fricative.

16. *El Tiempo* was a daily newspaper written in Judeo-Spanish in Latin letters and published in Tel Aviv from 1950 to 1968.

17. The Hebrew word *azpan* is also used to mean "insolent".

18. See the section on Judeo-Spanish morphology in this chapter.

19. See chapter 4, note 10.

20. The *Pirkei Avot* literally "Chapters" or "Ethics of the Fathers" is a treatise of the Mishnah and contains the ethical maxims of the early rabbis.

21. See chapter 11, section 7 (p.208) on the multilingualism of the Sephardim.

22. A variation of this proverb is: *El gameyo no mira su korkova, ma mira la delfrente.* 'The camel does not look at his hump, but he looks at the one in front (of him)'.

23. For a list of works on Judeo-Spanish proverbs and collections of *refranes* consult Besso 1980 and Bunis 1981:141–145.

24. According to M. Molho, the Hebrew loans in Judeo-Spanish are ten times less numerous than those in Yiddish, which has borrowed about four thousand Hebrew words comprising more than 15 percent of the total Yiddish vocabulary (M. Molho 1960:6).

25. During Atatürk's regime efforts were made to remove all foreign influences from the country. In Atatürk's efforts for westernization, the Arabic alphabet was outlawed as the Latin-based one was adopted in November 1923. Atatürk also devoted much time to "liberating the language from the yoke of foreign languages," which meant eliminating Arabic and Persian loan words from Turkish. See chapter 3, p. 46.

26. Notice the similarity of *almenara* to the Hebrew word [menora] 'a candelabra of seven branches' which, according to Díaz-Mas, probably reinforced its use in Judeo-Spanish (Díaz-Mas 1986:108).

27. See note 3 of this chapter.

28. Sephiha questions the Portuguese origin of *akavidarse,* which, he writes, could also have resulted in changes from the Spanish past participle *precavida* to *akavida* and finally to *akavidar* (1987a:201).

29. According to Sephiha, *burako* (Modern Portuguese *buraco*) is also widespread in the Northwest of Spain and in some parts of Latin America (Sephiha 1987a:203).

30. Sephiha suggests that *birra* or *embirra* could also be attributed to *birria* of Leonese origin, since in Portuguese it does not have the meaning of "anger" but rather, "stubborness" or "obstinacy" (1987a:203).

31. The Portuguese origin of the *-tes* second person plural preterite verb endings is questioned by Sephiha (1966:102), and Renard attributes this ending to linguistic dissimilation plus the addition of final *-s* by analogy to other tenses, which he reports also occurs in Portuguese (Renard 1966a:119).

32. The pronunciation of *jornal* with the palatal affricate [ǰ] sound was probably influenced by the same Italian sound in *giornale,* while *žurnal* pronounced with the palatal fricative [ž] sound was influenced by the French pronunciation of *journal* (See the following section on French influences).

33. See chapter 11, sections 6 and 7 on the role or influence of the Italian and French schools on the Sephardim in the Levant.

34. See note 32 above.

35. *Arrivar* could also have originated from Italian *arrivare.*

36. *Pasha* was often used as a term of praise or endearment in Judeo-Spanish.

37. *Chakshir* referred to Turkish trousers with a broad band around the waist and light leather boots attached to the ankles, while *shalvares* were the Turkish baggy trousers.

38. *Fustan* is also of Arabic-Iberian origin. In certain South American countries it means "petticoat"; "undershirt".

39. *Parlak* means "bright" in Turkish.

40. The word for "black" or "carbon" in Judeo-Spanish carried a fatal connotation. Besides euphemistic use of Turkish based *kimur* or *komur,* the Sephardim also used *blanko.* See Note 10 of chapter 4 for the euphemistic use of *blanko* to mean "carbon, tar," and "black."

41. *Bayram* is a religious feast day, especially the festival following the fast of Ramadan.

42. The Turkish word *uydurmasyon* found in the Turkish dictionary (Hony, H. C. 1976. *A Turkish-English Dictionary,* second edition. Oxford: Clarendon Press/ Oxford University Press) was described as "an invented word" used "jokingly" or as "slang." I suggest that, since the Judeo-Spanish *-sion* (Modern Spanish *-ción*) ending is not a regular Turkish ending, the possibility exists that this word form with the *-syon* ending may have been derived from Judeo-Spanish.

43. The Turkish *fal* 'fortune' and *falci* 'fortune teller' were also used. *Goral* is used in various expressions such as *avrir goral* meaning "to consult an oracle".

44. *Celebi* was formerly a title for a royal prince; educated man; gentleman. It was also a title given to men of certain religious orders.

45. According to Hony's (1976) *Turkish-English Dictionary,* both meanings "family" and "wife" were given. However, my Turkish informant reports that the Modern Turkish word *familya* is no longer used to designate "wife".

46. The Spanish verb *fumar* 'to smoke' was also used.

47. M. Weinreich attributes *apotripos* and *aver* to the Hebrew component since they entered Hebrew during the talmudic period (M. Weinreich 1980:140).

48. *Meldar* was introduced into the language before expulsion (Renard 1966a:134). See comments on the origin of *meldar* in chapter 4.

49. The fork was unknown in Spain in the sixteenth century. Thus the word *tenedor* did not exist in Judeo-Spanish. When forks were later introduced, Judeo-Spanish adopted a variation of the Greek term.

Chapter 6. The Survival of Judeo-Spanish in the Ottoman Empire

1. See note 4, chapter 3.

2. The Jews, like other non-Muslim minorities in the Empire, were exempt from military service until 1909. See chapter 3, note 13.

3. Altabé cites the emigration of large numbers of Sephardic *conversos* and the different work habits of the Sephardim versus the Ashkenazim, who came from and were influenced by an intolerant shtetl culture, as possible explanations for the exclusion of Yiddish as a language of prayer. See Altabé (1981).

4. The Bible translations were done some centuries before expulsion, together with versions published later in the sixteenth century in the Diaspora, such as the famous Ferrara Bible published in 1553, as well as the Constantinople *Pentateuch* printed in 1547 (See chapter 4).

5. This was a situation similar to that of the Roman Catholics in the past with regard to the use of Latin in their masses.

6. The various sources I consulted included Galante 1935, Gaon 1965, Díaz-Mas 1986, Papo 1987, and Shaw 1991. Often these sources listed different years of publication, so many of the dates will be approximations. However, they should still give an idea of the popular Judeo-Spanish newspapers and reviews which were published in the Levant. I take full responsibility for all errors.

7. There have been only a few Judeo-Spanish newspapers printed in Latin characters: *El Luzero de la Pasensia,* published in Turnu Severin, Rumania from 1886 to 1890, and the three papers published in Tel Aviv: *El Tiempo* (1950–1968), *La Verdad* (1949–1972), and *La Luz de Israel,* which was published from 1972 until 1990. There are also some sporadic journals published today in Judeo-Spanish in Latin characters as well. See Appendix E for a list of present-day journals.

8. Even though Turkish was written with the Arabic alphabet (until Atatürk's reforms in the 1920s), the first Arabic/Ottoman printing press was not brought to Istanbul until early in the eighteenth century.

9. *Lingua Franca* or *Sabir* was the Romance-based pidgin used in the Mediterranean area from about the time of the Crusades until the late nineteenth or early twentieth century. It was often used by sailors not only to communicate in their ports of call, but also to communicate among themselves, since many crews were multinational (Collier 1976).

10. The situation of Judeo-Spanish in the Empire before the 1800s can be compared to that of Catalan in Catalonia. Woolard writes:

> We can see that the question, "Why do low-prestige languages persist?", is not appropriately asked about Catalan, which is not a low-prestige language in the people's minds or ears . . . The higher status of Catalan helps explain why Catalonia is almost unique among European minority languages in maintaining and even recruiting speakers. (Woolard 1989:125)

11. See the articles written by Kosover (1954:753–84) and Angel-Malachi (1946:103–4) concerning Judeo-Spanish lexical borrowings in the Yiddish of the Ashkenazim living in Palestine.

12. *Giffoot* was derived from the Turkish word *çıfıt* which was a derogatory term used to designate a Jew (Benardete 1982:135).

13. Salonika was the largest Jewish city in Southeastern Europe. It had about 23,001 Jews in 1518; 23,942 in 1589; and 22,767 in 1613. Due to plagues, fires, and other natural disasters, this figure remained the same until the end of the eighteenth century, making Salonika the only large city of the Empire where Jews constituted a majority of the population (Shaw 1991:38).

14. However, as the Sephardim and their language began to lose prestige (especially to French) in the Empire, it was the resulting different attitudes and behavior of the mothers and women in general, which later worked against the maintenance of Judeo-Spanish (Sala 1970a:33). See chapter 12 on negative language attitudes.

Chapter 7. The Sephardic Communities: New York, Israel, Los Angeles

1. Shearith Israel, commonly known as the Spanish and Portuguese Synagogue, is located on 70th Street and Central Park West. It has been referred to

as the "mother synagogue of American Jewry," and it was the leading synagogue in North America until the mid nineteenth century (Elazar 1989:167).

2. Both estimates include a certain number of Jews from Arab or Moslem countries like Syria, Iraq, and Iran, as well as Greek Jews from Janina, none of whom were Judeo-Spanish speakers.

3. After 1907 the Sephardim on the Lower East Side were concentrated on Allen, Chrystie, Broome, Orchard, and Eldridge Streets and on streets in the general vicinity (Angel 1981:4).

4. See Goren (1970:20–21) for a discussion of the Ashkenazic *landsmanschaft* principle and identity.

5. The coffeehouses, especially on the Lower East Side, were the real centers of immigrants, for both Ashkenazim and Sephardim. Rischin refers to them as "Jewish saloons" (Rischin 1962:141). Elazar informs us that many of them that were frequented by the Sephardim even resembled the former coffeehouses in the Balkans (Elazar 1989:171). However, Papo, like the Sephardi press, criticized the Sephardi coffeehouses, which did not help to develop young Sephardi men mentally or socially, diverting them from efforts to improve their levels of education (Papo 1987:27).

6. Various larger Sephardic organizations like the Federation of Oriental Jews begun in 1913 and the Central Sephardic Jewish Community of America founded in 1941, were not terribly successful in uniting the whole Sephardi community in New York. See Papo (1987) and Angel (1982) for detailed discussions of a lack of any central uniting organizations and forces in the United States. Also see chapter 11, section 21.

7. "Grandees" was the term used to describe these earlier American Sephardic Jews who considered themselves to be America's Sephardic elite and the "nobility of Jewry." According to Elazar, after emigrating to the United States,

They moved quickly to establish their own institutions and punctiliously sought to preserve the institutional forms that combined their Iberian heritage with Jewish tradition; and they did so in a manner so aristocratic that they became known as grandees. (1989:163)

See Stephen Birmingham's book *The Grandees, America's Sephardic Elite* (published in 1971 by Harper and Row) in which he describes these well-educated, aristocratic families who played an important role in United States history.

8. This limited number of Judeo-Spanish papers illustrates the small size of the Judeo-Spanish-speaking population in New York as compared to the Yiddish speakers. Rischin informs us that between 1885 and 1914, over 150 daily, weekly, monthly, quarterly, and festival journals and yearbooks appeared in Yiddish (Rischin 1962:119).

9. See Appendix E for a list of current Sephardic organizations and institutions in New York.

10. The *Shulhan Arkuh* was first published in Salonika in 1568 and twice again in Venice in 1602 and in 1712 under the title *Meza del alma* (Altabé 1981:12). It became the standard guide to Jewish law and practice.

11. The Chief Rabbi or *Hahambashi* was not only the head of Jewish religious matters, but was also the official in charge of all civil matters for the Jewish community. He enjoyed the respect and cooperation of the Ottoman authorities.

12. *Kashrut*—the regulations governing dietary laws and the killing and preparing of Kosher meat.

13. There are currently two newspapers in the world which are *partially* written

in Judeo-Spanish. *Şalom* 'Peace' is a weekly published in Istanbul. However, since the end of September 1984, only one of its eight pages is written in Judeo-Spanish while the other seven pages are written in Turkish. In the past the proportions were the opposite with Judeo-Spanish being the predominant language. The other paper is a recent one, just started in 1991 in Tel Aviv by Turkish Jews in Israel. It is called *Haber* (the Turkish word for "news" and the Hebrew word for "friend") which is also printed mostly in Turkish, with only two pages written in Judeo-Spanish. Unfortunately *Haber* temporarily ceased publication in 1992. See Appendix E.

14. See chapter 11 for a discussion of the decline of Judeo-Spanish in Israel.

15. I use the term *Oriental* to refer to the Jews who are neither of Ashkenazic (Eastern European) or Sephardic (Spanish or Portuguese) background. These Jews, for the most part, originated in Arab or Moslem countries.

16. See Elazar (1989:14–15) for the strict definition of the terms *Sephardi* and *Sephardim*.

17. Papo informs us that

> Natives of the Island of Rhodes showed a special ability for working with horticultural products and soon began to operate produce and flower stands and, in time, opened food markets and florist shops of their own. (1987:294)

In fact, the Rhodeslis were/are often known for their high quality flower shops.

18. This high percentage of Sephardic membership differs from that of New York's Shearith Israel which is about 50 percent Ashkenazic.

19. Until very recently, there have been no rabbinical schools in the United States for the training of Sephardic rabbis. With the inception of the Sephardic Studies Program at Yeshiva University in New York in the late sixties, a number of Sephardi students have enrolled and been ordained. But as Papo reminds us, not all ordained Sephardic rabbis assume Sephardi pulpits (Papo 1987:193–94).

20. One exception is the Sephardic Hebrew Academy, which was founded in 1970 and is the first Sephardic Hebrew Day School to be established in the United States. However, it is run by Syrian Jews who are not Judeo-Spanish speakers. Sitton informs us that the Syrian Jews (like many Ashkenazim) have successfully established Jewish educational centers in the United States. He writes that among the Sephardic groups, "the Syrian Jewish communities are considered the best organized American communities both spiritually and materially" (1985:329).

21. See Appendix E for a list of Sephardic organizations and institutions in Los Angeles.

Chapter 8. The Informants

1. See chapter 11, section 6 and chapter 2, note 1.

2. According to Samarin:

> A representative speaker has had built into him all the linguistic rules needed for interacting efficiently with the other members of the speech community. We can say that he has within him a microcosm of the linguistic structure. (1967:28)

3. I do mention some variations attributable to dialect differences, but I make no statistical analyses of these variations.

4. The parents of these informants were from different Balkan regions. For

example, an informant might have a mother from Istanbul while his father was from Salonika.

Chapter 9. Present Language Domains

1. See chapter 1, note 5 on Rashi script.
2. *La luz de Israel* was the only Judeo-Spanish newspaper (written totally in Judeo-Spanish) in the world after 1972. It appeared weekly in Tel Aviv and was printed in roman letters. It ceased publication in 1990.
3. See Appendix E for more detailed information on *Aki Yerushalayim*.
4. See Appendix E for a more detailed description of *Vidas Largas*.
5. See Appendix E for more on *Şalom*.
6. See chapter 6, section 6 (p. 125) for a description of the *Me'am Lo'ez*.
7. Fourteen informants never knew their grandparents, six had no children, twenty-eight had no grandchildren, one was unmarried and one had no siblings.
8. See Fasold (1984:235, 237) for an example of the implicational scale used to demonstrate choice of either Tiwa or English by Tiwa speakers, and Gal (1979:120–21) for an implicational scale on the use of Hungarian or German in Oberwort, Austria.
9. *Djoha* stories—David Altabé writes:

> *Djoha* is an anagram for "hodja" referring to Nasreddin Hodja who lived in Asia Minor in the thirteenth century. Tales of Nasreddin Hodja are famous throughout the Moslem world. His character is somewhat similar to that of the *schlemiel* in Yiddish humor. He does and says seemingly nonsensical things, but when carefully studied, they are filled with clever wit and wisdom. (1985:9)

Altabé feels that the character *Djoha* must have also been popular in Greek, Armenian, and Bulgarian folktales as well as those of other nationalities who lived under Turkish rule.

Chapter 10. Characteristics of Current Spoken Judeo-Spanish

1. See Appendix D for a copy of the word list used in New York and Israel in 1978 and in Los Angeles in 1985.
2. *Marketa* is an English word with a Spanish ending and is also found in New York Puerto Rican Spanish as well as dialects of Chicano Spanish in the United States. Poplack suggests that this word might now be an example of integration into the code of Puerto Rican Spanish (Poplack 1983:120). Altabé reports that *marketa* was used back in the 1930s even before there was a significant number of Puerto Ricans in New York (Altabé 1992 editing notes).
3. Some of these words, especially *parkear* (spelled *parquear* in Modern Spanish), are also found in other Spanish dialects spoken in the United States as well as in certain Spanish-speaking countries.
4. It is difficult to determine the amount of Hebrew influence because so many Hebrew words such as *haham* 'rabbi; intelligent' have been a part of the language since before expulsion. However, certain Modern Hebrew words were clearly not part of the Judeo-Spanish dialects spoken in the Balkans. Some examples are Modern Hebrew *hag* 'holiday' instead of Hebrew *moed* or Judeo-Spanish *dia*

bueno; Hebrew *uga* 'cake' instead of the Judeo-Spanish *pastel* or *pan d'espanya;* or Modern Hebrew *mitbach* 'kitchen' instead of Judeo-Spanish *kuzina.* In this chapter, I am concentrating on English, French, and Modern Spanish influences.

5. Luria's analysis of Judeo-Spanish in New York circa 1930 shows a variance of *m* and *n* in words like *nuzotros—muzotrus* (Modern Spanish *nosotros*) depending on the origin of the speaker (Luria 1930–31:14).

6. The topics of the free conversation samples are described in the section on code-switching.

7. I left these words off the word elicitation list used in Los Angeles in 1985. See Appendix D.

8. Altabé informs me that [naranǰa] was also used to mean "orange" in Salonika (1992 editing notes).

9. The influence of Modern Spanish on the language of the Israeli informants was the result of their either having lived or extensively traveled in countries where Spanish was spoken, or of having studied the language.

10. The plural of the Spanish noun *parte* is *partes* but it means "portion" or "part of something", not a "role" (Modern Spanish *papel*).

11. *Regreto* and *returnar* could also be considered legitimate Judeo-Spanish words of French and Italian origins that were in use prior to World War I. However, in my samples both words were pronounced as in English with the *-o* or *-ar* endings added.

12. I have not included code-switching examples of concepts or objects that did not exist in the same form in the Balkans. Examples are words denoting forms of education like *high school, junior high school, college,* or American concepts or inventions such as *downtown, freeway, pie, sandwiches, old age home,* and so on.

13. Notice the incorrect use of *yo* (instead of *me*). Grammatical errors were common in the speech of the informants who, for the most part, have never studied Judeo-Spanish. See chapters 10 and 11.

14. *Mishpaha* was also used in pre–World War I Judeo-Spanish.

15. These terms were used by Poplack (1982:244).

16. Notice phonological interference from Modern Spanish in the word *verdad* instead of the metathesized Judeo-Spanish form *vedrad.*

17. Today it is rare to find a person under the age of fifty or fifty-five who can still converse in Judeo-Spanish. See Malinowski (1979) and Harris (1979, 1985).

18. The Judeo-Spanish courses that have been offered in the past concentrate on the history and development of the language or on Sephardic literature written in Judeo-Spanish, but are not devoted to teaching the language. See chapter 12, note 5.

Chapter 11. Reasons for the Decline of Judeo-Spanish

1. See chapter 3, note 13 on the *cizye.*

2. See chap. 7, note 13 on *Şalom.*

3. See chapter 7 and Angel (1982) for a discussion of Gadol and *La America.*

4. See Rabin (1958), Fellman (1985), and Fishman (1991: chap. 10) for a discussion of the revival or vernacularization of Hebrew.

5. See Appendix E for a list of Sephardic organizations in Israel.

6. Max Nordau (1849–1923) was a famous philosopher and Zionist leader. He was a physician and journalist as well as a novelist and playwright. He joined

Theodor Herzl at the beginning of the Zionist movement, and his addresses at all the Zionist Congresses were enthusiastically received. He also drew up the 1897 Basle Program.

7. E. Papo also writes of the *kuatrolinguizmo* 'quadrilingualism' of the Jews of Sarajevo, that is, they spoke Judeo-Spanish in the home, Serbo-Croatian (Serbesko) in the street, Turkish in commercial dealings, and used Hebrew in the synagogue (E. Papo 1992:39).

8. *Homophonic calque* was the term originally used by Uriel Weinreich (1953:49).

9. See chapter 10 for examples of individual variations in Judeo-Spanish found among the New York informants (Harris 1979).

10. The same can be said for Yiddish. Fishman informs us that even though Yiddish was the medium of Judaic study, it was/is "rarely taught as a language in its own right" (Fishman 1991:209).

11. *Los españoles sin patria* was Dr. Angel Pulido's phrase as well as part of the title of his book published in 1905—*Los españoles sin patria y la raza sefardí.*

12. See chapter 2 concerning the names of the language.

13. See chapter 7, note 19 on Sephardic rabbinical training in the United States.

14. There are exceptions of course. Rabbi Ott of Tifereth Israel in Los Angeles and Rabbi Marans of the Sephardic Temple in Cedarhurst, Long Island, as well as other Ashkenazic rabbis around the country, have done a tremendous amount to foster education in Sephardic culture and to promote Sephardic practices among their congregations.

15. This is not true of Tifereth Israel and the Sephardic Hebrew Center in Los Angeles, whose memberships are still between 85 percent and 95 percent Sephardic. See chapter 7.

16. The same thing has happened with Yiddish in America. Fishman describes the lack of geographic concentration of secularist Yiddish-speaking circles as one of the reasons for the current attrition of Yiddish in the United States (Fishman 1991:202).

17. Juan Eugenio Hartzenbusch (1806–1880) was a Spanish playwright and director of the Biblioteca Nacional (National Library) of Spain.

18. The Judeo-Spanish department of Radio Kol Israel in Jerusalem broadcasts one daily program of approximately fifteen minutes in length in Judeo-Spanish. These programs cover the news as well as topics of Sephardic cultural interest. See Appendix E.

19. See Appendix E for a list and a description of the role of various organizations in promoting Sephardic culture.

Chapter 12. Negative Language Attitudes

1. Macnamara also gives the examples of Catalonians who have learned Castilian in addition to Catalan, and the people of Provence who have accepted French in place of Provençal (Macnamara 1973:37). Many more such language shift examples abound where the speech communities have a positive instrumental attitude accompanied by a negative integrative attitude.

2. According to D. Bunis:

Numerous are the incidents related in the research literature of linguists who, while traveling through the Balkans, chance to hear some Jewish shopkeeper or merchant conversing with a coreligionist in a language with a Hispanic flavor. Their scholarly curiosity piqued, the linguists inevitably ask "Are you speaking Spanish?" and are often answered "No, I'm speaking Jewish (Ĵidiyo)." (1975a:32)

Also see chapter 11, note 15.

3. See chapter 10 for a detailed discussion of code-switching or shifting in contemporary Judeo-Spanish.

4. See chapter 14 for a discussion of the ethnic revival.

5. Woolard reports that there is "a tendency to underreport proficiency because of linguistic insecurity" which is often a characteristic of minority-language communities (Woolard 1989:106).

6. Judeo-Spanish has been taught in New York at Columbia University and at New York University in the mid to late seventies by David Bunis, at Sephardic House by Joe Tarica and David Altabé, and at the University of Judaism (continuing education branch) in Los Angeles by Tracy Harris. In Israel courses have been taught by Moshe Giora at Bar Ilan University, David Gold at the University of Haifa, David Bunis at Hebrew University, and other courses have been offered at Ben Gurion University of the Negev and Beer Sheva University. However, these courses either emphasize(d) the reading of religious texts, or were/are concerned with the development of the historical or cultural role of the language, rather than with the acquisition of linguistic skills for conversational purposes.

7. There are exceptions such as *Los Amigos Sefardis* which was started in Oakland, California in 1985 to help preserve Sephardic culture. The group sponsors meetings and concerts and practices speaking Judeo-Spanish together. The *Sircolo de Kultura Djudeo-Espanyola* in Jerusalem has monthly meetings and conferences given in Judeo-Spanish on themes pertaining to various aspects of Sephardic culture. However, both of these groups are relatively small, and are made up predominantly of older speakers.

8. Woolard reminds us of the effects of speakers' attitudes on their behavior "since speakers are also their own auditors" (Woolard 1989:124).

Chapter 13. Judeo-Spanish and Language Death

1. Figures were obtained from a personal interview with Rosa Yaech and Nissim Bueno, the editors of *La luz de Israel,* in August, 1978.

2. See chapter 10 for examples of individual variation.

3. See chapter 11, sections 11, 12, and 13.

4. See chapter 10 for a detailed discussion of code-switching in current Judeo-Spanish speech.

5. See chapter 11, sections 13 and 14 concerning the writing system of Judeo-Spanish.

6. See chapter 12 for a discussion of the language attitudes of the female informants.

7. See Rabin (1958), Fellman (1985), and Fishman (1991, chapter 10), for a discussion of the revival of Hebrew.

8. The latest figures for the population of Yiddish speakers in the world today is somewhat over three million (Fishman 1991:194), compared to my estimate of approximately sixty thousand remaining Judeo-Spanish speakers in the world (see section b under *Signs of the Impending Death of Judeo-Spanish* in this chapter). But these figures are misleading because as Fishman reports, of the 1¼ million of Yiddish mother tongue population in the United States today, roughly only 300,000 are still active Yiddish speakers (Fishman 1991:194).

9. But this group of Yiddish speakers is relatively isolated. As Fishman points out,

> The substantial strength of ultra-Orthodox Yiddish is . . . no consolation to secular Yiddishists because these two sectors are virtually completely separated from each other, each representing a completely unacceptable life-style to the other. (1991:215)

Chapter 14. Prospects for Judeo-Spanish and Sephardic Ethnicity

1. Fishman reminds us that "intergenerational mother tongue transmission and language maintenance are not one and the same," although they are related. "Without intergenerational mother tongue transmission no language maintenance is possible," and without language maintenance, there will be fewer and fewer people able to transmit the mother tongue to succeeding generations (Fishman 1991:113).

2. The exceptions are the Israeli publication *Aki Yerushalayim* and the Judeo-Spanish broadcast on *Kol Israel*. However, both efforts are generally aimed at an older audience.

3. The revival of Hebrew in Israel was possible due in large part to government support, which backed all efforts to revive the language. See Fishman (1991, chapter 10), Fellman (1985), and Rabin (1958) for a discussion of the revival of Hebrew.

4. Sephardic House, which was originally associated with Congregation Shearith Israel in New York City, has recently (1992) become an independent organization dedicated to researching and promoting Sephardic history and culture. See Appendix E for a more detailed description.

5. Fishman describes a similar situation for Yiddish. He reports that Yiddish courses given by various synagogue affiliated afternoon and Sunday schools focus mostly on "Yiddish appreciation" rather than oral or literacy skills (Fishman 1991:206). Also, even though Yiddish is taught as a foreign language at between fifty and sixty American colleges and universities, they are mostly elementary courses. Columbia University was the only university which offered a graduate major in Yiddish through the Linguistics department. However, the future of the Yiddish program is doubtful due to the elimination of this department. (Fishman 1991:214).

Bibliography

Agard, Frederick. 1950. Present-day Judaeo-Spanish in the United States. *Hispania* 33: 203–10.

Agnew, J. 1981. Language shift and the politics of language: the case of the Celtic languages of the British Isles. *Language problems and language planning* 5: 1–10.

Akriche, Reine. 1987. Refranes i ditchas de mi avuela sefardita. *Vidas largas* 6: 11–12.

Aldrete, Bernardo de. 1614. *Varias antigüedades de España, Africa y otras provincias.* Antwerp.

Alhadeff, Léon. 1991a. Les communautés séphardies sous l'Empire Ottoman, 1ère partie. *Los muestros,* no. 4 (September): 8–9.

———. 1991b. Les communautés séphardies sous l'Empire Ottoman, 2ème partie. *Los muestros* no. 5 (December): 10–11.

Altabé, David F. 1977–78. The romanso, 1900–1933: a bibliographical survey. *The Sephardic Scholar* III: 96–106. New York: American Society of Sephardic Studies.

———. 1981. Judeo-Spanish as a language of liturgy and religious identification. In *The Americanization of a Hispanic group: The Sephardic experience in the United States,* 11–23. Proceedings of a conference sponsored by Sephardic House at Shearith Israel, New York. 5 April.

———. 1985. Sephardic humor. Paper read 3 December at Shearith Israel in New York.

Y ———. 1992. The significance of 1492 to the Jews and Muslims of Spain. *Hispania* 75: 728–31.

Angel, Marc D. 1971. Sephardic Culture in America. *Jewish Life 38, no. 4 (March–April): 7–11.*

———. 1974. *The Sephardim of the United States: An exploratory study.* New York: Union of Sephardic Congregations.

———. 1978. *The Jews of Rhodes: The history of a Sephardic community.* New York: Sepher-Hermon Press, Inc.

———. 1981. The literary, social and cultural life of the Judeo-Spanish Sephardim during the immigrant generation (early 1900's). In *The Americanization of a Hispanic group: The Sephardic experience in the United States,* 2–10. Proceedings of a conference sponsored by Sephardic House at Shearith Israel, New York. 5 April.

———. 1982. *La America: The Sephardic experience in the United States.* Philadelphia: The Jewish Publication Society of America.

———. 1987a. The Jews of Rhodes: The challenge of Mediterranean culture. In

The Sephardim: A cultural journey from Spain to the Pacific coast, ed. Rabbi Joshua Stampfer, 74–94. Portland, Ore.: The Institute for Judaic Studies.

―――. 1987b. The Planting of Sephardic Culture in North America. In *The Sephardim, a cultural journey from Spain to the Pacific coast,* ed. Rabbi Joshua Stampfer, 95–113. Portland, Ore.: The Institute for Judaic Studies.

―――. 1991. *Sephardi voices 1492–1992, A study guide.* New York: The Women's Zionist Organization of America.

Angel-Malachi, Saul. 1946. "Ha spaa't ha-Ladino al ha-Iddish" (The influence of Ladino on Yiddish). *Edoth* (Jerusalem) I: 103–4.

―――. 1978. Judeo-Espanyol—the language of Sephardi Jewry. Paper presented at the First International Congress for the Study of the Heritage of Sephardi and Oriental Jewry, Jerusalem. 27 June.

Armistead, Samuel G., and Joseph H. Silverman. 1965. Influencias griegas en el folklore sefardí, La balada del Puento de Arta. *Davar* (Buenos Aires) 107: 97–104.

―――. 1970. Exclamaciones turcas y otros rasgos orientales in el romance judeo-español. *Sefarad* 30: 177–93.

Ascher, Gloria Joyce. 1976. Words of the Sephardim, Izmirli proverbs and songs from the Bronx, no. 1. A series of annotated selections. New York: *Adelantre,* The Judezmo Society.

Attias, M., A. Capdevila, and C. Ramos-Gil. 1964. Supervivencia del judeoespañol. *Cuadernos israelíes* 9 (Jerusalem): 15–31.

Balch, Trudy, 1980. Do you speak Jewish? Photocopy.

Barker, George C. 1947. Social functions of language in a Mexican–American community. *Acta Americana* 5: 185–202.

Bar-Lewaw, I. 1968. Aspectos del judeo-español de las comunidades sefardíes en Atlanta y Montgomery. *Actas del XI Congreso internacional de lingüística y filología románicas,* 2109–2126.

Barocas, David N. 1976. *Ladino, Judezmo and the Spanish Jewish dialect.* The Sephardic Storm Lamp, Tract no. XI. New York: The Foundation for the Advancement of Sephardic Studies and Culture.

Baruch, Kalmi. 1930. El judeoespañol de Bosnia. *Revista de filología española* 17: 113–54.

―――. 1935. Les Juifs balkaniques et leur langue. *Revue internationale des études balkaniques* 2: 173–9.

Belon, Pierre. 1588. *Les observations de plusieurs singularitez et choses memorables trouvées en Grece, Asie, Judée, Egypte, Arabie et autres pays estrangers.* Paris: H. de Marnel et UVe G. Cavellat.

Benabu, Isaac, and Joseph Sermoneta, eds. 1985. Preface in *Judeo-romance languages,* ix–xi. Jerusalem: Misgav Yerushalayim and The Hebrew University of Jerusalem.

Benardete, Mair José. 1982. *Hispanic culture and character of the Sephardic Jews.* New York: Sepher-Hermon Press, Inc. (Reprint of 1953 edition.)

Benbassat, David. 1987. Quelques exemples de l'influence de la langue turque sur le judéo-espagnol. *Vidas largas* 6 (May): 49–53.

Bendiner, Elmer. 1983. *The rise and fall of paradise: when Arabs and Jews built a kingdom in Spain.* New York: G. P. Putnam's Sons.

Ben-Rubi, Itshak. 1950. *"Chimon, Chimon"—Aqui vos avla Chimon, Chimon,* humorous sketches of Chimon Chimon on the Radio Kol Israel, s.l.n.d. Tel Aviv.

Besso, Henry V. 1961. Judeo-Spanish literature. *Le Judaïsme Séphardi* 23: 1016–22.

———. 1963. Situación actual del judeo-español. *Arbor* 55: 155–72. (Reprinted in *Presente y futuro* 1964, 307–24).

———. 1970. Decadencia del judeo-español. Perspectivas para el futuro. In *Actas del primer simposio de estudios sefardíes* 1964, ed. Iacob Hassán, 249–61. Madrid: Instituto Arias Montano.

———. 1971. Judeo-Spanish—its growth and decline. In *The Sephardi heritage,* ed. R. Barnett, 604–35. London: Vallentine, Mitchell and Co.

———. 1980. Judeo-Spanish proverbs: an analysis and bibliography. In *Studies in Sephardic culture,* ed. Marc D. Angel, 21–55. New York: Sepher-Hermon Press, Inc.

Birmingham, Stephen. 1971. *The Grandees, America's Sephardic elite,* New York: Harper & Row.

Birnbaum, Solomon. 1944. Jewish languages. In *Essays in Honor of The Very Reverend Dr. J. H. Hertz,* eds. I. Epstein, E. Levine, and C. Roth, 51–67. London: E. Goldstein.

Blom, Jan P., and John J. Gumperz. 1972. Social meaning in linguistic structure: code-switching in Norway. In *Directions in sociolinguistics,* ed. Gumperz and Hymes, 407–34. New York: Holt, Rinehart and Winston.

Blondheim, David S. 1925. *Les parlers judéo-romans et la vetus latina.* Paris: Eduoard Champion.

Bortnick, Rachel A. 1991. From the editor. *A.A.J.F.T. Newsletter* 2, no. 1 (March): 2.

———. 1992a. Turkish Jews in Israel. *A.A.J.F.T. Newsletter* 3, no. 1 (March): 3–4.

———. 1992b. Turkish-Jewish Women, 1992. *A.A.J.F.T. Newsletter* 3, no. 1 (March): 8.

———. 1992c. The state of Ladino as a spoken language. *A.A.J.F.T. Newsletter* 3, no. 2 (May): 13.

Bumaschny, Perla H. 1968. *La historia del ladino.* Buenos Aires: Congreso Judío Mundial.

Bunis, David M. 1974. The historical development of Judezmo orthography: a brief sketch. In *Working papers in Yiddish and East European Jewish studies,* no. 2 (October). New York: YIVO.

———. 1975a. Problems in Judezmo linguistics. In *Working papers in Sephardic and Oriental Jewish Studies #1.* New York: The American Sephardi Federation.

———. 1975b. *A guide to reading and writing Judezmo.* New York: Adelantre.

———. 1978a. Notes on Judezmo "Jewish language, language of Eastern Sephardic Jews." Photocopy.

———. 1978b. Response (to Denah Lida's paper on Ladino language and literature). In *Jewish languages: Theme and variations,* ed. Herbert Paper, 93–102. Cambridge, Mass.: Association for Jewish Studies.

———. 1981. *Sephardic studies, a research bibliography.* New York: Garland Publishing Company.

————. 1982a. Types of nonregional variation in early modern eastern spoken Judezmo. *International Journal of the Sociology of Language* 37: 41–70.

————. 1982b. Judezmo language and literature: an experiment at Columbia University. In *The Sepharadi and Oriental Jewish heritage,* ed. Issachar Ben-Ami, 383–402. Jerusalem: The Magnes Press, The Hebrew University.

Camhy, Ovadia. 1966. Certaines caracteristiques linguistiques du judéo-espagnol. *Kol-Sépharad* 2: 18–20.

————. 1971. Le judéo-espagnol—facteur de conservation pendant 4 siècles. In *The Sephardic heritage,* ed. R. Barnett, 560–603. London: Vallentine, Mitchell and Co.

Canfield, D. Lincoln. 1981. *Spanish pronunciation in the Americas.* Chicago: University of Chicago Press.

Cantera, Jesús. 1964a. Longevidad y agonía del judeo-español de Oriente. *Arbor* (Madrid) 58, no. 222: 148–156.

————. 1964b. Una lengua que desaparece: el judeoespañol. *Las ciencias* (Madrid), Año 29, no. 4: 252–57.

————. 1972–73. Notas sobre el judeoespañol de Oriente. *Filología moderna* 13, no. 46–47: 105–15.

Castro, Federico Pérez. 1971. España y los judíos españoles. In *The Sephardi heritage*, ed. R. Barnett, 314–22. New York: Ktav.

Chetrit, Joseph. 1985. Judeo-Arabic and Judeo-Spanish in Morocco and their sociolinguistic interaction. In *Readings in the sociology of Jewish languages,* ed. Joshua A. Fishman, 261–79. Leiden: E.J. Brill.

Chumaceiro, Rita Mendes. 1982. Language maintenance and shift among Jerusalem Sephardim. *International Journal of the Sociology of Language* 37: 25–39.

Collier, Barbara. 1976. Lingua Franca or Sabir. Department of Linguistics, Georgetown University. Photocopy.

Cooper, Robert L. 1985. Language and social stratification among the Jewish population of Israel. In *Readings in the sociology of Jewish languages,* ed. Joshua A. Fishman, 65–81. Leiden: E.J. Brill.

Coteanu, I. 1957. A propos des langues mixtes (sur l'istro-roumain). In *Mélanges linguistiques,* published on the occasion of the VIII International Congress of Linguists in Oslo, 5 to 7 August, 129–48. Bucharest: Editions de l'Académie de la République Populaire Roumaine.

Crantford, Carey S. 1991. Variants in the classification of Judeo-Spanish as a language. Paper presented at the Second International, Interdisciplinary Conference on Sephardic Studies, S.U.N.Y. Binghampton. April 21.

Crews, Cynthia M. 1935. *Recherches sur le judéo-espagnol dans les pays balkaniques.* Paris: Droz.

————. 1954. Some Arabic and Hebrew words in Oriental Judeo-Spanish. *Vox romanica* 14: 296–309.

————. 1961. Reflections on Judeo-Spanish by a Spanish Jew. *Vox romanica* 20: 327–34.

Danon, Abraham. 1896. Recueil des romances judéo-espagnoles chantées en Turkie. *Revue des études juives* 32: 102–23.

————. 1903–4. Essai sur les vocables turcs dans le judéo-espagnol. *Kelete szemle* no. 4: 216–29; no. 5: 111–26.

——. 1913. Le turc dans le judéo-espagnol. *Revue hispanique* 29: 5–12.

——. 1922. Les éléments grecs dans le judéo-espagnol. *Revue des études juives* 75: 211–16.

Del Río, Angel. 1963. *Historia de la literatura española*. Tomo I. New York: Holt, Rinehart and Winston.

Denison, Norman. 1977. Language death or language suicide? *Linguistics* 191: 13–22.

Deutsch, Karl W. 1942. The trend of European nationalism—the language aspect. *American Political Science Review* 36: 533–41.

Díaz-Mas, Paloma. 1986. *Los sefardíes-historia, lengua y cultura*. Barcelona: Riopiedras Ediciones.

Díez-Echarri, E., and J. M. Roca Franquesa. 1966. *Historia de la literatura española e hispanoamericana*. Madrid: Aguilar.

DiPietro, Robert J. 1976. Language as a marker of Italian ethnicity. *Estratto da studi emigrazione/études migrations* 42: 202–18.

Donnell, Rabbi Shelton. 1987. At the end of the frontier: Sephardim in the Western United States. In *The Sephardim, a cultural journey from Spain to the Pacific coast*, ed. Rabbi Joshua Stampfer, 114–37. Portland, Ore.: The Institute for Judaic Studies.

Dorian, Nancy C. 1973. Grammatical change in a dying dialect. *Language* 49: 413–38.

——. 1977. The problems of the semi-speaker in language death. *Linguistics* 191: 23–32.

——. 1980. Language shift in community and individual: the phenomenon of the laggard semi-speaker. *International Journal of the Sociology of Language* 25: 85–94.

——. 1981. *Language death: The life cycle of a Scottish Gaelic dialect*. Philadelphia: University of Pennsylvania Press.

Dressler, Wolfgang, and Ruth Wodak-Leodolter. 1977a. Introduction. *Linguistics* 191: 5–11.

——. 1977b. Language preservation and language death in Brittany. *Linguistics* 191: 33–44.

Eastman, Carol M. 1984. Language, ethnic identity and change. In *Linguistic minorities, policies and pluralism*, ed. J. Edwards, 259–76. London: Academic Press.

Edwards, John. 1982. Attitudes toward Gaelic and English among Gaelic speakers in Cape Breton Island, Nova Scotia. Paper presented at the Sixth Congress of the International Association of Cross-Cultural Psychology, Aberdeen.

——. 1984a. Language, diversity and identity. In *Linguistic minorities, policies and pluralism*, ed. J. Edwards, 277–310. London: Academic Press.

——. 1984b. Irish and English in Ireland. In *Language in the British Isles*, ed. P. Trudgill, 480–98. Cambridge: Cambridge University Press.

——. 1985. *Language, society and identity*. Oxford and New York: Basil Blackwell.

Elazar, Daniel J. 1989. *The other Jews, the Sephardim today*. New York: Basic Books.

Entwistle, W. J. 1951. *The Spanish language together with Portuguese, Catalan and Basque*. London: Faber & Faber.

Esh, Shaul. 1970. Some observations on the place of the Sephardim in modern Jewry. In *Actas del primer simposio de estudios sefardíes 1964,* ed. Iacob Hassán, 131–40, 395–99. Madrid: Instituto Arias Montano.

Estrugo, José M. 1933. *El retorno a Sefarad cien años después de la Inquisición.* Madrid: Imprenta Europea.

——. 1958. *Los sefardíes.* Havana: Editorial Lex.

Farhi, Gentille. 1937. La situation linguistique du Séphardite à Istanbul. *Hispanic Review* 5: 151–8.

Fasold, Ralph W. 1975. Code-Switching and implications. Department of Linguistics, Georgetown University. Mimeo.

——. 1984. Language maintenance and shift. In *The sociolinguistics of society,* by Ralph Fasold, 213–45 (Reprint 1985). Oxford and New York: Basil Blackwell.

Fellman, Jack. 1985. A sociolinguistic perspective on the history of Hebrew. In *Readings in the sociology of Jewish languages,* ed. J. A. Fishman, 27–34. Leiden: E.J. Brill.

Fishman, Joshua A. 1964. Language maintenance and language shift as fields of inquiry. *Linguistics* 9: 32–70.

——. 1965. *Yiddish in America: Sociolinguistic description and analysis.* The Hague: Mouton.

——. 1966a. *Language loyalty in the United States.* The Hague: Mouton.

——. 1966b. *Hungarian language maintenance in the United States.* Bloomington: Indiana University Press.

——. 1972. Language maintenance in a supraethnic age. In *Language and sociocultural change,* ed. Anwar S. Dil, 48–75. Stanford, Calif.: Stanford University Press.

——. 1973. The third century of non-English language maintenance and non-Anglo ethnic maintenance in the United States of America. *TESOL Quarterly* 7, no. 3 (September): 221–33.

——. 1977. Language maintenance and language shift as a field of inquiry: revisited. In *Language in sociocultural change,* ed. Anwar S. Dil, 76–134. Stanford, Calif.: Stanford University Press.

——. 1985. The sociology of Jewish languages from a general sociolinguistic point of view. In *Readings in the sociology of Jewish languages,* ed. Joshua A. Fishman, 3–21. Leiden: E.J. Brill.

——. 1991. *Reversing language shift.* Philadelphia: Multilingual Matters Ltd.

Fishman, J., et al. 1985. *The rise and fall of the ethnic revival.* Berlin: Mouton de Gruyter.

Fontanella de Weinberg, María B. 1976. El judeospañol. In *La lengua española fuera de España,* by M. B. Fontanella de Weinberg, 124–48. Buenos Aires: Editorial Paidos.

Franco, M. 1897. *Essai sur l'histoire des Israélites de l'Empire Ottoman, depuis les origines jusqu'à nos jours.* Paris: A. Durlacher.

Gal, Susan. 1979. *Language shift: Social determinants of linguistic change in bilingual Austria.* New York: Academic Press.

Galante, Abraham. 1935. La presse judéo-espagnole mondiale. *Hamenora* 13: 3–16.

Gampel, Benjamin. 1987. The Decline of Iberian Jewries: Pogroms, inquisitions and expulsions. In *The Sephardim: A cultural journey from Spain to the Pacific coast,* ed. Rabbi Joshua Stampfer, 36–57. Portland, Ore.: The Institute for Judaic Studies.

Gans, H. 1979. Symbolic ethnicity: the future of ethnic groups and cultures in America. In *On the making of Americans: Essays in honor of David Riesman,* ed. H. Gans et al., 193–220. Philadelphia: University of Pennsylvania Press.

Gaon, M. D. 1965. *A bibliography of the Judeo-Spanish (Ladino) press.* Jerusalem: Ben Zvi Institute.

Gardner, R. C., and W. E. Lambert 1972. *Attitudes and motivation in second language learning.* Rowley, Mass.: Newbury House.

Gartner, Lloyd P. 1974. Immigration and the formation of American Jewry, 1840–1925. In *The Jew in American society,* ed. Marshall Sklare, 31–50. New York: Behrman House, Inc.

Garvin, Paul L., and Madeleine Mathiot. 1972. The urbanization of the Guaraní language: a problem in language and culture. In *Readings in the sociology of language,* ed. J. A. Fishman, 365–74. The Hague: Mouton. (Reprint from 1956.)

Gellner, E. 1964. *Thought and change.* London: Weidenfeld & Nicolson.

Gerber, Jane. 1991a. Paper presented at the Symposium *Yom Limud: 1391—The destruction of Spanish Jewry,* Sephardic House, New York, 12 May.

———. 1991b. Decade of despair: the last days of Jewish life in Spain. The Morris Levy Memorial Lecture, Queens College, New York, fall.

Gil, Rudolfo. 1909. La lengua española entre los judíos. *España moderna* 21: 30–43.

Gold, David. 1981. Jewish intralinguistics as a field of study. *International Journal of the Sociology of Language.* 30:31–46.

———. 1991. Judezmo: Once the chief language of Sephardic Jewry. *Language International* 3.5:32–34.

Goldberg, Harriet. 1993. The Judeo-Spanish proverb and its narrative context. *PMLA* 108, no. 1 (January): 106–20.

Gonzalo de Illescas. 1606. *Historia pontifical y cathólica,* Barcelona: Iayme Cendrat.

Goren, Arthur A. 1970. *New York Jews and the quest for community: The Kehillah experiment, 1908–1922.* New York: Columbia University Press.

Graur, Alexandru. 1960. Cum moare o limba. Limbi mixte. In *Studii de lingvistica generala* by A. Graur, 434–39. Bucharest: Editura Academiei Republicii Populare Romine.

Gregor, D. 1980. *Celtic: A comparative study.* New York: Oleander.

Güleryüz, Naïm. 1991a. The history of the Turkish Jews, a brief review. Condensed from a lecture presented July 1989. New York: The Quincentennial Foundation of Istanbul (United States).

———. 1991b. Les Juifs en Turquie. *Los muestros,* no. 4 (September): 10–11.

Haberman, Clyde. 1990. Where 16 synagogues stand among the Minarets. *New York Times International,* 30 July.

Haim, Abraham. 1988. Introduction. In *Jewish roots in Spain-Raíces judías en España,* ed. K. Chamorro et al., 1–9. Madrid: Acor Artes Gráficas.

Halio-Torres, Joe. 1980. Writing the Spanish-Jewish dialect. In *Studies in Sephardic culture,* ed. Marc D. Angel, 95–104.

Harris, Tracy K. 1979. The prognosis for Judeo-Spanish: its description, present status, survival and decline, with implications for the study of language death in general. Ph.D. diss., Georgetown University, Washington, D.C.

———. 1982. Reasons for the decline of Judeo-Spanish. *International Journal of the Sociology of Language.* 37: 71–97.

———. 1983. Foreign interference and code-switching in the contemporary Judeo-Spanish of New York. In *Spanish in the U.S. setting: Beyond the southwest,* ed. L. Elías-Olivares. Washington, D.C.: National Clearinghouse for Bilingual Education.

———. 1985. The decline of Judezmo: problems and prospects. In *Readings in the sociology of Jewish languages,* ed. Joshua A. Fishman, 195–211. Leiden: E.J. Brill.

———. 1987. The current status of Judeo-Spanish in the Los Angeles Sephardic community. Paper presented at the 69th Annual Meeting of the AATSP (American Assoc. of Teachers of Spanish and Portuguese) in Los Angeles, California, 15 August.

———. 1990. Prospects for Judeo-Spanish, Sephardic ethnicity and culture. Paper presented at the 106th MLA Convention, Chicago, 28 December.

———. 1991. Code-switching in contemporary Judeo-Spanish. Paper presented at the Second International, Interdisciplinary Conference on Sephardic Studies, S.U.N.Y. Binghamton, 21 April.

Hassán, Iacob. J. 1963. Perspectivas del judeo-español. *Arbor* 55: 175–84.

———, ed. 1970. *Actas del primer simposio de estudios sefardíes 1964.* Madrid: Instituto Arias Montano.

Hasselmo, Nils. 1970. Code-switching and modes of speaking. In *Texas studies in bilingualism,* ed. G. Gilbert, 179–210. Berlin: de Gruyter.

Haugen, Einer. 1978. Bilingualism, language contact and immigrant languages in the United States. In *Advances in the study of societal multilingualism,* ed. J. A. Fishman, 1–111.

Hermon, Simon R. 1961. Explorations in the social psychology of language choice. *Human Relations* 14: 149–64.

Herzog, Marvin I. 1978. Yiddish. In *Jewish languages: Theme and variations,* ed. H. H. Paper, 47–58. Cambridge, Mass.: Association for Jewish Studies.

Hill, Jane H. 1978. Language death, language contact and language evolution. In *Approaches to language: Anthropological issues,* ed. W. McCormac and S. Wurm, 45–78. The Hague: Mouton.

Hirsch, Ruth. 1951. A study of some aspects of a Judeo-Spanish dialect as spoken by a New York Sephardic family. Ph.D. diss., University of Michigan, Ann Arbor.

Hofman, John E. 1985. The commitment to Modern Hebrew: value or instrument? In *Readings in the sociology of Jewish languages,* ed. Joshua A. Fishman, 51–64. Leiden: E.J. Brill.

——— and Haya Fisherman. 1972. Language shift and language maintenance in Israel. In *Advances in the sociology of language,* Vol. 2, ed. J. A. Fishman, 342–64. (Reprint from *International Migration Review* (1971) 5:204–26).

Huffines, Marion L. 1980. Pennsylvania German: maintenance and shift. *International Journal of the Sociology of Language* 25: 43–57.

Immanuel, Jon. 1989. Lucky Jews. *The Jerusalem Post International Edition,* week ending 28 October, p.1.

Israel, Gerard. 1960. *L'Alliance Israélite Universelle 1860–1960. Cent ans d'efforts pour la libération et la promotion de l'homme par l'homme. Cahiers de l'Alliance Israélite Universelle* no. 127, Numéro Spécial (February). Paris: L'Ecole Normale Israélite Orientale.

Jochnowitz, George. 1978. Judeo-Romance languages. In *Jewish languages: Theme and variations,* ed. H. H. Paper, 65–74. Cambridge, Mass.: Association for Jewish Studies.

———. 1981. Ladino. In *Midstream,* February: 29–32.

Kahane, Henry. 1973. Review of *Estudios sobre el judeo-español de Bucarest* and *Phonétique et phonologie du judéo-espagnol de Bucarest,* by Marius Sala. *Language* 49: 943–48.

Kahane, Henry, and Sol Saporta. 1953. The verbal categories of Judeo-Spanish. *Hispanic Review* 21: 193–214; 322–36.

Kamen, Henry. 1990. The Converso or Crypto-Jewish community in Spain and the founding of the Spanish Inquisition. Paper presented at the *Expulsion 1492 Conference* organized by the S.E.C. at Tifereth Israel, Los Angeles, 9 November.

Ke Xaber? (What's New?) 1976–77. Newsletters of *Adelantre,* ed. D. Bunis and S. Levy. New York: *Adelantre:* The Judezmo Society.

Kiddle, Lawrence B. 1978. Response to G. Jochnowitz's paper on Judeo-Romance languages. In *Jewish languages: Theme and variations,* ed. H. H. Paper, 75–77. Cambridge, Mass.: Association for Jewish Studies.

Koch, Yolanda Moreno. 1978. The Taqqanot of Valladolid of 1432. *The American Sephardi* IX: 58–145.

Koen-Sarano, Matilda. 1986. Dichas i refranes en la vida matrimoniala Djudeoespanyola. *Aki Yerushalayim,* Anyo 8, January–July, no. 28–29: 72–75.

———. 1988. Las paras en el reflán Djudeo-Espanyol. *Aki Yerushalayim,* Anyo 10, Enero-Djunio, no. 36–37: 39–41.

Kolonomos, Žamila, ed. 1976. *Poslovice i izreke sefardskih jevreja bosne i hercegovine (Proverbs and sayings of the Sephardi Jews of Bosnia and Herzegovina).* Belgrade: The Federation of Jewish Communities in Yugoslavia.

Kosover, Mordechai. 1954. Ashkenazim and Sephardim in Palestine (A study in intercommunal relations). In *Homenaje a Millas-Vallicrosa,* vol. 1, 753–84. Barcelona: Consejo Superior de Investigaciones Científicas (CSIC).

Kraus, Karl. 1951. Judeo-Spanish in Israel. *Hispania* 34: 261–70.

———. 1952. El judeo-español en Israel. *Boletín de filología* (Montevideo) 7: 385–419.

Labov, William. 1966. *The social stratification of English in New York City.* Washington, D.C.: Center for Applied Linguistics.

Lamouche, Léon. 1907. Quelque mots sur le dialecte espagnol parlé par les Israélites de Salonique. *Romanische Forschungen* 23: 969–91.

Lapesa, Rafael. 1968. *Historia de la lengua española.* 7th ed. Madrid: Escelicer, S.A.

Lathrop, Thomas A. 1986. *The evolution of Spanish: An introductory historical grammar,* revised edition. Newark, Del.: Juan de la Cuesta.

Lavender, Abraham D. 1977. The Sephardic revival in the United States: A case of ethnic revival in a minority-within-a-minority. In *A coat of many colors: Jewish subcommunities in the U.S.,* ed. A. Lavender, 305–317. Westport, Conn.: Greenwood Press.

Lazar, Moshe. 1972. Introduction. In *The Sephardic tradition: Ladino and Spanish-Jewish literature,* ed. M. Lazar, 13–29. New York: W.W. Norton.

Lestchinsky, Jacob. 1946. *Bilan de l'extermination.* Brussels: Congrès Juif Mondial.

Levy, Denah. 1952. El sefardí esmiriano de Nueva York. Ph.D. diss., University of Mexico, Mexico.

Levy, Isaac J., and Dale E. Enwall. 1986. Dichas i refranes de los sefardíes. In *Aki Yerushalayim* Anyo 8, January–July, no. 28–29: 25–27.

Levy, Rebecca Amato. 1987. *I remember Rhodes.* New York: Sepher-Hermon Press, Inc.

Levy, Sam. 1948. El judeo-espaniol quedara el de vivir? *La Boz de Türkiye* (Istanbul) año IX, no. 197: 232.

———. 1949. La langue maternelle des Séphardis-grandeur et décadence du Ladino. IV. *Les cahiers séfardis* (Paris) vol. 3: 46–51.

Lewis, Glyn. 1978. Migration and decline of the Welsh language. In *Advances in the sociology of language,* vol. 2, ed. Joshua A. Fishman, 263–352. The Hague: Mouton.

Lida, Denah. 1962. The vanishing Sephardim. *Le Judaïsme séphardi* 24: 1035–40.

———. 1978. Ladino language and literature. In *Jewish languages: Theme and variations,* ed. H. H. Paper, 79–92. Cambridge, Mass.: Association for Jewish Studies.

Lieberson, Stanley and Timothy J. Curry. 1981. Language shift in the United States: Some demographic clues. In *Language diversity and language contact: Essays by Stanley Leiberson,* 158–72. Stanford, Calif.: Stanford University Press.

Luria, Max A. 1930. *A study of the Monastir dialect of Judeo-Spanish based on oral material collected in Monastir, Yugo-Slavia.* New York: Instituto de las Españas.

———. 1930–31. *Judeo-Spanish dialects in New York City.* Reprint from *Todd Memorial Volumes,* 7–16. New York.

———. 1954. Judeo-Spanish dialects and Mexican popular speech. In *Homenaje a Millas-Vallicrosa,* vol. 1, 789–810. Barcelona: CSIC.

La Luz de Israel 1978–79. Various issues, biweekly newspaper, Tel Aviv, Israel. Ed. Rosa Yaech Bueno and Nissim Bueno.

Mackey, William F. 1970. Interference, integration and the synchronic fallacy. Bilingualism and language contact. In *Georgetown University round table on languages and linguistics 1970,* ed. J. E. Alatis, 195–227. Washington, D.C.: Georgetown University Press.

Macnamara, John. 1971. Successes and failures in the movement for the restoration of Irish. In *Can Language be planned?,* ed. J. Rubin and B. Jernudd, 65–94. Hawaii: University Press of Hawaii.

———. 1973. Attitudes and learning a second language. In *Language attitudes: Current trends and prospects,* ed. R. Shuy and R. Fasold, 36–40. Washington, D.C.: Georgetown University Press.

Maimon, Sam. 1980. Ladino-English dictionary. In *Studies in Sephardic culture*, ed. Marc D. Angel, 107–178. New York: Sepher-Hermon Press, Inc.

Malaji, A.R. 1939. El porvenir del ladino. *Judaica* (Buenos Aires) 13: 78–9.

Malinowski, Arlene. 1979. Aspects of contemporary Judeo-Spanish in Israel based on oral and written sources. Ph.D. diss., University of Michigan, Ann Arbor.

———. 1982a. A report on the status of Judeo-Spanish in Turkey. *International Journal of the Sociology of Language* 37: 7–23.

———. 1982b. Review of Haïm Vidal Sephiha's *L'agonie des Judéo-Espagnols* [Paris: Editions Entente, 1977]. *La corónica* (Fall): 103–105.

———. 1983. Judeo-Spanish language maintenance efforts in the United States. *International Journal of the Sociology of Language* 44: 137–51.

———. 1985. Judezmo in the U.S.A. today: Attitudes and institutions. In *Readings in the sociology of Jewish languages*, ed. J. A. Fishman, 212–24. Leiden: E.J. Brill.

Marcus, Jacob Rader. 1989. *United States Jewry 1776–1985*. Vol I. Detroit: Wayne State University Press.

Marcus, Simon. 1962. A-t-il existé en Espagne un dialecte judéo-espagnol? *Séfarad* 22: 129–49.

Matza, Diane. 1990. Sephardic Jews transmitting culture across three generations. *American Jewish History* (spring): 336–354.

Mendoza y Bobadilla, Cardenal Francisco de. 1849. *Tizón de la nobleza de España*. Madrid: D. Saavedra y Companía.

Mézan, Dr. Saul. 1925. *Les Juifs espagnols en Bulgarie, 1: Histoire, statistique, ethnographie*. Sofia: Edition d'Essai.

———. 1936. *De Gabirol à Abravanel, Juifs espagnols promoteurs de la Renaissance*. Paris: Librairie Lipschutz.

Miller, Wick R. 1971. The death of language or serendipity among the Shoshoni. *Anthropological Linguistics* 13: 114–120.

The Minority within a minority. 1976. *Human Behavior* 5, no. 6 (June): 62.

Mizrahi, Judith. 1987. Sources of diversity in Sephardim. Ph.D. diss., New York University.

Molho, Isaac R. 1961. La terminologie arabe dans le vocabulaire judéo-espagnol. *Tesoro de los judíos sefardíes* 4: 64–68.

Molho, Michael. 1950. *Usos y costumbres de los sefardíes de Salónica*. Madrid: Instituto Arias Montano.

———. 1960. *Literatura sefardita de Oriente*. Madrid: Instituto Arias Montano.

———. 1963. Penetración de extranjerismos en el español de Oriente. *Actas del I congreso de instituciones hispánicas* 1: 325–34.

Molho, Rena. 1992. The Jewish presence in Macedonia. *Los muestros*, no. 6 (March): 5–9.

Nahir, M. 1977. The five aspects of language planning: a classification. *Language Problems and Language Planning* 1: 107–23.

Nahirny, Vladimir C., and Joshua A. Fishman. 1965. American Immigrant groups: Ethnic identification and the problem of generations. *The Sociological Review* 13, no. 3: 311–326.

———. 1966. Ukrainian language maintenance efforts in the United States. In

Language loyalty in the United States, by J. A. Fishman et al., 318–57. The Hague: Mouton.

Nebrija, Antonio de. 1492. *Gramática de la lengua castellana.* Salamanca. Edition prepared by Antonio Quilis 1980. Madrid: Edición Normal.

Nehama, Joseph. 1936. *Histoire des Israélites de Salonique, t. III, L'age d'or du séfaradisme salonicien (1536–1593)*, 206–7. Salonika: Librairie Molho.

———. 1965. Salonique au XVIIIème siècle. Instruction et culture juives. In *Studies in honor of M.J. Benardete*, ed. I. Langnas and B. Sholod, 337–47. New York: Las Americas.

———. 1977. *Dictionnaire du judéo-espagnol.* Madrid: Instituto Arias Montano (C.S.I.C.).

Nemer, Julie F. 1981. Sound patterns and strategies—loanwords in Judeo-Spanish. Ph.D. diss., Indiana University, Bloomington.

North, Roger. 1890. *The lives of the Right Hon. Francis North . . . and the Hon. and Rev. Dr. John North*, vol. 3, ed. Augustus Jessopp. D.D. London: George Bell and Sons.

Papo, Eliezer. 1992. Kuatrolinguizmo de los Djudios de Sarajevo. *Aki Yerushalayim*, Anyo 13, no. 46: 38–40.

Papo, Joseph M. 1946. The Sephardic community in America. *The Reconstructionist* 12: 370–88.

———. 1980. The Sephardic Jewish community of New York. In *Studies in Sephardic culture*, ed. Marc D. Angel, 65–94. New York: Sepher-Hermon Press, Inc.

———. 1987. *Sephardim in twentieth century America, in search of unity.* San Jose, Calif.: Pele Yoetz Books.

Perez, Avner. 1992. El soletreo. *Aki Yerushalayim*, Anyo 13, no. 46: 33–37.

Perles, F. 1925. Jüdisch-Deutsch und Jüdisch-Spanisch. *Der Morgen* 1: 370–388.

Poplack, Shana. 1982. "Sometimes I'll start a sentence in Spanish y termino en español": Toward a typology of code-switching. In *Spanish in the United States: Sociolinguistic aspects*, ed. J Amastae and L. Elías-Olivares, 230–263. New York: Cambridge University Press.

———. 1983. Bilingual competence: linguistic interference or grammatical integrity. In *Spanish in the U.S. setting: Beyond the southwest*, ed. L. Elías-Olivares, 107–29. Rosslyn, Va.: Clearinghouse for Bilingual Education.

Porter, David. 1835. *Constantinople and its environs.* In a series of letters exhibiting the actual state of the manners, customs, and habits of the Turks, Armenians, Jews and Greeks, as modified by the policy of Sultan Mohammed. By an American. 2 vols. New York: Harper and Bros.

Prinz, Joachim. 1973. *The secret Jews.* New York: Random House.

Pulido á Fernández, Angel. 1905. *Españoles sin patria y la raza sefardí.* Madrid: E. Teodoro.

Quilis, Antonio. 1970. Causas de desaparición de formas dialectales. In *Actas del primer simposio de estudios sefardíes 1964*, ed. I. Hassán, 225–32. Madrid: Instituto Arias Montano.

Rabin, Chaim. 1958. The revival of Hebrew. Second edition. *Israel Today*, no. 5. Jerusalem: Israel Digest.

Ramos-Gil, C. 1959. La lengua española en Israel. *Tesoro de los judíos sefardíes* 1: 32–40.

Renard, Raymond. 1961. L'Influence du français sur le judéo-espagnol du Levant. *Revue des langues vivantes* 27: 47–52.

———. 1965. Le système phonique du judéo-espagnol. *Revue de phonétique appliquée* 1: 23–33.

———. 1966a. *Sépharad: le monde et la langue judéo-espagnol des Séphardim.* Belgium: Annales Universitaires de Mons.

———. 1966b. L'Influence du mode de transcription sur le système phonique du judéo-espagnol. *Revue phonétique appliquée* 1: 35–40.

———. 1971. La mort d'une langue: le judéo-espagnol. *Revue des langues vivantes* 37:719–22.

———. 1991. La mort d'une langue: le judéo-espagnol. *Los muestros* no. 5 (December): 60–61.

Resnick, Salomon. 1933. La evolución idiomática de los judíos. El judeo-español. *Judaica* (Buenos Aires) 4:155–59.

Révah, Israel S. 1938. Notes en marge du livre de Mrs. Crews. *Bulletin hispanique* 40: 78–95.

———. 1964. Formation et évolution des parlers judéo-espagnols des Balkans. *Tesoro de los judíos sefardíes* 7: 41–48.

———. 1970. Hispanisme et judaïsme des langues parlées et écrites par les Séfardim. In *Actas del primer simposio de estudios sefardíes 1964,* ed. I. Hassán, 233–42. Madrid: Instituto Arias Montano.

Rischin, Moses. 1962. *The promised city: New York's Jews 1870–1914.* Cambridge: Harvard University Press.

Rodrigue, Aron, 1990. *French Jews, Turkish Jews: The Alliance Israelite Universelle and the politics of Jewish schooling in Turkey, 1860–1925.* Bloomington and Indianapolis: Indiana University Press.

Rohlfs, Gerhard. 1957. *Manual de filología hispánica,* Bogota: Talleres Editoriales de la Librería Voluntad Limitada.

Romey, David. 1981. Judeo-Spanish as a language of communication, folklore and cultural identity. In *The Americanization of a Hispanic group: The Sephardic experience in the United States,* 24–35. Proceedings of a conference sponsored by Sephardic House at Shearith Israel, New York, 5 April.

Romey, David, and Marc D. Angel. 1980. The ubiquitous Sephardic proverb. In *Studies in Sephardic culture,* ed. Marc D. Angel, 57–64. New York: Sepher-Hermon Press, Inc.

Roth, Cecil. 1970. *A history of the Jews.* New York: Schoken Books.

Sala, Marius. 1970a. Observaciones sobre la desaparición de las lenguas. In *Estudios sobre el judeoespañol de Bucarest,* 9–45. Mexico: Universidad Nacional Autónoma. (Reprint from *Revue linguistique* 6 [1961]: 185–202.)

———. 1970b. La desaparición de las lenguas y la polysemía. In *Estudios sobre el judeoespañol de Bucarest,* 46–65. (Reprint from *Revue de linguistique* [Bucharest] 7 [1962]: 289–99.)

———. 1970c. Como contribuye una lengua románica a la desaparición de otra. In *Estudios sobre el judeoespañol de Bucarest,* 74–130. (Reprint from *Actes du x congrès de linguistique romane* [Strasbourg] [1965a]: 1375–77.)

———. 1970d. La organización de una 'norma' española en el judeo-español. In *Estudios sobre el judeoespañol de Bucarest,* 131–42. (Reprint from *Anuario de letras* 1965b, [Mexico] 5: 175–82.)

————. 1970e. Elementos balcánicos del judeo-español. In *Estudios sobre el judeoespañol de Bucarest*, 143–55). (Reprint from *Actas del xi congreso internacional de lingüística y filología románicas* (Madrid) [1968] IV: 2151–60.)

————. 1971. *Phonétique et phonologie du judéo-espagnol de Bucarest*. The Hague: Mouton.

Salazar-Cano, Djamila. 1987. Quelle langue parlaient les Juifs en Espagne avant 1492? *Vidas largas*, no. 6 (May): 59–62.

Salomon, H. P., and Tomás L. Ryan. 1978. Review of *The Sephardic storm lamp: Ladino, Judezmo and the Spanish Jewish dialect* (Tract 11), by David N. Barocas. *The American Sephardi* 9: 155–6.

Samarin, William J. 1967. *Field linguistics*. New York: Holt, Rinehart and Winston.

Sanua, Victor D. 1967. A study of the adjustment of Sephardi Jews in the New York metropolitan area. *The Jewish Journal of Sociology* 9: 25–33.

————. 1977. Contemporary studies of Sephardic Jews in the United States. In *A coat of many colors: Jewish subcommunities in the U.S.*, ed. Abraham D. Lavender, 281–288. Westport, Conn.: Greenwood Press.

Saville-Troike, Muriel. 1982. *The ethnography of communication*. Oxford and New York: Basil Blackwell.

Schieffelin, Bambi B. 1990. *The give and take of everyday life: The language and socialization of Kaluli children*. New York: Cambridge University Press.

Schlieben-Lange, Brigitte. 1977. The language situation in Southern France. *Linguistics* 191: 101–8.

Sephiha, Haïm-Vidal. 1971. The "real" Ladino. *The American Sephardi* 5:50–58.

————. 1973a. The present state of Judeo-Spanish in Turkey. *The American Sephardi* 6: 22–29.

————. 1973b. *Le ladino (judéo-espagnol calque), Deutéronome, versions de Constantinople (1547) et de Ferrare (1553)*. Paris: Editions Hispaniques.

————. 1977. *L'agonie des Judéo-Espagnols*. Paris: Editions Entente.

————. 1981. Néologie en judéo-espagnol—les euphémismes (1), *Ibérica III, cahiers ibériques et ibéro-americains de l'Université de Paris—Sorbonne*, 113–123.

————. 1984. La société judéo-espagnole à travers ses proverbes ou dis-moi tes proverbes je te dirai qui tu es. In *Richesse du proverbe*, vol. 2, *Typologie et fontions, actes du colloque de parémiologie* (Lille 6 to 8 March 1981), Etudes réunies par François Suard et Claude Buridant. Université de Lille.

————. 1986. *Le judéo-espagnol*. Paris: Editions Entente.

————. 1987a. *Le dictionnaire du judéo-espagnol* de Joseph Nehama. References abusives au portugais. *Arquivos do Centro Cultural Português* 23: 199–207.

————. 1987b. La gallomanie des Judéo-Espagnols de l'Empire Ottoman, un pas vers l'émancipation? Extract from *Politique et religion dans le judaïsme moderne: des communautés à l'émancipation* (Actes du colloque tenu en Sorbonne les 18–19 November 1986), 155–66. Paris: Sorbonne.

Shaul, Moshe. 1990. El djudeo-espanyol en Israel i la actividad en este kampo de la emision djudeo-espanyola de Kol Israel. *Aki Yerushalayim*, Anyo 11, no. 42: 20–25.

————. 1991. El djudeo-espanyol en muestros dias. *Los muestros*, no. 5 (December): 59.

Shaw, Stanford Jay. 1976. *History of the Ottoman Empire and modern Turkey.* Vol. 1: *Empire of the Gazis: The rise and decline of the Ottoman Empire, 1280–1808.* New York: Cambridge University Press.

———. 1989. Decline and Revival of Ottoman and Turkish Jewry, 17th–20th centuries. Paper presented at Sephardic Temple Tifereth Israel, Los Angeles, 24 April.

———. 1991. *The Jews of the Ottoman Empire and the Turkish Republic.* New York: New York University Press.

———. 1992. The story of Turkish Jewry: Five hundred years of peace and harmony. *Los muestros,* no. 6 (March): 17–21.

Sherman, Charles Bezalel, 1965. *The Jew within American society: A study in ethnic individuality.* Detroit: Wayne State University Press.

Silva-Corvalán, Carmen. 1983. Code-shifting patterns in Chicano Spanish. In *Spanish in the U.S. setting: Beyond the southwest,* ed. L. Elías-Olivares, 69–87. Rosslyn, Va.: Clearinghouse for Bilingual Education.

Sitton, David. 1985. *Sephardi communities today.* Jerusalem: The Council of the Sephardi and Oriental Communities.

Sjoestedt, M. L. 1928. L'Influence de la langue anglaise sur un parler local irlandais. *Etrennes de linguistique offertes par quelques amis à Emile Benveniste,* 81–122. Paris: Librairie Orientaliste Paul Geuthner.

Sklare, Marshall. 1971. *America's Jews.* New York: Random House.

———. 1974. *The Jew in American society.* New York: Behrman House.

Smith, Anthony D. 1981. *The ethnic revival.* New York: Cambridge University Press.

Sombart, Werner. 1923. *Les Juifs et la vie économique.* Paris: Payot.

Sowell, T. 1978. Ethnicity in a changing America. *Daedalus* 107, no. 1: 213–37.

Spaulding, Robert K. 1965. *How Spanish grew.* Berkeley: University of California Press.

Spitzer, Leo. 1939. El judeo-español de Turquía. *Judaica* (Buenos Aires) 13: 9–14.

———. 1944. Origen de las lenguas judeo-románicas. *Judaica* (Buenos Aires) 11: 175–87.

Stampfer, Rabbi Joshua. 1987. Introduction. In *The Sephardim: A cultural journey from Spain to the Pacific coast,* ed. Rabbi J. Stampfer, 13–21. Portland, Ore.: The Institute for Judaic Studies.

Stankiewicz, Edward. 1964. Balkan and Slavic elements in the Judeo-Spanish of Yugoslavia. In *For Max Weinreich on his seventieth birthday,* 229–36. The Hague: Mouton.

Stern, Stephen. 1977. The Sephardic Jewish community of Los Angeles: A study in folklore and ethnic identity. Ph.D. diss., Indiana University, Bloomington, Indiana.

———. 1982. Ethnic identity among the Sephardic Jews of Los Angeles. In *The Sepharadi and Oriental Jewish heritage,* ed. Issachar Ben-Ami, 133–44. Jerusalem: The Magnes Press, The Hebrew University.

Studemund, Michael. 1975. *Bibliographie zum Judenspanischen.* Hamburg: Helmut Buske Verlag.

Swadesh, Morris. 1948. Sociologic notes on obsolescent languages. *International Journal of American Linguistics* 14, no. 4: 226–35.

Taboret-Keller, Andrée. 1972. A contribution to the sociological study of language maintenance and language shift. In *Advances in the sociology of language II,* ed. J. A. Fishman, 365–76. The Hague: Mouton.

Tamir, Vicki. 1979. *Bulgaria and her Jews: The history of a dubious symbiosis.* New York: Sepher-Hermon Press, Inc.

Terracini, A. Benvenuto. 1951. Como muere una lengua. In *Conflictos de lenguas y de cultura,* by A. B. Terracini, 11–42. Buenos Aires: Ediciones Iman.

Timm, Lenora A. 1980. Bilingualism, diglossia and language shift in Brittany. *International Journal of the Sociology of Language* 25: 29–41.

Toledano, Mauricio Hatchwell. 1991. History, Sefarad 92. *Los muestros,* no. 4 (September): 6–7.

Ullman, Joan. 1991. The impact of the expulsion on the Spanish national consciousness. Paper presented at *Expulsion 1492 Conference,* at Sephardic Temple Tifereth Israel, Los Angeles, 11 November.

Umphrey, G. W., and Emma Adatto. 1936. Linguistic archaisms of the Seattle Sephardim. *Hispania* 19: 255–64.

Unamuno, Miguel de. 1905. Letter written to don Angel Pulido Fernández. In *Los españoles sin patria y la raza sefardí,* by Angel Pulido á Fernández, 104–5. Madrid: E. Teodoro.

Van der Plank, Pieter. 1978. The assimilation and non-assimilation of European linguistic minorities: A sociological retrospection. In *Advances in the study of societal multilingualism,* ed. J. A. Fishman, 423–56. The Hague: Mouton.

Vendryes, J. 1921. Contact et mélange des langues. In *Le langage, introduction linguistique à l'histoire,* by J. Vendryes, 330–48. Paris: La Renaissance du Livre.

———. 1933. La mort des langues. In *Conferences de l'Institut de Linguistique de l'Université de Paris,* 5–15.

Vidas, Albert de. 1991. The language controversy among the Sephardim of the Ottoman Empire at the turn of the century. *AAJFT Newsletter* 2, no. 4 (November): 8–9.

———. 1992. Dr. Angel Pulido and the Sephardim in the Ottoman Empire at the turn of the century. *AAJFT Newsletter* 3, no. 1 (March): 13.

Wagner, Max Leopold. 1909. Los judíos españoles de Levante, Kritischer Rückblick bis 1907. *Revue de dialectologie romane* (Brussels) 1: 470–506.

———. 1923. Algunas observaciones generales sobre el judeo-español de Oriente. *Revista de filología española* 10: 225–44.

———. 1925. Los dialectos judeo-españoles de Karaferia, Kastoria y Brusa. In *Homenaje ofrecido a Ramón Menendez Pidal* 2, 193–203. Madrid: Hernando.

———. 1930. Caracteres generales del judeo-español de Oriente. *Revista de filología española,* Anejo 12.

———. 1950a. Espigueo judeo-español. *Revista de filología española* 34: 9–106.

———. 1950b. As influências recíprocas entre o português e o judeo-espanhol. *Revista de Portugal* 15: 189–95.

———. 1954. Calcos lingüísticos en el habla de los sefarditas de Levante. In *Homenaje a Fritz Kruger,* vol. 2, 269–81. Argentina: Mendoza.

Weiker, Walter F. 1988. *The unseen Israelis: The Jews from Turkey in Israel.* Lanham, Md.: University Press of America.

Weinreich, Max. 1953. Yiddishkayt and Yiddish: On the impact of religion on language in Ashkenazic Jewry. In *Mordecai M. Kaplan jubilee volume,* 481–514. New York: Jewish Theological Seminary of America. (Reprinted in *Readings in the sociology of language* [1972], ed. J. A. Fishman, 382–413. The Hague: Mouton.)

————. 1956. The Jewish languages of Romance stock and their relation to earliest Yiddish. *Romance Philology* 9: 403–28.

————. 1980. Yiddish in the framework of other Jewish languages. In *History of the Yiddish language,* tr. Shlomo Noble and Joshua A. Fishman, 124–53. Chicago: University of Chicago Press. (First appeared in *Geshikte fun der yiddisher shprak 1973.*)

Weinreich, Uriel. 1953. *Languages in contact.* 5th printing 1967. The Hague: Mouton.

Wertheimer, Elaine C. 1977. Jewish sources of Spanish blood purity concerns. In *Working papers in Sephardic and Oriental Jewish Studies #3.* New York: *Adelantre,* The Judezmo Society.

Wharncliffe, Lord, ed. 1970. *The letters and works of Lady Mary Wortley Montagu.* Vol. 1. New York: AMS Press. (Reprinted from the 1861 edition, London.)

Woolard, Kathryn A. 1989. *Double talk: Bilingualism and the politics of ethnicity in Catalonia.* Stanford, Calif.: Stanford University Press.

Yahuda, A. S. 1915. Contribución al estudio del judeo-español. *Revista de filología española* 2: 339–70.

Yeshaia, Samuel B. 1970. Jerusalén y sus comunidades sefaraditas. In *Actas del primer simposio de estudios sefardíes 1964,* ed. I. Hassán, 95–105. Madrid: Instituto Arias Montano.

Zamora, Vicente A. 1974. Judeoespañol. In *Dialectología española,* by Vicente A. Zamora, 349–377. Madrid: Editorial Gredos.

Zengel, Marjorie S. 1962. Literacy as a factor in language change. *American Anthropologist* 64: 132–39.

Zimmels, Hirsch J. 1958. *Ashkenazim and Sephardim: Their relations, differences and problems as reflected in the rabinnical responsa.* London: Oxford University Press.

Index